Before Truth

Before Truth

Lonergan, Aquinas, and the Problem of Wisdom

JEREMY D. WILKINS

The Catholic University of America Press
Washington, D.C.

Library of Congress Cataloging-in-Publication Data

Names: Wilkins, Jeremy D. (Jeremy Daniel), author.
Title: Before truth : Lonergan, Aquinas, and the problem of wisdom /
    Jeremy D. Wilkins.
Description: Washington, D.C. : Catholic University of America Press,
    2018. | Includes index.
Identifiers: LCCN 2018030458 | ISBN 9780813233154 (alk. paper)
Subjects: LCSH: Lonergan, Bernard J. F. | Thomas, Aquinas, Saint,
    1225?-1274. | Truth—Religious aspects—Christianity. | Wisdom—
    Religious aspects--Christianity.
Classification: LCC BX4705.L7133 W55 2018 | DDC 230/.2092—dc23
LC record available at https://lccn.loc.gov/2018030458

Coniugi dilectissimae et filiis carissimis

Contents

Chapter Four: Aquinas and Lonergan's Turn to the Subject   96

Chapter Five: Self-Appropriation as First Philosophy   131

Chapter Six: Foundational Methodology and Theology   180

PART 2: WISDOM AS OBJECT   233

Chapter Seven: Doctrine and Meaning   235

Preface

This is a book about Bernard Lonergan and, in a way, his model and most important teacher, St. Thomas Aquinas. It is also a book about a problem. The problem, approximately, is the place of truth in theology. For Aquinas, that place was first. The articles of faith, revealed by God, provided the first principles for his *sacra doctrina*. The Gospel message has not ceased to be true and divine. Nevertheless, it does not seem possible to adopt Aquinas's position without further ado. The message was not originally given as a body of truths. The theologians transplanted it from its native soil in narrative and symbol to the cooler clime of propositional truth and explanatory meaning. Our doctrines, as formulated, are the product of their labors. We cannot reasonably impugn those labors, for intelligence and exactitude are as worthwhile in religious as in other matters. If, however, we admit that our doctrines have a contingent history, that they have developed and are developing still, we must also admit that there are theological operations that do not presuppose formulated doctrines and are before them. 'Before truth,' then, names a problem of theological wisdom, of ordering theological activities and establishing theological criteria.

Behind the theological problem lies an existential issue of some cultural moment. Given any sufficiently complex question, evidence can be arranged on different sides, or shown to be inconclusive, or disregarded as 'fake.' Assent divides along tribal lines, and there are prophets (and profits!) abroad to declare the truth dead. The truth turns out to be an arduous good, and our culture seems short on the hope of attaining it. Getting things right—reaching the truth in the ordinary sense of true predication—requires intellectual preparation, moral seriousness, and a readiness to be changed. 'Before truth,' then, also names a problem of measuring up, of existential truthfulness.

Measuring up also means being measured. Objectively, the truth is not our possession, but we are its. Prior to the adequacy of true judgment, prior to the adequacy of honesty and preparation, there is a kind of natural law of self-transcendence, a summons to self-surrender before truth. Without a satisfactory philosophical elucidation, however, the entailments of this natural law are readily obscured.

These are large issues. To the extent that they admit of a solution, it will not be a new articulation of principles, instruction in rules of inference, or the discovery of some overlooked evidence. The radical solution, if it is indeed radical, must involve a new stage in human self-understanding and a form of honesty resisting all obscurantism, especially in oneself.

It was Lonergan's aim to get a handle on the compound problem 'before truth.' He succeeded in ways I find helpful and expect others might find helpful, too. This book is about his project and is also a case for it. It is addressed not only to his confirmed disciples (though, I hope, it will be useful to them) but also to readers fundamentally concerned about the contemporary state of theology, church, and culture and perhaps doubtful that Lonergan is part of the solution and not part of the problem. They are apt to be troubled, as Lonergan was and as I am, by widespread disregard for doctrinal issues,[1] a tendency even to "consider dogmas meaningless,"[2] but if they have heard anything of Lonergan they are likely to suspect him of underwriting this tendency. They may admire Thomas Aquinas but doubt that Lonergan could help them read him, let alone inherit a portion of his spirit. To them, I wish to present a side of Lonergan that may not be known, a Lonergan who believed and loved the mysteries of faith, whose paramount concern was for the possibility of a theology carrying forward the best achievements of Catholic tradition, a serious disciple for whom Aquinas exemplified the right way to do theology, not only for the brilliance of his thought but also for his courage and honesty in the face of the real and pressing challenges of his time.

---

1. Bernard J. F. Lonergan, "Horizons and Transpositions," in *Philosophical and Theological Papers 1965–1980*, ed. Robert C. Croken and Robert M. Doran, Collected Works of Bernard Lonergan 17 (Toronto: University of Toronto Press, 2004), 409–32, here 427. Volumes in the series Collected Works of Bernard Lonergan are henceforth abbreviated CWL.

2. Bernard J. F. Lonergan, "Christology Today: Methodological Reflections," in *A Third Collection*, ed. John D. Dadosky and Robert M. Doran, CWL 16 (2017), 70–93, here 86.

This book, then, is both a study of Lonergan's approach to a problem and an inductive introduction to his project. As a study, it is a work of interpretation. As an introduction, it is also a work of persuasion, illustrating what he is up to in (I hope) a fresh and compelling way for those to whom Lonergan is just a name freighted with a (probably misleading) reputation. The argument here corrects, or at least disrupts, common perceptions of Lonergan and makes a case for his basic importance. I cannot hope to reproduce here the pedagogy of self-discovery he sought to enact in *Insight*, though I hope some will come away feeling the struggle must be worth it.

"This book is, I am afraid, a patchwork in date, in style, in treatment, in inspiration," if I may channel Ronald Knox for a moment.[3] In one sense, its chapters might be taken as nothing more than a series of soundings, *sondages*, but the soundings are cumulative and strategic. If they are not the whole of Lonergan's thought, they are meant to convey a sense of the whole *in* his thought, its overall thrust, its fundamental shape and coherence, and some of its unifying threads.[4] Our key is the interplay of method and performance, for Lonergan's remarks on method arose out of reflection on his own efforts in theology. "One must begin from the performance, if one is to have the experience necessary for understanding what the performance is."[5] This means that the performance and its reflection—the theology and the proposed method in theology—should be mutually illuminating. Lonergan's method can hardly exclude his own theology, a fact which ought to disturb at least some interpretations of its entailments.[6]

Persuasive exposition is not without its risks. It blurs the line between indirect discourse—reporting what Lonergan said and explaining what

3. Ronald A. Knox, *Essays in Satire* (London: Sheed & Ward, 1928), 15, quoted in Philip McShane, *Process: Introducing Themselves to Young (Christian) Minders* (Halifax: Mount Saint Vincent Press, 1990), xii. Accessed December 27, 2017. http://www.philipmcshane.org/wp-content/themes/philip/online_publications/books/process.pdf.

4. I have in mind Lonergan's characterization of metaphysics as the whole in knowledge but not the whole of knowledge. See Bernard J. F. Lonergan, *Insight: A Study of Human Understanding*, ed. Frederick E. Crowe and Robert M. Doran, CWL 3 (1992), 416.

5. Bernard J. F. Lonergan, "Christ as Subject: A Reply," in *Collection*, ed. Frederick E. Crowe and Robert M. Doran, CWL 4 (1988), 153–84, here 174.

6. This particular argument has been developed by Charles C. Hefling Jr., "The Meaning of God Incarnate According to Friedrich Schleiermacher; or, Whether Lonergan Is Appropriately Regarded as 'A Schleiermacher for Our Time,' and Why Not," *Lonergan Workshop* 7 (1988): 105–77.

he meant—and advocacy for the value, significance, and relevance of his meaning. The result is an uneasy compound of Lonergan's insights and judgments and my own. Of course, it must be frankly admitted that my own insights and judgments are largely derivative. In any case, I accept the risks for the purpose at hand.

Underlying the exposition is an exegetical case with a twofold goal. The first is to show a thematic progression and unity of ideas, what I have called 'the whole' in Lonergan's project. The second is to attend to the chronological development of his thought. The overarching structure of the book is not chronological but thematic. Yet Lonergan did not stand still. An interpreter has to face the fact that Lonergan's thought is a moving target and underwent sometimes profound transformations. Within each chapter, and sometimes between chapters, careful attention is paid to the way Lonergan's thought developed over time. Usually the developments are important clues to his questions and concerns. Without pretending to an exhaustive study of his development on any single point, I hope to convey a sense both of the important shifts and also of the major threads of continuity in his questions, convictions, and approach.

In sum, this book is an exercise in interpretation and exposition. Its object is 'the whole' in Lonergan's thought, the unifying thread of his project. Its procedure is to illuminate the method by studying the theology and to resist tendencies to interpret the method as if it appeared in a vacuum. As his theology and its questions become better known, it will become clearer what problems he sought to address and how his method is related to them. By and large, these problems remain the problems of theology today, and the invitation and challenge of this book is to give his proposal a new hearing.

Acknowledgments

Gratitude is among the happiest offices of the spirit. Its expression, however, must be among the most perilous. The plain fact is that my debts, both personal and intellectual, are too numerous and too severe even to enumerate. Nevertheless, some acknowledgment must be made of my more egregious benefactors.

As a young undergraduate with more zeal than sense, it was my remarkable fortune to encounter J. Patout Burns. By his teaching he introduced me to theology. By his example he introduced me to intellectual probity as an element of Christian vocation. Seeing the direction of my interests, he pointed me to Lonergan as a thinker of fundamental importance and arranged my first exposure to *Insight* in a course by William Shea. That pointing was the start of a great adventure in learning. It would lead me to the feet of some of Lonergan's greatest students.

In Toronto, Gordon Rixon hooked me on the archival papers. Robert Doran encouraged me to study Lonergan's Latin textbooks, and Gilles Mongeau accompanied me through *Method* for the first time. Later, at Boston College, Patrick Byrne midwifed the 'startling strangeness' of intellectual conversion. Charles Hefling, who suffered my services as his teaching assistant, reinforced like no other the value of clarity and precision. With exceptional kindness, Matthew Lamb taught me the impossibility of interpreting Lonergan without measuring Lonergan's involvement with Thomas Aquinas. When therefore I decided to begin an apprenticeship to Aquinas, Stephen Brown took me under his wings and kept me honest. The wise and generous Frederick Lawrence put an unmistakable seal on my reading of Lonergan and, by his conversation and unfailing friendship, continues to enlarge my understanding of theology as a Christian service.

I am indebted to many friends and colleagues who gave valuable feedback on drafts, some of whom went to exceptional lengths to be of service. Among the first is Philip McShane, who graciously read every scrap I sent his way and gently pricked my complacent incomprehension. Anna Moreland pressed me to transcend my native 'Lonerganese.' Other generous commentators include Clinton Brand, Daniel De Haan, Thomas Harmon, Grant Kaplan, Murray Johnston, Ryan Miller, Mark Miller, Ligita Ryliškytė, Michael Vertin, and my able research assistants Matthew Thollander (in Toronto) and John Kern (in Boston), as well as two anonymous readers for the Press. If this book is not only helpful but also readable, it is largely thanks to them, despite my slowness to learn. To their names might be added many others whose godly conversation was invaluable: Matthew Petillo, Eric Mabry, Brian Bazjek, Boyd Coolman, Holly Taylor Coolman, Daria Spezzano, and Michael Ryall; one must stop somewhere. I am grateful, finally, to John Martino for shepherding with extraordinary care the transition from manuscript to book, and to Kristen Schubert for her meticulous, intelligent, and efficient copyediting.

Finally, there are debts of a most personal nature. Joe and Raylene gave me a bright and warm place to work without asking anything in return. My parents and siblings share neither my Christian convictions nor my preoccupation with religious questions but have been constant and unsparing in their support. In the long gestation of this project, none have borne more and spared less, however, than my beloved bride, Maureen, and our sons, Abraham and Thomas. In token return of their goodness to me, this book is for them.

Benedicam Dominum qui tribuit mihi intellectum.

Parts of chapter 7 previously appeared in *Studies in Religion/Sciences Religieuses*. An earlier version of chapter 8 was published in *The Thomist*, and an earlier version of chapter 9 in *Pro Ecclesia*. In each case the material has been significantly revised. I wish to thank their respective editors and publishers for their kind permission to present my work here.[1]

The lion's share of work on this book was conducted while I was director of the Lonergan Research Institute at Regis College, Toronto; it would not have been possible without the generosity of the Institute's friends. I also benefited enormously from a pilot project applying the discovery analytics of Crivella West to Lonergan's corpus. I am grateful, finally, for support from the Boston College Lonergan Institute.

1. "(Mis)Reading Lonergan's *Way to Nicea*: A 'More Generous Interpretation,' in Conversation with Jane Barter Moulaison," *Studies in Religion/Sciences Religieuses* 42, no. 4 (2013): 429–447; "Method, Order, and Analogy in Trinitarian Theology: Karl Rahner's Critique of the 'Psychological' Approach," *The Thomist* 74, no. 4 (2010): 563–92; and "Love and Knowledge of God in the Human Life of Christ," *Pro Ecclesia* 21, no. 1 (2012): 77–99.

A Note on Citations

As a rule, the works of Lonergan are cited in the Collected Works of Bernard Lonergan (CWL) edition, published by the University of Toronto.

Three volumes of very recent appearance in the CWL supersede older and widely available published editions: *A Second Collection*, *A Third Collection*, and *Method in Theology*.[1] Citations to the two collections refer to specific papers, so that even those without convenient access to the CWL editions should be able to locate references in the older editions with a minimum of effort. An exception is made for *Method in Theology*. It is cited in both the ubiquitous 1974 edition (with its numerous Toronto reprints) and the CWL edition.

The major works of Lonergan are normally cited without his name, but shorter papers with less familiar titles are not.

For Thomas Aquinas, the *Summa theologiae* is abbreviated *STh*; the *Summa contra gentiles*, *ScG*.

---

1. Bernard J. F. Lonergan, *A Second Collection*, ed. William F. Ryan and Bernard J. Tyrrell (Philadelphia: Westminster, 1974) = *A Second Collection*, ed. John D. Dadosky and Robert M. Doran, CWL 13 (2016); Bernard J. F. Lonergan, *A Third Collection: Papers*, ed. Frederick E. Crowe (New York: Paulist, 1985) = *A Third Collection*, ed. John D. Dadosky and Robert M. Doran, CWL 16 (2017); Bernard J. F. Lonergan, *Method in Theology* (New York: Herder and Herder, 1972) (reprinted numerous times by University of Toronto Press) = *Method in Theology*, ed. John D. Dadosky and Robert M. Doran, CWL 14 (2017).

Introduction

I give you the end of a golden string;

Only wind it into a ball,

It will lead you in at Heaven's gate,

Built in Jerusalem's wall.[1]

WILLIAM BLAKE

Augustine relates that for many years he found Scripture coarse, impenetrable, absurd; he thought God must be a finely diffused body. In time, he came to realize it was he himself who had been coarse, impenetrable, absurd.[2] To reach adequate answers to his most important questions, he had to transcend both the chaos of his loves and the grossness of his mind in its thrall to imagination. It is easy to suppose no one today could make so obvious a mistake as to imagine God diffused through space and time, but currently fashionable reveries of a God who suffers, who improves with time, who is 'relational' and 'open' and somehow, perhaps, interiorly perfected through dramatic extroversion into the world, are evidence to the contrary. Augustine's experience represents, in short, a problem every theologian must face, and its neglect as a topos hardly improves the likelihood of its satisfactory resolution.[3]

1. William Blake, "Jerusalem," Plate 77 (E 231), quoted in Northrop Frye, *Fearful Symmetry: A Study of William Blake*, Princeton Paperbacks (Princeton, N.J.: Princeton University Press, 1969), 143.

2. Augustine, *Confessions*, ed. James J. O'Donnell (Oxford: Clarendon Press, 1992), 7.1.2.

3. Matthew L. Lamb, *Eternity, Time, and the Life of Wisdom* (Naples, Fla.: Sapientia Press of Ave Maria University, 2007), 1–12.

Today the problem of transcendence is compounded, however, by a problem of historical contingency. Modernity represents a profound revolution in human self-understanding exhibited in transformations of natural science, historical scholarship, and culture. Its denouement so far has been the emergence of postmodernity, the more or less wholesale renunciation of the universal, the permanent, and the same in honor of the different, the contingent, and the relative and particular. For Christians, the upshot has been a series of crises in their religious self-understanding and the demolition of its intellectual superstructure. For theologians, it means a new set of problems added to the old. To operate on the level of our time, there has to be an open-eyed reckoning with the contingency of a tradition that has developed and is developing still, whose historical legacy has been not merely a matter of logical deduction nor even of patient learning, but a compound of attention and inattention, intelligence and stupidity, truth and error, responsibility and moral renunciation. Even if we wholly prescind from the complicated histories of politics, culture, economics, institutions, and the like to consider solely the development of doctrine and theology, we are faced with questions about the transitions, the continuity between stages or orderings of doctrine, the criteria for preferring one ordering to another, and the shift toward increasingly systematic orderings which inevitably are further removed from the largely narrative order of the sources.[4] Such transitions present an acute problem for discernment, compounded enormously by widespread tendencies to relativism, subjectivism, scientism, and historicism.

Sacra doctrina, in the scholastic paradigm, could begin from the received articles of faith in a way no longer available to us. If as believers we simply bow to mystery, as theologians we are called to articulate the transcultural basis of our normative claims. It cannot be the claims themselves as formulated, for the formulations have a history. We must penetrate to the light that grounds assent, commitment, discernment, interpretation. Before the formulated axioms of a particular logic or a philosophy, there are the immanent, natural norms of human reason, the spontaneously operative criteria of question and answer.[5] Before

---

4. See Frederick E. Crowe, "Lonergan's Search for Foundations: The Early Years, 1940–1959," in *Developing the Lonergan Legacy: Historical, Theoretical, and Existential Themes*, ed. Michael Vertin (Toronto: University of Toronto Press, 2004), 164–93, here 185.

5. Aristotle recognized the prior task of dialectic but did not penetrate to an explicit possession of

the stated doctrines of Christian faith, there is our interrogation by the word, the Word. Before the truth expressed in propositions, there is the existential truthfulness by which we measure up to questions, develop understanding, reach balanced judgment.

Augustine's problem—measuring up to the transcendence of the Beloved—may have gone underground, but it has not gone away. But today we also have to face a problem of historical contingency whose dimensions are still coming into view. A contemporary Christian wisdom, in short, is not only a matter of ordering the contents of faith and the testimonies of tradition but also of discerning the order in successive stages of tradition, of putting in order the diverse forms of inquiry adequate to our questions (e.g., making sense of authors, of historical developments, and of fundamental conflicts; articulating principles, making truth claims, understanding the mysteries of faith, and presenting them to widely different audiences), of promoting order in the theological community adequate to the contemporary problems of theology. Theologians have to face relativity, subjectivity, and history honestly, but without falling for relativism, subjectivism, or historicism, or, alternatively, an irresponsible fideism. We have to discern the sapiential principles by which what God has revealed beyond human invention progresses in the church.[6]

However tempting it might be to settle for piecemeal adjustments, Bernard Lonergan came to the conclusion that the valid achievements of our tradition would be best served by their insertion into a new paradigm. In his judgment, the contemporary situation calls for a development as thoroughgoing as the reorganization and transformation of theology at the hands of Aquinas in the thirteenth century. His proposal for method in theology is an attempt to meet the issue. He is fundamentally important only if he proposed a workable solution, and I wish to contend that he did. Unfortunately, it seems to me Lonergan's proposal

---

the operational first principles necessary to meet today's issues.

6. This progress is, of course, itself affirmed as doctrine: see Vatican Council II, Dogmatic Constitution *Dei Verbum*, no. 8 (November 18, 1965), in Norman P. Tanner et al., eds., *Decrees of the Ecumenical Councils*, 2 vols. (Washington, D.C.: Georgetown University Press, 1990), 2:974. Christine Helmer suggests theology today contends with 'the end of doctrine'—whether it is possible, meaningful, purposeful, or legitimate. See Helmer, *Theology and the End of Doctrine* (Philadelphia: Westminster John Knox, 2014); see too Grant Kaplan, *Answering the Enlightenment* (New York: Crossroad Publishing, 2006).

has been ignored and dismissed before a proper hearing. It is perceived as needlessly complicated, unwieldy, stilted; as somehow dismissive of specialized work in positive theology; as a species of Hegelianism; as a brief for secularism; as wrought in isolation.

This book offers an interpretation of Lonergan's proposal in the context of its problem, strategy, inspiration, and performance. His strategy for meeting the contemporary problem of Christian wisdom rests not on a system or logic to be followed, but on a kind of asceticism. Lonergan intended a program of practices to bring under explicit scrutiny one's spontaneous preoccupation (cognitionally as well as morally) with 'relevance to me.' Through a "self-attention of scientific dimensions,"[7] he proposed, one might gather up into luminous self-possession the norms, operative and prior to every system, of reason illumined by faith. To recognize them in oneself, to surrender to them, is to come into the strangeness of a self-possession that is also self-displacement. For by it, one recognizes knowing as a form of self-surrender. One knows oneself as a bit player in a vast universe of being, a universe gradually coming to light for us in the long collaborative fermenting toward the intelligible, explanatory truth by which we know things in their relations to one another.

This ascetic strategy naturally involves a turn to the subject. Its superficial resemblance to the programs of Descartes and Kant has frequently led to Lonergan's quick dismissal as a second-tier avatar. His true inspiration, however, is a Christian tradition of self-knowledge he learned first from Augustine and John Henry Newman and whose fruits he later recognized in Thomas Aquinas. His project took the particular shape it did because of the 'Augustinian' orientation he brought to his apprenticeship to Aquinas. The real bearing and value of Lonergan's program, therefore, are not grasped by vague and ominous vituperations about the dangers of Cartesian subjectivism, but rather in the context of his own efforts, however imperfect, to work it out and implement it in

---

7. The expression is from Philip McShane, "Lonerganism," in *Philosophical Dictionary*, ed. Walter Brugger and Kenneth Baker (Spokane, Wash.: Gonzaga University Press, 1972), 230–33. It is not my aim to reenact Lonergan's pedagogy of self-appropriation, but to give some reasons to think it might be worth pursuing. There is no substitute for *Insight*, which Lonergan intended as a kind of workbook. The reader interested in an alternative pedagogy might profitably consult Joseph Flanagan, *Quest for Self-Knowledge: An Essay in Lonergan's Philosophy* (Toronto: University of Toronto Press, 1997); McShane, *Process*; and Mark D. Morelli, *Self-Possession: Being at Home in Conscious Performance* (Chestnut Hill, Mass.: Lonergan Institute at Boston College, 2015).

theology. I propose, therefore, to expound Lonergan's method by con-textualizing it within his own development and theological performance.

Lonergan's own theological writings, despite their limitations, are still the best available exemplification of his method at work, and they show how strange and one-sided are commonly prevailing assessments of its portent. Here I propose a consideration of strategic problems from his theological work as a way into the heart, moment, and value of his method. Method, after all, is reflection on performance, and it may be that Lonergan's proposal for method in theology is opaque in roughly the same measure that his theology itself—much of it, until very recently, cocooned in rare Latin textbooks—is unknown. Moreover, Lonergan's transpositions of Aquinas are more explicit in the theological textbooks than they are in his more frequently mentioned English works, *Insight* and *Method*. Thus, expounding the method by way of the theology has the further merit of building a bridge to Lonergan from the better known terrain of Aquinas and of situating Lonergan within a tradition. It also brings into the light the kinds of concrete theological problems the method was designed to surmount. My contention is that Lonergan's way of proceeding is his most important offering, and there is no better entry into his project than to watch him at work on it. Thus, I propose something of an inductive approach by way of soundings in his theology.

Aquinas and Lonergan's Grammar of Wisdom

Lonergan has a reputation as an isolated thinker; this reputation, if not quite deserved, is not without cause. As far as I can tell, none of the great theologians of his age—a remarkable generation—were among his most important conversation partners. He took no direct part in the patristic *ressourcement* that animated them. A fierce critic of neo-scholasticism, he nevertheless soldiered on loyally in institutions committed to it. He hardly involved himself in the quotidian fray. He had formed strong opinions about grace and nature, but the ferment around de Lubac's *Surnatural* elicited only the most oblique commentary. His influence at Vatican II was remote. He lectured on the educational psychologist Jean Piaget but not (though he knew his work) a theological giant like von Balthasar. His most personal works, *Insight* and *Method in Theology*, and his Latin textbooks on Trinity and Christology devote little time to the discussion of contemporary theological or philosophical views. His interests moved on another level that, to him, seemed more fundamental. He had conceived the idea of an underlying problem that he called by that Cartesian bugbear, method.

Lonergan's was a lonely climb to a lonely peak. Lonergan has remained lonely, because by and large theologians have not known what to do with him. It would be wrong, however, to take his recusal from his contemporary scene for isolation. It is the roman-tic fashion to oppose creativity and dependence. Original think-ers, though, are creative because they are conversational, they "enter / into each other's bosom . . . / in mutual interchange," as Blake has it.[8] Not only do we think through our questions in conversation with others, but most often the questions themselves would not even come to light otherwise. It is true that Lonergan attended his own rhumb, unmarked by others, but it is also true that he was constantly learning from them: Augustine, Newman, Piaget, Voegelin, mathematicians and physicists and historiographers.[9] None left a deeper mark or exerted a more lasting fascination than Aquinas, the master of thought to whom Lonergan apprenticed himself.[10] Although I do not propose here a complete study, still less a defense, of Lonergan's reading of Aquinas, I do wish to suggest that the arc of Lonergan's thought

---

8. Blake, "Jerusalem," Plate 88 (E 246), quoted in Frye, *Fearful Symmetry*, 143.

9. He had pivotal encounters with, among others, Christopher Dawson, John Henry Newman, Plato via John Alexander Stewart, Augustine, and later the phenomenological, existentialist, and hermeneutical strands in European philosophy. See Richard M. Liddy, *Transforming Light: Intellectu-al Conversion in the Early Lonergan* (Collegeville, Minn.: Liturgical Press, 1993), esp. 16–40 (on Newman), 41–49 (Plato), 50–73 (Augustine), 91–119 (Aquinas); Frederick E. Crowe, *Lonergan*, Outstanding Christian Thinkers (Collegeville, Minn.: Glazier, 1992), 39–57 (Aquinas); Frederick G. Lawrence, "Lonergan's Search for a Hermeneutics of Authenticity: Re-Originating Augustine's Hermeneutics of Love," in *Lonergan's Anthropology Revisited: The Next Fifty Years of Vatican II*, ed. Gerard Whelan (Rome: Gregorian and Biblical Press, 2015), 19–56; Matthew L. Lamb, "Bernard Lonergan SJ: The Gregorian Years," in Whelan, *Lonergan's Anthropology Revisited*, 57–80; and Mark D. Morelli, *At the Threshold of the Halfway House: A Study of Bernard Lonergan's Encounter with John Alexander Stewart* (Chestnut Hill, Mass.: Lonergan Institute at Boston College, 2007).

10. "Eventually perhaps there arrives on the scene a master capable of envisaging all the issues and of treating them in their proper order." *Method* (1972), 345, or CWL 14, 319. There is no doubt he means, in the first place, Thomas Aquinas. See Bernard J. F. Lonergan, *The Triune God: Systematics*, ed. Robert M. Doran and H. Daniel Monsour, trans. Michael G. Shields, CWL 12 (2007), 72–73.

cannot be fully understood without appreciating not only what he learned from Aquinas but also how he was inspired by him.

The Aquinas who captured Lonergan's heart and imagination was not the sclerotic figure of the manuals, highly praised but seldom imitated. It was, rather, the adventurer who squared up to Aristotle, "aiming excessively high and far" and laying "under tribute Greek and Arab, Jew and Christian" in the service of Christian wisdom.[11] In doing so, Lonergan observed, Aquinas was resisting "the diehard traditionalism of the current Christian Platonists and, at the same time, [inaugurating] historical research by appealing to the real Aristotle against the Parisian Averroists."[12] In the epilogue to *Insight*, Lonergan wrote of the personal transformation wrought by his eleven years of apprenticeship.

> After spending years reaching up to the mind of Aquinas, I came to a twofold conclusion. On the one hand, that reaching had changed me profoundly. On the other hand, that change was the essential benefit. For not only did it make me capable of grasping what, in the light of my conclusions, the *vetera* really were, but also it opened challenging vistas on what the *nova* could be. . . . Once [the mind of Aquinas] is reached, then it is difficult not to import his compelling genius to the problems of this later day.[13]

For the rest of his life, Lonergan stretched out toward those vistas. In doing so, he understood himself to be attempting for our day what

---

11. Bernard J. F. Lonergan, *Grace and Freedom: Operative Grace in the Thought of St Thomas Aquinas*, ed. Frederick E. Crowe and Robert M. Doran, CWL 1 (2000), here 144 and 142.

12. *Grace and Freedom*, 142.

13. *Insight*, 769. See also the preceding paragraph: "To penetrate to the mind of a medieval thinker is to go beyond his words and phrases. It is to effect an advance in depth that is proportionate to the broadening influence of historical research. It is to grasp questions as once they were grasped. It is to take the *opera omnia* of such a writer as St Thomas Aquinas and to follow through successive works the variations and developments of his views. It is to study the concomitance of such variations and developments and to arrive at a grasp of their motives and causes. It is to discover for oneself that the intellect of Aquinas, more rapidly on some points, more slowly on others, reached a position of dynamic equilibrium without ever ceasing to drive towards fuller and more nuanced synthesis, without ever halting complacently in some finished mental edifice, as though his mind had become dull, or his brain exhausted, or his judgment had lapsed into the error of those that forget man to be potency in the realm of intelligence."

Aquinas achieved for his: a new entente between the Christian message and the best available thought, an architectonic structure for theology on the level of our time. His twist was that a paradigm adequate to today has to face explicitly the problems of historicity that were largely implicit to Aquinas.[14]

In his retrieval of Aquinas's doctrine of wisdom, Lonergan drew attention to a duality in wisdom, an object- and a subject-pole: "Principally, [wisdom] regards the objective order of reality; but in some fashion it also has to do with the transition from the order of thought to the order of reality."[15] The object of wisdom is the order of things; wisdom in this sense is "the highest, architectonic science, a science of sciences."[16] Because Aquinas distinguished a twofold mode of truth, a natural and a supernatural order, he also distinguished a wisdom that is metaphysics from a wisdom subalternate to the mysteries held in faith, a *sacra doctrina*.[17] Of itself, philosophic wisdom is incomplete. It is, as Lonergan puts it, "only hypothetically wisdom, and the hypothesis is not verified. It is [not philosophical but] theological wisdom that judges all things in the actual order of the universe."[18] Besides wisdom's object, there is wisdom's subject, the wise person. Only one who is wise is qualified to select appropriate principles, order operations, and pass judgment on results. If wisdom as object is the science of sciences, wisdom as an aptitude in the subject is a capacity for every science.[19] However, in us here below, the perfection of wisdom is not from learning but a gift of the Spirit,

---

14. See *Insight*, 765; also Lonergan, "The Scope of Renewal," in *Philosophical and Theological Papers 1965–1980*, CWL 17, 282–98, here 293.

15. Bernard J. F. Lonergan, *Verbum: Word and Idea in Aquinas*, ed. Frederick E. Crowe and Robert M. Doran, CWL 2 (1997), 79–80. ("Principally, it regards the objective order of reality; for the wise [person] contemplates the universal scheme of things and sees each in the perspective of its causes right up to the ultimate cause. . . . Still, wisdom is not merely an ontology or a natural theology; it also has some of the characteristics of an epistemology.") See *Verbum*, 99, 101.

16. *Verbum*, 79.

17. See *Verbum*, 99–101; on Aquinas's conception of theology as a science, see Bernard J. F. Lonergan, "Theology and Understanding," in *Collection*, CWL 4, 114–32, here 117–27.

18. Bernard J. F. Lonergan, *Early Works on Theological Method 1*, ed. Robert M. Doran and Robert C. Croken, CWL 22 (2010), 106; see too Bernard J. F. Lonergan, "The Natural Desire to See God," in *Collection*, CWL 4, 81–91, here 85.

19. ". . . virtus quaedam omnium scientiarum . . ." Thomas Aquinas, *Sententia libri Ethicorum*, ed. R.-A. Gauthier, Opera Omnia 47, Leonine ed. (Rome: Ad Sanctae Sabinae, 1969), bk. 6, lect. 5, quoted in Lonergan, *Verbum*, 80.

"making us docile to his movements, in which, even perceptibly, one may be '*non solum discens sed et patiens divina*,'" not only a learner but also a sufferer of divine things.[20]

Theology is involved with special problems because it regards both the utter brightness of divine mystery and the utter darkness of sin, objective falsity. To divine mystery—including the judgment and ordering of sin—only divine wisdom is strictly proportionate. The wisdom of a theologian and the wisdom of a theology, however, are another, inferior wisdom.

> The wisdom of the theologian is not divine wisdom, not the wisdom of the blessed, not the wisdom of divine revelation or inspiration, not the wisdom of the infallibility of the church, but something that has to be learned. . . . The proportionate principle for passing judgment on the mysteries is not any human acquisition; it is divine wisdom. And it is only insofar as the theologian obtains wisdom through revelation, through the virtue of faith and the gifts of the Spirit, that he can venture to make theological judgments. And because his participation in divine wisdom, which alone is proportionate to passing judgment on the object, is an imperfect participation, the theologian is always ready to submit his judgment to the judgment of the church.[21]

Theology, then, participates in divine wisdom in different ways, both in the object of its contemplation—the world-order actually established by divine wisdom—and in the subject who contemplates, the theologian, as more or less learned, more or less discerning, more or less docile to the Spirit, more or less ready to recognize the higher, participated wisdom that infallibly determines ecclesial faith.[22] What is certain is that unless they are content merely to repeat words without grasping their meaning, theologians cannot avoid making judgments of their own. We know too

---

20. *Verbum*, 101.

21. *Early Works on Method 1*, 105–6; compare *Method* (1972), 320–26, or CWL 14, 298–303; see too his 1977 "Questionnaire on Philosophy: Response," in *Philosophical and Theological Papers 1965–1980*, CWL 17, 352–83, here 374, on the "disastrous effects" of positions unable to account for dogma; and see the apologetic for an infallible church in *Insight*, 744.

22. See Lonergan, "Theology and Understanding," 125–26.

well from history that church teaching does not operate in a vacuum but depends in some way upon theologians. We cannot sidestep the problem of developing our wisdom.

Wisdom in this life is a contemplation of the order of things, a *sacra doctrina* connecting faith and reason, a virtue of right judgment, and an instinct for listening to the Spirit. There is no doubt Lonergan conceived his program in terms of wisdom; in fact, the essential point of both *Insight* and *Method in Theology* is the development of wisdom. Wisdom puts matters in order, and Lonergan's overarching concern for method is for "envisaging all the issues and . . . treating them in their proper order."[23] The defining questions of his work—order in the knower (self-appropriation, conversion, self-surrender in love), order in the known (metaphysics, theology), and order in the coming to know (method)—are parsing the grammar of wisdom. In his English (but not in his Latin) writings, Lonergan preferred, however, to use another idiom, to speak of conversion and differentiation of consciousness, of religious, moral, and intellectual self-transcendence, of ordering operations methodically, of moving toward a comprehensive or universal viewpoint, though, as Ivo Coelho has shown, it is certain that in speaking this way he meant to address the problem of becoming wise.[24] Perhaps he shifted his language simply to have a fresh vocabulary, rooted in his own hermeneutics of interiority, by which to distinguish different aspects of wisdom and to bring an ancient tradition into living contact with present problems.

In the chapters that follow, I wish to trace Lonergan's interaction with this grammar of wisdom, not exhaustively but suggestively, as he sought to bring history into theology.

The Structure of the Book

The book is divided into a prelude and two main parts. The prelude contextualizes the overall argument of the book in relation to widespread perceptions of Lonergan and in relation to the cultural and intellectual crisis of our time as he saw it.

23. *Method* (1972), 345, or CWL 14, 319.

24. This is an important thread in Ivo Coelho, *Hermeneutics and Method: The "Universal Viewpoint" in Bernard Lonergan* (Toronto: University of Toronto Press, 2001).

The first part, Wisdom as Subject, addresses Lonergan's 'foundational methodology' in four sketches: (1) his fundamental strategy for meeting the crisis of our time, (2) the emergence of this strategy in his encounter with Aquinas, (3) its development and implementation in *Insight*, and (4) his subsequent proposal for ordering theology. The second part, Wisdom as Object, explores how Lonergan developed and, insofar as he was able, implemented his program in the theology he wrote. That theology was both the expression of his ideas on method and also the impetus for their further development. The selection of problems is strategic. One chapter deals with doctrine in its development, another with method and order in systematic theology, and a third with the wisdom expressed in Christ's human life.

The division into Wisdom as Subject and as Object is suggested by *Insight*, which Lonergan divided into halves, 'Insight as Activity' and 'Insight as Knowledge.' Its meaning is somewhat different, however. Lonergan's purpose in 'Insight as Activity' was to construct a kind of workbook, a series of strategic examples in which to notice the occurrence of insight, its methodical development, and its characteristic derailments, culminating in the decisive act he called 'self-appropriation.' In 'Insight as Knowledge,' he executed a series of forays into metaphysics, the foundation of ethics, the question of God, and the expectation of divine revelation to illustrate how self-appropriation might be methodically exploited in the development of knowledge. Our Wisdom as Subject, however, does not intend a pedagogy of self-discovery, but only to show how, why, and with what fundamental implications Lonergan took his 'turn to the subject.' Our Wisdom as Object exemplifies the fecundity of this program by showing how it was actually applied to theological questions.

The prelude comprises two chapters. In the first chapter, I examine representative assessments of Lonergan and the portent of his project. The incoherence of conventional wisdom about him underscores the desirability of a new encounter with Lonergan. The second chapter, A Crisis of Normativity, frames the cultural and intellectual crisis of our time as Lonergan diagnosed it. I sketch the major cultural and intellectual shifts of modernity and postmodernity, with their outcome in a crisis of normativity. The chapter does not aim to be a complete theory of modernity or postmodernity, but a somewhat updated orientation to the problems as Lonergan tended to read them and to which he intended to respond. I show why he came to believe that only a science of inquiry or methods could meet the fundamental issue of the day. Although the present context of theology is significantly different from the one in which Lonergan operated, I suggest that the deep underlying problems remain unchanged and unresolved. The need for new theological foundations adequate to contemporary natural science and historical and cultural understanding is with us still. I argue that Lonergan's way of linking wisdom as self-surrender to a program of wisdom through self-interrogation and self-knowledge offers a distinctive way forward.

The first part, Wisdom as Subject, begins in earnest with the third chapter, A Wisdom of the Concrete. Here I present Lonergan's turn to the subject as an effort to meet the crisis of normativity. Rather than describe his cognitional theory, I try to situate his turn argumentatively in relation to alternative approaches to the foundational problems of theology today. I argue that in any case what Lonergan is about is really a kind of asceticism whose fruits cannot properly be conveyed by describing them, but only attained by practice. I also invert, so to speak, the order of his discovery. In Lonergan's development and his typical presentation, the normativity of wonder and cognitional structure lead, but I start from the normativity of love and worship which was, in a sense, the point upon which his thought was converging.

Chapters 4 and 5 pursue the thread of Lonergan's methodological itinerary: how and why he came to propose his program of self-knowledge and self-appropriation as 'first philosophy.' I begin by situating this program in terms of his interaction with Augustine and Aquinas, before tracing the main stages by which it developed and he realized that he had moved out of the ambit of a metaphysical psychology and into an analysis of intentionality.

Chapter 6 explores the existential significance of his method in theology as subalternating all of theology to conversion and faith. I give a brief account of Lonergan's proposal for a functionally specialized theology and outline some of its more notable implications. I argue, further, that Lonergan's method effects a twofold transposition of Aquinas's articulation of the relationship of theology to faith and of the speculative or systematic office of theology to doctrine.

The second part, Wisdom as Object, turns more directly to Lonergan's implementation of this program in theology. Chapters 7, 8, and 9 take up the problems of order, criteria, and method in theology. Special attention is given to the relationship between doctrine and systematic theology. Chapter 7 addresses the problem of doctrinal development by examining Lonergan's analysis of the process from the New Testament to the Council of Nicaea. Lonergan characterized that process as a movement from one kind of clarity to another, from the clarity of narrative and symbol to the clarity of systematic meaning. The development in doctrine presupposed a concomitant and proportionate development in theologians to become able to operate securely in a new stage of meaning. Further considerations regard doctrine as knowledge, that is, the function of doctrines as truth claims about the world. Doctrines have a cognitive truth-intention that is not merely the expression of our immanent religious experience. Although doctrine is carried by language, for Lonergan it was fundamentally about authentic judgment and therefore wisdom.

Chapter 8 is a case study of the problem of order in systematic theology, but it is also an exercise in what Lonergan meant by theological dialectic. The case in point is Lonergan's transposition of Aquinas's 'psychological analogy' for the Trinity. Aquinas's approach has come under heavy criticism in recent decades, but I argue that the critics miss the point. Systematic theology has its own internal criteria for ordering questions and for measuring success, and Lonergan argued that, if measured by the appropriate criteria, Aquinas's treatise on God in the *Summa theologiae* was the apex of speculative theology in the scholastic tradition. Here, furthermore, method becomes content, as it were: by knowing ourselves knowing and loving, we conceive God as infinite Knowing and Loving.

Chapter 9 turns to Lonergan's own theological understanding of Christ's wisdom. The chapter serves several important purposes. In the first place, by showing how Lonergan developed the achievement of Thomas Aquinas on the question of Christ's human knowledge, it illustrates both continuity and progress in theology, showing once more how Lonergan sought to meet more recent objections by consolidating and developing the achievements of the tradition rather than scrapping them. Then, too, because the topic is knowledge, it provides another opportunity to illustrate the bearing of Lonergan's account of knowing.

It also exemplifies his approach to the systematic part of theology as subalternate to doctrines. Finally, because the topic is the wisdom of Christ, the supreme teacher of wisdom, it serves as a fitting coda to a book on wisdom. For all of theology is subalternate to faith, to the personal adherence of the theologian to Christ, wisdom incarnate. Lonergan's articulation of Christ's human knowledge is not only his account of Christ as the supreme teacher and definitive revelation of God but also a personal confession of his Christian conviction. If theology is an integral part of the wisdom proportionate to the actual order of this universe, it is because we are involved with the mystery given and declared in Christ.

Prelude

CHAPTER ONE

Apprehensions and Misapprehensions

*Centuries are required to change mentalities, centuries. You don't
get a change of mentality by introducing a few fads.*[1]

BERNARD LONERGAN

B RILLIANT ARGUMENTS," WRITES R. R. Reno of Lonergan in a
poignant essay, "are not the same as intellectual influence."[2] A quick
glance at Lonergan's standing in the contemporary academy may give
the impression of health. There are established Lonergan centers all
over the world, annual conferences devoted to his thought, and working
groups at major professional societies; there is a steady stream of dis-
sertations and theses, books and articles. Among his pupils are bright,
rising stars. Yet, I feel, all is not well. The Lonergan project, if not a
ghetto, is in danger of becoming one. Over four decades since the
appearance of *Method in Theology* and almost six since *Insight*, even his
questions seem to be slipping away. Philosophically and theologically
an outlier and relentlessly demanding on his readers, Lonergan makes
a poor casual interlocutor. His ideas are difficult and obscure; his style
is often elliptical and sometimes awkward and confusing. Now, past
evensong's psalmody for the last generation of his immediate students,
Lonergan's isolation seems more complete than ever. His thought-
world can seem like an exotic club whose management has set too

---

1. Bernard J. F. Lonergan, *Caring about Meaning: Patterns in the Life of Bernard Lonergan*, ed. Pierrot
Lambert, Charlotte Tansey, and Cathleen Going, Thomas More Institute Papers 82 (Montreal:
Thomas More Institute, 1982), 173.
2. R. R. Reno, "Theology After the Revolution," *First Things* 173 (2007): 15–21.

steep a cover charge; those who are not persuaded to pay up in youth are unlikely ever to do so.

Reliable introductions exist,[3] but the genre suffers endemic limitations. A conceptual overview, however valuable and exact, does little to bring Lonergan's method to life. It is all too easy to give the impression that 'getting Lonergan' is a matter of learning a special language game ("five levels, four biases, three conversions . . . and zero understanding"[4]). Merely learning the language, unfortunately, is not 'getting Lonergan' and generally leaves things more or less as they were, unless, worse, it gelds him.

Surely less harm has been done Lonergan by superficial acquaintance, however, than by the unconscious conscription of his language into games of power or self-delusion.[5] I do not exempt myself from this critique. It would be dishonest to ignore how many colleagues have been turned off completely by encounters with some autarkic 'Lonerganian' smugly endowed with the answers to everyone else's questions, or affecting to be deeper, more serious, more 'authentic' than others, or simply unable to break the monologue for a real conversation. Consequential ideas are always let in for abuse, perhaps especially in a culture, like ours, so given to the individualisms of utility and self-expression, but Lonergan's project may be unusually intoxicating because it portends, in a way, a new game.

---

3. For introductions to Lonergan's life and work, see Crowe, *Lonergan*; Pierrot Lambert and Philip McShane, *Bernard Lonergan: His Life and Leading Ideas* (Halifax: Axial Press, 2010); and William A. Mathews, *Lonergan's Quest: A Study of Desire in the Authoring of* Insight, Lonergan Studies (Toronto: University of Toronto Press, 2006). Flanagan, *Quest for Self-Knowledge*, is a reliable way into Lonergan's philosophy; Mark T. Miller, *The Quest for God and the Good Life: Lonergan's Theological Anthropology* (Washington, D.C.: The Catholic University of America Press, 2013), is a theological introduction pitched to undergraduates; and Vernon Gregson, ed., *The Desires of the Human Heart: An Introduction to the Theology of Bernard Lonergan* (New York: Paulist Press, 1988), is addressed to a lay readership without prior familiarity with Lonergan's work. Two dated but still valuable guides are Michael C. O'Callaghan, *Unity in Theology: Lonergan's Framework for Theology in Its New Context* (Lanham, Md.: University Press of America, 1980), which relates *Method in Theology* to the German context of the later twentieth century; and David Tracy, *The Achievement of Bernard Lonergan* (New York: Herder and Herder, 1970), an important study conducted before the appearance of *Method in Theology*.

4. Lonergan would reportedly conclude his Trinity course at the Gregorian University by wryly quipping that Trinitarian theology has "five notions, four relations, three persons, two processions, one God, and zero understanding." (Grant Kaplan tells me he heard this from Stephen Duffy; I have heard it from others, too.)

5. Frederick G. Lawrence, *The Fragility of Consciousness: Faith, Reason, and the Human Good*, ed. Randall S. Rosenberg and Kevin M. Vander Schel (Toronto: University of Toronto Press, 2017), 277.

At the very least, a strong dose of repentance and humility is in order. Nevertheless, the fact remains that theologians (and philosophers), by and large, have not known what to do with Lonergan, have not caught the real bearing of his project, and have not been motivated to come to grips with it.

To urge a new hearing is to allege the insufficiency of the earlier. In this chapter, I illustrate that insufficiency by passing in review a representative selection of interpretations, or rather, misinterpretations so contradictory to one another that manifestly they cannot all be right. In fact, they are mostly wrong. Outside the small circle in which he is taken with utmost seriousness, Lonergan is a shade whose cast depends on one's own proclivities, philosophical, theological, or both.

My sampling of misreadings invites a fuller dialectic than the chapter offers. The result may seem somewhat peremptory, and I can only ask the reader's patience. There are many defective interpretations but, in principle, only one correct interpretation. It would be tedious to correct errors one by one, so in the main I limit myself here to illustrating their existence. The reply, so to speak, is the rest of the book.

Quarantine

Lonergan has been likened to a dilatory tinker, stropping his knife to postpone carving.[6] He was doomed to press his theology into neoscholastic molds even as he sought to break them. Publishing three Latin textbooks in 1964 was no recipe to gain a readership. Then, too, his pupils at the Gregorian University were largely bound for parish and prelacy, not the professoriate. These factors tended to keep the main body of his theological work obscure, so that his methodological indications, already cryptic to many, suffered further from want of illustration. But even if the theology had been better known, it was not the embodiment of his method but the constrained performance upon which method reflects. We will never know the theology Lonergan might later have written, for after *Method in Theology* he turned his hand to economics.[7]

6. Hearsay imputes a remark to this effect to Karl Rahner.

7. Lonergan's interest in economics dates back to the 1930s, i.e., the decade before his apprenticeship to Aquinas: "His interests . . . were economic, political, sociological, cultural, historical, religious, rather than gnoseological and metaphysical" (Frederick Crowe, writing in the editors'

The Latin textbooks he did write are finally appearing in English at a moment when there is almost no context to receive them. Disciples of Aquinas might be better prepared than most to appreciate Lonergan's theological achievements, but first they must be persuaded to read him. For many in the wide and ecumenical circle of theologians and philosophers for whom Aquinas is a major conversation partner, Lonergan seems simply a closed world, deserving perhaps of a passing remark but basically unrelated and unrelatable to anything else. I find it strange that the community struggling to reach up to Aquinas finds so little to recognize in Lonergan's project, but they seem to have largely given him up.

The negligence is mutual: deep knowledge of Aquinas is rare in Lonergan circles, as if reaching up to Lonergan supersedes grappling with Aquinas and could be achieved without it. In fairness, there is more to Lonergan than scholarship on Lonergan; no knowledge of Aquinas is required to benefit from the exercises of self-appropriation that are the heart of Lonergan's project and relevant to many applications beyond theology and philosophy. Yet scholars of Lonergan sometimes appear to know of Aquinas only what Lonergan tells them, repeated with diminishing returns for want of context. This reflects, of course, a general state of disarray in contemporary theology; deep knowledge of the *vetera* is rare. But such practical supersessionism among Lonergan scholars has a palpable irony. "It is quite impossible," Lonergan insisted, "to tell anyone what Aquinas meant while omitting mention of the historical origin and the nature of the blocks he pieced together."[8] But Aquinas, it seems to me, was as important to Lonergan as Aristotle had been to Aquinas. As

---

preface to Lonergan, *Verbum*, vii). The experience of the Depression persuaded Lonergan that the social doctrine of the church needed a sound economic footing if it would advance beyond vague platitudes on economic justice. See Bernard J. F. Lonergan, *Macroeconomic Dynamics: An Essay in Circulation Analysis*, ed. Frederick G. Lawrence, Patrick H. Byrne, and Charles C. Hefling Jr., CWL 15 (1999); Bernard J. F. Lonergan, *For a New Political Economy*, ed. Philip McShane, CWL 21 (1998); Bernard J. Lonergan and Michael Shute, *Lonergan's Early Economic Research: Texts and Commentary*, ed. Michael Shute, Lonergan Studies (Toronto: University of Toronto Press, 2010); and Michael Shute, *Lonergan's Discovery of the Science of Economics* (Toronto: University of Toronto Press, 2010). Frederick Crowe remarked, apropos Lonergan's last decade of work, that "though he has given, through the lectures of this period, scattered hints on a return to theology, the work of implementing his method was left to be undertaken by his theological heirs." "Bernard Lonergan as Pastoral Theologian," in *Appropriating the Lonergan Idea*, ed. Michael Vertin (Washington, D.C.: The Catholic University of America Press, 1989), 127–44, here 138.

8.   Bernard J. F. Lonergan, "On God and Secondary Causes," in *Collection*, CWL 4, 53–65, here 61.

for the theologians, in any case, Lonergan had no wish to replace the tradition; his aim was to help us measure up to it.

Among professing Thomists, Lonergan is under a cloud of suspicion. His iconoclasm towards the commentators is rebarbative; his 'turn to the subject' smacks of apostasy. Gilson's alarum about ceding the game to idealism seems to have become the prevailing sentiment, so that a 'direct' and 'immediate' realism is widely presumed unsafe even to doubt, *non potest tuto dubitari*—and, perforce!, the authentic doctrine of Aquinas.[9] "Adjectivally transcendental, substantively Thomism" was Schubert Ogden's summary judgment on 'transcendental Thomism'[10]—the box into which Lonergan is most often put—but to professing Thomists it seems the other way around. Indeed, today the very exegetical and speculative questions Lonergan addressed are often debated as if Lonergan—even his strictly exegetical studies, *Grace and Freedom* and *Verbum*—had simply never happened.[11] When Lonergan's Trinitarian systematics first

---

9. Étienne Gilson, *Réalisme thomiste et critique de la connaissance* (Paris: Librairie philosophique J. Vrin, 1939), chap. 2. "Qui commence en idéaliste finira nécessairement en idéaliste." Gilson, *Le réalisme méthodique* (Paris: Chez Pierre Téqui, 2007), 4.

10. Schubert Miles Ogden, "The Challenge to Protestant Thought," *Continuum* 6, no. 2 (1968): 236–40, here 239; a similar judgment was entered by Edward MacKinnon, "The Transcendental Turn: Necessary but Not Sufficient," *Continuum* 6, no. 2 (1968): 225–31, here 225; see too Bernard A. M. Nachbar, "Is It Thomism?," *Continuum* 6, no. 2 (1968): 232–35.

11. Here I can only give a few examples representing conversations in which Lonergan made significant interventions that are no longer even afforded the courtesy of a rebuttal. On insight and inner word—the central topic of *Verbum*—an exception is Mark D. Jordan, *Ordering Wisdom: The Hierarchy of Philosophical Discourses in Aquinas*, Publications in Medieval Studies 24 (Notre Dame, Ind.: University of Notre Dame Press, 1986), who devotes nine pages to a thoughtful dissent from certain aspects of Lonergan's interpretation of the inner word. On the other hand, one might expect more than a tangential reference to *Verbum* in John O'Callaghan, *Thomist Realism and the Linguistic Turn: Toward a More Perfect Form of Existence* (Notre Dame, Ind.: University of Notre Dame Press, 2003). Jeffrey E. Brower and Susan Brower-Toland, "Aquinas on Mental Representation: Concepts and Intentionality," *The Philosophical Review* 117, no. 2 (2008): 193–243, argue directly contrary to Lonergan's thesis, but *Verbum* is not engaged except for a listing among the references. It is not even in the bibliography of Gilles Emery, *The Trinitarian Theology of Saint Thomas Aquinas*, trans. Francesca Aran Murphy (New York: Oxford University Press, 2007); nor Emmanuel Perrier, *La fécondité en dieu: la puissance notionnelle dans la Trinité selon saint Thomas d'Aquin*, Bibliothèque de la Revue thomiste, Études de théologie 3 (Paris: Parole et silence, 2009). Thomas Joseph White's monumental *The Incarnate Lord: A Thomistic Study in Christology* (Washington, D.C.: The Catholic University of America Press, 2015) is involved with an enormous range of conversation partners within and apart from the Thomist tradition, on topics to which Lonergan made signal contributions; he makes a modest appearance in the bibliography but none in the text. On self-knowledge in Aquinas, Lonergan does not exist for Therese Scarpelli Cory, *Aquinas on Human Self-Knowledge* (New York: Cambridge University Press, 2013), though he might have helped her escape taking self-awareness for a kind of self-perception. Mark D. Jordan's discussion

appeared in 1959, the achievement was heralded in the *Bulletin Thomiste* with a warm encomium by Albert Patfoort;[12] it reappeared half a dozen years ago as unexploded ordnance.

The Subversive

Neglect may be preferable to some attentions. Here I would like to notice the strictures of John Finnis and Tracey Rowland, John Milbank and Catherine Pickstock. In doing so, I do not intend so much to pick on them, particularly, as to exemplify a simple point: an indefensible verdict on Lonergan has become, in many circles, conventional wisdom.

Finnis was grateful to Lonergan, because *Insight*, he felt, had helped lead him to the church.[13] His later disenchantment, however, verges on contempt. Finnis found he could not follow the hermeneutical turn Lonergan took in *Method in Theology*, which, in his judgment, sundered

---

of the same topic in *Ordering Wisdom* mentions Lonergan's interpretation but engages it only obliquely. On grace and freedom, Steven A. Long, *Natura Pura: On the Recovery of Nature in the Doctrine of Grace*, 1st ed., Moral Philosophy and Moral Theology (New York: Fordham University Press, 2010), repristinates Banezianism without a mention of Lonergan's scathing critique. On this question, however, exceptions have begun to appear. See, e.g., Joshua R. Brotherton, "The Integrity of Nature in the Grace–Freedom Dynamic: Lonergan's Critique of Bañezian Thomism," *Theological Studies* 75, no. 3 (2014): 537–563; Robert Joseph Matava, *Divine Causality and Human Free Choice: Domingo Báñez, Physical Premotion, and the Controversy de Auxiliis Revisited* (Boston: Brill, 2016); and Steven A. Long, Roger W. Nutt, and Thomas Joseph White, eds., *Thomism and Predestination: Principles and Disputations* (Naples, Fla.: Sapientia Press of Ave Maria University, 2016). On the relationship of philosophy and science, one of the central problems of *Insight*, William A. Wallace, *The Modeling of Nature: Philosophy of Science and Philosophy of Nature in Synthesis* (Washington, D.C.: The Catholic University of America Press, 1996), gives a lot of ink to outlining various positions without taking any notice of Lonergan.

12. "For this speculative work and its pedagogical communication, Fr Lonergan has a very vivid and extremely lucid sense, and he realizes his design in a powerfully structured work, following a method profoundly rethought and truly re-created. . . . It is long since anyone has spoken of the grandeur and fruitfulness of speculative theology with such conviction and such precision; and it is long, we will add, since anyone has exemplified it so vigorously." Albert Patfoort, review of *Divinarum Personarum Conceptio Analogica*, by Bernard J. F. Lonergan, *Bulletin Thomiste* 10, no. 2 (1959): 531–34, here 532, my translation. *Divinarum Personarum* is an earlier published edition (originally 1957) of Bernard J. F. Lonergan, *De Deo Trino 2. Pars Systematica* (Rome: Gregorian University Press, 1964); this 1964 text is now presented with English translation in *Triune God: Systematics*.

13. Finnis credits *Insight* with an instrumental role in his conversion: see his personal biography at http://www.twotlj.org/Finnis.html (third paragraph) and the descriptions of his conversations with Germain Grisez at http://www.twotlj.org/grisez_collaborators.html (right-hand column).

the gates to nihilism,[14] or at least to proportionalism (apparently an earlier station on the same track).[15] His strictures alight on two perceived weaknesses in particular: Lonergan's later account of moral objectivity and his "cloudy rhetoric about the significance of cultural change."[16] First, as Finnis reads him, Lonergan "denies that goods ('values') are understood"[17] and has somehow "overlooked the truly decisive difference between the good as merely experienced and the good as understood."[18] The bottom line seems to be that Lonergan abandoned rational ethics for fine feeling. On cultural change, next, Finnis charges him with outright incoherence, partly because Lonergan did not assign a date for the shift from one world-view to another,[19] and partly because he finds Lonergan still using theoretical techniques that, Finnis supposes, Lonergan somehow ruled out,[20] but mostly because he just cannot figure out what exactly is meant. "Sometimes the distinction seems to be little more than: between having an education focused on the Greek and Latin classics, and then expanding one's horizons by reading Christopher Dawson on comparative religion."[21]

Finnis's criticisms of Lonergan are really declarations of anxiety that tell us nothing about Lonergan, or rather, what they tell us is wrong. What is astonishing about Finnis's criticisms, however, is not that Lonergan is difficult and Finnis misunderstood him. It is Finnis's breezy misidentification of his incomprehension with Lonergan's incoherence.[22]

14. See John Finnis, *Fundamentals of Ethics* (Oxford: Clarendon Press, 1983), 30–32, 42–45; Frederick G. Lawrence, "Finnis on Lonergan: A Reflection," *Villanova Law Review* 57, no. 5 (2012): 849–925, here esp. 851–52.

15. John Finnis, *"Historical Consciousness" and Theological Foundations* (Toronto: Pontifical Institute of Medieval Studies, 1992), 1–2. This is basically an unjust critique erected on a wholly inadequate interpretation. Further discussion of Lonergan's critique of 'classicism' in the next chapter.

16. John Finnis, *Religion and Public Reasons*, Collected Essays, vol. 5 (New York: Oxford University Press, 2011), 272; see also 58 and 58n13; compare *"Historical Consciousness,"* 1–4.

17. Finnis, *Fundamentals of Ethics*, 54 (II.4); see 32n18, 42–44; *"Historical Consciousness,"* 12–14.

18. Finnis, *Fundamentals of Ethics*, 44. This is a rather remarkable thing to say about a person who, in practically everything he had to say about ethics and every other topic, emphasized the distinction between experience and understanding.

19. Finnis, *"Historical Consciousness,"* 2.

20. Ibid., 12–16.

21. Ibid., 2n4.

22. See, e.g., Finnis, *"Historical Consciousness,"* 12–13; *Fundamentals of Ethics*, 42–45. The whole discussion of Lonergan in these places is an object lesson in the limitations of proof-texting.

To Lonergan on culture we return in the next chapter, but it might bear notice here that Finnis's construal of Lonergan on value is worthless.[23] He imputes to Lonergan a counterposition that Lonergan refutes most explicitly.[24] Lonergan himself characterized his development on value this way:

> In *Insight* the good was the intelligent and the reasonable. In *Method* the good is a distinct notion. It is intended by questions for deliberation: Is this worthwhile? Is it truly or only apparently good? It is aspired to in the intentional response of feeling to values. It is known in judgments of value made by a virtuous or authentic person with a good conscience. It is brought about by deciding and living up to one's decisions. Just as intelligence sublates sense, just as reasonableness sublates intelligence, so deliberation sublates and thereby unifies knowing and feeling.[25]

According to Lonergan, deliberation does not replace intelligence and reasonableness with feeling, but brings them together into a higher synthesis. We raise questions about value; by raising them we proceed to criticism and judgment of values; in judging we distinguish objectively true values from false, the truly worthwhile from the merely pleasant; correct evaluations and good decisions presuppose correct understanding of reality; and as it is the virtuous, self-transcending person who is a competent judge in matters moral and, indeed, feels the right way about things, so it is the person who feels the right way about things who is likely not only to notice but also to honor what is worthwhile.[26] If

---

23. Finnis himself records his surprise that the kind of analysis Lonergan performs does not seem to fit with what he, Finnis, took him to mean (*"Historical Consciousness,"* 12–16). But, for some reason, the felt dissonance does not seem to have occasioned a reconsideration.

24. *Insight*, 629–30.

25. Bernard J. F. Lonergan, *"Insight* Revisited," in *A Second Collection*, CWL 13, 221–33, here 277.

26. *Method* (1972), 34–41, or CWL 14, 35–42; note also the fascinating remarks in "An Interview with Fr Bernard Lonergan, S.J.," in *A Second Collection*, CWL 13, 176–94, here 188; for interpretations, see Patrick H. Byrne, *The Ethics of Discernment: Lonergan's Foundations for Ethics* (Toronto: University of Toronto Press, 2016), 169–203; Brian Cronin, *Value Ethics: A Lonergan Perspective*, Guide to Philosophy 13 (Nairobi: Consolata Institute of Philosophy, 2006), 209–324; and Mark J. Doorley, *The Place of the Heart in Lonergan's Ethics: The Role of Feelings in the Ethical Intentionality Analysis of Bernard Lonergan* (Lanham, Md.: University Press of America, 1996).

Lonergan coherently meant all these things, he was no more a sentimentalist than Plato, who, after all, had a point about music and moral education.

Patrick Brown suggests Finnis might be reacting less to Lonergan himself than to decidedly whiggish (if nominally approving) conscriptions of his critique of 'classicist' culture.[27] I suspect there is a much broader story to be told here about Lonergan's indirect role in the public furor over Paul VI's 1968 encyclical *Humanae Vitae*. I am not aware of any study of Lonergan's role in these events. As far as I know, he did not intervene publically in the fracas. Privately, however, he opined that the encyclical's biological assumptions were antiquated and, accordingly, its moral analysis missed the point. Lonergan was likely the most illustrious Canadian theologian at that time, and it seems probable that his low opinion of Paul VI's argument had some influence, at least through his Jesuit confrere and Regis College colleague Edward Sheridan, SJ, upon the Canadian bishops at their Winnipeg conference in September 1968. Judging at least from the effective history of their Winnipeg statement, the Canadian bishops declined to support the encyclical's judgment on contraception, offering Canadian Catholics a way out by appeal to conscience. Many leaders of the organized opposition in the United States, moreover, starting with Charles Curran, claimed the mantle of Lonergan, particularly his critique of 'classicism.'[28] I surmise Finnis, and others of Lonergan's critics, have been more or less aware of these connections, which fuel their perception of Lonergan as subversive.

The perception, however, has taken on a life of its own. Finnis had read and learned from Lonergan; he was not just channeling the diminishing returns of conventional wisdom. Tracey Rowland's version of Lonergan

27. Patrick Brown, "Classicism: A Prelude" (paper presented at the West Coast Methods Institute, Loyola Marymount University, Los Angeles, Calif., April 2013). For instances of somewhat distorting haute vulgarization, Brown points to Mark Stephen Massa, *The American Catholic Revolution: How the Sixties Changed the Church Forever* (New York: Oxford University Press, 2010), 10–13; Charles E. Curran, *Catholic Moral Theology in the United States: A History*, Moral Traditions (Washington, D.C.: Georgetown University Press, 2008), 103–4; Richard P. McBrien, *Catholicism*, rev. ed. (New York: HarperSanFrancisco, 1994), 610, 911; and Richard M. Gula, *Reason Informed by Faith: Foundations of Catholic Morality* (New York: Paulist Press, 1989), 30–33.

28. See Richard McCormick, "*Humanae Vitae* 25 Years Later," *America Magazine*, July 17, 1993, 6–12.

is, as far as I can tell, derived from Finnis's. In her narrative, he is not an interlocutor but a bête noire: 'Lonergan' is a name attached to positions she is totally against. She formulates these positions in a manner that resembles things he said, but taken with a meaning he never intended. It is the meaning one might derive from reading Finnis's critique without coming to grips with Lonergan himself.

For Rowland, Lonergan symbolizes an 'open narrative' of adaptation to the Zeitgeist—what used to be called 'modernism' in Catholic circles—whereas she would have a critique of modernity from the resources of Christian tradition.[29] What she is for, he is supposed to be against: a personal formation oriented to what is normative, committed to excellence, "recognizing grades of distinction in the achievement of the norm."[30] As we will see in due course, this imputation is not merely wrong on some point of nuance; it is so completely wrong that her summary description of what Lonergan is purportedly against could stand as a description of his dearest concern: grounding transcultural normativity.

Ex falso sequitur quodlibet. Confident of his 'modernism,' Rowland makes Lonergan her example of those who advocate "abandoning 'what the Church gained from her inculturation in the world of Greco-Latin thought.'"[31] The charge is dispiriting, for Lonergan wrote hundreds of pages—granted, very many of them in Latin—defending the exact opposite. In one of the most unsparing essays of his career, he demolished the position Rowland imputes to him in the form of Leslie Dewart's dehellenization program. He faulted Dewart for rejecting truth as correspondence (without which it would be impossible to mean anything), propositions, dogma, and, most to the point, "the Greek miracle that effected the triumph of logos over mythos": logic and metaphysics.[32]

29. See Tracey Rowland, "Catholic Theology in the Twentieth Century," in *Key Theological Thinkers: From Modern to Postmodern*, ed. Svein Rise and Staale Johannes Kristiansen (Burlington, Vt.: Ashgate, 2013), 37–52.

30. Tracey Rowland, *Culture and the Thomist Tradition: After Vatican II*, Routledge Radical Orthodoxy (New York: Routledge, 2003), 72.

31. Ibid., 45. The internal quotation is from John Paul II, *Fides et Ratio*, Encyclical Letter (September 14, 1998), §72. On Benedict's advocacy of the positive legacy of Hellenism, see James V. Schall, *The Regensburg Lecture* (South Bend, Ind.: St. Augustine's Press, 2007); Joseph Ratzinger, *Introduction to Christianity*, trans. J. R. Foster, rev. ed. (San Francisco: Ignatius Press, 2004), 94–104.

32. Bernard J. F. Lonergan, "The Dehellenization of Dogma," in *A Second Collection*, CWL 13, 11–30, here 19; this is an essay review of Leslie Dewart, *The Future of Belief: Theism in a World Come of Age* (New York: Herder and Herder, 1966). These are Lonergan's settled views on the questions at hand.

Dewart, in Lonergan's assessment, was just sloganeering: "Let's liquidate Hellenism."[33] It is bizarre, then, that Lonergan should himself make Rowland's list of liquidators, and one wonders how.[34]

Let us round out this small sampling by briefly noting the critique of Lonergan offered by John Milbank and Catherine Pickstock. They aver that (for Aquinas, but also for them) judgment is attained not through a discursive canvassing of the evidence interrupted by a grasp of its sufficiency, but through an intuition of essence by which the mind "partakes infallibly of the divine power of intuitive recognition."This is contrasted to Lonergan's purportedly "neo-Kantian" account of (Thomist) judgment as "synthesis."[35] As the chapters to follow will show, their version of Lonergan is unrecognizable, intuitively or otherwise, and could not possibly survive contact with the evidence.[36]

Despite my rather pointed remarks, I would not wish to do to these thinkers what they have done to Lonergan. They all have something important to say in their own right, though this is not the place to get at it. All I really want to say here is that in casting Lonergan as the villain of their tales, they have done him, their readers, and themselves wrong.

The Paradox

Reputation is a funny thing. Lonergan's fundamental concern was for order in theology, but he has obviously come to be seen as a harbinger of disorientation. To very many he is simply among the villains who brought

33. Lonergan, "The Dehellenization of Dogma," 21. The slogan is Lonergan's take on Dewart, not Dewart's own phrase. Lonergan appreciated the achievements and permanent contributions of Greek thought, but he sifted them carefully. See too his paper "Aquinas Today: Tradition and Innovation," in *A Third Collection*, CWL 16, 34–51.

34. There are two neutral paragraphs on the Lonergan school in Rowland's essay on twentieth-century Catholic theology, but they do not go beyond general knowledge about his project: Rowland, "Catholic Theology in the Twentieth Century," 50.

35. John Milbank, *Truth in Aquinas*, Routledge Radical Orthodoxy (New York: Routledge, 2001), 22; see the critique by Paul J. DeHart, *Aquinas and Radical Orthodoxy: A Critical Inquiry*, Routledge Studies in Religion 16 (New York: Routledge, 2012).

36. See Neil Ormerod, "'It Is Easy to See': The Footnotes of John Milbank," *Philosophy and Theology* 11, no. 2 (1999): 257–264; Martin J. De Nys, "Lonergan and Radical Orthodoxy" (paper presented at the West Coast Methods Institute, Loyola Marymount University, Los Angeles, Calif., April 2017).

the house down: a subjectivist, a misbegotten Kantian in philosophy, a stillborn Schleiermacher in theology.[37] Yet to others, he has not gone nearly far enough, philosophically, theologically, or both.

Charles Davis, in his relation to Lonergan, is almost the anti-Finnis. The one felt Lonergan led him to the church; the other felt he had liberated him from it.[38] Both felt Lonergan sowed seeds of destruction, Finnis to his horror and Davis to his Promethean release. Reading Lonergan, Davis tells us, "freed the spiritual dynamic within" him while at the same time failing to persuade him "of the validity of the chief purpose of all his [Lonergan's] work." This was because (Davis charged) Lonergan assumed an infallible church without scrutiny, while Davis could not.[39] Davis accused Lonergan of hanging on to retrograde Catholicism despite his own better angels:

Lonergan's excellent analysis of the transition from classical to modern culture, when read without his [Catholic, dogmatic] presuppositions, urges, I suggest, the opposite conclusion to his own: namely, that the Roman Catholic insistence on unchanging dogmas, an infallible magisterium and a hierarchically

37. Criticisms of this kind began from the time of the first of the *verbum* articles, for instance, Matthew J. O'Connell, "St. Thomas and the Verbum: An Interpretation," *The Modern Schoolman* 24, no. 4 (1947): 224–34. For more recent examples, see, e.g., Charles James, "Falling into Subjectivism," *New Oxford Review*, September 2003; Julian Burt, "Lonergan Doctrine: Is It Orthodox?," *Homiletic and Pastoral Review*, January 1986, 26–32, 50–53; John F. X. Knasas, *The Preface to Thomistic Metaphysics: A Contribution to the Neo-Thomist Debate on the Start of Metaphysics* (New York: Peter Lang, 1990); John F. X. Knasas, "Aquinas's Metaphysics and Descartes's Methodic Doubt," *The Thomist* 64, no. 3 (2000): 449–72; and David F. Ford, "Method in Theology in the Lonergan Corpus," in *Looking at Lonergan's Method*, ed. Patrick Corcoran (Dublin: Talbot Press, 1975), 11–26. T. F. Torrance is not among the Catholics but similarly takes Lonergan for a subjectivist and "Schleiermachian": see "The Function of Inner and Outer Word in Lonergan's Theological Method," in *Looking at Lonergan's Method*, 101–26, here 120–24. The story of Lonergan's relationship to Catholic modernism has not, to my knowledge, yet been told. There is no doubt, however, that he was preoccupied with the problem of dogmatic permanence and historicity and that he (in this respect, like Pius X in *Pascendi Dominici Gregis*, Encyclical Letter, September 8, 1907) diagnosed the underlying issue in terms of insufficient, or insufficiently considered, philosophic assumptions (or the interconnection of metaphysical and methodological commitments).

38. Charles Davis, "Lonergan and the Teaching Church," in *Foundations of Theology: Papers from the International Lonergan Congress 1970* (Notre Dame, Ind.: University of Notre Dame Press, 1971), 60–75, here 62.

39. Ibid., 62–63.

constituted church belongs to the classical culture and will have to be given up.[40]

In fact, Davis hypothesized, it was Lonergan's commitment to dogma and infallibility that fundamentally vitiated his whole project. It was, in the end, "an overdevelopment or excess of the theoretic and systematic," for the sake of "a vast ideological superstructure" to save his dogmatic faith by "creating the illusion that all the appropriate answers will be available" while masking the real situation.[41] Davis (rightly) disagrees with Rowland about Lonergan's intentions but shares nonetheless the suspicion that Lonergan's method is corrosive of dogma. This suspicion invites a fuller analysis than we can give here, but in subsequent chapters I aim to show it unfounded.

Davis is hardly the only critic for whom Lonergan did not go nearly far enough or was trying to have it both ways.[42] James Mackey dismissed Lonergan wearily as the bondservant of the imperial Logos-God whose "obituary is recorded in the death-of-God movement."[43] For Mackey, God may change and the church should change, but he is a votary of Consistency when it comes to reading Lonergan. Lonergan's analogical, developing, and historically sedimented use of 'transcendence' strikes him as a "poor alibi for lack of precision in a man's thought."[44] In Mackey's sage verdict, what Lonergan has to say in *Method in Theology* "will be as

---

40. Ibid., 74.

41. Charles Davis, review of *The Achievement of Bernard Lonergan*, by David Tracy, *Journal of Religion* 53, no. 3 (1973): 384–87, here 386–87. The critique takes in view *Method in Theology*, which appeared two years after Tracy's book (see 385).

42. For instance, William Richardson, "Being for Lonergan: A Heideggerian View," in *Language, Truth, and Meaning: Papers from the International Lonergan Congress 1970* (Notre Dame, Ind.: University of Notre Dame Press, 1972), 272–83; MacKinnon, "The Transcendental Turn"; Donal Dorr, "'Conversion,'" in *Looking at Lonergan's Method*, 175–85; J. P. Jossua, "Some Questions on the Place of Believing Experience in the Work of Bernard Lonergan," in *Looking at Lonergan's Method*, 164–74; Nicholas Lash, "Method and Cultural Discontinuity," in *Looking at Lonergan's Method*, 127–43; and J. P. Mackey, "Divine Revelation and Lonergan's Transcendental Method in Theology," in *Looking at Lonergan's Method*, 144–63.

43. Mackey, "Divine Revelation and Lonergan's Method," 151–52. For Mackey, Lonergan's 'classical' type of transcendentalism "could work only during the reign of the classical transcendent God of the West, the self-revealing Logos, and . . . both the method and the divinity are now either obsolete or obsolescent" (147).

44. Ibid., 145, criticizing Lonergan's use of "transcendental." *Sapientis non est curare de nominibus.*

much use . . . as the hearty advice: 'use your head and do the best you can with what you have.'"[45]

Protestant readers may be less prone to disenchantment, perhaps, but generally of similar mind. T. F. Torrance, George Lindbeck, and Schubert Ogden (to take three examples) all felt Lonergan was trying to have it both ways. "Torrance wanted to know if Lonergan was an old-style Roman Catholic or a new-style Tillich, and . . . felt Lonergan's work would not allow him to decide."[46] In the end, he misjudged Lonergan's project for a "neo-Catholic theology . . . collapsing into a form of neo-Protestant *Glaubverständnis* that takes its basic cue from an anthropological starting point."[47] Lindbeck found Lonergan difficult to square with his model. It seemed to him that Lonergan was stumbling through a routine of "complicated intellectual gymnastics" to hold together 'cognitivist' and 'experiential-expressivist' accounts of doctrine.[48] Ogden, like Finnis but from the other side of the question, indicted Lonergan as a smuggler whose banner was the 'subjectivist principle' but whose trade was in foreign goods.[49]

In fairness, Lonergan is genuinely riddlesome, and not just from circumstance. He couples a disquieting constancy with constant movement. Lonergan remarked that Aquinas never ceased "to drive towards fuller

45. Ibid., 163.

46. Ibid., 158, reporting on discussions at a seminar on *Method in Theology* at St. Patrick's College, Maynooth, Ireland, in the spring of 1973.

47. Torrance, "The Function of Inner and Outer Word in Lonergan's Theological Method," 122; compare Lonergan, "Theology and Understanding," esp. 117.

48. George A. Lindbeck, *The Nature of Doctrine* (Philadelphia: Westminster, 1984), 17; see 16–17, 31–32; Mike Higton, "Reconstructing *The Nature of Doctrine*," *Modern Theology* 30, no. 1 (2014): 1–31. Discussion of Lindbeck's criticisms in Neil Ormerod, *Method, Meaning, and Revelation: The Meaning and Function of Revelation in Bernard Lonergan's "Method in Theology"* (Lanham, Md.: University Press of America, 2000), 29–32, 192–205; and Charles C. Hefling Jr., "Turning Liberalism Inside Out," *Method: Journal of Lonergan Studies* 3, no. 2 (1985): 51–69. It may be, as my friend Murray Johnston suggests (in personal correspondence), that the debate between Lindbeck and David Tracy—both serious but ultimately unpersuaded readers of Lonergan—in the 1980s and into the 1990s overshadowed *Method in Theology* before its insights could be absorbed. For Tracy's questions to Lonergan, see David Tracy, "Lonergan's Foundational Theology: An Interpretation and a Critique," in *Foundations of Theology: Papers from the International Lonergan Congress 1970* (Notre Dame, Ind.: University of Notre Dame Press, 1971), 197–222; see too Tracy's earlier book, *The Achievement of Bernard Lonergan*; and T. Howland Sanks, "David Tracy's Theological Project: An Overview and Some Implications," *Theological Studies* 54, no. 4 (1993): 698–727.

49. Schubert Miles Ogden, "Lonergan and the Subjectivist Principle," in *Language, Truth, and Meaning: Papers from the International Lonergan Congress 1970* (Notre Dame, Ind.: University of Notre Dame Press, 1972), 218–35.

and more nuanced synthesis, without ever halting complacently in some finished mental edifice, as though his mind had become dull, or his brain exhausted, or his judgment had lapsed into the error of those that forget man to be potency in the realm of intelligence."[50] In its own way, this was also true of himself. He therefore left a job of work for "the second-rate men, though most useful in their place," as Newman has it, "who prove, reconcile, finish, and explain."[51] Some wonder if he did not simply change his stripes and make reconciliation impossible. At the same time, however, from end to end his work displays a fundamental conviction so unwavering that many find it unsettling.[52]

Though sharply critical of a theological and ecclesiastical regime investing enormous energy controlling what questions would be permitted a serious hearing, Lonergan, like many others who lived through the 'revolution,' was as dismayed by the derailments of the new theology as he had been by the inadequacies of the old.[53] He decried a tendency to disregard settled doctrine, to reject it, to reject even its very possibility. He lamented a loss of contact with important questions and content, a fragmentation of theology, a love of novelty for its own sake. He insisted that what was needed was not a new Gospel but a new mediation of the one Gospel into a radically changed cultural situation.[54] For him, the

---

50. *Insight*, 769.

51. John Henry Newman, *An Essay in Aid of a Grammar of Assent*, ed. Ian T. Ker (Oxford: Clarendon Press, 1985), 380.

52. Let Charles Davis express a disquiet that is doubtless shared by others. "Lonergan's thought, in my opinion, represents an overdevelopment or excess of the theoretic and systematic. It is an enormous constructive effort, leading to the erection of a vast ideological superstructure. The system—it is a system whatever is said to the contrary—has an immense digestive capacity. It voraciously tries to consume the whole of modern knowledge. But everything loses its own consistency as it is assimilated into the system. The reader does not meet other authors in Lonergan; under various names he finds only elements extracted to serve the enclosed dynamism of Lonergan's own thought. I do not mean that other writers are misinterpreted. They are simply not present; their writings are raided." Review of *The Achievement of Bernard Lonergan*, 386. Similar criticisms are leveled by Jane Barter Moulaison, "Missteps on *The Way to Nicea*: A Critical Reading of Lonergan's Theory of the Development of Nicene Doctrine," *Studies in Religion/Sciences Religieuses* 38, no. 1 (2009): 51–69; in reply, Wilkins, "(Mis)Reading Lonergan's *Way to Nicea*."

53. See Lonergan, "The Scope of Renewal"; also the interviews in Fehmers, *The Crucial Questions*; Joseph Ratzinger, *Dogma and Preaching: Applying Christian Doctrine to Daily Life*, ed. Michael J. Miller, trans. Michael J. Miller and Matthew J. O'Connell (San Francisco: Ignatius Press, 2011), 175–76.

54. Bernard J. F. Lonergan, "Dimensions of Meaning," in *Collection*, CWL 4, 232–45, here 244.

function of method was twofold: to transcend the limits of inadequate procedures, but also to discern and resist "the exaggerations or deficiencies to which the new age itself is exposed."[55] "Knowledge of method"— that is, figuring out what we are doing in theology and what we might do to get better at it—"becomes a necessity when false notions of method are current and more or less disastrous."[56] Disastrous, as in destructive of the possibility of dogma; that was Lonergan's example. Charles Davis never properly understood Lonergan, but he was not wrong to suggest that "the struggle of a Catholic believer to reconcile his dogmatic faith precisely as dogmatic with modern ways of thinking" was, in some sense, "decisive . . . for the problematic of Lonergan."[57]

So it is that today, what Lonergan has to say practically disappears into the fissure dividing those who would repristinate not only the traditional questions but also the old answers of scholastic theology from those to whom the old questions seem irrelevant and the old answers implausible. If to some his ontology smells fishy, to others the whole idea is absurd. If some distrust his orthodoxy, others find his doctrinal convictions breathtakingly quaint. By virtually all he is pinned, labeled, set aside: noxious, genus uncertain. For most, at least the geography is settled: Lonergan's *Method in Theology* is "yet another tributary belatedly flowing into the great stream of liberal theology"[58]—wherever that lets out. In my experience, most graduate students pick up on the lay of the land by a kind of osmosis; before page one they have Lonergan figured for a thoroughgoing modern, a discredited Cartesian propounding an "individualistic foundational rationalism,"[59] a transcendental subjectivist

---

55. Lonergan, "Christology Today," 74.

56. Lonergan, "Questionnaire on Philosophy," 374.

57. Davis, review of *The Achievement of Bernard Lonergan*, 387; see the poignant obituary by Adrian Hastings, "Obituary: Charles Davis," *The Independent*, February 5, 1999, http://www.independent.co.uk/arts-entertainment/obituary-charles-davis-1068782.html. On his relationship to Lonergan, Davis remarked, "The paradox is this. I am convinced that I myself should never have been able to leave the Roman Catholic Church, had it not been for my reading of Lonergan." He does not mean that Lonergan argued him out of the church, of course, but that "Lonergan freed the spiritual dynamic within me from the heteronomy that had severely circumscribed and oppressed it." "Lonergan and the Teaching Church," 62.

58. Hefling Jr., "Whether Lonergan Is Appropriately Regarded as 'A Schleiermacher for Our Time,' and Why Not," 106.

59. George A. Lindbeck, *The Church in a Postliberal Age* (Grand Rapids, Mich.: William B. Eerdmans, 2002), 7 (Lonergan is not mentioned by name here).

"wedded to outmoded interests and conceptions."[60] Neither those who, like Nehemiah, would rebuild the walls of the city, nor those who, like David before the Ark, would dance in liberated exultation can have much use for the project commonly assigned to 'Lonergan.'

Lonergan, angel of disarray, Samsonesquely pulling the temple down onto his own head, and Lonergan, warmed-over Thomist; Lonergan, Kantian subjectivist trapped in immanentism, and Lonergan, Hegelian rationalist, complacently propounding a dogmatic metaphysics; Lonergan, Cartesian foundationalist, and Lonergan, liberal-modernist Schleiermacher for our time. How such disparate classifications came to be applied to a single project would make a fascinating tale in the sociology of knowledge. My premise is that all of them are, more or less, wrong. Uncomprehending couturiers have robed him in swatches of disapproval, a "king of shreds and patches."[61] The coat does not fit. Lonergan has been assimilated to existing paradigms, though he explicitly intended a new one.

The Real Import

Declaring a new paradigm, actually effecting one, and making oneself understood are three different things. Lonergan scrabbles for purchase because he has not been widely understood. I have suggested various factors: his own shortcomings and choices, the failings of his disciples, the constraints of his circumstance, the limitations of his readers, and unwholesome aspects in the culture of the academy. Nevertheless, probably the most decisive factor has been the novelty and difficulty of his project, which requires a "self-attention of scientific dimensions."[62]

60. J. Augustine Di Noia, "Karl Rahner," in *The Modern Theologians: An Introduction to Christian Theology since 1918*, 3rd ed., Great Theologians (Malden, Mass.: Blackwell, 2005), 118–33, here 131 apropos of Rahner. "It was Rahner's contention that Catholic theology must appropriate the transcendental, anthropological, and subjective turns characteristic of modern thought. Thus, in an intellectual climate in which philosophers and theologians are increasingly critical of precisely these elements of modern thought, Rahner's theological program will seem to be wedded to outmoded interests and conceptions."

61. William Shakespeare, "Hamlet, Prince of Denmark," in *The Complete Works of William Shakespeare* (New York: Avenel Books, 1975), 1071–1112, here 1096 (act 3, scene 4). Thanks to Nicholas DiSalvatore for suggesting the image.

62. McShane, "Lonerganism."

It has been easier by far to make sense of his larger program as a variation on Kant's 'revolution in methodology,'[63] or, because its implications proved to be so thoroughgoing, to take it for some kind of omnivorous, homogenizing system,[64] than to develop the practical skills required for self-discovery on the scale he envisioned, and with the requisite honesty and humility. Lonergan's own willingness, after *Insight*, to settle for quick summaries of his results may have been a bad bargain, undercutting his ascetical program. The first thread of the argument here is that 'system' is the wrong paradigm for understanding Lonergan's project; his fundamental idea is not the execution of a logic but a program of practices.[65]

To be sure, Lonergan has his share and more of 'brilliant arguments,' but I dare say they are almost incidental to his real significance. His fundamental contribution is not an argument, theory, system, or logic, but his practical program of self-appropriation with all it entails for our development and practice as theologians. He explicitly recognized all theory, system, and logic as limited in scope and provisional in nature, with the one exception he called 'cognitional theory.' As I explain in the chapters to follow, however, what he has in mind here is not theory in any conventional sense, but the discovery in oneself of how the elements of our knowing form a dynamic, ordered whole. The gravamen of Lonergan's project is not an accumulation of arguments but a pedagogical "invitation to a personal, decisive act."[66]

Many have pointed out that theology's perennial first problem is the wisdom of the theologian. What distinguishes Lonergan and at the same time makes him genuinely unsettling is his practical program for promoting it. His turn to the subject is not a withdrawal into self-enclosed Cartesian or Kantian uncertainty, a disengaged modern rationality struggling to 'get out,' but an Augustinian decentering through

---

63. Giovanni B. Sala, *Lonergan and Kant: Five Essays on Human Knowledge*, ed. Robert M. Doran, trans. Joseph Spoerl (Toronto: University of Toronto Press, 1994).

64. On Lonergan's relationship to Hegel, see Mark D. Morelli, "Lonergan's Reading of Hegel," *American Catholic Philosophical Quarterly* 88, no. 3 (2014): 513–534.

65. Just what this means cannot be determined from general considerations, but there is at least a family resemblance to the thesis of Pierre Hadot, *Philosophy as a Way of Life: Spiritual Exercises from Socrates to Foucault*, trans. Arnold I. Davidson (Malden, Mass.: Blackwell, 1995).

66. *Insight*, 13; see 766. *Insight* is many things, but probably the best way to think of it is as a kind of workbook, a set of exercises.

self-knowledge. He never shared the strange conviction that the turn to the subject should mean the loss of objects, for the same reason he never bought into the widespread notion that we apprehend the world intuitively or not at all. It was Kant who posited, at the very head of his Transcendental Aesthetic, that cognition is related to objects immediately only through intuition, and "for two hundred years," Lonergan dryly remarks, "people have been swallowing [it]."[67] In fact, it is our questions that relate us immediately to cognitional objects; answers are related to objects through the questions they respond to. Sense experience is just part of the matter of our total apprehension of the world. Apart from the little matter of wonder, of asking and answering questions, no measure of experience would result in more than association, conditioning, and habituation.

Lonergan's aim was a program for the development of theologians (and everyone, really) that would help us bring into focus the complex and deficient manners in which we are already involved with the world, in order to get a purchase on what might need to happen in us if we are to measure up to the realities we care about. Adequate knowledge of anything, let alone of ourselves, our limitations and lapses, is not achieved at a stroke but only through a long and arduous effort.[68] There are pressing problems in theology that will be met only if we become better persons and better theologians; it behooves us to know what that might mean and to envision, to the extent possible, what might be involved in getting there. That is the heart of Lonergan's whole effort.

In Reno's appreciative but wistful telling, there is no context for Lonergan because Lonergan and his generation unwittingly helped destroy it. I demur boldly. Lonergan's moment has not passed; it has not yet come.[69] Theology is a field strewn with objects of niche fascination, but Lonergan should not be one of them. He aimed to be an agent of the new kind of order needed today, but we have not been ready for it. Lonergan was dominated by his sense that wisdom had suffered greatly

---

67. Lonergan, archival note 2851D0E070, quoted in Mark D. Morelli, "Meeting Hegel Halfway: The Intimate Complexity of Lonergan's Relationship with Hegel," *Method: Journal of Lonergan Studies*, n.s., 6, no. 1 (2015): 63–98, here 66n4.

68. See *Insight*, 18.

69. I mean this partly in view of what I take to be his real novelty and partly in view of the manifest perplexity of his contemporaries and the constraints under which he was bound to operate.

from a neglect of the efforts involved in becoming wise. A restoration and renewal in this vein became his life's work. His itinerary of wisdom as self-knowledge, wisdom as theology, and above all, wisdom as self-surrender is a golden string, not only to be followed, but also to be gathered up, *ad maiorem Dei gloriam.*

CHAPTER TWO

A Crisis of Normativity

Non-thinking, which seems so recommendable a state for political and moral affairs, has its perils. By shielding people from the dangers of self-examination, it teaches them to hold fast to whatever the prescribed rules of conduct may be at a given time in a given society. What people then get used to is less the content of the rules, a close examination of which would always lead them into perplexity, than the possession of rules under which to subsume particulars.[1]

HANNAH ARENDT

SOMETHING ABOUT LONERGAN feels subversive. His ideas are not only difficult to understand but also at least vaguely unsettling; they threaten to upend the world. Critics on both sides have felt that, somehow, he lays the axe to the tree of his own tradition, underwriting intellectual, moral, and cultural anarchy, or perhaps, from another perspective, liberation.

Anarchy could not be farther from Lonergan's true object. They are not wholly wrong, however, who take Lonergan for a radical. He was indeed radical, in the same kind of way Thomas Aquinas was so radical as to have once been mistaken for a revolutionary (until, bleared and caponized, he became the tradition).[2] His program, rightly understood,

1. Hannah Arendt, *Thinking* (New York: Harcourt Brace Jovanovich, 1978), 177.

2. See Jean-Pierre Torrell, *Saint Thomas Aquinas: The Person and His Work*, trans. Robert Royal (Washington, D.C.: The Catholic University of America Press, 1996), 296–316.

must offer as little comfort to the theological and cultural Jacobins as to the dreamers of restoration. If Lonergan seems to toll the bells of revolution, it was not to ring in cultural disgorgement or political decapitation but to urge a thorough renovation of Christian thought, its permanent achievements intact, from the ground up.[3] In this, his inspiration lay in that profound reorganization of theological science of which Aquinas represents the signal achievement.[4] Lonergan, like his exemplar Aquinas, meant to resist both the liquidation and the ossification of Christian thought by articulating a new basis of integration and control.

The need for some such articulation must have been felt at least since Denis Pétau's novel treatment of dogma in its historical development,[5] but its explicit moment came with Newman's *Essay on the Development of Christian Doctrine* (and the nearly contemporaneous labors of the Catholic Tübingen school).[6] Newman's *Essay* took aim at a criteriological problem unmet by the logical and metaphysical reconciliations of scholastic theology. The scholastic project originally could not, and later (as neo-scholasticism) would not, come to terms with the full extent of its involvement in historical problems. A tradition that knows it has developed, a tradition self-consciously aware that it is developing still, has to ask of itself whence and whither with eyes wide open.[7] It cannot assume its doctrines, institutions, and practices as foundational first principles, for they are known to be derivative and contingent. The articles of faith, as formulated, far from being the starting point for Christian theology, are contingent deliverances of its history, whose meaning depends upon a context. Acknowledgment of this fact raises questions

3. See Bernard J. F. Lonergan, "Revolution in Catholic Theology," in *A Second Collection*, CWL 13, 195–201.

4. Bernard J. F. Lonergan, "A New Pastoral Theology," in *Philosophical and Theological Papers 1965–1980*, CWL 17, 221–39, here 236–39.

5. Alfred Vacant, Eugene Mangenot, and Emile Amann, eds., *Dictionnaire de théologie catholique: contenant l'exposé des doctrines de la théologie catholique, leurs preuves et leur histoire* (Paris: Letouzey et Ané, 1908), s.v. "Pétau, Denys," column 12, accessed May 28, 2016, http://archive.org/details/dictionnairedet03vaca.

6. Gunter Biemer, *Newman on Tradition*, trans. and ed. Kevin Smyth (New York: Herder and Herder, 1967), 48–57, 126–35; Ian Ker, *The Achievement of John Henry Newman* (Notre Dame, Ind.: University of Notre Dame Press, 1990), 109–20. On the Catholic Tübingen school, see Kaplan, *Answering the Enlightenment*.

7. *Method* (1972), 361–67, or CWL 14, 333–38.

of validity and permanence. Of validity, for it may seem that what is not a necessary deduction from self-evident premises can be no more than an accidental and perhaps arbitrary outcome. Of permanence, for it may seem that meanings settled within one context cannot be transposed to another. In short, historical mindedness has problematized an older sense of normativity without putting anything palpable in its place. The result is a crisis of normativity and, especially, a crisis about the possibility of permanently valid religious and moral claims.

Lonergan's basic question was whether there is a rock upon which to rebuild Christian thought and culture. For some, the question is otiose and Lonergan's answer preposterous.[8] For others, Lonergan's reputation as a subversive rests on his unwillingness to settle for unsatisfactory answers. But answers respond to questions, and they satisfy intelligence and reason in the measure they fulfill criteria implicit in questions. To understand Lonergan's answers we have to work our way into his questions. The present chapter, then, attempts to bring some salient dimensions of the underlying issue into focus. It is not intended as a complete diagnosis of our contemporary situation, but a sketch intended to achieve two goals. First, we have to understand how Lonergan in particular read the lay of the land if we would grasp the basic problem he meant to face. At the same time, I would like to suggest that though times change, this problem has not gone away and, if anything, has intensified.

The chapter has three parts. First, I outline paradigm shifts in the natural sciences and historical scholarship, together with their repercussions on culture and education. Next, I briefly sketch 'scientism' and 'historicism' as ideological fallout from these transformations. Third, finally, we consider the inadequacy of Christian efforts to come to terms with modernity, culminating in the collapse of neo-scholasticism and the contemporary disarray of Christian thought and culture.

---

8. Thomas G. Guarino, *Foundations of Systematic Theology*, Theology for the Twenty-First Century (New York: T&T Clark International, 2005), 1–25, provides a useful summary of the contemporary problem of theological foundations. Michael H. McCarthy, *Authenticity as Self-Transcendence: The Enduring Insights of Bernard Lonergan* (Notre Dame, Ind.: University of Notre Dame Press, 2015), 5–24, 109–49, 182–206, offers an interpretation mostly complementary or overlapping with the argument of this chapter.

Science and History

From the stern we can only imagine how disruptive to Christian bearings, public and personal, were the voyages of a Columbus, the discoveries of a Copernicus, Reimarus's criticism of the Gospels, and Darwin's assault on fixed and immutable species, including Adam's.[9] Scholastic thought revered traditional authority and presupposed teleology in ways that were long out of sync with modernity's frank repudiation of past authority in the name of future progress and the disappearance of teleology from its science. The modern turn away from tradition meant old answers would not be taken for granted, while at the same time science's break from teleology had the effect of undercutting the epistemological foundations upon which any solution to the problem of how to live well might claim to be objectively adequate.[10] A profound reorientation of apprehensions of space and time, history, culture, and human identity was underway, and rearguard efforts to thwart it were doomed.[11] As Lonergan read it, far more important than particular amendments to our picture of the world and ourselves was a series of transformations in the very notions of science, history, and culture.

Natural science was long considered a domain of philosophy ('natural philosophy'), but in the scientific revolution, its subalternation to metaphysics came to an end. Modern natural sciences are an autonomous set of inquiries with no reference to end, agent, matter, or form, to substance or the categories. Contemporary natural science makes no appeal to the ideal of certitude formulated in the *Posterior Analytics* ('*certa per causas cognitio*'). It does not equate its fundamental concepts and verified laws with the necessary principles of nature. It knows it must settle for a succession of hypothetical approximations. Its basic concepts are not

9. Brief discussion, largely consonant, in Ratzinger, *Dogma and Preaching*, 131–32, 172–76.

10. Leo Strauss, *Natural Right and History*, Charles R. Walgreen Foundation Lectures (Chicago: University of Chicago Press, 1953), 12; Ernest L. Fortin, "The New Moral Theology," in *Ever Ancient, Ever New: Ruminations on the City, the Soul, and the Church*, ed. Michael P. Foley, Collected Essays 4 (Lanham, Md.: Rowman & Littlefield, 2007), 113–29, here 127. Epistemology in some sense seems the typical project of modern philosophy. Classical and scholastic thought gave accounts of knowledge and, of course, faced the obvious problems of skepticism. But it was the moderns who, in their break with the medieval reverence for authority, felt the need to justify certitude by way of an epistemology. Nowhere does this feel more obvious than in Descartes's strategy of methodic doubt.

11. Lonergan, "Questionnaire on Philosophy," 353–54.

fixed and immutable but open to continuous revision with increasing explanatory power, still only a gradual approximation to the intelligibility immanent in natural processes. Contemporary science has no use for absolute space and time; it acknowledges reference frames and relativity. A modern science cannot be a *habitus* in a single mind but is an ongoing, open-ended collaboration distributed, both in its content and in its skill sets, across a community of scientists. The foundation of such a science is not in basic concepts but in its method.[12]

A similar transformation affected historical knowledge. Even the most historically sensitive premodern writers handled their sources differently from contemporary scholars. As astute a reader as Thomas Aquinas tended to enter his authorities into the ledger as if they were more or less contemporaneous pieces of the same puzzle.[13] He may or may not have been able to control for their imperfections, errors, or overgeneralizations. But he could hardly know, and did not realize how much depended on knowing their historical contexts. The coherence of the tradition for him was, as it were, synchronic, a problem of fitting testimonies together; for us it is diachronic, a problem of change over time. Historical questions are not put to rest by the report of credible testimonies; historians are after a hypothetical reconstruction of the past on the basis of critically sifted evidence (including, of course, the evidence of testimony). Hypothetical reconstructions are subject to revision, and both the reconstructions and the revision depend not only on the availability of evidence but also on the kinds of questions posed and the qualities of those who pose them. There arises ineluctably a problem of historical perspective and the unsettling prospect of an endless series of conflicting interpretations.[14]

12. A useful starting point is Lonergan, "Aquinas Today"; Lonergan's most expansive statement on method in the natural sciences is *Insight*, 93–125. On science in Aristotle, see Patrick H. Byrne, *Analysis and Science in Aristotle*, SUNY Series in Ancient Greek Philosophy (Albany: State University of New York Press, 1997).

13. Compare Finnis, *"Historical Consciousness,"* 22–23. Aquinas "tended to read the sources available to him as if the main problem with them was their as yet imperfect unity, as if they were pieces in a jigsaw puzzle which could fit together as a whole without drastic reworking." Finnis goes on to note that Aquinas did not adequately control for the mistakes and overgeneralizations of his sources, but the present point is that he also did not adequately control for context.

14. Discussed at length in *Method* (1972), 175–234, or CWL 14, 164–219. See Thomas J. McPartland, *Lonergan and Historiography: The Epistemological Philosophy of History* (Columbia, Mo.: University of Missouri Press, 2010).

Almost inevitably, these tectonic shifts affected culture and education. Their cumulative effect is to heighten a sense of contingency that unsettles commonsense self-understanding very directly. Because common sense as such is incapable of examining its presuppositions, the default orientation of any group of people regards its ways not only as possible, workable solutions but as *the* correct solutions to the problem of living together. This translates into a supposition that the way of one's own people is the normative way and other ways are inferior. Even when this spontaneous conviction is subjected to scrutiny, as it was by the ancient distinction between nature and convention, education may cultivate rather than undermine the feeling that one's own culture is the standard, its manners the correct manners, its noblest aesthetic achievements "the models of all beauty, past, present, and future," the embodied standard of taste and refinement, rectitude and excellence.[15] In this perspective, culture is the opposite of barbarism; it is something acquired through proper formation.

It was such an educational regime and its assumptions that Lonergan seems to have had in mind as the downside of 'classicism.' His proximate model was the regime in which he was educated.[16] In its positive moment, "classicism in its best sense, the Greek achievement," was "a pure development of human intelligence," "the emergence of the intellectual pattern of experience," that is, the differentiation of the norms of rationality from the criteria of practical success.[17] This permanently valid step—which Lonergan had no intention of renouncing—lent itself to a preference for the permanent over the changing, the typical over the merely accidental, the universal over the particular, the law over the case, so that, by implication, the concrete and contingent is merely incidental to an

---

15. Régine Pernoud, *Those Terrible Middle Ages: Debunking the Myths*, trans. Anne Englund Nash (San Francisco: Ignatius Press, 2000), 25; a Renaissance version is described at 21–30. Brief but illuminating descriptions of a Confucian version of classicism in late imperial China are afforded by Frederic E. Wakeman, *The Fall of Imperial China*, The Transformation of Modern China Series (New York: Free Press, 1977), 23–24, 212–13.

16. Lonergan knew this world intimately: "Classical culture [was] something I was brought up in and gradually learned to move *out of*" ("An Interview," 177). Despite his strictures on the limitations of classicism, Lonergan appreciated the perspective it opened up for him: see *Caring about Meaning*, 11–12; *Topics in Education: The Cincinnati Lectures of 1959 on the Philosophy of Education*, ed. Robert M. Doran and Frederick E. Crowe, CWL 10 (1993), 205–7.

17. *Topics in Education*, 75; see 75–76.

understanding of reality.[18] Lonergan wished to free the valid achievement from its involvement in untenable assumptions about the possibility of a unitary and permanent 'catholic' culture. It should not need mention (but, unfortunately, it does) that an honest acknowledgment of the problems of cultural relativity and of the brittleness of classicist assumptions is no endorsement of relativism, no cry for the liquidation of Christian practice, nor a renunciation of care for intellectual achievement and seriousness.

Today, the educated strata of society know perfectly well that cultures and the social arrangements they invest with meaning are not self-evidently correct, but the result of choosing from among many different possible arrangements. In this perspective, culture is regarded empirically and ethnographically, not as normative per se. A culture invests a way of life with meaning and there are as many valid cultures as there are tribe and tongue, people and nation.[19] Every culture is "essentially a moral order," but none is *the* moral order.[20]

This realization, while correct, tends to provoke a crisis of standards, especially once it penetrates social consciousness in a kind of post-theoretic

18. Bernard J. F. Lonergan, "Natural Right and Historical Mindedness," in *A Third Collection*, CWL 16, 163–76; see Charles Norris Cochrane, *Christianity and Classical Culture: A Study of Thought and Action from Augustus to Augustine*, rev. and corr. (New York: Oxford University Press, 1944), 3–30, 82–124. Caesar Augustus, for instance, imagining himself enacting a permanent solution to the crisis of the late Republic, shared with Plato and Aristotle the hope that the instruments of polity might bring release from the ephemeral flux. (It is because classicism represents both an achievement and the characteristic deformations of that achievement that Lonergan can say what Finnis finds so confounding, that it was typical of a stage of development and that the best minds were never imprisoned by its negative proclivities.)

19. Lonergan credited Christopher Dawson with introducing him "to the anthropological notion of culture and so began the correction of my hitherto normative or classicist notion" ("*Insight Revisited*," 222). He is referring to Dawson, *The Age of the Gods: A Study in the Origins of Culture in Prehistoric Europe and the Ancient East* (New York: Sheed & Ward, 1934). Dawson elsewhere puts the matter this way: "To the average educated man culture is still regarded as an absolute. Civilization is one: men may be more cultured or less cultured, but in so far as they are cultured, they are all walking along the same high road which leads to the same goal. . . . Humanism, the Enlightenment and the modern conceptions of the 'democratic way of life' and the 'one world' all presuppose the same idea of a single universal ideal of civilization toward which all men and peoples must move. Against this we have the anthropologist's and ethnologist's conception of a culture as an artificial creation. . . . The cultures are as diverse as races and languages and states. A culture is built, like a state, by the labor of generations which elaborate a way of life suited to their needs and environment and consequently different from the way of life of other men in other circumstances." *Christianity and European Culture: Selections from the Work of Christopher Dawson*, ed. Gerald J. Russello (Washington, D.C.: The Catholic University of America Press, 1998), 46.

20. Dawson, *Christianity and European Culture*, 21.

way. Most people feel qualitative differences among arrangements but cannot give an adequate accounting of them. They feel responsible to values but cannot adequately articulate either the values or their responsibility for them. Van Harvey feared that "orthodox belief corrodes the delicate machinery of sound historical judgment,"[21] but more palpably today it is superficial awareness of cultural and historical differences, whose real significance is not understood, that is corroding the old and once seemingly obvious orthodoxies of public morality. We may be facing, as Ernest Fortin suggested, a cultural crisis without precedent.

> Westerners were unable to defend the superiority of their civilization for the simple reason that they had renounced the standards by which that superiority could be established. They were at a loss to demonstrate that truth should prevail over error because they had finally concluded that the distinction between them was unclear. Nothing was true or false, everything was relative.[22]

Now, while I find the question of cultural superiority rather beside the point, I find the renunciation of standards discomfiting. The educated members of our society feel keenly the contingency of their—and any—social mores. Unless they are also prepared to sift through the real meaning of this contingency and the real bearing of their feelings toward it, in all likelihood they will feel the conventions of public morality are not binding on them and, worse, are merely stultifying and oppressive. What is contingent and not always and everywhere self-evident is readily confused with the merely arbitrary. Society divides into two camps: those for whom the public morality is still taken for granted and is therefore perceived as binding and obviously correct; and those who cannot take it for granted but also, by and large, are unequipped to carry out the kind of interrogation that would reauthenticate it. In their mutual incomprehension, one side sees lawlessness and the other, oppression.

---

21. Van A. Harvey, *The Historian and the Believer; the Morality of Historical Knowledge and Christian Belief* (New York: Macmillan, 1966), 119.

22. Ernest L. Fortin, "A Note on Dawson and St. Augustine," in *The Birth of Philosophic Christianity: Studies in Early Christian and Medieval Thought*, ed. J. Brian Benestad, Collected Essays 1 (Lanham, Md.: Rowman & Littlefield, 1996), 115–22, here 116; quoted in Lawrence, *Fragility of Consciousness*, 288.

As the received moral language breaks down, value tends to be accounted for by appeal to the objects of immediate, experiential satisfaction that, if they are not also perceived as directly harmful, seem irrefragably good. Thus we become consumers and, in school, learn the skills to 'consumerize' others: consuming them for the sake of our consumption.[23] This breakdown, unfortunately, does not put to rest the puritanical instinct. It is evidently compatible with the strictest forms of groupthink, with a profession of multiculturalism devoid of more than aesthetic interest in other cultures, even resentful of the moral alternatives they represent. It may be even worse, for a culture in the thrall of relativism and historicism seems hardly able to perform what Lonergan regarded as the most important office of culture, namely, the critique of moral preferences on the way to a normative, even if unscientific, self-knowledge. Thus, unless awareness of cultural and historical relativity is complemented by other developments in self-understanding, it opens up a broad and easy highway to out-and-out moral relativism impatient of challenge.[24]

Scientism and Historicism

The classical and scholastic distinction between nature and convention measures convention by an order of things we receive but do not originate. Modernity, by contrast, rests on an apprehension of human beings as the originators of order. Thus, where an older, teleological narrative told of obedience and disobedience, conformity to an order revealed, or at least discovered, a newer, nonteleological narrative features our creativity and progress; we are makers of our own world and of ourselves.[25] As Strauss

23. I am grateful to Sue Lawrence and Jean Ponder Soto for conversations that helped me appreciate this point. These issues are helpfully discussed in Nicholas Boyle, *Who Are We Now? Christian Humanism and the Global Market from Hegel to Heaney* (Notre Dame, Ind.: University of Notre Dame Press, 1998); Lawrence, *Fragility of Consciousness*, 296–325; Randall S. Rosenberg, *The Givenness of Desire: Concrete Subjectivity and the Natural Desire to See God* (Toronto: University of Toronto Press, 2017), 184–200.

24. See Lamb, *Eternity, Time, and the Life of Wisdom*, 125–52.

25. Leo Strauss argues that "natural right in its classic form is connected with a teleological view of the universe . . . [which] would seem to have been destroyed by modern science" (*Natural Right and History*, 7–8). In Strauss's reading, modern political philosophy originates with an open-eyed break from the abstract teleological commitments that structured the older tradition; it is a tradition unified in this explicit breach. See Strauss, "The Three Waves of Modernity," in *An Introduction to*

put it, "'man is the measure of all things' is the very opposite of 'man is the master of all things'"[26]—the former involves us with an independent standard, but the latter might mean the only standard is arbitrary choice. In one sense, then, it might be said that modernity knows no problem of order in the soul, because a problem of order arises only in relation to a standard supplying criteria for ordering; hence, perhaps, our culture's present insouciance about the problem of spiritual order. In another sense, however, it might be said that modernity has involved a rediscovery of the problem of order because it knows all solutions as radically contingent and can take none for granted. We have stumbled anew onto the fundamental problem, that we are responsible for the orders within which we live—and are there any criteria for our ordering? What is known as contingent is also readily perceived as arbitrary and therefore violable; as Richard Rorty sums it up, the new norm is there are no norms, "no criterion that is not an appeal to such a criterion, no rigorous argumentation that is not obedience of our own conventions."[27]

The classical critique of convention in light of nature presumed that nature was not only knowable but also normative in some relevant sense. There have always been skeptics to cast doubt on the knowledge, but today the normativity, too, is doubted. This is due partly to paradigmatic features of modern natural science, and partly to its cultural ascendancy in the form of ideological 'scientism.' Paradigmatically, modern natural science supplants the narrative of special creation with a narrative of chance emergence and disregards teleology in favor of experimentally verified correlations. Science in this mode seems to leave little room

---

Political Philosophy: Ten Essays, ed. Hilail Gildin, Culture of Jewish Modernity (Detroit: Wayne State University Press, 1989), 81–98; compare John Thornhill, *Modernity: Christianity's Estranged Child Reconstructed* (Grand Rapids, Mich.: William B. Eerdmans, 2000), who interprets modernity as an ideological "reaction to the cultural assumptions of medievalism." Lonergan's own brief account is given in "The Transition from a Classicist World View to Historical Mindedness," in *A Second Collection*, CWL 13, 3–10. One gets a feel for the breach by comparing the introit to Augustine's *Confessions* to the opening of Rousseau's book of the same name; the suggestion is from Charles T. Mathewes, "The Presumptuousness of Autobiography and the Paradoxes of Beginning in *Confessions* Book One," in *A Reader's Companion to Augustine's Confessions*, ed. Kim Paffenroth and Robert Peter Kennedy, 1st ed. (Louisville, Ky.: Westminster John Knox, 2003), 7–24, here 10.

26. Strauss, "Three Waves," 85.

27. Richard Rorty, "The Fate of Philosophy," *The New Republic*, October 18, 1982, 32, quoted in Frederick G. Lawrence, "Language as Horizon?," in *The Beginning and the Beyond: Papers from the Gadamer and Voegelin Conferences*, ed. Frederick G. Lawrence (Chico, Calif.: Scholars Press, 1984), 13–34, here 16.

for classical and Christian conceptions about the end of human beings and their difference from other animals. The discrediting of teleology as a valid mode of analysis sidelines the serious interrogation of our purpose as human beings. But some kind of teleological consideration seems necessary to underwrite both the objectivity of moral claims and the dialectical analysis of sin—without which the data set on human beings is intractable. Nature, then, is seen as basically irrelevant to moral and existential questions. If it is knowable, it is through the experimental sciences, but the nature so known is not normative; it is as often irrational as rational and, at best, might afford some tangential clues for moral consideration.

Yet it is the cultural ascendancy of natural science under the guise of 'scientism' that really compounds the havoc to our self-understanding. 'Scientism' is a bevy of mistaken but mutually reinforcing assumptions and their attendant narratives about knowing, reality, and, in consequence, human existence. The conspicuous success and empirical orientation of natural science lend it an air of unquestionable authority as *the* valid and 'objective,' and therefore uniquely 'public' and 'neutral,' form of knowing. Thus, in popular culture, the most banal assertions—'smiles are contagious,' 'we are all connected'—are regularly buttressed by appeals to science. This aura is embedded in a narrative about science as (neutral and objective) 'knowledge' in contrast to religion and morality as matters of (tribal and subjective) 'belief.' Assumptions about what knowing is correspond to assumptions about what reality is, and the assumptions of scientism are reductive. What is, is matter; what counts, is countable. Such assumptions have far-reaching implications for our common life. They shape how we might conceive, for instance, the purposes of education, the studies worth pursuing, and the measures of success. They abet a narrative of inevitable progress toward 'neutral' secularity. Under the double-barreled assault of modern science and its ideological screen, 'scientism,' 'nature' comes to mean the physical only and has nothing to say about behaviors beyond diet and exercise.

The ideological counterparts to scientism in the sphere of the natural sciences are historicism and relativism in the humanities. Historicism denies the possibility of transcultural norms. For historicism, and for the culturally ascendant relativism it has sponsored, the only standard that might possibly be relevant is not just extrinsically but intrinsically conditioned by history (time) and society (space). On this view, transhistorical or transcultural normativity is impossible because measurement presupposes a reference frame, and the valid frames are all internal to a time and place. This implies, unfortunately, that there are no norms we ourselves do not create, or if there are, they are imposed upon us arbitrarily, beyond our knowledge or reach. Accordingly it is neither charity nor justice but tolerance that is enthroned as the chief virtue of true religion, and diametrically opposed to tolerance in this mode is the (intolerable because presumed intolerant) assertion of a transcendent or transcultural standard. In default of criteria, self-ascribed identities demand assent and approval without question. Objective truth is the first casualty of antinomian decisionism, but it is the transcendental subject, alienated, truncated, pent up beyond recognition, who suffers the most.

Institutions and practices of public morality that can no longer be taken for granted lose their power to bind. Profound confusion about their sources in our orientation to transcendence leaves us with the brute fact that we decide, on the basis of who knows what criteria. From the standpoint of a practical decisionism, the constraints of traditional institutions seem arbitrary and are readily abandoned. Venerable traditions of moral, religious, even legal reasoning are now brushed aside as though no cogent account ever had been or could be offered for them. At the same time, insoluble conflicts are never far off between groups who lack the resources to understand one another, in a world where convenient facts can be manufactured for the right price, the seeds of confusion are genetically modified, and public discourse is watered by an unhealthy dose of public mistrust. As Christopher Dawson put it, "custom and tradition and law and authority have lost their old sacredness and moral prestige. They have all become the servants of public opinion and of the will of society."[28] But without them and the institutions they legitimate, there will be little shelter from the chill winds of illiberalism.

North American culture is at sea without bearings, and theology is in the same boat. We are well aware that our practices and institutions, our teachings and values have a contingent history. They are not necessary conclusions from self-evident first principles or from the red-lettered

28. Dawson, *Christianity and European Culture*, 66.

words of Christ.[29] They are not the permanent things, and their emergence and development has not been anything like a straightforward deduction from whatever the permanent things are. They are conditioned, collective, seemingly accidental, and, in the opinion of many, arbitrary outcomes of history. It has become downright incredible to many that doctrines, known to have a contingent history, were once for all revealed by God. Whether they are still even meaningful, let alone normative, is widely questioned. It is all too easy to urge that there is no Gospel, only another competition for attention and control. Even if we politely decline the leap into relativism and arbitrariness, we have to face relativity and contingency squarely.

The Crisis of Christian Thought and Culture

On the whole, Catholics seem to have badly misread the advent of modernity as nothing more than "a series of regrettable aberrations that unfortunately were widely accepted."[30] For some, doubling down on classicist suppositions seemed the only secure defense against relativism, immanentism, and 'modernism' (the theological version of 'historicism'); their dominant reflex was to fend off the new questions with dogmatic proofs and an authoritarian crouch.[31] The resulting intellectual program was neo-

29. Here is a neat problem. Aquinas, for instance, established the form of the Eucharist from a fairly uniform tradition known to him, but today's question is whether any of the diverse forms, recognized as canonically valid, in which it is and has been celebrated can claim to be normative. See Robert F. Taft, "Mass Without the Consecration?: The Historic Agreement on the Eucharist between the Catholic Church and the Assyrian Church of the East Promulgated on 26 October 2001," in *Theological Dimensions of the Christian Orient* (Kottayam, India: Oriental Institute of Religious Studies, 2005), http://www.liturgia.it/addaicongress/en/study/3Taft_en.pdf. Another index of the same problem is Aquinas's notorious denial of the Immaculate Conception, a truth revealed by God (according to Pius IX), but not one of the articles of faith presupposed by Aquinas's *sacra doctrina* and, unless we are to accuse him of a merely logical error, not deducible from the truths he did presuppose. I find helpful for thinking about this problem Ben F. Meyer, *The Early Christians: Their World Mission and Self-Discovery*, Good News Studies 16 (Wilmington, Del.: Michael Glazier, 1986).

30. Lonergan, "Questionnaire on Philosophy," 354.

31. Consider the elaborate control regime laid out in *Pascendi Dominici Gregis* (1907), initiated by the highest authorities and implemented in dioceses and seminaries throughout the world: interdiction and censorship of books (§§50–2), watch councils in every diocese (§55), the restriction of clergy congresses (§54), neo-scholasticism in clerical formation (already prescribed by Leo XIII) (§45–7), all monitored by compulsory triennial reports from every diocesan ordinary to the Holy See (§56) and bolstered in 1910 with the Oath against Modernism. There is something to Hannah

scholasticism, "the attempt to solve the modern crisis . . . [with] a timeless, unified theology that would provide a norm for the universal church."[32]

Some version of scholasticism held the field in Catholic thought for some eight centuries. It provided both theology and philosophy a set of common questions and a standard framework for articulating results. It developed an impressive synergy with ecclesiastical doctrine. It was embedded in a culture, a system of education, and serried institutions. Regrettably, neo-scholasticism came to epitomize the weakness more than the glory of scholasticism: a penchant for ahistorical orthodoxy, abstractness, antiquated science; a predilection for logic over discovery, proof over understanding; a posture of defense rather than creativity.[33] Insoluble disputes led to philosophical gimmickry masquerading as profundity. It went hand in glove with a culture pretending to normativity and universality, resistant to innovation, blind to meaningful difference and to the positivity of pluralism. A tendency to sacralize Aristotelian philosophy and science, antique cosmology, and particular cultural and political forms contributed to the scandal of faith and the

Arendt's claim that "authority precludes the use of external means of coercion; where force is used, authority itself has failed." Arendt, "What is Authority?," in *Between Past and Future: Exercises in Political Thought* (London: Faber, 1961), 92–93. Pius X was quite correct to warn that principles of method could not be free of metaphysical suppositions, but his repressive prescriptions did nothing to promote, and probably inhibited, the development of real solutions, and at the cost of a great deal of personal suffering (Yves Congar compared his experiences in the decade 1946–56 to physical captivity: *Journal d'un Théologien, 1946–1956*, ed. É. Fouilloux et al. [Paris: Editions du Cerf, 2001]). Censorship and often other more severe sanctions were imposed on such serious Catholic thinkers as Marie-Joseph Lagrange, Pierre Battifol, Henri de Lubac, Marie-Dominique Chenu, Yves Congar, and Karl Rahner, many of whom were later publicly vindicated by church authorities. Such measures were especially systematic in the anti-Modernist era (1907–1960s), but they seem of a piece with the generally defensive posture adopted by, e.g., Pius IX, and not without antecedents dating to seventeenth-century responses to the new science and the new criticism. See C. J. T. Talar, "'The Synthesis of All Heresies'—100 Years On," *Theological Studies* 68, no. 3 (2007): 491–514 (Talar also underscores the extent to which "Modernism" was a cultural and not merely an intellectual crisis); Fergus Kerr, *Twentieth-Century Catholic Theologians: From Neoscholasticism to Nuptial Mysticism* (Malden, Mass.: Blackwell Publications, 2007), 1–16. Jürgen Mettepenningen argues that the Nouvelle Théologie represented a third way between neo-scholasticism and Modernism, and it was this third way (not Modernism) that prevailed at Vatican II. See "The 'Third Way' of the Modernist Crisis, Precursor of Nouvelle Théologie: Ambroise Gardeil, O.P., and Léonce de Grandmaison, S.J.," *Theological Studies* 75, no. 4 (2014): 774–94.

32. Walter Kasper, *Theology and Church*, trans. Margaret Kohl (London: SCM Press, 1989), 1, quoted in Kerr, *Twentieth-Century Catholic Theologians*, vii. Kasper opines, "Without doubt, the outstanding event in the Catholic theology of our [twentieth] century was the surmounting of neo-scholasticism."

33. See Lawrence, "Lonergan's Search for a Hermeneutics of Authenticity."

empowerment of secularists.[34] A preventive defense never was tenable, and when, inevitably, it was abandoned for lost, the storm was all the fiercer for the wait.

Almost in the twinkling of an eye, the whole effort was swept away, and with it many older and more admirable achievements. The pent-up fury was such that most students I meet know neo-scholasticism only as ruins from 'the bad old days.' Some, like R. R. Reno, suggest Lonergan's generation tragically destroyed the context for its own work.[35] That feels a bit like a postmortem blaming the physicians for prescribing too hard a remedy. If the crisis after Vatican II presents an important lesson, it is probably not about the alleged incontinent nest-fouling of Congar and Chenu, Rahner and Ratzinger, de Lubac and Lonergan, whatever their real failings. It is that burking questions has a price. A party line, backed by oaths and condemnations, interdiction and censorship, surveillance and constraint, cannot succeed forever in the face of real problems whose urgency is only intensified by repression. When Vatican II finally took the lid off the pot, it boiled over with a vengeance because positive solutions were long overdue.[36]

34. Augustine, *Confessions*, 5.5.9, complained of the scandal caused by those who mistake their falsifiable, extrascientific opinions on empirical questions of cosmology for Catholic truth. It might be objected that secularism drove ecclesiastical policy and not the other way round; I do not suppose it was a one-way street.

35. Reno, "Theology After the Revolution."

36. *Pace* Bruce Marshall, "Reckoning with Modernity," *First Things* 258 (2015): 23–30. According to Marshall, "for the Catholic Church, the basic fact about modernity, the event with an impact that exceeded any other, was not the rise of modern science or the emergence of historical criticism, but the French revolution," which "establish[ed] secularism . . . as a basic feature of European politics and culture" (26, 27). He goes on to advance a thesis about the timeliness of Vatican II, "the Church's decisive reckoning with modernity," which came neither "too soon" nor "too late" (28). I would distinguish Marshall's thesis on three points. First, the cultural conditions for aggressive secularism were prepared in part by a sacralized cosmology and, later, a defensive sacralization of scholarship, "the extension of the mantle of religion over the opinions of ignorant men" that led to an outright rejection of the church as "the futile champion of a dead and unlamented past." Bernard J. F. Lonergan, "Sacralization and Secularization," in *Philosophical and Theological Papers 1965–1980*, CWL 17, 259–81, here 274; Lawrence, *Fragility of Consciousness*, 193–226; Lamb, *Eternity, Time, and the Life of Wisdom*, 73–104; see too Charles Taylor, *A Secular Age* (Cambridge, Mass.: Belknap Press of Harvard University Press, 2007), esp. 90–99, 159–71; and, on a facet of unintended Christian intellectual complicity, Michael J. Buckley, *At the Origins of Modern Atheism* (New Haven: Yale University Press, 1987). The revolution may have been decisive as a trauma, but it was a symptom, not a cause, of cultural transformation. Next, the Council may not have come "too late" in the sense that it occurred when it realistically could occur (see Marshall, 28–29), but it certainly came too late in the sense that a more creative response was long overdue. Third, it

The denouement, in any case, was catastrophic. Neo-scholasticism was the intellectual arm of a culture, and its disappearance was not only the failure of an intellectual project but also the destruction of a cultural form. The collapse of that world left many educated Catholics in a "state of almost complete disorientation," feeling themselves "confronted with an endless relativism" and unequipped "to deal effectively and successfully with the premises set forth by relativists."[37] The disorientation is with us still. It is, in fact, inseparable from a wider cultural crisis in the West, a crisis of meaning and value, identity and purpose that has destroyed "our working relation to the past."[38]

In the vacuum, Christians in the West, bereft of a native tongue, have inherited foreign ones: possessive individualism ('life, liberty, and the pursuit of furniture,' as my colleague Brian Braman puts it, but it could almost be a quote from Locke), expressive individualism ('to thine own self be true'), and relative perspectivism ('works for me') have become our first languages. These cultural idioms are inept vehicles for the Gospel and almost as a rule result in its devaluation.[39] The challenge for theology in this context is to help Christians re-create a native language. While there is no question of forgetting what we have learned from our involvement in the reflective techniques of Greek culture,[40] still

---

seems to me the Council can be called a "decisive reckoning with modernity" in the sense that it acknowledged problems and meant to face them squarely, but not in the sense that it solved them. The reorientation of theology to its real problems and the needed revision of methods to meet them is still fragmentary.

37. Bernard J. F. Lonergan, "Doctrinal Pluralism," in *Philosophical and Theological Papers 1965–1980*, CWL 17, 70–104, here 75–76.

38. Michael H. McCarthy, describing what he calls a crisis of philosophy in the Anglo-Analytic tradition, puts it this way: "This crisis concerns the common meanings and values by which we live together, our working relation to the past, and our understanding of what it is to be human. This crisis has come about because our inherited religious and moral traditions have lost their authority. . . . Since the beginning of the scientific revolution modernity has struggled with the fact of tradition. It could no longer accept tradition's authority as the great medieval theologians once did. The most influential modern thinkers viewed tradition as an inherited burden, as something from which to be liberated. But, in the course of the next two centuries, they gradually created an alternative tradition that Harold Rosenberg has called the tradition of the new." McCarthy, *The Crisis of Philosophy* (Albany: State University of New York Press, 1990), xx, referring to Harold Rosenberg, *The Tradition of the New* (New York: Horizon, 1959).

39. Lawrence, *Fragility of Consciousness*, 326–52; Lamb, *Eternity, Time, and the Life of Wisdom*, 73–104.

40. See Lonergan, "The Dehellenization of Dogma." Compare Joseph Ratzinger: "The Fathers did not just mix into the gospel a static and self-contained Greek culture. They could take up a

our present challenge will not be met merely by recovering a language that has been lost; it must be a new inculturation, a new mediation of the faith into our culture.

To Lonergan's mind, the need of the hour was a great effort of creativity:

> One has to be creative. Modernity lacks roots. Its values lack balance and depth. Much of its science is destructive of man. Catholics in the twentieth century are faced with a problem similar to that met by Aquinas in the thirteenth century. Then Greek and Arabic culture were pouring into Western Europe and, if it was not to destroy Christendom, it had to be known, assimilated, transformed. Today, modern culture, in many ways more stupendous than any that ever existed, is surging around us. It too has to be known, assimilated, transformed. That is the contemporary issue. The contemporary issue, then, is a tremendous challenge. Nor should one opt out on the speciously modest plea that one is not another Aquinas. There could have been no Aquinas without the preceding development of Scholasticism. There would have been no Aquinas if there had not been the students to whom he lectured and for whom he wrote. Finally, there would have been a far more successful Aquinas, if human beings were less given to superficial opinions backed by passion, for in that case the work of Aquinas would not have been so promptly buried under the avalanche of the Augustinian-Aristotelian conflict that marked the close of the thirteenth century.[41]

Yet if this creativity is not to be compromised by its own involvement in the spiritual disorders of our culture, we must acknowledge that we are not exempt from them. As Frederick Lawrence points out, the

---

dialogue with Greek philosophy and could make it an instrument of the gospel, wherever in the Hellenistic world the search for God had brought into being a self-criticism of that world's own culture and its own thought. Faith links the various peoples . . . not with Hellenistic culture as such, but with Hellenistic culture in the form in which it transcended itself, which was the true point of contact for the interpretation of the Christian message." Ratzinger, *Truth and Tolerance: Christian Belief and World Religions*, trans. Henry Taylor (San Francisco: Ignatius Press, 2004), 200.

41. Bernard J. F. Lonergan, "Belief: Today's Issue," in *A Second Collection*, CWL 13, 75–85, here 85.

languages of our culture have "invaded us."[42] If we would learn Christ, or take up Lonergan's foundational practices, we start not with a blank slate but with conversion, repentance, a new asceticism. We are turning away from the ways our culture offers us to interpret our desires and needs, our conflicts and struggles. We are dissenting from the scale of values implied by and embedded in our social practices and institutional arrangements. We must become like children and learn anew a Christian language. But we must be adults in working out what that may mean here and now. Charles Taylor likens us to Matteo Ricci,[43] strangers in a culture estranged from the Gospel and from its own history.

The fundamental problem is not noetic but 'metanoetic.' Nevertheless, it has a noetic dimension. For what has been lost and can never be regained is the normativity that once was presumed to reside in cultural forms, institutions, and universal propositions. It is not merely that one set of meanings has passed away and another has taken its place. It is that the very foundations of meaning are called into question. We have learned that cultures are our products (and we are theirs) and our products are not normative. From this discovery we (in the West) have been altogether too quick to conclude that our way of life—and we ourselves—can be, then, whatever we want. A new basis for dialectical critique of cultures is essential. Without it, we cannot find our footing as Christians and cannot render a service urgently needed by our culture and our church.

---

42. Lawrence, *Fragility of Consciousness*, 343. ("My own sense is that conversion and repentance are crucial to the process of learning Lonergan's foundational language precisely because the languages of liberalism or nihilism are so dominant in our culture. They do not just exist 'out there' or 'in them.' If my own experience is not unique, these languages have invaded us. They affect our day-to-day life-choices and our overall way of life both in the manner in which we individually and collectively interpret our desires and needs and in the ordering of the values incorporated in the already understood and agreed upon solutions to the problem of living together that make up our institutions. These languages are the symptom of our implicatedness in what today is commonly called 'structural sin.'") Compare Ratzinger, *Dogma and Preaching*, 168–69. ("The world exists in [Christians] too . . . and thus the dialogue with the world is always to some extent dialogue of Christians with themselves. . . . What is Christian never exists in an entirely wordless way.")

43. See Charles Taylor, "A Catholic Modernity," in *A Catholic Modernity: Charles Taylor's Marianist Award Lecture*, ed. James L. Heft (New York: Oxford University Press, 1999), 13–37. On differences between Taylor's and Lonergan's meanings of authenticity, see Brian J. Braman, *Meaning and Authenticity: Bernard Lonergan and Charles Taylor on the Drama of Authentic Human Existence* (Toronto: University of Toronto Press, 2008).

Conclusion

The contemporary crisis of culture is a crisis of normativity attendant upon a transition to a new stage in the history of human meaning.[44] Classicism assumed its traditions were normative. Neo-scholasticism assumed that universal norms meant universal propositions and rules of inference. Paradigm changes in the natural sciences, history, and culture have steadily eroded the viability of these suppositions. An adequate solution cannot consist in bluntly reasserting the normativity of some lost, sacrosanct cultural form.[45] But that does not mean acquiescence in cultural liquidation, either. What is desirable is a way between the false alternatives.

> There is bound to be formed a solid right that is determined to live in a world that no longer exists. There is bound to be formed a scattered left, captivated by now this, now that new development. . . . But what will count is a perhaps not numerous center, big enough to be at home in both the old and the new, painstaking enough to work out one by one the transitions to be made, strong enough to refuse half-measures and insist on complete solutions even though it has to wait.[46]

44. Lonergan distinguishes three stages of meaning: the linguistic and literary, the logical, and a third stage, which we are now entering, in which it becomes clear that transpositions from one horizon or culture to another, and the process of discovery itself, are not logical and therefore raise a different kind of question of validity (*Method* [1972], 85–96, or CWL 14, 82–93). The idea is not that logic becomes irrelevant; it retains its uses for clarifying positions at any given stage of development. But the successful application of logic presupposes the attainment of univocal propositions in a static state. Moreover, logic is not the instrument of discovery, because, logically, nothing is in the conclusion that is not already in the premises. The prior and more basic issue is the discovery and validation of the premises. For further discussion with special reference to historiography, see McPartland, *Lonergan and Historiography*, 111–52. For a brief, accessible introduction, see William P. Loewe, *Lex Crucis: Soteriology and the Stages of Meaning* (Minneapolis: Fortress, 2016), 1–11; the whole book is a worthwhile experiment with some possible theological implications of this notion.

45. Joseph Ratzinger, commenting on the inescapability of Christian self-mediation in the 'world,' underscores the risks of internecine warfare—playing off one historical form of Christian existence against another—out of a failure to discern the requirements of one's age. "What is Christian never exists in an entirely wordless way. . . . This interweaving of what is Christian with the world can easily lead to the situation of an apparent conflict between faith and the world, while in reality what is Christian is not being defended against the world but, rather, just one particular historical form of Christian involvement in the world against another." *Dogma and Preaching*, 169.

46. Lonergan, "Dimensions of Meaning," 245.

The call to a 'not numerous center' may sound like arrogant 'beyondism,' a pox on all houses, but really it is an invitation to the hard work that truly needs done. To the left it is an invitation to become at home in the old and acknowledge the real claims of the past upon our present. To the right it is an invitation to recognize that the giants of *ressourcement*, the Congars and the Torrells, were so because they faced squarely the challenges presented by historicity.

The alternative to the center is a dialectical feedback loop. The need for norms is felt. Until it is met in a satisfactory manner, many will perceive the rejection of classicist pretense as a rejection of all norms. Not a few rejoice at the liberation. They furnish abundant evidence to confirm suspicions on the solid right, where the revival of something very like neo-scholasticism in thought and classicism in culture cannot but seem the appropriate remedy. A scattered left will resist what is seen as revanchism. The way forward, nevertheless, is to acknowledge relativity without becoming relativist, to be historically honest without becoming historicist, to find a cultural norm above every cultural form so that we may face contingency squarely without succumbing to arbitrary decisionism.

Lonergan remains timely, I submit, because his asceticism of self-discovery can meet the crisis of normativity and its portents for our self-understanding. He was not tempted to involve himself in passing controversy; he "saw that there were genuine intellectual problems forced on Christian thinkers and set about solving them rather than attacking the enemy."[47] Today he is a reproach to both houses: to a solid right unequal to the tradition's best achievements and questions, and to a scattered left that has no use for them.

> In the name of phenomenology, of existential self-understanding, of human encounter, of salvation history, there are those that resentfully and disdainfully brush aside the old questions of cognitional theory, epistemology, metaphysics. I have no doubt, I never did doubt, that the old answers were defective. But to reject the question as well is to refuse to know what one is doing when one is knowing; it is to refuse to know why doing that is

47. William M. Shea, "A Vote of Thanks to Voltaire," in *A Catholic Modernity*, 39–64, here 50.

knowing; it is to refuse to set up a basic semantics by conclud-
ing what one knows when one does it. That threefold refusal is
worse than the mere neglect of the subject, and it generates a far
more radical truncation. It is that truncation that we experience
today not only without but within the church, when we find
that the conditions of the possibility of significant dialogue are
not grasped, when the distinction between revealed religion and
myth is blurred, when the possibility of objective knowledge of
God's existence and his goodness is denied.[48]

It is not enough to name what is not normative, to cast down the idol
of misplaced normativity. We have to name and to know in ourselves
what is genuinely normative. There is no other way we as theologians
can measure up to our tradition and calling. What Lonergan proposes
is a difficult but essential remedy.

---

48. Bernard J. F. Lonergan, "The Subject," in *A Second Collection*, CWL 13, 60–74, here 74.

.

PART 1

Wisdom as Subject

CHAPTER THREE

A 'Wisdom of the Concrete'

Wisdom for us is not only about knowing God, as with the philosophers, but also about directing human life.[1]

ST. THOMAS AQUINAS

Like most other discourses, contemporary theology, outside of a few precincts, is no longer much influenced by the Aristotelian conceptuality of scholastic thought. Lonergan's involvement in scholasticism and his critique of its limitations can lend an air of quaintness to his project or a tint of ambiguity to his aims. But he had the crisis of normativity clearly in his sights, and his proposal for getting a handle on it is a program of normative self-knowledge as relevant and as vital now as it was forty years ago. What he proposed is not a theory or a logic or a system pretending to permanence and normativity. It is, fundamentally, a practical asceticism of self-appropriation, of methodical collaboration, of promoting intellectual, moral, and religious order in the soul by bringing their dimensions into practical focus.

The crisis of normativity arises because the real principles of human development, cultural, scientific, or religious, cannot be adequately objectified in any set of propositions, no matter how basic. A principle is first in some order. If we conceive the problem of order principally in terms of scientific formulations, then the principles are premises, as in the model of science presented in Aristotle's *Posterior Analytics*, where

---

1. Thomas Aquinas, *Summa theologiae* (New York: Editiones Paulinae, 1962), 2–2 q. 19 a. 7c (henceforth *STh*); "sapientia secundum nos non solum consideratur ut est cognoscitiva Dei, sicut apud philosophos; sed etiam ut est directiva humanae vitae" (my rather free translation).

the first principles are the premises for scientific syllogisms, or in Aquinas's *sacra doctrina*, where the first principles are the articles of faith, or again in the neoscholastic arrangement of tractates, where fundamental theology presented those doctrines whose acceptance would lead to the acceptance of the others.[2] In each of these cases, the ordered set consists of propositions, and those propositions are first whence the others are somehow derived. But Lonergan's primary concern was not with the ordering of theological and philosophical contents, but with the still-prior business of ordering theological and philosophical operations. Just as what is foundational to modern natural sciences is not some set of primitive contents but the collaborative operations of the community of scientists, so Lonergan aimed for a theology whose foundations would reside in the collaborative operations of theologians. But the ordering of theological operations cannot be separated from the ordering of the operating subjects, that is, of theologians.

To that end, in *Insight* Lonergan sought to enact a pedagogy that could lead readers to a strategic set of judgments through a "self-attention of scientific dimensions."[3] *Insight* is meant to guide an interrogation of one's own wonder, of the basic patterns to be found within the activities of asking and answering questions. Through it, one reaches a limited but strategic set of judgments concerning the structure of one's own knowing, that is, the structural relationships among such recurring acts as inquiry, phantasm, insight, formulation, reflection, and judgment. Self-knowledge of this kind, Lonergan hoped, could give a sound basis to further kinds of self-knowledge—for instance, of one's proclivity to bias, inattention, obtuseness, irrationality, and so on. Above all, it could reground the wisdom that it is impossible to live fully as a human being without surrendering oneself to transcendent mystery beyond our comprehension and control.

---

2. In Aristotle's *Posterior Analytics*, a first principle generally means a self-evident premise in a scientific syllogism: "the premises of demonstrated knowledge must be true, primary, immediate, better known than and prior to the conclusion, which is further related to them as effect to cause." In Aquinas's attempt to put *sacra doctrina* on a scientific basis in this mode, the first principles are the articles of faith, self-evident to God and the blessed if not to us. In the neoscholastic division of tractates, the treatises of 'fundamental' theology set forth the set of first doctrines upon which the others follow. This general meaning of first principle is not the only meaning and does not exclude the fact that Aristotle and Aquinas also acknowledged, in their own ways, the operational first principle that is understanding. See Byrne, *Analysis and Science in Aristotle*, 184–89.

3. McShane, "Lonerganism," 230.

In *Insight* Lonergan took the further step of relating this fundamental structure to the method of metaphysics, and in the sequel, *Method in Theology*, he related it to the tasks of a theology that recognizes the historicity of its doctrines without relativizing their truth. The essential point, however, is not the objectification of the structure or the formulation of such universal principles as the first precepts of speculative and of practical intellect. The judgments in view do not supply premises for any kind of further deduction. Rather, for Lonergan, what is ineluctably basic (foundational) is the reality about whom the judgments are to be made: the self-transcending subject, ordered potentially to all of being through his or her transparency to the demands of wonder and love. This reality is oneself as belonging to what is greater than we: to the traditions that take our measure, and above all to the uncreated light that ontologically grounds such intelligence as we can call our own.

The purpose of the objectification is to mediate a concrete knowledge of and efficacious commitment to one's own rationality as a created participation of uncreated light. Lonergan called this objective 'self-appropriation.' For Lonergan, then, what is first in theology is the intelligence and rationality of the theologian, illumined by faith, motivated by love, and heightened in its efficacy by a deliberate program of recollection and scrutiny, penetration and self-possession. It is these, not as objectified in some theoretic synthesis, not as impossibly abstracted from involvement with God and history, not—whatever one might think—as providing some basic abstract scheme, one size to fit all, for the assimilation of all data without further ado; it is intelligence and reason simply as discovered and verified and embraced in oneself.

The office of wisdom is to discover first principles and put matters in order. Because Lonergan's program attempts to bring order to theological and philosophical inquiry and knowledge beginning not from universal principles but from the concrete structure of intelligence and reason, it is a 'wisdom of the concrete.' It is a program for the development of wisdom, that is, for a deepening possession of first principles; but it is of the concrete, a wisdom not through the appropriation of a system but through appropriation of oneself as a created participation of uncreated light, an incarnation of intelligence, reason, responsibility. Its first principles are not first propositions but the operational principles of our intelligent, rational, moral, and religious being. The essential point of his most personal work is utterly lost if it is taken—as it frequently is—for a mere accumulation of arguments to be followed rather than an "invitation to a personal, decisive act,"[4] an asceticism of self-discovery and self-appropriation to be gathered up. 'Know thyself' has been easy to affirm and difficult to achieve ever since the Delphic oracle. If Lonergan was right to suppose that it is the only way to get a proper handle on the crisis of normativity, then today it is also a matter of fundamental urgency.

As I noted in the introduction, there is no possibility of re-creating anything like Lonergan's pedagogy here. What I hope to do is dispel misunderstandings and give some reasons to think his program might be a worthwhile investment. To that end, this chapter sketches the basic meaning and bearing of Lonergan's approach to the development of wisdom in three steps: wisdom as self-surrender, the question of God, and wisdom as self-knowledge.

Wisdom as Self-Surrender

If the fundamental problem for theology is the adequacy of theologians to their vocation, the one thing most necessary is the one thing God alone can give: loving and listening to God. Needless to say, Lonergan was not a Pelagian and did not think a pure and unconditional love of God could be mediated by philosophy. But he wanted to prepare a way for a clear and unreserved acknowledgment of its normativity. Lonergan realized that our most important involvement with the world is through our loves and our questions—but we must measure up to them. He was also well aware of the fact that the wisdom of the theologian is an imperfect wisdom and no human effort will make it perfect. He acknowledged a higher wisdom than the wisdom of learning that knows the order of things in the mirror of the soul; it is a wisdom of listening, of docility to the Spirit, who is divine personal Listening.[5] Thus, for Lonergan, what above all is normative in us is the wisdom of listening, of transparency

---

4. *Insight*, 13; see 766.

5. Lonergan conceived the Spirit as divine personal Listening. Bernard J. F. Lonergan, *The Triune God: Doctrines*, ed. Robert M. Doran and H. Daniel Monsour, trans. Michael G. Shields, CWL 11 (2009), 638–85; Lonergan, *Caring about Meaning*, 20–21, 61–62.

to God, of suffering divine things. It is not normative as a theory about grace. It is not normative as named, objectified, formulated, affirmed. It is normative as a reality in persons, in Christians, in theologians, not as windowless monads but as the way of their relation to the world, to one another, to Christ. Thus the normativity of otherworldly love is correlative to the beloved, to God in Christ, reconciling the world; it involves us with divine mystery ineluctably. Thus, the central purpose of Lonergan's pedagogy of self-discovery, his turn to the subject, was not to enclose but to decenter the subject by bringing to light the inherent relatedness of subjectivity to the world.[6] The humility of recognizing our situatedness, horizon, brokenness, and blindness need not involve us in relativism.

In underscoring the existential normativity of conversion, Lonergan was transposing Aquinas's notion of an infused wisdom transforming reason and feeling alike. Thus, there is a wisdom acquired through study, and it is metaphysics and self-knowledge. Still higher is theology as reason ordered by faith. Its supreme rule, the wisdom highest in us, is a wisdom of listening, an infused wisdom. Lonergan explains that, for Aquinas,

> wisdom through self-knowledge is not limited to the progress from empirical through scientific to normative knowledge [of ourselves]. Beyond the wisdom we may attain by that natural light of our intellects, there is a further wisdom attained through the supernatural light of faith, when the humble surrender of our own light to the self-revealing uncreated Light makes the latter the loved law of all our assents. Rooted in this faith, super-natural wisdom has a twofold expansion. In its contact with human reason, it is the science of theology, which orders the data of revelation and passes judgment on all other science. But faith, besides involving a contact with reason, also involves a

6. See Lawrence, *Fragility of Consciousness*, 229–77, esp. 244; also Nicholas Plants, "Decentering Inwardness," in *In Deference to the Other: Lonergan and Contemporary Continental Thought* (Albany: State University of New York Press, 2004), 11–32; Martin J. Matustik, *Mediation of Deconstruction: Bernard Lonergan's Method in Philosophy: The Argument from Human Operational Development* (Lanham, Md: University Press of America, 1988); James Marsh, "Postmodernism: A Lonerganian Retrieval and Critique," *International Philosophical Quarterly* 35, no. 2 (1995): 159–73; and Jerome A. Miller, *In the Throe of Wonder: Intimations of the Sacred in a Postmodern World* (Albany: State University of New York Press, 1992).

contact with God. On that side wisdom is a gift of the Holy Spirit, making us docile to his movements, in which, even perceptibly, one may be 'non solum discens sed et patiens divina.'[7]

If theology is a wisdom higher than metaphysics, it is because it is rooted in the wisdom highest in us, docility to the Spirit. That highest wisdom is the basis for our hearing, the loved law of our assent, and the source and measure of the questions that follow upon it.

Under the tutelage of Aquinas, Lonergan initially conceived religious conversion in terms of the reorientation of desire, a change in antecedent willingness.[8] For Aquinas, as Lonergan reads him, God is always the transcendent author of our freedom. By granting us to desire, God opens up an existential 'space' for us to deliberate and choose. That is, prior to the wanting, there are no prospective objects of deliberation; it is only when we begin to desire that we are presented the possibility of a choice. Conversion in this sense, that is, the process that for Aquinas leads to the infusion of sanctifying grace, is the special case of a radical, stable reorientation of the will. Not only external performance but also internal decisions—to believe, to hope, to revere God—are cooperative responses made possible by God plucking the heart of stone.[9]

As Lonergan brought this perspective into conversation with the problems brought to light by hermeneutical and existentialist philosophy, further dimensions opened up for him.[10] The grace of conversion, religious conversion, is not only the gift of a new heart but also of a new world. The old self not only does not love the right things; the old self cannot even properly notice or conceive them; they fall outside the horizon, the effective range of openness, interest, and concern. Conversion, then, relates a problem of desire to a problem of horizon. One's horizon settles what one is prepared to notice, to appreciate as a possibility, to care for. In the old horizon, incarnation and resurrection seem laughably fraudulent; in the

---

7. *Verbum*, 101 (internal citations omitted).

8. See Lonergan, "*Insight* Revisited," 646, 711, 747.

9. *Grace and Freedom*, 141–42; see 128 on conversion; also 132–142 on the difficulties of interpreting Aquinas regarding the exterior act and the grounds for taking the *actus exterior* to include even internal acts of the will.

10. Compare *Insight*, 451–58 ("major flexibility is the selection of a new goal"); and *Method* (1972), 40–41, or CWL 14, 41 ("vertical liberty").

new, they are hauntingly right. Falling in otherworldly love, responding to the Spirit's gift of charity, opens a new self to a new world. Conversion dismantles the previous horizon and establishes a new one, in an exercise of freedom Lonergan's Gregorian colleague Joseph de Finance taught him to call 'vertical liberty.'

Lonergan generalized the notion of conversion to conceive a threefold reversal, rather startling when objectified, in one's operational criteria for assent, evaluation, and devotion.[11] The reversal is also a decentering from the givenness of one's animal sensorium to a properly human orientation in the strange and far vaster universe of being, or from the ultimacy of human projects to a collaboration with God. By distinguishing conversion into its moral, intellectual, and religious or affective dimensions, Lonergan resisted the reduction of our spiritual pathology to one single dimension. There is a conflict between reason and the passions, but it is not the only conflict, and it is not alone relevant to the reductions

---

11. There are many relevant, and largely parallel, discussions in Lonergan's corpus, e.g., see *Method* (1972), 267–69, or CWL 14, 251–52; "Unity and Plurality: The Coherence of Christian Truth," in *A Third Collection*, CWL 16, 228–38, here 236–38. My discussion here draws proximately from "Reality, Myth, Symbol," in *Philosophical and Theological Papers 1965–1980*, CWL 17, 384–90, here 389–90: "Insofar as one is inauthentic there is needed an about-turn, a conversion—indeed, a threefold conversion: an intellectual conversion by which without reserves one enters the world mediated by meaning; a moral conversion by which one comes to live in a world motivated by values; and a religious conversion when one accepts God's gift of his love bestowed by the Holy Spirit." These conversions are distinct but not separate, just as holiness is a dimension distinct from moral goodness, and sin is not only moral fault but offense against God. See *Method* (1972), 242–43, or CWL 14, 228–29; *Early Works on Method 1*, 566. Religious conversion implies moral conversion, but holiness is a distinct dimension of life, and it is always possible to destroy one's moral being without losing one's faith (just as the scholastics distinguished acquired from infused virtues and acknowledged the possibility of a *fides informata* as well as a *fides caritate formata*). Both religious and moral conversions imply intellectual conversion, because adherence to revealed mystery and discernment about the concrete human good involve us inextricably with intelligible truth irreducible to sense. But as an explicit achievement of the kind Augustine narrates in *Confessions*—his discovery that he had been imagining God—it seems exceedingly rare. For an introduction to Lonergan's account of conversion, see Miller, *The Quest for God and the Good Life*, 143–74; see too Walter Conn, "Bernard Lonergan and Authenticity: The Search for a Valid Criterion of the Moral Life," *American Benedictine Review* 30, no. 3 (1979): 301–21; André Gilbert and Louis Roy, "La Structure Éthique de La Conversion Religieuse d'après B. Lonergan," *Science et Esprit* 32, no. 3 (1980): 347–60; and Michael L. Rende, "The Development and the Unity of Lonergan's Notion of Conversion," *Method: Journal of Lonergan Studies* 1, no. 2 (1983): 158–73. Finally, Robert M. Doran has proposed a fourth, 'psychic' conversion, most thoroughly in *Theology and the Dialectics of History* (Toronto: University of Toronto Press, 1989). A detailed exposition and examination of this notion lies beyond the purview of this book. For a relatively recent and compendious account, see Doran, "Reception and Elemental Meaning: An Expansion of the Notion of Psychic Conversion," *Toronto Journal of Theology* 20, no. 2 (2004): 133–57.

of scientism, the contraction of the spirit to the psychological management of tensions, the truncated instrumentalization of reason, or
postmodern alienation.

Moral conversion effects an evaluative shift from motives of pleasure
and pain—the criteria of sensitive extraversion spontaneously operative inasmuch as we are animals—toward properly human motives of
intelligible value. It is exemplified in Socrates's fantastic contention that
it is far better to suffer than to do wrong, or again by Augustine's flat
dismissal of the evil we suffer as a trivial problem compared to the evil we
do. Moral conversion responds to the struggle for dominance between
the higher and the lower appetites, but it is not the total remedy because
that struggle is not the total problem. Similarly, intellectual conversion
effects a cognitive break from the criteria of sensitive extroversion—
again, spontaneously operative in us as animals—into the properly
human criteria of rational judgment, intelligible truth, and sufficient
evidence. It is exemplified in Socrates's push for explanatory concepts, or
again by Augustine's realization that God is not the name of an imaginable extension and duration but the intelligible eternity that creates time
and space.[12] It responds to the problem of ascending from the cave of
appearance to the sunlit world of the intelligible and true, but it does not
represent the pathology of reductionism as the only problem. Religious
conversion, finally, is a displacement away from the human-centered
loves of the earthly city into a theocentric friendship with God above all,
and with all in God and for God's sake. It is exemplified by Augustine's love
of God even to the contempt of self, or again by that supreme friendship
with God that, for Aquinas, is above even the friendly love of creature
for Creator. It involves us implicitly with value, for the world is God's
good creation. It involves us with intelligible truth, for God, the right
order of the soul, and the revealed mysteries are not, strictly speaking,
imaginable; they are attained through true judgments.

Although intellectual and moral conversion, like knowledge of God's
existence, lie within the range of possible human achievement, in the
actual conditions of this life they are almost certainly never achieved
without involvement with divine grace, and Lonergan considered that
ordinarily, consent to divine love—religious conversion—comes first. In

---

12. See Lamb, *Eternity, Time, and the Life of Wisdom*, 29–53.

its first moment, the reality of religious conversion is the illumination of the Spirit that precedes and grounds decision. In itself, love has the character of a 'yes' prior to concrete decisions and particular questions; it constitutes a horizon within which decisions and questions emerge and to which they bear witness. Apart from this first moment, there is as yet no decision to be made. Love is at once the basis for a decision and the demand for free and full commitment.[13]

There is, however, no transformation of subjects that is not mediated by an involvement in the world. It is not that we first have some immanent experience called 'religious' and subsequently decide to attach it to a tradition. It is rather that we experience ourselves as addressed, as summoned "to hearken and to hammer day and night."[14] And if we 'hearken' it is because we have hearts to hearken, ears to hear. Such an involvement is nothing if it is not concrete. As concretely Christian, it involves us in an explicit mutual self-mediation with Jesus Christ, who articulates definitively the full meaning of conversion. As he lived his life in relation to us, so we work out our lives in relation to him and those who belong to him—particularly those given to our care, but in some sense, to everyone.[15] In Christ we learn the wisdom of the cross as the touchstone of religious authenticity: God's purpose to overcome the malice of sin, not by power, but by love. This foundational claim is also a personal adherence to Christ, who says to each of us, without exception: Take up your cross and follow me.

Conversion is, therefore, conversational. It upends one's existing conversations and inaugurates new ones. We are not deracinated Enlightenment rationalists but conversational subjects receiving and carrying forward a tradition. This brings us back to the problem of a Christian native language raised in the previous chapter. For typical adults, language is the most versatile, sophisticated carrier of meaning.

13. See Bernard J. F. Lonergan, "Bernard Lonergan Responds (1)," in *Shorter Papers*, ed. Robert C. Croken, Robert M. Doran, and H. Daniel Monsour, CWL 20 (2007), 263–74, here 266–68; "Bernard Lonergan Responds," in *Foundations of Theology: Papers from the International Lonergan Congress 1970*, ed. Philip J. McShane (Notre Dame, Ind.: University of Notre Dame Press, 1971), 223–34, here 225–27.

14. Rainer Maria Rilke, *Letters to a Young Poet and The Letter from the Young Worker*, trans. and ed. Charlie Louth (New York: Penguin, 2011), 43. Possibly he is quoting back his correspondent, Kappus.

15. See *STh* 2-2 qq. 25, 26; 3 q. 8 a. 3.

It is therefore ordinarily essential to a sustained flow of thought. As Lonergan puts it, "Prizing names is prizing the human achievement of bringing conscious intentionality into sharp focus and, thereby, setting about the double task of both ordering one's world and orientating oneself within it. . . . Listening and speaking are a major part in the achievement" of conscious presence to the world.[16] He continues:

> So it is that conscious intentionality develops and is moulded by its mother tongue. It is not merely that we learn the names of what we see but also that we can attend to and talk about the things we can name. The available language, then, takes the lead. It picks out the aspects of things that are pushed into the foreground, the relations between things that are stressed, the movements and changes that demand attention. . . . The action is reciprocal. Not only does language mould developing consciousness but also it structures the world about the subject.[17]

Conversation is the link between the transcendental structures of conscious intentionality and their concrete unfolding in the world mediated by meaning. Its reciprocal action shapes our readiness and structures our world.[18]

In relation to that world, each of us is presented a fundamental problem of self-understanding to which an answer must be given. An answer is, in fact, already begun before ever we bring the question into the light of deliberate, adult freedom. One's first, native language—not as the abstract set of possibilities represented in dictionaries and grammars, but as a set of concrete resources for understanding and expression in ongoing conversations—is never a matter of deliberation and choice. For us, being is becoming, the becoming is conversational, and we are involved from the beginning. There are no atomic individuals and no pure perception; there are conversational subjects coming into being in a world overwhelmingly mediated by linguistic meaning, and with greater or less readiness to ask and answer and follow through on the most important questions.

16. *Method* (1972), 70, or CWL 14, 68.
17. *Method* (1972), 71, or CWL 14, 68.
18. See Lawrence, *Fragility of Consciousness*, 240–50.

Our authenticity in conversation is radically conditioned by the presence or absence of conversion, in ourselves and in others. In this life everyone is affected by internal disorder externally reinforced by what Augustine called the "infernal river of human custom"[19] and Lonergan "the social surd."[20] Everyone is also involved—prior to any decision and as a necessary condition for the most important decision—with the pull of divine love. 'Pure nature' is a valid line of reference, but not a condition in which anyone has ever lived, before the Fall or after, under the Law or under the Gospel.[21] If we are not dealing with historicity, sin, and grace, we are dealing in abstractions.

What is basic, then, is not proof, but authenticity in conversation.[22] That authenticity means standing by the light of our intelligence, reason, and responsibility. But concretely, it leads beyond our humanity by involving us also with grace; in the real world, "to be just a man is what man cannot be."[23] Such authenticity is not sustained in a vacuum but through friendships, in conversation. Lonergan reminded his students that to be of service to others, it is necessary that they first exist authentically themselves, lest the blind lead the blind. He enjoined them to promote conversion rather than controversy.[24] This was one way he had of putting "the eminently practical question" about the right way to live.[25] It turns out that the problem of understanding is intimately bound up with the problem of living, since "science, scholarship, philosophy, and theology can only be genuine in the measure that they 'head one into being authentically human.'"[26] In the end, knowing, like loving, is a kind

19. Augustine, *Confessions*, 1.16.25.

20. *Insight*, 254–63, 653–56, 710–15, 721–22, 748–50.

21. See *Grace and Freedom*, 17.

22. *Method* (1972), 337–39, or CWL 14, 312–14.

23. *Insight*, 750.

24. "Quae cum ita sint, si quis aliis subvenire voluerit, et (1) ipse ex-sistat necesse est ne caecus caecum ducat et (2) in aliis magis convertendis quam convincendis incumbat." Bernard J. F. Lonergan, *The Ontological and Psychological Constitution of Christ*, ed. Frederick E. Crowe and Robert M. Doran, trans. Michael G. Shields, CWL 7 (2002), 22.

25. Lawrence, *Fragility of Consciousness*, 231–32; Frederick G. Lawrence, "The Horizon of Political Theology," in *Trinification of the World: A Festschrift in Honour of Frederick E. Crowe in Celebration of His 60th Birthday*, ed. Thomas A. Dunne and Jean-Marc Laporte (Toronto: Regis College, 1978), 46–70, here 50.

26. Lawrence, *Fragility of Consciousness*, 11, quoting Bernard J. F. Lonergan, "Method: Trend and Variations," in *A Third Collection*, CWL 16, 10–20, here 20 ("Being a scientist is just an aspect of

of self-surrender, and the quality of the surrender cannot be disengaged from the quality of the self.[27]

The Question of God

The one question no one can evade is the question about the right way to live. In order to live, we are obliged to give it a practical answer. At least obliquely it involves us with God, because there is no waymaking in this life that does not involve us trying to understand, yielding to evidence, pursuing what seems worthwhile, asking what we should love. As Lonergan wrote in the epilogue to *Insight*,

> our first eighteen chapters were written solely in the light of human intelligence and reasonableness, without any appeal to the authority of the church and without any explicit deference to the genius of St Thomas Aquinas. At the same time, our first eighteen chapters were followed by a nineteenth and twentieth that revealed the inevitability with which the affirmation of God and the search of intellect for faith arise out of a sincere acceptance of scientific presuppositions and precepts.[28]

If we ask for explanation, we suppose the objective intelligibility of the universe. If we bow to evidence, we implicitly acknowledge a ground of being. If we pursue value and prize rectitude, we presume an objective right and good. If we yield ourselves in love, tacitly we raise the possibility of total self-surrender to a supreme loveliness whom we may love with all our hearts, without conditions, restrictions, or qualifications. The question of God arises, and its answer is cumulatively implied by the demand for complete explanation, the force of sufficient reason, the obligation of moral rectitude, the gift of a love stretching beyond the confines of this world.[29]

---

being human, nor has any method been found that makes one authentically scientific without heading one into being authentically human").

27. On self-surrender, see *Method* (1972), 105–15, 237–44, 267–69, 273, 277–78, or CWL 14, 101–11, 223–30, 251–52, 256, 260–61.

28. *Insight*, 765.

29. See Bernard J. F. Lonergan, "Philosophy of God, and Theology," in *Philosophical and Theological Papers 1965–1980*, CWL 17, 159–218, here 206–7.

Lonergan gradually concluded that the dominant note in this orientation was not the wonder so much as the love. Aquinas's celebrated 'five ways' each conclude with a statement to the effect that the being reached by the proof is what everyone means by God.

> But what is this meaning known by everyone? Is it that everyone in some fashion or other does prove the existence of God? Or is it that God gives sufficient grace to everyone, that the one sufficient grace is the gift of charity without which nothing else is of avail (1 Corinthians 13), that the gift orientates one to what is transcendent in lovableness, that that orientation can occur without any corresponding apprehension, that it can be, in Rahner's phrase, a content without a known object, that such a content is an orientation to the unknown, to mystery? Such an orientation to mystery, in my opinion, is a main source of man's search for God. As Pascal quoted in his *Pensées*, you would not be seeking for me unless you had already found me.[30]

In *Insight*, Lonergan worked out explicitly the argument from the demand for complete explanation: if being is completely intelligible, God exists. Intelligence demands complete explanation, but contingent being is not self-explanatory. The five ways of Aquinas he interpreted as so many illustrations of the incomplete intelligibility of contingent being; "there are as many other proofs of the existence of God as there are aspects of the incomplete intelligibility in the universe of proportionate being" (proportionate, that is, to our manner of coming to know, through inquiry into data).[31] The one correct answer to the

30. Bernard J. F. Lonergan, "Bernard Lonergan Responds (2)," in *Shorter Papers*, CWL 20, 275–81, here 278. Compare *Method* (1972), 341–42, or CWL 14, 315–16.

31. *Insight*, 701; see 692–99. On the context and internal development of Lonergan's philosophy of God, see Bernard J. F. Lonergan, "The General Character of the Natural Theology of Insight," in *Philosophical and Theological Papers 1965–1980*, CWL 17, 3–9; Bernard J. F. Lonergan, "Natural Knowledge of God," in *A Second Collection*, CWL 13, 99–113. For interpretations, see Patrick H. Byrne, "God and the Statistical Universe," *Zygon* 16, no. 4 (1981): 345–63; Alicia Jaramillo, "The Necessity of Raising the Question of God: Aquinas and Lonergan on the Quest after Complete Intelligibility," *The Thomist* 71, no. 2 (2007): 221–67; Robert J. Spitzer, *New Proofs for the Existence of God: Contributions of Contemporary Physics and Philosophy* (Grand Rapids, Mich.: William B. Eerdmans, 2010), 144–76; Paul St. Amour, "Bernard Lonergan on Affirmation of the Existence of God," *Analecta Hermeneutica* 2, no. 1 (2010): 1–9; Bernard J. Tyrrell, "The New Context of the

question of God is in some way already contained in our intelligent, rational, moral honesty.[32]

Consider, however, how large a stipulation that honesty really is. It supposes that one is intellectually curious, grasps the import of the question, and has the ability, formation, and leisure to address it. It supposes one will not flinch from uncomfortable answers, answers that may call one's concrete solution to the problem of living into question, complicate one's every relationship, overthrow settled preference and feeling. Besides honesty, a successful outcome also depends on luck. It supposes one hits upon a fruitful line of inquiry and is not derailed early and often by some fatal mistake. Concretely, it seems to suppose, too, an environment, a culture, a community of friends and interlocutors prepared to exercise a constructive rather than a distracting or even harmful influence.[33] So numerous, so weighty indeed are such stipulations that were God's existence not revealed, we might well conclude with Thomas Aquinas that it would be known with certainty only to very few, after a vast labor, and tinged with error.[34] The question of God arises for us and can be answered by us, but both the fruitful asking and, still more, the successful answering suppose the fulfillment of an enormous and demanding range of conditions—very few of which we fulfill all by ourselves.

Even an elementary reflection on the concrete factors reveals that the difficulty with the question of God is not so much the proof as its existential suppositions. It is not too difficult to formulate a valid syllogism, but it is something else to show its soundness. That requires what really is both difficult and rare: the prior sustained effort required to verify and accept the suppositions of the proof, to know just what is meant by affirming that being is completely intelligible, that it has a ground, that

---

Philosophy of God in Lonergan and Rahner," in *Language, Truth, and Meaning: Papers from the International Lonergan Congress 1970* (Notre Dame, Ind.: University of Notre Dame Press, 1972), 284–305; the most complete treatment is Bernard Tyrrell, *Bernard Lonergan's Philosophy of God*, American ed. (Notre Dame, Ind.: University of Notre Dame Press, 1974).

32. See *Method* (1972), 101–5, or CWL 14, 96–101.

33. These factors have recently been studied by Rosenberg, *The Givenness of Desire*.

34. See Thomas Aquinas, *Summa contra gentiles* bk. 1, chap. 4 (henceforth, *ScG*), in *Liber de Veritate Catholicae Fidei contra errores Infidelium, seu Summa contra Gentiles*, ed. Ceslas Pera, Pierre Marc, and Pietro Caramello, Leonine ed., 3 vols. (Turin: Marietti, 1961). See also *STh* 1 q. 1 a. 1; 2–2 q. 2 a. 4.

it is good; to know and accept that one's very intelligence, rationality, and responsibility bind one ineluctably to these affirmations.[35] Short of that luminosity, it is not only possible but in fact easy to throw up roadblocks, to regard the only adequate position as nothing more than "a dogmatic rationalist leap."[36]

What Lonergan meant by self-appropriation, then, has a double implication for the question of God. On the one hand, it makes the question unavoidable and, indeed, points inexorably to the one correct answer. On the other, it also brings into light how rarely the conditions for a successful answer may be concretely fulfilled. Lonergan came to the opinion that in the ordinary run of events, those conditions are usually not fulfilled except in the throe of otherworldly love, and never, de facto, apart from at least some influence of divine grace.[37] It is the

35. See Lonergan's 1967 retrospective on his 'natural theology' in his "Natural Theology of Insight." In a 1979 course on Method in Theology, Lonergan formulated an argument to the effect that "if the universe is intelligible, moral, and a field for personal relations, then God exists. But the universe is intelligible, moral, and a field for personal relations." Asked why the minor should be granted, he wrote: "One grants the minor premiss without difficulty if one has arrived at self-appropriation. Human understanding is an essential component in human knowledge; but one cannot positively understand what is unintelligible. Moral obligation is an essential component in the mature human being. But it is a nullified obligation if the universe (apart from man) has no part in morality. Human community is human through mature persons; and mature persons in human community have interpersonal relations; if intelligence has no intelligible object and moral obligation no objective basis, personal relations are destined to founder." Method in Theology seminar, Sept. 20, 1979, archival document 29610DTE070.

36. Oliva Blanchette, *Philosophy of Being: A Reconstructive Essay in Metaphysics* (Washington, D.C.: The Catholic University of America Press, 2003), 315; compare Richardson, "Being for Lonergan: A Heideggerian View," 277. Lonergan's brief reply to Richardson is "Bernard Lonergan Responds (2)," 280–81; "Bernard Lonergan responds," in *Language, Truth, and Meaning: Papers from the International Lonergan Congress 1970*, ed. Philip J. McShane (Notre Dame, Ind.: University of Notre Dame Press, 1972), 306–12, here 311.

37. Here are two soundings from the early 1970s: "The trouble with chapter 19 in Insight was that it . . . treated God's existence and attributes in a purely objective fashion. It made no effort to deal with the subject's religious horizon." Lonergan, "Philosophy of God, and Theology," 172. Again, "in *Method* . . . our basic awareness of God comes to us not through arguments or choices but primarily through God's gift of his love." "*Insight* Revisited," 233. Compare *Method* (1972), 337–38, or CWL 14, 312–13: (1) the normal expectation is that religious conversion precedes the effort to work out a rigorous proof, but (2) it may happen, "by way of exception," that the proofs precede and facilitate the conversion, and (3) in any case the knowledge attained through proof is natural in the sense of proportionate to human reason. Jeffrey A. Allen points out that Lonergan's shift in emphasis is mirrored by the shift from Vatican I to Vatican II in "Revisiting Lonergan's View of Natural Knowledge of God" (paper presented at the Lonergan Research Institute Graduate Seminar, Toronto, Ont., Dec. 2015). The former had treated first natural, then revealed knowledge of God; the latter reversed the order. On this point, see Avery Dulles, *The Assurance of Things Hoped*

moral and existential subject, the subject given over to love or at least moved by love, who apprehends the value of pursuing the question about God.

This may seem to elide the distinction between nature and grace that Steven A. Long has lately, and rightly, reaffirmed. Such existential qualifications, Long avers, seem to reduce the prospect of natural knowledge of God to "merely the faintest whiff of remote possibility."[38] In his view, when the First Vatican Council affirmed the possibility of sure natural knowledge of God,[39] it meant "not merely . . . real possibility but indeed . . . real proximate potency . . . for a human being *hic et nunc* can by the natural light of human reason know the one true God."[40] Yet, his asseveration seems doubly abstract, both from the existential context of the subject whose *hic et nunc* is meant and from the historical context of the conciliar decree he invokes.

There is an abstraction from the existential subject, for *hic et nunc* denote concreteness, but no concrete situation is named. Accordingly, the meaning of a 'real proximate potency' remains vague. Normally, as Aquinas observes, a subject is brought into proximate potency (*potentia propinqua*) to some last step by the orderly fulfillment of prior conditions.[41] Infants can learn to speak and normally do, but not in the *hic et nunc*

For: A Theology of Christian Faith (New York: Oxford University Press, 1994), 140; Dulles, "Faith and Reason: From Vatican I to John Paul II," in *The Two Wings of Catholic Thought: Essays on* Fides et Ratio, ed. David Ruel Foster and Joseph W. Koterski (Washington, D.C.: The Catholic University of America Press, 2003), 193–208; George H. Tavard, "Commentary on *De Revelatione*," *Journal of Ecumenical Studies* 3, no. 1 (1966): 1–35, here 12–13.

38. Long, *Natura Pura*, 102.

39. Vatican Council I, Dogmatic Constitution *Dei Filius* (April 24, 1870), chap. 2. "Eadem sancta mater Ecclesia tenet et docet, Deum, rerum omnium principium et finem, naturali humanae rationis lumine e rebus creatis certo cognosci posse . . ." with a corresponding canon: "Si quis dixerit, Deum unum et verum, creatorem et Dominum nostrum, per ea, quae facta sunt, naturali rationis humanae lumine certo cognosci non posse, anathema sit." Tanner et al., *Decrees of the Ecumenical Councils*, 2:806, 810.

40. Long, *Natura Pura*, 102–3 (internal emphasis omitted). I am grateful to Jeffrey A. Allen for bringing the importance of this passage to my attention in his paper "Revisiting Lonergan's View of Natural Knowledge of God."

41. *ScG* bk. 3, chap. 102, no. 6 (counting paragraphs in the Leonine manual edition). "Eiusdem rationis esse videtur quod aliquid operetur ex subiecto; et quod operetur id ad quod est in potentia subiectum; et quod ordinate operetur per determinata media. Nam subiectum non fit in potentia propinqua ad ultimum nisi cum fuerit actu in media. . . . Omnis autem creatura necesse habet subiecto ad hoc quod aliquid faciat: nec potest facere nisi ad quod subiectum est in potentia, ut ostensum est. Ergo non potest facere aliquid nisi subiectum reducat in actum per determinata media."

of the delivery room. Relativity and quantum theory, too, have always lain within the proportion of human intelligence, but they presuppose a tensor calculus and an eigenvalue analysis difficult to master and, it happens, fairly recently developed. In the actual order of things, quantum reality is understood with clarity and certitude by very few, after long and arduous investigation from the perch of other shoulders, and not without some admixture of error; indeed, if such knowledge were vital for salvation, it would seem best revealed. Yet, greater still is the moral and intellectual probity required to prove the existence of God.[42]

The conciliar doctrine also has a context, and, in fact, the conciliar *acta* raise questions Long did not face.[43] The third draft asserted explicitly that certain knowledge of God is possible, even to fallen human beings (*ab homine lapso*); the final constitution, however, declined to specify this condition.[44] Again, the third draft asserted that knowledge of God could be reached without help of a tradition of teaching, but many Fathers wished to say only that it could be reached without a positive, supernatural revelation, and in the event, the clause was dropped.[45] If, then, Long's 'real proximate potency' is enjoyed '*hic et nunc*' by anyone whatever, even one who is morally depraved and without proportionate formation, it is not the doctrine of Vatican I but a determination of

---

42. This is a rather obvious point that Aquinas also makes. *STh* 2–2 q. 2 a. 4c. (to prove the existence of God presupposes many other sciences).

43. The history and meaning of the text are discussed by Lonergan, "Natural Knowledge of God," 99–101. He provides some extracts from the *acta* and relies on Hermann D. Pottmeyer, *Der Glaube vor dem Anspruch der Wissenschaft. Die Konstitution Dei Filius des 1. Vatikanischen Konzils* (Freiburg: Herder, 1968), 168–204. See also Lawrence Moonan, "…*certo cognosci posse*. What Precisely Did Vatican I Define?," *Annuarium Historiae Conciliorum* 42, no.1 (2010): 193–202.

44. J. D. Mansi et al., *Sacrorum Conciliorum Nova et Amplissima Collectio*, 53 vols. (Arnhem: Hubert Welter, 1927), 53:164–169 at 168. Canon 1 *De Revelatione* read in draft, "Si quis negaverit, Deum unum et verum . . . per ea, quae facta sunt, naturali ratione ab homine lapso certo cognosci et demonstrari posse: anathema sit." Minutes of the discussion at 53:186–9; it was agreed to omit "lapso" and "demonstrari" from the canon. The final version reads, "Si quis dixerit, Deum unum et verum . . . naturali rationis humanae lumine certo cognosci non posse: anathema sit."

45. Mansi et al., *Sacrorum Conciliorum*, 53:165. Chapter 2 *De Revelatione* read in draft, ". . . ecclesia Deum, rerum omnium principium et finem, docet naturali humanae rationis lumine e rebus creatis certo cognosci posse, neque ad hoc traditam de Deo doctrinam omnino necessariam esse . . ." The discussion and context suggests what the Fathers wished to specify was that revelation was unnecessary and simply a mercy of God to us (53:184–5). The final version reads, ". . . ecclesia tenet et docet, Deum, rerum omnium principium et finem, naturali humanae rationis lumine e rebus creatis certo cognosci posse." Both the draft and the final version introduce the possibility of natural knowledge to underscore the gratuity of revelation.

questions the Council evidently preferred to leave open. The Council, it seems, was content to settle a matter of principle. It lies within our natural powers to truly conceive and certainly affirm the existence of God, without the light of revelation or faith—but not, perhaps, without proportionate intellectual formation, rare natural ability, long and diligent inquiry, repentance from sin, radical moral honesty, and a humble pursuit of the light. Such conditions, as a matter of fact, are not fulfilled in us apart from grace, unless someone believes that we, the fallen, can so order our own loves aright as to be capable of sustained moral effort and honesty without the help of grace—a supposition that would itself be contrary to faith.[46]

46. Hence Lonergan's conclusion: natural knowledge of God "is not attained without moral judgments and existential decisions," which "do not occur without God's grace" ("Natural Knowledge of God," 133). In this connection, note that the doctrine regarding the possibility of natural knowledge of God is not a freestanding doctrine but is also related to other doctrines that bear on the possibility of sustained moral effort apart from grace. See Josef Neuner and Jacques Dupuis, eds., *The Christian Faith: In the Doctrinal Documents of the Catholic Church*, 7th rev. ed. (Staten Island, N.Y.: Alba House, 2001) (hereafter ND); see also Henricus Denzinger and Adolfus Schönmetzer, eds., *Enchiridion Symbolorum Definitionum et Declarationum de Rebus Fidei et Morum*, 36th ed. (Frieburg: Herder, 1976) (hereafter DS). Note the following: (1) The Fall results in two consequences for all Adam's descendants: loss of innocence and loss of power for good (= moral impotence). No one is capable of remedying these defects by free will, apart from grace (ND 503, DS 239, *Indiculus* ca. AD 435–442). Grace is strength for good performance, not merely the remission of sins (ND 1901, DS 225, Council of Carthage XVI, AD 418); grace is not only instruction (ND 1902, DS 226, Carthage XVI). (2) Without grace, fulfillment of the commandments is not merely difficult, but impossible (ND 1903, DS 227, Carthage XVI). (3) All have truly sinned (ND 1904, DS 228, Carthage XVI) and stand in need of forgiveness (ND 1905, DS 229, Carthage XVI), even the saints (ND 1906, DS 230, Carthage XVI). No one is good without Christ (ND 1908, DS 240, *Indiculus*). (4) Even the baptized need God's help to persevere (ND 1909, DS 241, *Indiculus*). (5) Grace is prior to merit and prior to good will: The merits of the saints are more from God than from themselves (ND 1910, DS 243, *Indiculus*). Every good inspiration is from God more than from us (ND 1911, DS 244, *Indiculus*). All merits are preceded by grace, which liberates the will; God operates in us both to desire and to will (ND 1914, DS 248, *Indiculus*). Grace is prior to all human desire, will, or effort. Grace precedes good will; grace is the cause of good will (ND 1915, DS 373, Council of Orange, AD 529). Even the desire to be cleansed is from the operation of grace ("the infusion and action of the Holy Spirit") (ND 1916, DS 375, Orange). Not only the beginning but also the increase of faith is from the inspiration of the Spirit, not merely from our natural desire (ND 1917, DS 375, Orange). Grace makes us humble and obedient; humility and obedience are not the beginning of grace, but grace is the beginning of humility and obedience (ND 1918, DS 376, Orange). No one can believe the Gospel without grace (ND 1919, DS 377, Orange). (6) Everyone, without exception, stands in need of grace, because of the wound of original sin (ND 1920, DS 378, Orange). (7) "Free will has been so distorted and weakened by the sin of the first parent that thereafter no one could love God as was required, or believe in God, or perform for the sake of God what is good, unless first reached by the grace of divine mercy" (ND 1921, DS 396, Orange). These points do not, of course, negate the possibility of natural knowledge of God; they merely affirm the antecedent improbability of the requisite moral honesty occurring apart from some divine assistance.

My purpose, however, is not to dispute about the meaning of Vatican I's constitution, *Dei Filius*, but to underscore a foundational issue. There are questions that can be asked and answered only by those who are prepared for them, and there are problems in theology that can be solved only through the development of theologians. That development is not happening in a vacuum. It is traditional in modernity to pretend that modernity is not a tradition, and it is traditional in modern science to pretend that science is not a tradition. We, of all people, ought not to be taken in by Enlightenment bias against tradition or by the notion that our minds stand in no need of formation and renewal, transformation and enlargement, if we are to grapple successfully with the questions before us. We must not jejunely imagine answers will come easily if we but open our eyes and look.

If truth is the adequation of the mind to reality, *the* central issue in theology is the readiness of the theologian to measure up to the demands of our authentic tradition and the challenges of our culture. That adequacy is not in itself a theological operation, but the result of the momentous personal transformations Lonergan named religious, moral, and intellectual conversion, and of further measuring up through the differentiations of consciousness by which one becomes at home in prayer, in the rarefied world of theory, in discerning structural components of one's interior life, in the practical world of another time and place. Foundational for these developments is the recognition that it is impossible to live without giving ourselves to something beyond ourselves, and the height of wisdom in this life is self-surrender to otherworldly love.

Wisdom as Self-Knowledge and Self-Appropriation

As grace perfects nature, as infused virtue perfects acquired, as the love of God transforms human loving, so the wisdom of docility to the Spirit draws up and transforms the human love of wisdom and its pursuit through study. This transformation is not to the exclusion of cooperation but rather makes cooperation possible. Lonergan's program of self-appropriation was conceived as an instrument for cooperation in the love of wisdom.

Wisdom is not just any knowledge, but knowledge that is basic and comprehensive. As Lonergan's project developed, he parsed this out in

terms of the poles of cognitional theory and metaphysics, with epistemology in, as it were, the middle. Self-knowledge takes hold of what is
basic, metaphysics formulates what is comprehensive, and epistemology
articulates the link between cognitive performance and objective knowledge. He conceived these in relation to three basic questions: What
am I doing when I am knowing? Why is doing that (i.e., performing
these operations) knowing? What do I know when I do it? Later, he
added a fourth, in effect: What must I do if I would stand by the exigencies
entailed by the answers to the first three? Thus, Lonergan's basic and
total science became (1) cognitional structure, (2) epistemology, which
articulates the pivot from performance to knowledge, (3) metaphysics,
which sets up a basic semantics for inquiry, and (4) existential ethics.

Fundamentally, Lonergan's aim is to make programmatic the "wisdom
through self-knowledge," the discovery of the soul as the "dynamic norm"
of inquiry and action, that he discerned in Aquinas.[47] The story of how
this program developed will occupy us in the next three chapters. Its roots
are in Lonergan's own *ressourcement*, his apprenticeship to Aquinas. In
Verbum, Lonergan discerned a 'duality' in wisdom "between our immanent
intellectual light and the uncreated Light that is the object of its groping and straining."[48] The duality, in other words, is between wisdom as
subject—ourselves as created to the image and likeness of God—and
wisdom as object—God as the eternal Exemplar. This duality is "the
basic instance" of the opposition between the first-for-us and the first-
in-itself: "ontologically the uncreated Light is first; epistemologically our
own immanent light is first, for it is known not by some *species* but *per se
ipsum* as the actuating element in all intelligible *species*."[49] We know the
light of our minds not by grasping an intelligible form in matter, but by
coming to know what it means to be intelligent and rational; and it is
by coming to know ourselves that we are able to conceive God as infinite
intelligence in act.

> Normative knowledge has to rest upon the eternal reasons. But this
> resting, Aquinas explained, is not a vision of God but a participation

47. *Verbum*, 101.

48. *Verbum*, 100.

49. *Verbum*, 100.

and similitude of him by which we grasp first principles and judge all things by examining them in the light of principles.[50]

Lonergan sought to push this Thomist program a step further to bring into explicit focus not propositional but operational first principles. Self-knowledge as normative is the knowledge of oneself as a created participation of uncreated light, a knowledge of the pure, innate exigencies of intelligence.

Lonergan's program of self-knowledge and self-appropriation yields, he claimed, a transcultural and radically unrevisable position on knowing. So bold a claim has naturally raised some eyebrows as a display of "brazen naiveté" without respect for concrete circumstances.[51] It seems impossibly fallacious to suppose "a basic abstract scheme"[52] could account for the decisive structural factors in human knowing in the concrete. It is fashionable to insist that such a thing as Lonergan attempts cannot be done. The crisis of normativity rests on a critique of the possibility of transcultural, transhistorical, or transpolitical objectivity.[53] Claims to the contrary are regarded as 'dogmatic' in the pejorative sense that they are held to rest upon an arbitrary premise—the identification of being

50. *Verbum*, 101. The reference is to Thomas Aquinas, *De veritate* q. 10 a. 8c., in *Quaestiones disputatae De veritate*, Opera Omnia 12, Leonine ed. (Rome: Editori di San Tommaso, 1970).

51. Lonergan's assertion to have hit upon a radically unrevisable structure has "all the brazen naiveté and lack of respect for concrete circumstances of Catch 22." Mackey, "Divine Revelation and Lonergan's Method," 162. Similar concerns are raised, though from a somewhat more sympathetic stance, by Donald L. Gelpi, *Inculturating North American Theology: An Experiment in Foundational Method*, AAR Studies in Religion (Atlanta: Scholars Press, 1988).

52. Davis, "Lonergan and the Teaching Church," 72. Davis claims to discover a fallacy in Lonergan's retorsion argument, that is, his claim that anyone who would refute his cognitional theory would have to invoke experience, understanding, and judgment. "[Lonergan's] fallacy is to suppose that to discover a basic abstract scheme into which all cognitional activities will fit is to have discovered and formulated all the elements of determining importance in human knowledge in the concrete" (72). On the contrary, the fallacy in Davis's rebuttal is to have missed the point. It is not an abstract scheme that is unrevisable; it is the structure of such interrelated facts as: we are involved with questions, and the questions entail some criteria for what might count as an answer; our questions for understanding regard data, and the data are not simply raw but are schematically represented; our questions for judgment regard evidence, and the evidence is construed in relation to a possibility grasped by intelligence; and so forth. To put the point differently, anyone who wishes to say that knowing is not a matter of understanding correctly is welcome to point out the data that have been overlooked or the evidence that has been misconstrued.

53. See Charles Bambach, *Heidegger, Dilthey, and the Crisis of Historicism* (Ithaca, N.Y.: Cornell University Press, 1995).

with the intelligible. As William Richardson objected, "when one begins the discussion of being by simply declaring that it is the 'objective of the pure desire to know,' it does not take a very subtle analysis to infer that being is intelligible."[54] According to the historicist critique (as portrayed by Leo Strauss), history can be intelligible as a whole only if we dogmatically identify the whole with the intelligible, that is, with the object of inquiry. This identification "leads to the dogmatic disregard of everything that cannot become an object" for our knowing or our mastery. "The dogmatic character of [this] basic premise . . . is said to have been revealed by the discovery of history or of the 'historicity' of human life."[55]

'Historicity,' in other words, means the diversity of times and places is irreducible to intelligence; times and places are incommensurable. Behind the assertion is a question: On what grounds should we suppose that history conforms to the conditions for a successful inquiry into it? But one might just as well ask if there are compelling reasons to suppose that it does not, and here there are three points to be made in reply. First, the basic reason for expecting some kind of commensurability is that the women and men of other times and places are, like we ourselves, more or less attentive and inattentive, intelligent and obtuse, reasonable and silly, responsible and irresponsible. They may turn out to be quite different from us, but, knowing what we do of ourselves, we cannot be surprised, for we ourselves might have turned out quite differently, too. Second, the only way to know is to interrogate the matter. To know the extent to which two societies really are different, we would have to achieve some understanding of each and compare them. There is no honest way to the historicist conclusion that does not involve asking and answering the very questions that the historicist claims cannot be answered. Finally, and most basically, the objection misses the point. Lonergan is not proposing an a priori, abstract scheme, a system, an articulated theory, a set of propositions, or an argument in a book as normative and universal.

On the contrary, he implores each of us to verify for ourselves a performance. It is the performance, not the account of the performance, that is normative and basic. The performance is asking and answering

54. Richardson, "Being for Lonergan: A Heideggerian View," 277.

55. Strauss, *Natural Right and History*, 30–31.

questions, construing evidence and judging accordingly, appraisal and deliberation. 'Why' and 'whether' and 'what for' manifest the light of wonder that needs no critical justification. It needs no critical justification because it is the very demand for critical justification. Questions have their own immanent criteria for what may count as a satisfactory response, and those criteria are normative. The normativity of the criteria means, correlatively, the performative normativity of truth for intelligence and of value for decision. That basic normativity is not lodged in the objects of our inquiry, judgment, or choice. It is lodged in the immanent, rational criteria of inquiry, judgment, and choice.

The first principles Lonergan is after are operational, not propositional, firsts. His foundation is not a flat declaration, a dogmatic assertion, a logically first premise, or indeed a statement of any kind. It is simply cognitional fact.

> A principle is what is first in an ordered set, *primum in aliquo ordine*. If the ordered set consists in propositions, then a principle in the set will be the premises from which the rest of the propositions may be deduced. If the ordered set consists not in propositions but in real causes and real effects, then the principle consists in the causes. Now the theological principle is conversion itself. It is not knowledge of religious conversion, awareness of religious conversion, interpretation of the psychological phenomena of religious conversion, propositions concerning conversion. It is simply the reality of the transformation named conversion, and it is that reality whether or not its subject has the foggiest notion of what it is or whether it has occurred.[56]

Here Lonergan is speaking of the principle specifically first in theology. In *Insight* his concern is to bring to light the principle generally first in knowing.

Note that it is not the discovery or the verification of one's intelligence with its dynamic structure that is foundational. It is the reality itself of that dynamic structure. Nevertheless, Lonergan invites each of us to self-discovery. The central aim of his philosophical program is a verifiable

56. Lonergan, "Bernard Lonergan Responds (1)," 268.

series of performatively ineluctable discoveries about oneself. The first is that when we want to know what is the case, we ask questions. The second is that we know what actually is the case only by successfully answering questions. The third, finally, is that the criteria for a successful answer are already immanent in the questions, or, as Aquinas put it, all knowledge is somehow originally implanted in us in the light of agent intellect.[57] We cannot, for instance, affirm a square circle as a possibility, not because it is unimaginable and not because we have inspected every circle, but because it is unintelligible.

If it is objected that I am just dogmatically asserting the identity of what is with what may be known, the reply is that it is rather nonidentity that must be dogmatically asserted, for, *ex hypothesi*, it cannot be known. Only an involvement with obscurantism could permit one to affirm it. To put the matter more positively: there is no other way to settle whether the whole is identical or nonidentical with the intelligible than to ask and answer the relevant questions. The only position coherent with the performance of asking and answering questions is the affirmation that being is to be known through correct understanding, that is, by getting the right answers to the right questions. Every alternative must be under-written by some renunciation of the light.

Lonergan is frequently suspected, and sometimes accused, of reaching his realism arbitrarily. The complete intelligibility of being, however, is as ineluctable as the law of noncontradiction. Its affirmation is the opposite of arbitrary. It is really the alternative—the affirmation of some ultimate brute fact without any explanation whatsoever—that must be arbitrary. Nothing happens that cannot happen; there are no square circles, even hypothetically. Picture, for a moment, Socrates and friends discussing, say, the definition of justice. They do not waste their time entertaining evident nonsense with no bearing on the question. They entertain only those prospective answers that seem plausible, and they discard them as soon as they are shown implausible, whether because they lack internal coherence, because they are incompatible with the facts, or for whatever other reason. For a reason: that is just the point. The irrational is discarded as irrelevant to reality. The intelligible

57. *De veritate* q. 10 a. 6c. ("in lumine intellectus agentis nobis est quodammodo omnis scientia originaliter indita").

is entertained as possibly relevant. Reason in the sense of causes in reality and reason in the sense of critical intelligence in the subject are two sides of the same coin.

Someone might object that it is naive, perhaps even dangerous, to disregard the irrational as irrelevant to reality. Reality, as some postmoderns are wont to claim, is absurd.[58] They have a point. Sin, after all, is irrational, yet it is obviously relevant to human reality. Presently I shall try to explain why I do not think the point decisive. Before doing so, however, permit me to observe that both the objecting and the answering have conditions. Those conditions presuppose rather than undercut my claim that the real is rational. For the objection holds water if it supplies a reason to deny or distinguish my claim. Similarly, a reply meets the issue if it supplies a reason to negate or distinguish the objection. Ineluctably, we find ourselves committed to giving reasons. Ineluctably, we find that giving and sifting reasons has a mysterious relevance to determining what is so.

Nothing happens of which it cannot (in principle) be asked why. Though an answer may not be immediately forthcoming, still we do not draw the conclusion that there simply is no answer to be had, no rhyme or reason whatever. If I came home to evidence of a fire in my home, no one would try to persuade me it is rational to accept 'no reason' as the answer to my 'why.' If being were not completely intelligible, there could be no valid argument for the existence of God; for every valid argument turns upon the fact that contingent being, of itself, is incompletely intelligible because non-self-explanatory.[59] If being were not completely intelligible, there would be no point in the interrogations of a Socrates or, for that matter, for apologetic arguments of credibility and credentity. For if the absurd counts for an answer as well as the intelligible, then every answer is equally valid and everything believable with equal reasonableness.

---

58. For a friendly dialectic with postmodern concerns, see Lawrence, *Fragility of Consciousness*, 193–226, 229–77; Miller, *In the Throe of Wonder*; Marsh, "Postmodernism: A Lonerganian Retrieval and Critique"; Gordon A. Rixon, "Derrida and Lonergan on the Human Subject: Transgressing a Metonymical Notion," *Toronto Journal of Theology* 18, no. 2 (2002): 213–29; Rixon, "Derrida and Lonergan on Human Development," *American Catholic Philosophical Quarterly* 76, no. 2 (2002): 221–36; and Gerard Walmsley, *Lonergan on Philosophic Pluralism: The Polymorphism of Consciousness as the Key to Philosophy*, Lonergan Studies (Toronto: University of Toronto, 2008), esp. 256–61.

59. *Insight*, 674–80, 695–96.

It is a different matter, of course, to discover that one has been asking the wrong question. Newton's law of inertia emerged from an 'inverse' insight: it is not continual movement but rather change in movement that requires an explanation. But this is precisely *not* renouncing the light; it is discovering the wrong way to imagine a problem.[60] Likewise, sin (a full treatment of which would take us rather far afield) requires an inverse insight. One has to distinguish the contraction of consciousness, which is an irresponsible, irrational nonevent, from the sinful deed that results. The latter is a wrong action that, as action, as an event in the world, has its intelligibility, but as wrong, as proceeding from a contracted consciousness, lacks the order responsibility and reason would endow. In this case, we spontaneously expect an intelligibility—the enlargement of responsible consciousness—and by inverse insight grasp that no such enlargement has occurred. Basic sin, that is, the formal element of formal sin, is not being but nonbeing, not occurrence but nonoccurrence.[61]

The main point, however, is that there are fundamental alternatives. Either the real is being and being is intelligible, or the real is not being and being is not intelligible. The former alternative is reasonable. The latter is not reasonable. It makes no difference if one wishes to subdivide the real into a portion that is intelligible and a portion that is not. If there is a portion that is not intelligible, then the real includes brute facts ultimately without explanation. But the brute fact, without explanation, is absurd; and the absurd cannot be rationally affirmed. Let me put it another way. Being is what *is*. But what does *is* mean in that sentence? The rational meaning of *is*, is to be discerned in the performance of 'being reasonable.' For when I want to know what is the case, what is so, what is real, what is true, I ask for reasons. I yield to evidence and reasoned argument. If I wave them aside, I am being arbitrary. The rational meaning of 'is,' then, is the meaning performatively involved in questioning. If I am being rational, and being is what is, then being is intelligible.

The decisive issue is performative, not logical. There are logically coherent options for the reader who wishes to assert the existence of brute facts. But that assertion would itself be a brute fact for which

60. See *Insight*, 43–50.
61. *Insight*, 689–91.

no reason could be given. Does not the one who claims the world is absurd relinquish the right to expect reasons from me? Again, there are innumerable other ways to assign meaning to *is*. It is just that in the clear light of day, there is only one way that accords with our native rationality. To affirm the complete intelligibility of being, then, far from being arbitrary, is to utterly renounce arbitrariness.

There has been, then, no discovery that being is not intelligible, for such a thing would be impossible to discover and impossible to rationally affirm. What in fact was (re)discovered is that statements are answers to questions; questions arise within a context, and answers are formulated within a context; contexts change, and future contexts cannot be predicted.[62] Such are the unimpeachable premises of relativism.

From them it follows, however, only that judgments are relative to a context of questions, data, insights, and evidence, not that they are only relatively true. Contexts can be discovered, and "there are many true statements whose context is easily ascertained."[63] Again, because contexts change, a later context may demand further differentiations without negating the truths rightly affirmed in an earlier context. Investigation can reconstruct the original context and thereby recover the original truth to bring it forward into the new context. No doubt truth claims are conditional, but one does not have to know everything to know something. Many claims can be affirmed "on the fulfillment of a manageable number of conditions."[64] No doubt, finally, future changes in context cannot be predicted, but—as I will presently illustrate—"one can predict, for example, that the contexts of descriptive statements are less subject to change than the contexts of explanatory statements."[65]

Let me clarify relativity to context without relativity to truth, as well as the distinction between descriptive and explanatory contexts, by way of example. "The sun is a disc of light that rises and sets over the earth" is absolutely true as a descriptive statement about the relation of the sun to us and our senses, and as long as there are sighted human beings

62. See Lonergan, "Doctrinal Pluralism"; *Verbum*, 75–76; and Lamb, "The Gregorian Years," 66–68.

63. Lonergan, "Doctrinal Pluralism," 75.

64. *Insight*, 380.

65. Lonergan, "Doctrinal Pluralism," 76.

living on this earth, its context is unlikely to vary significantly. On the other hand, there are statements about the sun within the explanatory context of contemporary physics. They are formulated in terms of what physicists currently regard as the fundamental concepts of their science. As those concepts are revised or displaced, physicists' statements about the sun will be revised accordingly. However, such revision need not be a matter of falsifying what now is regarded as true; it may and in all likelihood will be a matter of more adequate explanation that accounts for all that current theory explains, as well as much that current theory cannot yet explain.

Similar shifts occur through paradigm transformations in theology. So, for instance, St. Cyril's affirmation of the one nature of the incarnate Word is not false in its intended sense but is also not adequate to the questions of a later, more differentiated context. Again, Augustine's doctrine of divine sovereignty and the prevenience of grace was substantially transposed, not negated, in the context of scholastic theorems regarding the supernatural, divine operation, habits and acts—a set of fundamental categories quite different from Augustine's.[66] Note, then, first, that truth claims formulated in a less differentiated context can be related to those of a later context; next, that this relating involves determining the initial context and the relevant differences in the later context; third, that it does not involve negating the truth of the earlier claims; and finally, that the later context, if it is more adequate, is so because it has greater explanatory power than the earlier.

---

66. See *Grace and Freedom*, 17. "We have already suggested that the best commentary on Augustine's speculation lies in the subsequent speculative movement. Now the twelfth-century theologians were steeped in Augustine, yet their unceasing efforts with a material which must have seemed hopelessly refractory terminated in the idea of the supernatural. The anachronistic thinkers of a much later age attempted to reverse that decision, but it is difficult to esteem them without being completely ignorant of the evolution of medieval thought. Especially is this so when one succeeds in grasping that the idea of the supernatural is a theorem, that it no more adds to the data of the problem than the Lorentz transformation puts a new constellation in the heavens. What Philip the Chancellor systematically posited was not the supernatural character of grace, for that was already known and acknowledged, but the validity of a line of reference termed nature. In the long term and in the concrete the real alternatives remain charity and cupidity, the elect and the *massa damnata*. But the whole problem lies in the abstract, in human thinking: the fallacy in early thought had been an unconscious confusion of the metaphysical abstraction 'nature' with concrete data which do not quite correspond; . . . [the] achievement was the creation of a mental perspective, the introduction of a set of coordinates, that eliminated the basic fallacy and its attendant host of anomalies."

Behind the hermeneutical point lies an important ethical point. Rational judgment—that is, the demand for evidence and the possibility of getting it—is the sine qua non for authentic conversation.

> It is quite true that objective knowing is not yet authentic human living; but without objective knowing there is no authentic living; for one knows objectively just in so far as one is neither unperceptive, nor stupid, nor silly; and one does not live authentically inasmuch as one is either imperceptive or stupid or silly. . . . To treat people as persons one must know and one must invite them to know. A real exclusion of objective knowing, so far from promoting, only destroys personalist values.[67]

If there is no possibility of attaining the virtually unconditioned—that is, of grasping that the conditions for a prospective judgment have, de facto, been fulfilled—then there is also no possibility of terminating any line of inquiry in a manner that is not 'dogmatic' in the pejorative sense, that is, arbitrary. In such a case the reader who would gainsay my argument is merely enacting an arbitrary preference. By the same token, there is no possibility for a conversation that makes progress by some means other than by some variety of coercion or groupthink.[68] The possibility of transcultural understanding, or of a genuine ecumenism, would vanish. It is the possibility of rational judgment—contingent, and perspectival, but nevertheless absolutely true as far as it goes—that makes conversation and shared understanding possible as well.

The possibility of the virtually unconditioned, then, is the possibility of significant dialogue. The eros of the mind is the immanent ground of questions, inquiry, and wonder. Inquiry has its own dynamic criterion, without which conversation must degenerate into power games or effete aestheticism. Lonergan acknowledges perspective because he recognizes that there is a conversational situation in which not everyone has the

---

67. Bernard J. F. Lonergan, "Cognitional Structure," in *Collection*, CWL 4, 205–21, here 220–21.

68. Frederick G. Lawrence, "Lonergan's Foundations for Constitutive Communication," *Lonergan Workshop* 10 (1994): 229–77, here 245. Lonergan commented on Karl Mannheim that he "was keenly aware that he had to avoid a relativism because he was a Jew who had been bounced out of Germany under the Nazis, and he did not want to accept anything at all of pure relativism, but he had some difficulty getting around it. It was his problem." *Early Works on Method 1*, 79.

same questions, and judgments are relative to contexts and questions. But he also recognizes the possibility of achieving (or more commonly, approaching) the virtually unconditioned, and therefore of arriving at judgments that are true in the intended sense and cannot be truthfully denied.[69] His is, in this sense, an *absolute* perspectivism (i.e., acknowledging truth as an absolute), in contrast to the relative perspectivism (or simply relativism) typical of postmodern culture.

At least in its darker, nihilist tendencies, the language of 'relative perspectivism' is also a language of tragic alienation that cannot be at home in the world, not because it yearns for another but because it is unable to trust the goodness of the whole and thus cannot summon hope. In effect, the relative perspectivist is in the profoundly alienated position of enunciating as true the claim that truth is what we make of it.[70] ("Historicism," says Strauss, "thrives on the fact that it inconsistently exempts itself from its own verdict about all human thought."[71]) The transition to postmodernity has been taken to mean the end of metaphysics as the end of the possibility of attaining any 'truth beyond the cave,' that is, beyond history.[72] If the reality of the subject is beyond the horizon and cannot be illuminated, we are bound to end up in one form or another of arbitrariness: either measuring by our own arbitrary preference or being measured by a standard that, because we cannot know it, is arbitrary to us. All human projects must rest, finally, on "unilluminated, and so irrational, decisions."[73]

Frederick Lawrence suggests that the real bearing of postmodern critique of the 'forgetfulness of being' (whatever Heidegger is thought to have meant) is the forgetfulness of the subject: forgetfulness, that is, of the priority of the truth of existence to propositional truth and especially to adequate self-knowledge, "forgetfulness of the inner light."[74] Thus we arrive at the prevailing cultural forms of the truncated consumer, the

---

69. See *Insight*, 296–303, 399–409; *Method* (1972), 214–24, 320–26, or CWL 14, 202–11, 298–303.

70. See Lawrence, "The Horizon of Political Theology," 58–61.

71. Strauss, *Natural Right and History*, 25.

72. See ibid., 11–12.

73. Lawrence, "The Horizon of Political Theology," 61–63.

74. Bernard J. F. Lonergan, "Theology and Praxis," in *A Third Collection*, CWL 16, 177–93, here 188.

self-enclosed romantic feeler, the alienated relativist bound to measure or be measured arbitrarily.[75] But to go all the way with a recovery of the subject as subject, it is necessary to arrive at an adequate account of the normative structures of consciousness, and particularly the normative orientation of intelligence to the truth and of responsibility to the good. Thus, whereas postmoderns generally hail the end of metaphysics, what is really 'over' is the Hegelian attempt "to fulfill the abstract-deductivist ideal of a complete system,"[76] to contain history in a logic, or to link normativity to a permanent form of thought or culture.[77]

Lonergan does not fall under this stricture of historicism insofar as he offers a path to self-knowledge that yields a nondogmatic (again, in the pejorative sense of 'dogmatic' as arbitrary) appropriation of the transcultural norms of attention, intelligence, reasonableness, responsibility, and self-surrender in love.[78] As Jerome Miller puts it, "Lonergan's way of thinking is neither trapped inside modernist presuppositions nor satisfied by the postmodern deconstruction of them but points to a kind of wisdom beyond both."[79] Lonergan takes relativity seriously without succumbing to relativism and "takes the absurdity and apparently random and chaotic dimensions of our world of experience fully seriously without capitulating to nihilism in any form."[80] He thus represents the possibility of an 'integral' postmodernity, a recognition of the fragility, situatedness, and historicity of human becoming without surrendering the normativity of truth for intelligence and value for decision.[81] Or, to put it differently, he represents the possibility of a 'fourth wave' of modernity beyond the utilitarian-individualist, romantic-expressivist,

75. This is how I understand Frederick Lawrence's analysis; see Jeremy D. Wilkins, "'Our Conversation Is in Heaven': Conversion and/as Conversation in the Thought of Frederick Lawrence," in *Grace and Friendship: Theological Essays in Honor of Fred Lawrence, from His Grateful Students*, ed. M. Shawn Copeland and Jeremy D. Wilkins, Marquette Studies in Theology 86 (Milwaukee, Wisc.: Marquette University Press, 2016), 319–53.

76. Lawrence, "The Horizon of Political Theology," 55–56.

77. See Bernard J. F. Lonergan, "A Post-Hegelian Philosophy of Religion," in *A Third Collection*, CWL 16, 194–213; also Lawrence, *Fragility of Consciousness*, 210–18.

78. See Lamb, *Eternity, Time, and the Life of Wisdom*, 125–52.

79. Miller, *In the Throe of Wonder*, iii.

80. Lawrence, *Fragility of Consciousness*, 230.

81. See Frederick G. Lawrence, "Lonergan's Postmodern Subject: Neither Neoscholastic Substance nor Cartesian Ego," in *In Deference to the Other*, 107–20.

and alienated-nihilist waves.[82] Having swept away the dream of an absolute, normative culture, modernity and postmodernity cry out for a new paradigm of human self-possession, what Lonergan calls a new stage of meaning governed through self-knowledge and not primarily through the objectified controls of theory and logic.[83]

The first principles of a philosophy in this new mode, Lonergan averred, are not "verbal propositions but [rather] the de facto invariants of human conscious intentionality,"[84] the invariants involved in the structure of question and answer, formulation and testing, reflection and judgment, evaluation and decision. This does not exclude the validity of propositions, or metaphysics, or a code of ethics, but these are not basic but derived. It means that what was called 'speculative intellect' names, in fact, a particular patterning of attention, inquiry, and rational reflection. It is an achievement, and the achievement is existential; it results from a moral deliberation, evaluation, and decision about the right way to proceed, a commitment to sticking to it, a gradual development of the requisite skills. "The primacy now belongs to practical intellect, and, perforce, philosophy becomes a philosophy of action."[85]

The exercise of self-appropriation is not bloodless theorizing; its existential presuppositions are severe, for one's own performance is under the microscope, and one's own performance invariably turns out to be spotty. Lonergan's program is, as Frederick Lawrence puts it, fundamentally a 'praxis issue.'

> Personally asking and answering the question about what I am *doing* when I am knowing in any and all areas of my living—which can only be done if one returns to the *Sache* as an empirically

---

82. See Lawrence, *Fragility of Consciousness*, 333–51.

83. See *Method* (1972), 85–99, or CWL 14, 82–95.

84. Lonergan, "Doctrinal Pluralism," 85.

85. Ibid. In the Preface to *Insight*, Lonergan describes his purpose as "a campaign against the flight from understanding" (7) that is eminently practical, for "insight into insight . . . will reveal what activity is intelligent, and insight into oversight will reveal what activity is unintelligent. But to be practical is to do the intelligent thing, and to be unpractical is to keep blundering about. It follows that insight into both insight and oversight is the very key to practicality" (8). See Liddy, *Transforming Light*, 84–90; Frederick G. Lawrence, "Dangerous Memory and the Pedagogy of the Oppressed," in *Communicating a Dangerous Memory: Soundings in Political Theology*, ed. Frederick G. Lawrence (Atlanta: Scholars Press, 1987), 17–33.

verifiable matter of psychological fact—also gets one into asking and answering for oneself the practical and political question about the most choiceworthy way to live. This is why Lonergan says in the Introduction to *Insight* that "more than all else, the aim of the book is to issue an invitation to a personal, decisive act." Hence, he proposed the personal appropriation of one's rational self-consciousness not as an idealist construction but as a practical and concrete program. And in what Lonergan, like Metz, has called "the end of the age of innocence," a consciousness cultured enough to execute that program needs to be morally and religiously converted.[86]

It is all too easy to repeat Lonergan with merely notional assent or to brush him aside with merely notional dissent, and either way to mistake his program as license to name the limitations and vices of the old regime while putting little in its place. Much more difficult is to accept and follow through with the ascetical program he presents: *gnōthi seauton*, wisdom as self-knowledge and self-appropriation.

Conclusion

The contemporary situation in the West is one of cultural crisis, a crisis of normativity. The dream of classicism, of timeless and unchanging liturgy, theology, and institutional forms, is over. The acknowledged fact is pluralism in culture, theology, and the church. The ongoing challenge for us is to make sense of pluralism, to judge wisely different kinds of difference, to acknowledge relativity without succumbing to relativism, to integrate natural science without falling for scientism, to deal with historical contingency without bogging down in historicism, to reaffirm the possibility of progressive and cumulative results despite the contingency of our every achievement.

To meet these challenges, theology today must be an ongoing, collaborative process of mediating the one Gospel into many different cultures. This does not mean a constant resetting. No doubt, the history

---

86. Lawrence, "Dangerous Memory," 33 (emphasis in original, internal references omitted); internal quotation of *Insight*, 13.

of theology is dialectical, a history of inadequacy and faithlessness as much as of fidelity and progress. Yet there is a genuine development of methods, of dogma, of theory, in the classification and ordering of materials, in the analysis of conflicts. There are permanently valid achievements in theology, and they may be authentically retrieved to enter into an ongoing mediation of the Gospel into cultures.

The present crisis brings into fresh focus theology's perennial problem: the adequacy of theologians to their vocation and tasks. Truth answers to questions and questions are not in a vacuum.[87] They may occur spontaneously, but worthwhile questions commonly strike those prepared for them, and only the trivial have obvious answers. Sufficient reason compels whether we like it or not; still, evidence has to be construed, and warrant enough for a Holmes leaves a Watson in the dark. The truth in matters of any importance normally has to be sought, and the seeking is fragile.[88] It puts us at risk; we may find ourselves, like Augustine, changing and changed, summoned to repentance and transformation. Before truth—the adequation of mind to reality—there is the little matter of permitting questions and facing them squarely, of devoted, sober, sedulous, and orderly inquiry, of measuring up, of solving problems, of acquiring skills, of overcoming one's limitations of disposition and preference, education, achievement, and fancy, and of enlarging, perhaps, one's readiness to consider, accept, believe, and commit.[89] Whatever the

87. The truths of faith, which are not properly understood and in some sense are accepted antecedently by faith, present a special case; we defer detailed discussion to chapter 7. However, note the following: (1) belief does not presuppose warrants on the matter believed, but does suppose warrants on the credentity and credibility of the one to be believed, and (2) the truths of faith are not so different from other truths as to preclude the development of doctrine. John Henry Newman draws a useful distinction between investigation and inquiry; the former concerns difficulties of understanding, the latter doubts as to truth. Newman, *An Essay in Aid of a Grammar of Assent*, 158–59, and Newman, *Apologia pro Vita Sua: Being a History of His Religious Opinions*, ed. Martin J. Svaglic (Oxford: Clarendon Press, 1967), 214.

88. So Aquinas observed about the question of God in *ScG* bk. 1, chap. 4. Aquinas had no doubt reason could prove the existence of God, but he added that were such knowledge not accepted on faith, it would be the preserve of a handful and riddled with falsehood even after a vast labor. The time before truth is named explicitly ("vix post longum tempus pertingerent") as is the problem before truth ("multa quae praeexigitur"). Compare *STh* 1 q. 1 a. 1.

89. The triplet "devoted, sober, sedulous" is suggested by Vatican I's call for theological understanding through inquiry that is "pie, sobrie, sedulo" (Vatican Council I, *Dei Filius*, chap. 4, no. 4, in Tanner et al., *Decrees of the Ecumenical Councils*, 2:808). Compare Hans-Georg Gadamer, *Truth and Method*, 2nd ed. (New York: Continuum, 2000), 269–70, 298–99.

laurels of speculative reason, what is concrete is the decision to admit questions, to prepare for them, and to labor to measure up to them.[90]

Therein lies the relevance of Lonergan's practical program, his pursuit of a 'wisdom of the concrete.' As Aristotle would not speak of virtue apart from the measure embodied in the *spoudaios*, the morally serious person,[91] so Lonergan refuses to consider the wisdom that is theology apart from the sapiential reality of the theologian, in love with wisdom, converted with a threefold conversion, at home in prayer, in theory and scholarship, and in the asceticism of self-knowledge. His program is to promote not a system, but conversion and personal development at every turn. His method would mediate the Gospel into a culture not by way of abstract principles, but by way of explicit attention to the performance of the mediators. His return to the concrete is a return to the imperfect wisdom of the theologian, whose horizon determines what questions even can arise and whose reality, as a created participation of uncreated light suffused with the love of God surpassing all understanding, is the concrete foundation for theology. Lonergan's call is for a wisdom of self-knowledge in humble acceptance of a higher wisdom of self-surrender.

90. Compare John Henry Newman on faith: "Although we must maintain most firmly that the truth which faith embraces is not merely subjective, but is one and the same to all, and immutable in anyone who believes rightly, it is nevertheless clear that the ways by which the mind attains to that truth are as many as the diversity of natural temperaments. Therefore, faith progresses subjectively to its object.... I am concerned ... not with reason considered in itself, in the abstract, but with the concrete question of how faith comes to be in particular minds, and of the kind of reasoning that leads to faith, which certainly is not the same in everyone." Carleton P. Jones, "Three Latin Papers of John Henry Newman: A Translation with Introduction and Commentary" (PhD diss., Pontificia Universitas S. Thomae in Urbe, 1995), 49.

91. Lonergan, "The Subject," 71; Lawrence, "Finnis on Lonergan," 851–59.

CHAPTER FOUR

Aquinas and Lonergan's Turn to the Subject

We do not know our intellect except by this:

that we understand ourselves to understand.[1]

ST. THOMAS AQUINAS

I N THE EPILOGUE TO *Verbum,* his once controversial and now largely forgotten study of the inner word in the thought of Thomas Aquinas, Lonergan felt called upon to respond to critics who could make little sense of his purpose or method. "My purpose," he wrote, "has been the Leonine purpose *vetera novis augere et perficere,*" to enlarge and perfect the old with the new, "though with this modality that I believed the basic task still to be the determination of what the *vetera* really were."[2] He went on to invoke the possibility of "a transposition of [Aquinas's] position to meet the issues of our own day."[3] Always a stickler about method, Lonergan drew a bright line between the tasks involved in understanding Aquinas and those involved in transposing him to a new key. In *Verbum,* he very deliberately limited himself "to determining on a restricted but, I believe, significant point what the *vetera* really were."[4]

Lonergan described his relationship to Aquinas as an eleven-year apprenticeship. Its chief literary fruits were the studies presented in

---

1. *In 3 De Anima,* lectio 9, no. 5, in *Sentencia libri De anima,* Opera Omnia 45, Leonine ed. (Paris: Librairie philosophique J. Vrin, 1984), 216 ("Non enim cognoscimus intellectum nostrum nisi per hoc, quod intelligimus nos intelligere").

2. *Verbum,* 222.

3. *Verbum,* 227.

4. *Verbum,* 227.

Grace and Freedom and *Verbum*—originally a mere nine articles, crisp, paradigm-shifting studies of precise, fundamental questions, but hardly the flood of verbiage demanded by present academic conventions, and seemingly too difficult or too compressed, or both, for widespread assimilation. One might be tempted to add the various, and sometimes substantial, Latin treatises he composed in the course of his teaching duties, which demonstrate a thorough appropriation of the principles, doctrine, and method of Aquinas. Yet in these texts the issues were almost never strictly exegetical, and Lonergan was speaking in his own voice out of the perspective consolidated through his apprenticeship.

Lonergan's image for his struggle to determine the *vetera* was 'reaching up.' His presupposition, it seems fair to say, was the priority of misunderstanding. His famous quip that objectivity is authentic subjectivity[5] does not mean that we inevitably make the world after our own image and likeness, but rather that doing otherwise takes considerable effort. It means, in other words, that the truth of predication rests on the prior truth of existence. Getting things right is not an exercise of power but of self-surrender; it is never as easy as making the world to the model laid up in our own private noetic heavens. Thus, Lonergan came to Aquinas knowing that understanding him in any deep manner could hardly be a matter of quoting and arguing, unless he would be content to assign his own meaning to someone else's words.[6] Looking back from the transom of *Insight*, Lonergan once again recalled the vast effort of reaching up to the difficult mind of Aquinas as a precondition for transposing his thought. The tremendous labors of historians, he wrote, have given us texts, sources, chronology, and exegetical studies.

> Above all, they have created a climate of opinion that has made it increasingly difficult to substitute rhetoric for history, fancy for fact, abstract argument for textual evidence. But however indispensable this work, it is in vain unless it is complemented by a further labor. To penetrate to the mind of a medieval

---

5. *Method* (1972), 292, or CWL 14, 273.

6. See *Verbum*, 223, on the "initial and enormous problem of developing one's understanding." If one "is content with the understanding he has and the concepts it utters, then all he can do is express his own incomprehension in the words but without the meaning uttered by the understanding of Aquinas."

thinker is to go beyond his words and phrases. It is to effect
an advance in depth that is proportionate to the broadening
influence of historical research. It is to grasp questions as once
they were grasped.[7]

This last point, it seems to me, is decisive. To transpose, one has first to
understand the original. To understand the original, one has to grasp its
originating questions. The possibility of perfecting and enlarging the old
depends on first understanding it, and deep knowledge seems hard to
come by. What is not first properly understood in its own context cannot
be meaningfully related to the present context.

Grasping questions as once they were grasped liberates us from the
constrictions of our age. It is easy to dismiss old answers we have not
understood, responding to questions we have forgotten how to ask or
failed to ask well. More difficult and more worthwhile is, as it were, to
let oneself be interrogated by them. We are bound to figure out what the
questions really mean if we are going to make any sense of the answers.
In this vein, Lonergan remarked about the sense, widely shared, that the
old dogmatic formulas have lost their meaning: "Personally I should urge
in each case one inquire whether the old issue still has a real import and,
if it has, a suitable expression for that import be found."[8] He was not
proposing that we set the ancient dogmas before the bar of contemporary sensibility, but that we open ourselves to the real importance of the
questions for today. Inquiry that begins with rediscovering the questions
we have forgotten how to ask, or groping toward questions we have not
yet learned to ask, involves us in a kind of self-surrender.

The question at the heart of Lonergan's *Verbum* inquiry was what
Aquinas meant by *intelligere* and *emanatio intelligibilis*. It was obviously a
matter of some importance, for the procession of the Word is characterized as 'intelligible' no fewer than six times in question 27 of the *Prima
pars*.[9] Yet the point, far from being satisfactorily explained, had obviously
been lost, for interpreters could assign no reason to restrict the *imago
Trinitatis* in human beings to their higher reason, nor make coherent

7. *Insight*, 769–70.

8. "Theology and Praxis," 193.

9. See *Verbum*, 206–8.

sense of the dependence of the procession of love on the procession of the inner word.[10]

In fact, the question about the meaning of Aquinas's *emanatio intelligibilis* was so seldom asked that Lonergan, for raising it, is frequently suspected—probably above all by those who have hardly read him—of sewing scraps of Aquinas into a Cartesian quilt. A far more important and also much more obvious inspiration than either Kant or Descartes was the Augustinian program of return to the self,[11] as well as Newman's practical approach in the *Grammar of Assent*.[12] If these and other influences prepared Lonergan to ask his question, however, there seems little doubt that the decisive influence was exercised by Aquinas himself, for it was in the execution of *Verbum* that Lonergan realized he could not give a satisfactory account of his data without appeal to the psychological realities. He did not think he was inventing an Aquinas *ad mentem Cartesianam* but piercing a heavy overlay of conceptualist interpretation. That is, in asking what Aquinas meant by intelligible emanation, he understood himself to be rediscovering Aquinas's original questions and something of his original itinerary; he did not think it possible to understand an author without figuring out what he was talking about, and he figured Aquinas had a point.[13] In the process he came to know experientially and not only theoretically what it means to be transformed through an encounter with genius.[14] The *Verbum* investigation led Lonergan to conclude that Kant's critique was irrelevant to Aquinas, a critique "not

---

10. *Verbum*, 11–13, 191–92, 209–13.

11. See Lonergan, "The Dehellenization of Dogma," 27–28; also Lawrence, "Lonergan's Search for a Hermeneutics of Authenticity."

12. Liddy, *Transforming Light*, 38, remarks that Newman's main importance for Lonergan's development seems to have been "the focus on the concrete, the interior, the facts of consciousness." On Lonergan's relationship to Descartes, Jeffrey A. Allen, "Ignatius's *Exercises*, Descartes's *Meditations*, and Lonergan's *Insight*," *Philosophy and Theology* 29, no. 1 (2017): 17–28, argues for certain similarities of influence, education, and method. *Pace* Allen, note the following: (1) Descartes, *Meditations on First Philosophy*, was probably important for Lonergan's question about foundations, but Lonergan's question was not motivated by methodic doubt; (2) in his letter to Henry Keane, 1935, Lonergan does mention the 'Cartesian cogito ergo sum' as the basis for developing a philosophy, but relates it immediately to the Thomist light of the mind, etc.; (3) Lonergan does not start with 'in here' and 'out there' in the sense of bodies; he does want to 'go back' from conception and formulation to the originating act of understanding.

13. See *Verbum*, 222–27; compare *Method* (1972), 156–58, or CWL 14, 148–50.

14. See *Insight*, 769; *Method* (1972), 161–62, or CWL 14, 152–53.

of the pure reason but of the human mind as conceived by Scotus."[15] "Kant for me was an afterthought," he reflected many years later.[16]

This may seem rather surprising and even implausible, because Lonergan's procedure, as he acknowledged (and as we shall presently explain), is in some sense the inverse of Aquinas's, and the inversion may suggest an opposition. The hypothesis urged here, however, takes Lonergan at his word. His investigation of the inner word (*verbum*) in Aquinas was the occasion for the key breakthroughs that would eventuate in several of his most distinctive positions, including his own version of the turn to the subject, his articulation of self-knowledge and self-appropriation as 'first philosophy,' and his approach to metaphysics via the explicit isomorphism of cognitional and ontological structure.

Here I spell this out in four steps. A first step sketches how Lonergan came to Aquinas and learned to read him. A second illustrates the 'introspective' approach he brought to his interpretation. A third shows how the main lines of Lonergan's later strategy for metaphysics were discovered in Aquinas. A fourth, finally, comes to the heart of the encounter: Lonergan's interpretation of Aquinas on consciousness and self-knowledge. The ulterior implementation and development of these discoveries in *Insight* and *Method* shall occupy us in subsequent chapters, so that over the course of three chapters we will see how Lonergan came to make his distinctive version of a 'turn to the subject' and accept its implications.

Finally, I have no hesitation in saying that Lonergan is an exceptionally astute and penetrating reader of Aquinas. His interpretations on the matters he treats are attentive, insightful, and precise in a rare way. Nevertheless, my aim here is to indicate some general contours of Aquinas's influence for his overall project in philosophy and theology. It is not to verify his exegesis and still less to vindicate it. It is obvious that until an author has been understood as he understands himself, confirming or

---

15. *Verbum*, 39; Lonergan's take on Scotus and his influence was indebted to Peter Hoenen; see *Caring about Meaning*, 10–11.

16. *Caring about Meaning*, 10; see also 15. In a letter to Frederick Crowe, July 23, 1958, he reports, "I have been working out the relations between *Insight* and Kant's *Critique of Pure Reason*," in connection with his preparations for the lectures on *Insight* subsequently published as *Understanding and Being*. Thus, it was only after *Insight* that Lonergan got down to the problem of Kant. See the editors' preface to *Understanding and Being: The Halifax Lectures on Insight*, ed. Frederick E. Crowe, CWL 5 (1990), xiv.

confuting his claims are out of the question. Getting hold of Aquinas's meaning as Lonergan took it is a big affair because the fingerprints of Aquinas are everywhere in Lonergan.

Discovery

Aquinas was not Lonergan's first love; before him and of special importance were John Henry Newman and Augustine.[17] It seems highly probable that Augustine and Newman encouraged Lonergan in the habits of concrete self-attention that would be decisive in his encounter with Aquinas and the trajectory of all his subsequent thought. A precise judgment on the matter is complicated, however, by the fact that our evidence on his relationship to them is largely indirect and not embodied in the kind of full-scale studies we have from his apprenticeship to Aquinas.

Of Newman, Lonergan tells us that the *Grammar of Assent* became a kind of *vademecum* during the years of his philosophy studies at Heythrop (he also earned degrees in mathematics and classics at the University of London during the same period). Lonergan reread its analytic parts, he reports, five or six times during his third year in philosophy.[18] Newman, he says, made him an "existentialist of sorts," meaning, I take it, that Newman brought home to Lonergan the problem before truth, the priority of the truth of existence to the truth of predication (i.e., truth in the ordinary sense of true judgment). Lonergan expressed this aptly in a fragment, probably written in the 1930s, on the 'morality' of assent in Newman:

> The essential morality of assent is the supreme contention of the *Grammar of Assent*. Assent is moral in its prerequisite of moral living, in its appeal to men of good will, in the seriousness with which it is to be regarded, in its reaction upon our views of what right morality is, in its being an *actus humanus*, in its norm—

---

17. See "*Insight* Revisited," 221–23; also the letter to Henry Keane (Lonergan's provincial), January 1935, reproduced in Lambert and McShane, *Bernard Lonergan*, 144–54, esp. 146–47. On Lonergan's early involvements with (inter alia) Newman and Augustine, see Liddy, *Transforming Light*, 16–40, 50–73.

18. "*Insight* Revisited," 221; compare *Caring about Meaning*, 13–14.

a real apprehension of human nature. We are to determine our assents not merely by artificial standards of logic, a mere common measure of minds, but by the light that God gives us, by our judgment, by our good sense, by our *phronesis*, by the facts as we know them to be. The right assent is not according to rule but by the act of a living mind. It has no criterion, no guarantee external to itself. It is to be made with all due circumspection, with careful investigation and examination, as the nature of the case demands and circumstances permit.[19]

Lonergan says that Newman's illative sense became *Insight*'s reflective understanding (insight into the relative sufficiency of the evidence on a question).[20] By the time Lonergan came to Aquinas, then, he had already developed a preference for Newman's strategy of concrete self-attention, rather than metaphysical analysis, as the route to self-knowledge. What impressed Lonergan most about Newman might be aptly summed up in an observation from Newman's biographer Ian Ker: "Newman's own starting point was . . . an examination of the actual mental process by virtue of which somebody is a believer or an unbeliever."[21]

Of Augustine, we know that Lonergan studied the early Cassiaciacum dialogues with great care; that he was struck by Augustine's concern with *veritas* and *intelligere*; that in *Verbum* he repeatedly drew attention to various manners in which Augustine's concerns were transposed by Aquinas.[22] It may be that Augustine prompted his first foray into interiority in general and cognitional theory in particular: "Augustine," he wrote, reminiscing over his early years in 1973, "was so concerned with understanding, so unmindful of universal concepts, that I began a long period of trying to write an intelligible account of my convictions."[23] In his textbooks of the Gregorian years, moreover, he would recur to Augustine to illustrate fundamental notions about consciousness, the subject, and presence, to which we shall return in due course. It seems

19. From p. 36 of a fragment which may represent a lost essay on assent, quoted in Liddy, *Transforming Light*, 39, from archives of the Lonergan Research Institute, Toronto.

20. *Caring about Meaning*, 13–15.

21. Ker, *The Achievement of John Henry Newman*, 36.

22. Liddy, *Transforming Light*, 50–73.

23. *"Insight* Revisited," 222.

likely enough that this was a convenient expedient given the formation and expectations of his students, but we may at least wonder if Augustine was Lonergan's own first teacher in these matters. In the introduction Lonergan wrote, some twenty years after the original investigation, for the first book edition of *Verbum*, Augustine represents attention to the psychological subject in contrast to Aristotelian analysis of the powers of the soul. "For Augustine," we read, "the mind's self-knowledge was basic; it was the rock of certitude on which shattered Academic doubt; it provided the ground from which one could argue to the validity both of the senses of one's own body and, with the mediation of testimony, of the senses of the bodies of others."[24]

Lonergan first met Aquinas by way of (mainly Suarezian) textbooks.[25] He was not impressed. Encounter at first hand, though, proved transformational. Wryly he reported to his provincial, in the flush of love's first light, his newfound suspicion "that St Thomas was not nearly as bad as he is painted."[26] He regarded the manual tradition, on the whole, as relatively inauthentic to the principles, method, and doctrine of Aquinas. At best, the manuals represented an ahistorical orthodoxy prepared to sacrifice understanding at the altar of certitude, "a predominantly logical approach whose penchant for anachronism violated virtually every precept of sound hermeneutics."[27] At their worst, they embodied a tradition of systematized incomprehension, unequal to its own best questions and reluctant to face new ones. In his dissertation on operative grace, Lonergan lamented the pseudometaphysical fog shrouding basic problems in scholastic thought. When he later tartly described a tendency to use "the text [of Aquinas] as a sort of cement to make a wall of a private heap of stones,"[28] he may well have had in mind the Banezian account of *praemotio physica*.[29] At any event, his summary verdict coincided, at least

24. *Verbum*, 9.

25. This seems to have been common in Jesuit formation at the time. De Lubac reports the same experience in his studies at Jersey.

26. Letter to Henry Keane, p. 3, in Lambert and McShane, *Bernard Lonergan*, 147.

27. Lawrence, "Lonergan's Search for a Hermeneutics of Authenticity," 42.

28. Lonergan, "On God and Secondary Causes," 60.

29. See Lonergan's contrast between the Banezian doctrine and the doctrine of Aquinas: "De Ente Supernaturali/The Supernatural Order," in *Early Latin Theology*, ed. Robert M. Doran and H. Daniel Monsour, trans. Michael G. Shields, CWL 19 (2011), 52–255, here 214–27 (Latin with interleaf translation). Further discussion in J. Michael Stebbins, *The Divine Initiative: Grace,*

in substance, with Gilson's: "the true meaning of the Christian philosophy of Saint Thomas had been lost" in the 'school Thomism' of the turn of the century.[30]

In Lonergan's judgment, 'school Thomism' exemplified the inauthenticity of a tradition within which one might "believe himself completely authentic, a most faithful disciple . . . completely free from any originality or personal opinions of his own," all the while systematically misrepresenting the thought of the master.[31] He deemed the radical cause for this state of affairs to be the occlusion of self-knowledge and, concomitantly, of the authentic psychology of Aquinas. Through the subterranean influence of Scotus, later reinforced by anxieties about Descartes and Kant,[32] the assumption prevailed among later scholastics that knowing

---

World-Order, and Human Freedom in the Early Writings of Bernard Lonergan (Toronto: University of Toronto Press, 1995), esp. 183–211, 266–69, 278–87; Brotherton, "The Integrity of Nature in the Grace–Freedom Dynamic." There is a brief but illuminating contrast between Lonergan's and John of St. Thomas's approaches to Aquinas on cognition in *Early Works on Method 1*, 11–12. Of course, ironically it is Lonergan who is often accused of building his own philosophy with Aquinas's stones. I note, however, at least one dissenting voice for whom Lonergan's forte is scholarship and his weakness is philosophy: C. J. F. Williams, in a rather uncomprehending review of the 1968 edition of *Verbum*. "The scholarship displayed in *Verbum* is impressive. Lonergan is thoroughly at home in the Aristotelian as well as in the Thomist *corpus*. What is lacking is a more critical philosophical spirit." Williams proceeds to admit he does not understand what Lonergan means by 'conceptualism,' to note the contrast between Lonergan's and Geach's respective interpretations of *intelligere* as 'understanding' and 'thought,' to expound the latter but not the former, and to use Geach as a springboard to lay out his own theory of Aquinas's supposedly jejune grasp of propositional analysis, before recalling himself to the book under review. Williams concludes, "Father Lonergan's labours are, I believe, largely frustrated by his failure to bring the discoveries of recent philosophical logic to bear on the theories of medieval philosophical psychology. But the scholarship to which this volume is such abundant evidence will not be wasted if it provokes philosophers who *have* learned the lessons of Frege and Wittgenstein to go back to the Aristotelian and Thomist sources to which Lonergan so carefully directs us. . . . The prizes will be won only by those who have as much scholarship as Lonergan and as much philosophical insight as Geach; and the going will be heavy." C. J. F. Williams, review of *Verbum: Word and Idea in Aquinas*, by Bernard J. F. Lonergan, *Religious Studies* 8, no. 1 (1972): 80–82, here 81–82. Perhaps the retort may be supplied from Lonergan's own words: "To the superficial philosopher, whose grasp of philosophic thought begins and ends with an exact use of language . . ." (*Verbum*, 37).

30. Étienne Gilson, *The Philosopher and Theology*, trans. Cécile Gilson (New York: Random House, 1962), 157; the French original is Gilson, *Le philosophe et la théologie* (Paris: A. Fayard, 1960), 172. See Lonergan, *Early Works on Method 1*, 16–17.

31. *Early Works on Method 1*, 16. The description cannot but call to mind Bañez's habit of insistence upon a fidelity to Aquinas so thorough that not so much as the breadth of a fingernail could separate them. See John Volz, "Domingo Bañez," in *The Catholic Encyclopedia* (New York: Robert Appleton, 1907), accessed November 7, 2016, http://www.newadvent.org/cathen/02247a.htm.

32. See *Verbum*, 19, 38–39, 83.

must consist not in learning, but in something like looking, a kind of spiritual intuition. Ironically, then, while 'school Thomism' understood itself as resisting Descartes, in fact it had become unwittingly enthralled with the same basic supposition: that knowledge is a matter of erecting a bridge from the 'in here' of the *res cogitans* to the 'out there' of the *res extensae*. Lonergan, by contrast, maintained that coming to know is a matter of learning; attention to detail is an indispensable first step, but so far from completing properly human knowledge, it is not even, as an activity on the sensitive level, in the same genus as the activities specific to intelligence. Aquinas had claimed *intelligere* as the proper operation of the mind, and this Lonergan took to mean the act of understanding. Aquinas had distinguished a *duplex operatio*, and these Lonergan took to mean direct insight into phantasm and reflective insight into the sufficiency of evidence.[33] For Aquinas, as Lonergan read him, coming to know is not a matter of erecting a bridge from 'in here' to 'out there' but of perfecting a potency through a process of inquiry into data and reflection on evidence.

Both in practice and in doctrine, Lonergan found, Aquinas prized understanding where the manuals were preoccupied with certitude.[34] In the practice of Aquinas, the *quaestio* was a living technique for developing understanding; the manuals had replaced it with the pedagogy of the thesis whose aim was not understanding but proof. In the doctrine of Aquinas, knowing was a discursive process whose central moment is insight into phantasm. It gradually developed through the refinement of increasingly adequate conceptual apparatus; its adequacy was not intuited but judged by wisdom.[35] Insight into phantasm meant that intelligence was not primarily a matter of comparing and relating concepts, but of turning over data, finding ways to think about problems that would be

---

33. This sufficiency is an extrinsic intelligibility, as distinct from form, an intrinsic intelligibility. On the *duplex operatio*, see, e.g., *De ente et essentia* chap. 4, no. 6, in *Opuscula IV*, ed. H.-F. Dondaine, Opera Omnia 43, Leonine ed. (Rome: Editori di San Tommaso, 1992), 377; *In De Trin.* q. 5 a. 3c., in *Super Boetium de Trinitate | Expositio Libri Boetii de Ebdomadibus*, Opera Omnia 50, Leonine ed. (Paris: Editions du Cerf, 1992), 147; and *In 3 De anima* lect. 11 §§746–47, in *Sentencia libri De anima*, 224–28. A wealth of texts is sampled by Frederick E. Crowe, "St Thomas and the Isomorphism of Knowing and Its Proper Object," in *Three Thomist Studies* (Chestnut Hill, Mass.: Lonergan Institute at Boston College, 2000), 207–35.

34. See Lonergan, "Theology and Understanding."

35. See *Verbum*, 38–46, 61–71, 78–87.

conducive to the emergence of understanding.[36] The development of concepts, and the development of an understanding that grasps many concepts in a single view, meant that the ordering of questions was as integral to Aquinas's achievement as were the individual solutions he proposed.[37]

An 'Introspective' Reading

Lonergan's eventual decision to take, in *Verbum*, an approach he called 'introspective' or 'psychological,' rather than beginning from the metaphysical analysis, probably owed much to his prior devotion to Newman and Augustine. But it also upset the 'logic' of the matter that he had internalized through his scholastic formation. He reports that in the composition of *Verbum*, he found himself almost constrained by the matter itself to begin "not from the metaphysical framework, but from the psychological content of the Thomist theory of intellect: logic might favor the opposite procedure but, after attempting it in a variety of ways, I found it unmanageable."[38] If the proximate problem was how to state his interpretation—that is, with whether it would be more effective to proceed from the psychological to the metaphysical principles or the other way round—the issue in the background was getting back to the realities themselves.

Lonergan's thesis in *Verbum* was that most interpreters had skipped over the meaning of 'intelligible' in Aquinas's discussion of 'intelligible emanations' in God. This had occurred, he was inclined to think, largely through oversight of insight, of the act of understanding. In other words, most commentators did not grasp what 'intelligere' meant and perforce could not understand the meaning of intelligible emanation. The commentators, Lonergan judged, had been too preoccupied with what intellect does to attend to what it is. This state of affairs was lamentable but

---

36. "Though Aquinas derived the doctrine [of insight into phantasm] from Aristotle, he also affirmed it as a matter of experience: 'Quilibet in se ipso experiri potest, quod quando aliquis conatur aliquid intelligere, format sibi aliqua phantasmata per modum exemplorum, in quibus quasi inspiciat quod intelligere studet.'" *Verbum*, 38. The reference is to *STh* 1 q. 84 a. 7c.

37. See *Verbum*, 213–22.

38. See *Verbum*, 59; Lonergan reflects on this reversal in *"Insight*: Preface to a Discussion," in *Collection*, CWL 4, 142–52.

also deeply ironic, because intellect can be known as what it is not only by what it does, as with material things, but also, because it is conscious, by what it is.[39] This, as we will see in the next chapter, would become the basis for his claim that cognitional theory is unique among explanatory sciences because its explanatory terms and relations are not hypothetical extrapolations from data but immediately given, if not immediately understood, within the data of consciousness.

In effect, Lonergan claims, the reader who would follow Aquinas's discussion of psychological realities must pay close attention to the relevant experiences in his or her own consciousness.

> Behind such a historical accident [as the failure of the commentary tradition to grasp the meaning of *intelligere*] there are deeper factors and they come to light as soon as one endeavors to explain the differences between the conceptualism of Scotus and . . . the quite distinct rational psychology of Aquinas. For then the issues of historical interpretation are complicated by the self-knowledge of the interpreter, by his difficulty in grasping clearly and distinctly just what he is doing when he understands and conceives, reflects and judges. Nor is this difficulty to be overcome in any easy fashion, for it has all the complexity of the critical problem.[40]

In *Verbum*, then, his decision was to begin with a presentation of the first and then the second acts of the mind as psychological events. Each has its respective inner word: direct insight into quiddity and its word, the concept or definition; reflective insight into the sufficiency (or not) of evidence and its word, the judgment. Only after the psychological interpretation is stated does he clarify a series of metaphysical issues before turning, at last, to the *imago Trinitatis* and an interpretation of Aquinas's Trinitarian theology. In order to catch on to what he is doing, however, it is not enough to notice that the organization of the project prioritizes the 'psychological' over the metaphysical. His

---

39. *Verbum*, 192–99.

40. Lonergan, "Theology and Understanding," 131–32. The general failure he illustrates by the widespread acceptance of the spurious *De natura verbi intellectus* with its quite different psychological suppositions.

guiding insight was that a correct exegesis of Aquinas on the mind and its acts could not occur without a concomitant exegesis of his own experience of those acts. A few examples will bring to light what that meant on the ground.

The 'three degrees of abstraction' is a scholastic topos derived from Aristotle's division of the theoretical sciences into physics (i.e., natural philosophy), mathematics, and metaphysics on the basis of their ascending degrees of separation from matter and movement.[41] As a preliminary clarification, we should insist that it is not abstraction to notice, for instance, that every tire on every automobile in my neighborhood is round. Abstraction is not some automatic process by which we notice 'commonalities' in groups of particulars[42] or recognize friendly Fido, bounding our way, as an instance of dog.[43] "Those are all dogs!" is something most toddlers can tell you, and it represents their understanding of how to use a name in connection with appropriate data of sense; it does not mean they have understood (abstracted the species) 'dogness.' Fido, for that matter, also knows the difference between cats and dogs without abstracting their species. If, as Aquinas suggests in the prologue to his conference on the Apostles' Creed, we have so far failed to grasp the nature of a single gnat,[44] then, strictly speaking, 'dogness' is what the zoologist is trying to understand, not something a toddler abstracts walking around the park practicing a new word. For Aquinas, to recognize what is common to instances is the function of the sensitive *vis cogitativa* or "particular reason," which "compares individual intentions as the intellectual reason compares universal intentions."[45]

---

41. See *In De Trin.*, q. 5 a. 1.

42. *Pace* Knasas, *The Preface to Thomistic Metaphysics*, 78–79.

43. *Pace* Cory, *Aquinas on Human Self-Knowledge*, 10–11.

44. "In Symbolum Apostolorum, scilicet 'Credo in Deum' expositio," in *Opuscula theologica 2*, ed. Raymund M. Spiazzi, 2nd ed. (Turin: Marietti, 1953), 191–217.

45. "Ratio particularis . . . est enim collativa intentionum individualium, sicut ratio intellectiva intentionum universalium." *STh* 1 q. 78 a. 4c. See *Verbum*, 43–46, 52–55; Julien Peghaire, "A Forgotten Sense: The Cogitative, According to St. Thomas Aquinas," *The Modern Schoolman* 20, no. 1–2 (1943): 123–40, 210–29, here 135–40; and more recent discussion of the intentionality of the *cogitativa* in Daniel D. De Haan, "Perception and the *Vis Cogitativa*: A Thomistic Analysis of Aspectual, Actional, and Affectional Percepts," *American Catholic Philosophical Quarterly* 88, no. 3 (2014): 397–437.

Abstraction is not an unconscious, automatic operation of the logic machine, but a conscious activity of intelligence.[46] Abstraction is an intelligent and conscious disregard for whatever is irrelevant to understanding. It is not a matter of noticing that data are similar but of penetrating to the intelligible ground of the similarity. If we move from the observation that all the tires are round to ask about the nature of roundness (geometry), or about rolling resistance (physics), or about the necessary and sufficient conditions for contingent being (metaphysics), then we are moving toward the abstract. Thus, "the very point of the celebrated three degrees of abstraction" is 'psychological': it is "the elimination by the understanding of the intellectually irrelevant because it is understood to be irrelevant."[47]

Abstraction, then, is a function of understanding, and interpreters who confuse the activities of the cogitative power with the abstraction proper to intellect have evidently failed to appreciate what the act of understanding properly is. According to Aquinas, the act of understanding is what properly distinguishes the intellect and perfectly demonstrates its power.[48] The concept, the inner word, is derived from understanding; "conceptualization is the expression of an act of understanding; such self-expression is possible only because understanding is self-possessed, conscious of itself and its own conditions as understanding." There is a first degree of abstraction if those conscious conditions include reference to sense but not to 'here' and 'now' as such (physics, natural philosophy); a second degree if they include reference to the imaginable, but not to the sensible order (mathematics); and a third, finally, if the conditions are all in the intelligible order (metaphysics).[49] The three degrees are not fundamentally a metaphysical theorem but a psychological fact: the intelligent disregard for what is irrelevant to the question.

A similar 'introspective' approach is taken to the genesis of the concept of being, *ens*, in our experience of conceiving possibilities. Lonergan does not claim that Aquinas made an explicit attempt "to describe the virtualities of the act of understanding in its self-possession to conceptualize

---

46. On abstraction, see *Verbum*, esp. 162–179.

47. *Verbum*, 53.

48. *STh* 1 q. 88 a. 2 ad 3.

49. *Verbum*, 53–56; see 76, 167–68, 187.

reflectively the preconceptual act of intelligence that utters itself in the concept 'being,'" but only that such an analysis undergirds Aquinas's explicit claims with amazing accuracy.[50] Contingent being is realized possibility. "Intelligibility is the ground of possibility, and possibility is the possibility of being."[51] Thus, he explains, the concept of being, *ens*, "is not just another concept" but is any and every concept considered "in relation to its own *actus essendi*," its act of existence.[52] Wherefore the concept is analogous, that is, a function of a similar proportion differently verified in different instances. "The identity of the process [of conception] . . . necessitates the similarity of the proportion, and it is the diversity of the content that makes the terms of the proportion differ."[53] To state the matter a little differently, questions regard possibilities and actualities: what might be the case and whether indeed it is the case, or, to reverse the order, whether something is the case and how it is the case. In response to questions of the 'what' or 'how' type, we conceive possibilities. In doing so, we understand a possibility as what might be the case and indeed would be the case if certain conditions were fulfilled. The many possibilities yield a diversity of contents, but in conceiving them, we understand that all are similarly related, as possibilities, to being. In this sense, being cannot be unknown to us, for it is conceived from any act of understanding. The concept of being "is the first concept; what is prior to the first concept is, not a prior concept, but an act of understanding; and like other concepts, the concept of being is an effect of the act of understanding."[54]

It is because intelligence is conscious of its own conditions as understanding that the decisive element in judgment is not synthesis (composition or division) as such, nor even the correspondence of mental and real synthesis; the decisive element is the *known* correspondence between mental and real synthesis. Synthesis itself is achieved through the coalescence of insights.[55] But judgment is a matter of positing

50. *Verbum*, 58.
51. *Verbum*, 57; see 69.
52. *Verbum*, 96.
53. *Verbum*, 58–59.
54. *Verbum*, 57 (internal citations omitted).
55. *Verbum*, 61–71.

synthesis, and it includes a survey of all the evidence on a question in light of the principles of intelligence.[56] In this process the principle of noncontradiction is naturally known because it is a criterion consciously implicated in posing a question for judgment. That is, in asking whether something is the case, we naturally know that the correct answer cannot be both yes and no in the same respect. In this sense the intellect knows by measuring things as if against its own principles.[57]

Another of Aquinas's standard illustrations of a naturally known first principle is that the whole is greater than the part. That this principle should be known *per se* presents no difficulty, for anyone who grasps the meaning of 'whole' grasps, in the same insight, the meaning of 'part.' But this seems to be something one learns by learning the meaning of its component terms; in this sense, it is different from the principle of contradiction, which is spontaneously operative in posing yes-or-no questions. Lonergan suggests, however, that there is a sense in which part and whole are also contained in questions, since in querying data to understand them, we implicitly realize that the phenomena are not the whole, that there is an intelligible component. Likewise, in interrogating evidence to posit being, we implicitly realize that a contingent act of existence adds something to finite essence; the existent is greater than the essential.[58]

We have noted very briefly four particular points of exegesis, and only in overview: the degrees of abstraction, the concept of being, synthesis and judgment, and whole and parts. In each case, Lonergan took it that Aquinas's discussion of the mind was ultimately founded on Aquinas's own attention to the relevant realities. Since those realities were also immediately accessible to Lonergan in the data of his own consciousness, his practice was to interpret the data of the text in conjunction with the data of consciousness. In this way, what Aquinas said directly about cognition might be properly understood and verified, and what he said about implicitly related matters, such as the origins of the concept of being, might be shown to have a sound basis. It was these related matters, perhaps, that led Lonergan to the celebrated 'isomorphism' of knowing

56. *Verbum*, 71–78.

57. *Verbum*, 72.

58. *Verbum*, 69–70.

and being that, in *Insight*, became foundational for his program of metaphysics. To that question we now turn.

The 'Logico-Ontological Parallel'

In a patient and suggestive article, Lonergan's disciple Frederick Crowe pieced together some of "the rudiments of isomorphism" in the doctrine of Thomas Aquinas.[59] It is not our present business to reduplicate his labors or even rehearse his argument, because what is at stake here is not an interpretation of Aquinas, nor a verification of Lonergan's interpretation, but the hypothesis, complementary to Crowe's, that Lonergan's encounter with Aquinas led him to the discovery of the isomorphism. It was not Aquinas but Lonergan who conceived the isomorphism explicitly, affirmed it, and made it a principle of control for the articulation of metaphysics. In this section, however, I would like to present some evidence suggesting that he hit upon it during his apprenticeship to Aquinas. Lonergan suggested more than once that he understood his proposal for metaphysics as an effort to make explicit a methodical principle that Aristotle and Aquinas had leveraged implicitly.

To begin, we may call upon Crowe's summary conclusion for a clear statement of the basic issue as it appears in light of the Thomist accounts of knowing and of being:

> What human intellect cannot do is conceive properly any form that is not intrinsically related to matter, or understand except by data given on the sensitive level, or judge rationally except by reflection on conception and data to reach truth in the affirmation of existence. And the conditions of knowledge on the side of the subject are matched by parallel conditions on the side of the object. Thus, we can conceive, analogically, objects that are not conditioned by time and space, even extrinsically; but properly, the objects proportionate to our knowledge are intelligibilities in matter. On the side of the knowing, there is a composition of sensitive apprehension, intellectual apprehension, and rational

59. Crowe, "St Thomas and the Isomorphism," 208.

judgment; on the side of the known, there is a parallel composition of potency, form, and act.[60]

The parallel, in the first instance, is between the composition of the knowing and the composition of the known. In both the knowing and the known, there is a coalescence of three elements. In the knowing, these are (as a first approximation) sensible presentations, insight into quiddity, and reflective grasp of sufficient evidence. In the object, these are potency, form, and act. These run parallel to one another, such that

presentations : potency :: insight : form :: judgment : act.

Moreover, if we analyze the knowing as itself an instance of being, then its potential component is experience (presentations), its formal component (first act, second potency) is the insight, and its actual component (second act) is the reflective understanding that grasps the sufficiency of evidence and, therefore, rationally posits "the correspondence between the mental and the real *composition*."[61] "Truth and reality are parallel."[62]

The parallel is also a proportion. Human knowing is proportioned to its proper object, *quidditates rerum materialium*, through a combination of operations on the sensitive and intellectual levels. The material singular is attained on the level of sense, intelligible form is attained through the first operation of the intellect, and contingent act is attained through judgment. The operations not only combine; they are cumulative or compounding, for understanding grasps the intelligibility in the matter, and judgment posits an intelligibility as contingently actual on the basis of evidence provided by the senses. This combining and compounding is proportioned to an object that itself is composed of matter, intelligible form, and contingent act.[63] With some regularity, therefore, Aquinas

---

60. Ibid., 234–35.

61. *Verbum*, 71.

62. *Verbum*, 81–82.

63. For example, see *In De Trinitate*, q. 5 a. 3c. "Duplex est operatio intellectus: una . . . qua cognoscit de unoquoque quid est; alia vero, qua componit et dividet . . . et hae quidem duae operationes duobus, quae sunt in rebus, respondent. Prima quidem operatio respicit ipsam naturam rei. . . . Secunda vero operatio respicit ipsum esse rei." ("The operation of the intellect is twofold: one . . . by which it knows of something what it is; another, by which it composes and divides . . . and these two operations correspond to two [elements] in the things. The first operation regards the nature

correlates *essentia* and *esse* with the first and second operations of the mind, respectively: as we understand essence by answering the question *quid*, so we arrive at knowledge of *esse* by answering the question *utrum*.[64]

Now, this thesis is at once a claim about being and a claim about knowing. Fundamentally, the claim is that being is the intelligible; it is what is attained through correct understanding. Hence, Lonergan writes,

> Aristotle's basic thesis was the objective reality of what is known by understanding. . . . The denial of the soul today is really the denial of the objectivity of the intelligible, the denial that understanding, knowing a cause, is knowing anything real.[65]

Direct understanding, grasping a quiddity, is attaining a real, intrinsic, and intelligible, but not imaginable, cause. Causality is never imaginable, because it is an intelligible dependence, either intrinsic (form) or extrinsic (efficient, final). The experience of 'this, then that' is not knowledge of causality; causality is known only through an intelligent grasp of 'because.'

Not only are the operations of the knowing subject proportioned to the known object, but also the elements on each side are proportioned to one another, and the proportions run parallel. The metaphysical elements of potency (matter), form, and act name a set of proportions—potency is to form, act is of form—that is differently verified in different instances. Similarly, the cognitional elements of sense experience, understanding, and judgment name a set of proportions—sense experience is for understanding, judgment regards the adequacy of understanding—differently verified in different instances. Thus,

> natural form stands to natural matter, as intelligible form stands to sensible matter; and when by a natural spontaneity we ask *quid sit*, we reveal our natural knowledge that the material or

---

of the thing. . . . The second operation regards its being" [my translation].) *Super Boetium*, 147. Compare *Sent.* 1, d. 19, q. 5, a. 1 ad 7.

64. An extensive collection of loci linking the two intellectual operations (understanding and judgment) to *essentia* and *esse*, respectively, may be found in Crowe, "St Thomas and the Isomorphism," 216–19, in text and notes.

65. *Verbum*, 34–35.

sensible component is only a part and that the whole includes a formal component as well. Similarly, when by a natural spontaneity we ask *an sit*, we again reveal our natural knowledge that the whole is not just a quiddity but includes an *actus essendi* as well.[66]

Again, in the synthetic judgment the terms correspond to the matter, the synthesis corresponds to the form, and the positing corresponds to the act of existence.[67] "The ground and cause of the composition that occurs in the mind and in speech is a real composition in the thing," so that truth "is the correspondence between mental and real synthesis" and knowledge of truth is knowledge of that correspondence.[68]

There are, then, two parallel structures, each representing a set of proportions and each also proportioned to the other. But it is important to notice the true locus of this parallel. It is not that the order of ideas is the order of realities, for the order of ideas is replete with unrealized possibilities. The true locus of the parallel is in the process or structure of the knowing and the process or structure of the known: the becoming of knowledge and the becoming of things; the being of knowledge and the being of things.[69] This Lonergan calls

> the logico-ontological parallel: as methodology [i.e., analysis] moves to discovery of the *quid*, so motion and generation move towards its reality; as demonstration [i.e., composition] establishes the properties from the *quid*, so real essences are the real grounds of real properties.[70]

Analysis ('methodology') is the becoming of knowledge, and movement and generation are the becoming of things. Synthesis or composition is the being of knowledge, that is, the demonstration of a science starting from the causes first in themselves, essences, just as properties of a thing are grounded in its essence.

66. *Verbum*, 70.
67. *Verbum*, 61–63.
68. *Verbum*, 63.
69. *Insight*, 511.
70. *Verbum*, 37.

There is a funniness to this parallel, and Lonergan knew it. It lies in the fact that analysis moves from the first-for-us to the first-in-itself, while movement and generation are governed by what is first-in-itself. To grasp the point of the parallel, then, one has to scratch beneath the surface. Analysis may begin from what is first-for-us, the phenomena, but, like movement and generation, the phenomena themselves are governed by what is first-in-itself. The analytic process is the gradual resolution of the phenomena into the causes first-in-themselves. Thus, Lonergan writes,

> in a sense the act of understanding as an insight into phantasm is knowledge of form; but the form so known does not correspond to the philosophic concept of form; insight is to phantasm as form is to matter; but in that proportion, form is related to prime matter, but insight is related to sensible qualities; strictly, then, it is not true that insight is grasp of form; rather, insight is the grasp of the object in an inward aspect such that the mind, pivoting on the insight, is able to conceive, not without labor, the philosophic concepts of form and matter.[71]

In other words, the matter of the insight—the phantasm—is not the matter of the thing, and therefore, in the first instance, what we come to understand are the presentations of things to our senses, as disposed by the cogitative power. "The act of understanding leaps forth when the sensible data are in a suitable constellation."[72] It is only through an accumulation and coalescence of such insights that we gradually work out the properties of a thing from its detectible activities and its essence from its properties. Finally, it is only by generalizing the proportions exhibited in this process that we conceive the metaphysical elements, form and potency.[73]

There is a related issue. Insight into phantasm (direct understanding) is the pivot between the particular and the universal. Its object is the

71. *Verbum*, 38.

72. *Verbum*, 28.

73. This interpretation seems to solve the puzzle noted by Frederick Crowe, *Verbum*, 256, editorial note n.

formal cause in 'this' matter, the quiddity of a material thing, for example, '*how* (or *why*) this wood is a house.' But *how* or *why* are not restricted to this particular instance, for, on the one hand, every relevantly similar instance would be understood just the same way, and, on the other hand, 'this' 'here' 'now,' just in themselves, are never among the relevancies. Thus, as 'into phantasm,' insight grasps the intelligibility of 'this': 'how this is what it is.' But as a grasp of 'how' (or 'why'), it involves the intelligent disregard of what always is irrelevant, namely, 'here' and 'now' simply as such.[74] Hence, by reflection back on the phantasm, we conceive this thing, this event, etc. By objectifying the intelligent disregard for the intellectually irrelevant 'here' and 'now,' we conceive the universal common to many, the essential definition, algorithm, etc., for example, '*what* a house is,' where 'what' means form and common matter.[75]

The formal cause, however, as immanent in this matter, is not in itself the universal idea but the concretely immanent *how* or *why* 'how' (form) that makes 'this' 'what' it 'is,' where 'this' denotes the matter, 'what' denotes the essence, that is, the composition of matter ('this') and form ('how,' 'why'), and 'is' denotes the act.[76] If, then, the reader of Aquinas knows what insight is, "it is impossible to confuse the Aristotelian form with the Platonic Idea. Form is the *ousia* that is not a universal, but a cause of being."[77] Form is the intrinsic 'how' intermediate between matter and the concrete being (*ens*), unity (*unum*), 'what' (*quid*) this is.

> On the cognitional side, form is known in knowing the answer to the question, Why are these sensible data to be conceived of as one thing, of a man, of a house? But knowing why and knowing the cause, like knowing the reason and knowing the real reason, are descriptions of the act of understanding. As, then, form mediates causally between matter and thing, so understanding mediates causally between sensible data and conception. By a stroke of genius Aristotle replaced mythical Platonic anamnesis by psychological fact, and, to describe the psychological fact,

74. See *Verbum*, 200–201.
75. *Verbum*, 189–90.
76. *Verbum*, 26–29.
77. *Verbum*, 195 (internal citations omitted).

eliminated the subsistent Ideas to introduce formal causes in material things.[78]

Thus, it is by pivoting from the intelligently abstracted idea back to the concrete and particularized 'how' that makes 'this' a 'what' that we work out the philosophic concepts of form ('how'), matter ('this'), and essence ('what,' i.e., the composition of form and matter) as intrinsic constituents of a being.

To summarize, the basic meaning of the parallel emerges from reflection on inquiry as proportionate to being. Propositions are meaningful because they are answers to questions, so that clarifying the question is prefatory to making sense of the answer. Answers come to light for us in two basic steps, which are indicated by Aquinas's *duplex operatio mentis*. Insight into phantasm grasps an intelligibility immanent in the matter. The reflective and judicial process grasps not a further intrinsic intelligibility but an extrinsic one: the fulfillment of the conditions for 'this' *to be* 'thus.' Form, potency, and act are, respectively, the intrinsic constituents or causes 'how' 'this' 'is,' where 'this' designates the matter as interrogated, 'how' designates the immanently intelligible form, and 'is' designates the intrinsic act that is, however, extrinsically intelligible.

As Lonergan suggested, and as we will explore in due course, his use of the 'logico-ontological parallel' as a methodological principle for the development of metaphysics was, in a sense, standing Aquinas on his head. For Aquinas, as Lonergan knew, the prior consideration scientifically regards what is first-in-itself, and absolutely speaking, that is the priority of divine causality. Thus, besides the parallel of analysis and becoming, synthesis and being,

> there is also interaction: the real is the cause of knowledge; inversely, the idea of the technician or artist is the cause of the technical or artistic product; and for Aquinas, the latter is the prior consideration, for God is the artisan of the universe.[79]

In the context of human living, this 'interaction' is substantial, for the human world is overwhelmingly the product of human knowledge and

---

78. *Verbum*, 195–96 (internal citations omitted).
79. *Verbum*, 37–38 (internal citations omitted).

choice. The causality of God's knowledge, however, is not properly 'interactive,' because God is not affected by the contingent order of being. It is rather the reverse side, the ontological ground, of the expectation that being is completely intelligible. Thus, being is completely intelligible because it is caused by Intelligence; and it is knowable by us because our minds are created participations in the mind of the Creator.

Self-Presence and Self-Knowledge

The isomorphism of knowing and being could become the methodical fulcrum of a metaphysics only if it could be articulated through a program of adequate self-knowledge. If it is possible to know the structure of knowledge and its proportionality to being, then it is possible to leverage that knowledge into a heuristic (i.e., anticipatory) account of the proportionate structure of being. This point, it seems to me, brings us to the real heart of Lonergan's encounter with Thomas Aquinas, for he emerged from his apprenticeship convinced that Aquinas himself must have undertaken some kind of program of self-attention. Furthermore, he concluded that an updated and explicit version of such a program could yield a normative self-knowledge and provide the key for meeting the issues of our day.

Aquinas distinguished three ways the soul knows itself,[80] which Lonergan described as 'empirical,' 'scientific,' and 'normative.'

> There is the empirical self-knowledge, actual or habitual, based upon the soul's presence to itself; there is the scientific and analytic self-knowledge that proceeds from objects to acts, from acts to potencies, from potencies to essence; but besides this pair . . . there is also a third. It lies in the act of judgment which passes from the conception of essence to the affirmation of reality. Still, it is concerned not with this or that soul, but with what any soul ought to be according to the eternal reasons; and

---

80. *De veritate* q. 10 a. 8c. "Sic ergo patet quod mens nostra cognoscit seipsam quodammodo per essentiam suam, ut Augustinus dicit: quodam vero modo per intentionem, sive per speciem, ut philosophus et Commentator dicunt; quodam vero intuendo inviolabilem veritatem, ut item Augustinus dicit." Compare ibid. q. 1 a. 9c.; *STh* 1 q. 87 a. 1c.

so the reality of soul that is envisaged is not sorry achievement but dynamic norm.[81]

These three are cumulative. Empirical self-presence is the basis for scientific self-knowledge, and scientific self-knowledge is the basis for normative self-knowledge. Let us consider each in turn.

Aquinas did not often speak expressly about the psychological subject, but he defined a person as a distinct subsistent in an intellectual nature. Ontologically, then, a person is an identity, a whole, a unity belonging to a certain grade of being, namely, the grade of spirit, which is intrinsically conscious being. Note that the spiritual subject just *is* conscious; empirical self-presence is not 'accessed' by what one does, it is given as what one is.[82] Lonergan contended that "an adequate account of consciousness is had by making more explicit the familiar Aristotelian-Thomist doctrine of the identity in act of subject and object." In an attendant note, he adds:

> The pure case of identity is the familiar tag, 'in his quae sunt sine materia idem est intelligens et intellectum.' . . . If I may hazard a surmise, I should say that the discovery of the subject, attributed to German idealism and subsequent philosophies, was simply an unbalanced effort to restore what implicitly existed in Aristotle and St Thomas but had been submerged by the conceptualist tendency.[83]

The conceptualist tendency to which Lonergan refers here is to be so fascinated with the products of the mind (for instance, logical formalizations) as to overlook its constitutive activities. Lonergan wished to redirect attention to the fact that an intellectual nature is also a conscious nature, for acts of understanding, knowing, and loving are conscious events, and the corresponding habits are inferred from the conscious events.

81. *Verbum*, 101.

82. See Cory, *Aquinas on Human Self-Knowledge*, 1–12, 69–133. In framing the problem in terms of 'self-access' and 'self-opacity,' Cory fails to break cleanly with thinking of the subject-as-object and penetrate to the subject-as-subject. Consciousness just *is* self-presence, presence to self in and through presence to objects.

83. Lonergan, "Christ as Subject," 179 and n50 (internal citations omitted).

Lonergan draws attention to several important places where the appeal to intellectual experience is explicit in Aquinas.[84] If a person is the ontological subject of an intellectual nature, then a person who is awake is also a subject in the psychological sense, the subject of intellectual and, if incarnate, also a sensitive consciousness. The psychological subject is the subject of consciousness, the subject of wonder, the subject of prayer, the 'I' who sees, hears, tastes, smells; inquires, understands, conceives, formulates; reflects and judges, deliberates and commits. One is always a person, but one is only a psychological subject when one is awake (or at least dreaming), when one is present to oneself as present to the world.

In distinguishing empirical self-awareness from the account of the soul achieved through scientific inquiry, Aquinas appealed to Augustine, who articulated a difference between the way the mind is present to itself as itself and the way it is present to the objects of its consideration. Here is Augustine:

> 'Know thyself' is not said to the mind in the way one says 'know the Cherubim and Seraphim'; for though they are absent, we believe what has been preached about them, that they are heavenly powers. Nor as it is said, 'know the will of that person,' which is not presented to us in any way to sense or to understand, except by way of signs bodied forth; and in such a way that we rather believe than understand. Nor as it might be said to someone, 'look at your face,' which can happen only in a mirror; for even our own face is absent from our view, because it is not somewhere we can direct our gaze. But when one says to the mind, 'know thyself,' by the very fact that it understands the meaning of 'thyself,' it knows itself; and for no other reason than that it is present to itself.[85]

---

84. *Verbum*, 89–91.

85. Augustine, *De Trinitate*, 10.9.12. "Non ita dicitur menti: *Cognosce te ipsam* sicut dicitur: 'Cognosce cherubim et seraphim'; de absentibus enim illis credimus secundum quod caelestes quaedam potestates esse praedicantur. Neque sicut dicitur: 'Cognosce uoluntatem illius hominis,' quae nobis nec ad sentiendum ullo modo nec ad intelligendum praesto est nisi corporalibus signis editis, et hoc ita ut magis credamus quam intellegamus. Neque ita ut dicitur homini: 'Vide faciem tuam,' quod nisi in speculo fieri non potest. Nam et ipsa nostra facies absens ab aspectu nostro est quia non ibi est quo ille dirigi potest. Sed cum dicitur menti: *Cognosce te ipsam*, eo ictu quo intellegit quod dictum est *te ipsam* cognoscit se ipsam, nec ob aliud quam eo quod sibi praesens est."

Expounding this passage, Lonergan distinguished three meanings of 'presence': the presence of bodies in a place, the presence of an intending subject to intended objects, and the presence of the intending subject to himself or herself, not as intended but as intending.[86] The distinction between the latter two kinds of presence grounded the meanings of two parallel sets of correlative terms in Lonergan's use: 'object' and 'subject,' 'intentional' and 'conscious.' These distinctions feature so prominently in Lonergan's thought, and are so decisive for the way he interprets what is going on in Aquinas, that some effort must be made to spell them out clearly.

A first meaning of presence, then, is local or spatial (e.g., the presence of Augustine's face on Augustine's body). A second meaning is intentional presence: the face, though locally present, is said to be absent from view when it is out of the line of sight, and present in view when attention is directed to its reflection in a mirror. Similarly, the angels, though absent from a place, are intended by the mind that hears and believes what is declared of them; the mind is present to them, or perhaps we may say they are present in the mind, by its intention. Again, someone may attempt to make known her wishes through external signs, but I become present to that meaning not by moving in space but through attention, wonder, understanding, judgment. It does not much matter whether we say that the objects are present in the mind, or that the mind is present to the objects, as long as we get clear what we are talking about. By intentional presence, a conscious subject is related to intended objects. An object in this sense is the intended content of any conscious act, for instance, the dreamt or imagined, the heard, smelled, or seen, the understood, the conceived, the believed, and so forth. Note that intentional, in this sense, merely means that the act apprehends some object; it does not necessarily mean that the act is under conscious control.

The intentional presence of objects depends, however, on the third sense of presence, the self-presence of the intending subject. One is present to oneself, not as intending oneself but just as conscious, as being

---

In *De Trinitate*, ed. W. J. Mountain and F. Glorie, Corpus Christianorum, Series Latina 50–50A (Tournhout: Brepols, 1968), 50:325–26. In *De veritate* q. 10, a. 8c, Aquinas refers to a different text from *De Trinitate* bk. 9 making a similar point about the mind's self-presence.

86. Bernard J. F. Lonergan, *The Incarnate Word*, ed. Robert Doran and Jeremy D. Wilkins, trans. Charles C. Hefling Jr., CWL 9 (2016), 474–76.

oneself. Colloquially, we speak of someone being 'self-conscious' who is preoccupied with his or her performance, his or her presentation to others; in this sense one is the object of one's own attention and concern. But we also speak of being conscious as opposed to being knocked out, unconscious. In this latter sense, unless one is conscious, there is no possibility of noticing anything at all, let alone directing attention to one's own performance. Not for nothing do we etherize the patient before cutting off a leg. Consciousness, self-presence, is not another kind of intentional presence; it is not presence to myself as the object of my attention or wonderment, understanding or reproach. It is rather that all of the intentional acts also presuppose one who is intending and who, as intending and not as intended, is also 'there.' It is by its self-presence that the mind knows what is meant when it hears the injunction "know thyself."

Thus, in Lonergan's idiom, the same acts are said to be both conscious and intentional. Such acts are intrinsically relational, and the relationality is constitutive of our awareness; in and through one and the same act, an object becomes present to the subject and the subject is, in a different sense, present to herself as regarding an object. As he put this point in a later context,

> although it is true that the subject is a knower, the act is a knowing, and the object is a known, the third of these is not converted such that only the object is known and every known is an object. For in every conscious act there is a threefold known [subject, act, object], but only one of these is the object: when someone who is seeing sees colors, not only the colors are known but also the subject himself or herself, the one who sees, is self-present; nor does one see by an unconscious act of seeing, but rather by a self-present act of seeing.[87]

Thus, the same act is conscious as rendering the subject self-present; intentional as rendering the subject present to an intended object. But Lonergan adds, further, that the acts occur in a flow and therefore are also related to one another. The flow may be fragmentary, as in a dream,

87. *Incarnate Word*, 488 (translation altered).

or it may be quite deliberately directed. Consciousness is a kind of field, then, relating a subject (consciously intending) to objects (consciously intended) through a structured flow of (conscious, intentional) operations.

It is this conscious relatedness among the acts that gives meaning to Aquinas's statement that the procession of the inner word is an 'intelligible emanation' (*emanatio intelligibilis*), and the procession of love from the word is an 'intelligible inclination' (*inclinatio intelligibilis*).

> There are two aspects to the procession of an inner word in us. There is the productive aspect; intelligence in act is proportionate to producing the inner word. There is also the intelligible aspect: inner words do not proceed with mere natural spontaneity as any effect does from any cause; they proceed with reflective rationality; they proceed not merely from a sufficient cause but from sufficient grounds known to be sufficient and because they are known to be sufficient. . . . Judgment is judgment only if it proceeds from intellectual grasp of sufficient evidence as sufficient.[88]

Similarly, love is rational only if it proceeds from a rational affirmation of value. In other words, these events are not merely cases where one act arises from another; they are cases where one act is consciously dependent upon another. The act of understanding (insight) depends on sense and imagination and wonder; conception or formulation or definition depends on insight; rational judgment depends on a grasp of evidence as sufficient; rational love depends on a rational affirmation of lovable good.[89]

To say that all this is present in consciousness, that it is involved in the mind's awareness of itself, is not to say that it is known in a full and properly human sense. Lonergan took the Thomist position to entail a rational realism: "the real is what is; and 'what is' is known in the rational act, judgment."[90] Thus, knowledge, in the properly human sense, is correct understanding known to be correct. There is an elementary sense in

88. *Verbum*, 207.
89. *Verbum*, 46–59, 204–13.
90. *Verbum*, 20; see 33–4.

which the given contents of outer and inner sensorium are 'known,' but 'knowing' in this sense is shared with the animals, and just the material element of a properly human knowing. Properly human knowledge is attained not through the given as given, but through the given as successfully interrogated, as understood and judged aright.

Scientific self-knowledge is a case of analysis and synthesis and, for Aquinas, takes the form of a faculty psychology that is generically metaphysical.

> Knowledge of soul, then, begins from a distinction of objects; specifying objects leads to a discrimination between different kinds of act; different kinds of act reveal difference of potency; and the different combinations of potencies lead to knowledge of the different essences that satisfy the generic definition of soul.[91]

What is central to this analysis are the activities of the soul. The analysis is not interested in the objects per se; it is interested in the objects just inasmuch as different kinds of objects specify different kinds of activities. Objects specify activities, activities are resolved into powers, and its powers demonstrate the essence of the soul. We do not achieve scientific knowledge of ourselves intuitively, like the angels, but through the kind of careful investigation Aquinas conducts across forty-five chapters (46–90) in the second book of the *Summa contra gentiles*. Self-understanding in this sense is achieved through abstracting the essential and disregarding the irrelevant in an aggregate of experiences.

The result of this analysis is an understanding of the proportion of nature, the objective intelligibility of a nature. Proportion means an equality of relations. The proportion of nature makes it possible to affirm and differentiate potencies from the occurrence of different kinds of operations. Again, natural proportion leads us to distinguish different kinds of animating principles, for instance, the material souls of animals from the spiritual souls of human beings.[92] Nature, in the Aristotelian sense, is not to be conceived as either an active or a passive potency,

91. *Verbum*, 87 (internal citation omitted).

92. Lonergan, "De Ente Supernaturali," 66.

but as the immanent principle of movement and rest. The Aristotelian concept of nature is

> a principle in the thing of movement in the thing; it is 'principium motus in eo in quo est motus.' It follows that nature is neither efficient potency nor receptive potency [i.e, *potentia activa* and *passiva* in the Aristotelian sense]. It is not efficient potency; for that is the principle of movement, not in self as self, but in the other or in self as other. It is not receptive potency; for that is the principle of movement, not in self as self, but by the other or by self as other.[93]

The relationship of efficient to receptive potency is exemplified by the order of agent to possible intellect, and of the will of the end to the will of the means. In each of these cases, the self is mover in one respect and moved in another. But the 'nature' is the form that orders efficient to receptive potencies, that is, that constitutes a proportion of cause to effect.

In the context of Aristotelian analysis, 'object' means an efficient or a final cause. In the matter at hand, however, the activities are all conscious, and their objects are also conscious contents of apprehension or appetition. The relevant acts are not merely events to be reduced to their causes; they are consciously related to their objects, and, therefore, the relationships among the acts and between the acts and their objects are immediately given within the field of our experience. The same is not true, however, of the essence and potencies of the soul, or of the habits informing those potencies; they have to be worked out, as Aquinas says, by diligent and subtle investigation.[94]

It remains that the intellectual and volitional activities of the soul are given in consciousness, and their givenness turns out to be not only the matter for interrogation but also the dynamic basis of the interrogation—which interrogation, after all, is a conscious inquiry into the nature of conscious events. Chief among these is the act of understanding (*intelligere*); it is by this act that we understand ourselves, and it is this

---

93. *Verbum*, 122–23.
94. See *STh* 1 q. 87 a. 1c.

very act that is the proper act of our soul, perfectly demonstrating its power and nature.[95] Hence the thesis of *Verbum*: "We must begin by grasping the nature of the act of understanding, . . . thence we shall come to a grasp of the nature of inner words, their relation to language, and their role in our knowledge of reality."[96] Again, "grasp the nature of your acts of understanding, and you have the key to the whole of Thomist psychology."[97]

Normative self-knowledge rests on scientific self-knowledge but goes beyond it. It is not analytic and theoretical but existential: it is knowledge in light of the eternal reasons. As scientific, self-knowledge yields a psychology; as normative, it grounds an epistemology. Augustine had accounted for rational knowledge by the vision of eternal truth. But Aquinas transposed that account into the soul to affirm the native light of human intellect as a created participation of uncreated light.[98] Normative self-knowledge is achieved inasmuch as we come to know this light in ourselves, grasping its virtuality as light.

> Now knowledge of the norm, of the ought-to-be, cannot be had from what merely happens to be and, too often, falls far short of the norm. Normative knowledge has to rest upon the eternal reasons. But this resting, Aquinas explained, is not a vision of God but a participation and similitude of him by which we grasp first principles and judge all things by examining them in the light of principles.[99]

By laying hold of this light, we grasp that inviolable truth by which we articulate, as much as we can, not only the nature of every human mind but also its normative order in light of the eternal reasons.[100]

95. *Verbum*, 90. See *STh* 1 q. 88 a. 2 ad 3 ("anima humana intelligit seipsam per suum intelligere, quod est actus proprius eius, perfecte demonstrans virtutem eius et naturam": the human soul understands itself by its act of understanding, which is its proper act, perfectly demonstrating its power and nature).

96. *Verbum*, 25.

97. *Verbum*, 90.

98. *Verbum*, 196–97.

99. *Verbum*, 101.

100. "Sed verum est quod iudicium et efficacia huius cognitionis per quam naturam animae cognoscimus, competit nobis secundum derivationem luminis intellectus nostri a veritate divina, in

Since understanding does not occur in every kind of knower and involves abstraction from the conditions of time and space, the Aristotelian agent intellect might have to be postulated as a condition for the possibility of understanding. At any rate, Aquinas debated with the Avicennists whether agent intellect was transcendent to all intellects or proper to each. On the other hand, we are all familiar with the flash of understanding ("Aha! Eureka!"); it is given in consciousness, even though most insights are unobtrusive, not game-changing. It is the effect and, we might say, the conscious evidence of agent intellect. It was in the immanence of understanding that Aquinas found his peremptory argument, against Avicenna, for an agent intellect immanent in each person: "this person understands."[101] The flash is a result of wonder and wonder, too, we have all felt. It is light in the mode of wonder that expresses itself in questions and provides the criteria for what might count as answers. It is light in the mode of clarity that guides the conception, the formulation, or the definition of what we understand by way of intelligible emanation. It is wonder in another mode that asks for evidence that bright ideas are true; we judge by the force of intellectual light.[102] These are not opaque metaphysical necessities but a dynamic structure within intellectual consciousness.

It is this structure, not only as the matter of interrogation but as itself the dynamic basis for the interrogation, that is the object of normative self-knowledge. Aquinas associates the achievement of this knowledge with the 'complete return' (reditio completa) to oneself mentioned in the Liber de causis. Although sensation is both true and conscious, it is not conscious of its own truth and can neither articulate nor verify it. Rational judgment, however, involves an initial return to oneself inasmuch as it knows its own truth and completes the return inasmuch as, penetrating to its own essence, it grasps its own proportion to its object, being.[103] This is why the self-understanding of intelligence is different from other cases of understanding. The mind knows itself not only through its products

---

qua rationes omnium rerum continentur, sicut supra dictum est. Unde et Augustinus dicit, in IX de Trin., intuemur inviolabilem veritatem, ex qua perfecte, quantum possumus, definimus non qualis sit uniuscuiusque hominis mens, sed qualis esse sempiternis rationibus debeat." STh 1 q. 87 a. 1c.

101. Verbum, 90–91.

102. Verbum, 95. See STh 1–2 q. 109 a. 1c.; 2–2 q. 173 a. 2c.

103. Verbum, 86–87. See De veritate q. 1 a. 9c.

and activities but through its own experience of itself; its self-knowledge is not a perfect identity, such that the mind's conception of itself is itself, as in God; but it is at least approaching identity, because the mind knows itself through itself and not only through its effects.[104]

The assertion that our mind is a created participation of uncreated light is an ontology of knowledge. It grounds the expectation of an isomorphism between the mind as *potens omnia* and the totality of being as its adequate object. Furthermore, it grounds the possibility of an epistemology, that is, a full account of the proportion of the mind to its objects. Untroubled by Enlightenment anxieties about certitude, Aquinas did not pursue this question to the end. "Aquinas himself did not offer an account of the procedure he would follow; so it is only by piecing together scattered materials that one can arrive at an epistemological position that may be termed Thomistic but hardly Thomist." The key to such an exercise, Lonergan became convinced, is self-knowledge of soul, "a development of understanding by which we come to grasp just how it is that our minds are proportionate to knowledge of reality. . . . It should seem that this act consists in a grasp of the native infinity of intellect; . . . from such infinity one can grasp the capacity of the mind to know reality."[105]

In this light, the critical problem is not the Cartesian 'bridge' from 'in here' to 'out there' but simply the determination of an infinite potency to a succession of finite objects. This process has its ground in conscious light and its determinant in data.[106] Intellectual light makes objects knowable, just as (Thomas thought) visible light makes colored objects visible.[107] Its implications may be expressed in principles, but it is somehow prior to principles, for it is the light that compels our assent: "Scientific conclusions are accepted because they are implied by first principles; but the assent to first principles has to have its motive too, for assent is rational; and that motive is the light that naturally is within us."[108]

---

104. *Verbum*, 204–08.

105. *Verbum*, 96.

106. *Verbum*, 92–94.

107. *Verbum*, 90–93. For texts and discussion, see Frederick E. Crowe, "Universal Norms and the Concrete *Operabile* in St Thomas," in *Three Thomist Studies* (Chestnut Hill, Mass.: Lonergan Institute at Boston College, 2000), 3–69, here 8–15.

108. *Verbum*, 91–92. The reference is to *In De Trin.* q. 3 a. 1 ad 4.

Conclusion

Aquinas's affirmation of a reflective process that grasps the nature of intelligence by grasping the nature of its proper act—understanding—gave Lonergan warrant to interrogate text and consciousness side by side. He learned from Aquinas how an articulation of consciousness might be the basis for a normative self-knowledge, the grounds for an epistemology completely free of Cartesian suppositions, and, because the mind is *potens omnia*, result in a general anticipation of what being could be—that is, a metaphysics.

When, in the composition of *Verbum*, Lonergan found himself constrained to begin from the psychological rather than the metaphysical content of the Thomist theory of understanding and conception, it was his way of going 'back to the things themselves.' It was a decision of tremendous moment, for it seems to have led him along the methodological path he sought to realize in *Insight's* pedagogy of self-appropriation. In particular, it seems likely that 'turning everything upside down' helped Lonergan notice an implicit isomorphism between the cognitional and ontological elements. The isomorphism made it possible to develop a critical method for metaphysics, but only if adequate self-knowledge could be attained. The key to adequate self-knowledge, he found, was bringing into focus one's own intelligence as a created participation of uncreated light.

CHAPTER FIVE

Self-Appropriation as First Philosophy

The same is for understanding as for being.

PARMENIDES

T HE MOST SHOCKING aspect of the book, *Insight*," Lonergan wrote to the American Catholic Philosophical Association at their 1958 annual meeting, "is the primacy it accords knowledge. . . . If Aquinas had things right side up—and that is difficult to deny—then I have turned everything upside down."[1] Idealism in the beginning, Gilson famously warned, leads to idealism in the end.[2] Lonergan, who made 'cognitional theory' his first philosophy, is a prime suspect. At least since he began publishing his interpretation of Aquinas on understanding and the inner word, he has been accused of idealist proclivities.[3] Many have seen in his procedure a thinly veiled acquiescence to Kantian premises that cannot have ended well, despite Lonergan's protestations to the contrary.

1. Lonergan, "*Insight*: Preface to a Discussion," 142. I am grateful to Saturnino Muratore for drawing my attention to the significance of this passage; see Muratore, "Bernard Lonergan and the Philosophy of Being," in *Going Beyond Essentialism: Bernard J. F. Lonergan an Atypical Neo-Scholastic*, ed. Cloe Taddei-Ferretti (Naples: Istituto Italiano per gli Studi Filosofici, 2012), 175–81, here 175.

2. Étienne Gilson famously urged that a critical realism was impossible, and whoever would attempt it was doomed to idealism; see Gilson, *Réalisme thomiste*, chap. 6. "Qui commence en idéaliste finira nécessairement en idéaliste." Gilson, *Le réalisme méthodique*, 4. Lonergan admired Gilson tremendously: see his two reviews of *Being and Some Philosophers*, both in *Shorter Papers*, CWL 20, 183–84, 185–88; also *Verbum*, 226. He recorded significant philosophical differences, however, briefly in the reviews but more notably in "Metaphysics as Horizon," in *Collection*, CWL 4, 188–204. See too Paul St. Amour, "Lonergan and Gilson on the Problem of Critical Realism," *The Thomist* 69, no. 4 (2005): 557–92; Neil Ormerod, "Gilson and Lonergan and the Possibility of A Christian Philosophy," *The Heythrop Journal* 57, no. 3 (2016): 532–41.

3. O'Connell, "St. Thomas and the Verbum: An Interpretation" at 228. See Lonergan, *Verbum*, 260, editorial note b.

There is no doubt that Lonergan did make cognitional theory his first philosophy, beginning, in effect if not in name, with *Insight*. The open questions are what he meant by doing so and what he achieved. The answer to the second question (what he achieved) can only come to light by considering his body of work, and in later chapters we will take a few soundings. To the first (what he meant), the answer comes to light, I suggest, by tracing the process by which he effectively made cognitional theory first, reflected on what he had done, and thought through its implications. Such is the topic of the present chapter. Lonergan's starting point, as we will see, is not an idealism, or some putatively immanent subject unrelated to the world. It is 'know thyself' in a distinctive sense. Its precepts are self-attention, self-understanding, self-knowledge, and the fundamental decision he named self-appropriation.[4]

In the main, my thesis is twofold. First, as my chapter title suggests and as I have been arguing explicitly, what Lonergan meant by cognitional theory is less an objectified set of terms and relations than a particular set of scientific practices (in a sense to be explained presently). Second, the process by which these practices became for him the first and basic task of philosophy was, at the same time, the transformation of a traditional model for conceiving the relationships among philosophic discourses. Lonergan's 'first philosophy' is not first in a hierarchy of discourses, but first in an order of methodical controls; it is not ontologically but methodologically basic and prior to particular sciences; it is first as the science of sciences in a context where sciences are defined by their methodologies rather than by their subjects. The meaning of these statements comes to light by following the itinerary of the development.

The result falls into four parts. First, I present *Insight*'s architectural and pedagogical enactment of the 'reversal' of the traditional order of metaphysics and psychology. Next, we turn to Lonergan's transitional reflections, in the aftermath of *Insight*, on the relationship of cognitional theory and metaphysics. A third section considers that relationship in

---

4. "Metaphysics was discovered, I should say, simultaneously with a satisfactory psychology and epistemology, but it was much easier to express the metaphysics, and then to express the psychology and epistemology in terms of the metaphysics, than to express the psychology and epistemology in a manner that was independent of metaphysics." Bernard J. F. Lonergan, *Phenomenology and Logic: The Boston College Lectures on Mathematical Logic and Existentialism*, ed. Philip J. McShane, CWL 18 (2001), 117.

further detail by examining some examples from Lonergan's metaphysics in practice. A final section sets forth brief and schematic clarifications by contrast with Kant and Descartes. Since the matter is exegetical, I may be pardoned for including what might otherwise be excessively numerous long quotations. Let me add that in this chapter perhaps more than elsewhere, we run the risk of describing Lonergan's results without really entering into his asceticism. That risk, which cannot be avoided here, adds the limitations of extrinsic description to the intrinsic difficulty of his thought. For this reason, I hope the complexities of the first two sections will be clarified somewhat by the illustrations of the latter two.

An Essay in Aid of Rational Self-Appropriation

If *Verbum* may be considered an experiment in interpretation, *Insight* is an experiment in pedagogy. In *Verbum*, Lonergan initiated an expository and performative 'turn to the subject': expository in the sense that it is restricted to a decision about how best to communicate the results of his investigation; performative in the sense that the enactment preceded adequate reflection on its meaning. It was, by his own admission, a strange experience. What in the composition of *Verbum* was a late realization, however, was programmatic for *Insight* from the first. *Insight* is the imperfect realization of Lonergan's intention to prepare "a set of exercises" for rational self-appropriation, starting with the psychological facts and grounding a transition to explicit metaphysics on the exercise of self-appropriation. Still, the enactment fell short of the vision, and subsequent reflection would reveal that the vision itself was, as yet, imperfectly comprehended.

In *Verbum*, Lonergan sought to interpret Aquinas's texts on understanding and the intelligible emanation of the inner word alongside the data of his own consciousness. In effect, he placed two data sets side by side. One consisted in Aquinas's statements about intelligence; the other consisted in his own experience of intelligence. This procedure was justified on the grounds that Aquinas was speaking of realities of the mind, and texts are always less opaque to readers familiar with the objects under discussion. Nevertheless, as Lonergan saw it, Aquinas had been interpreted for centuries by readers unfamiliar with the realities, fearful of self-attention, bewildered by merely verbal problems, and inclined to overcome their confusion by speculative invention. As a result, Lonergan's interpretation took on so novel an aspect as to be almost inscrutable to many, judging from the general failure to catch his drift or even understand—if only to refute—his thesis.

In *Insight*, Lonergan meant to address the underlying occlusion. He would formulate a workbook, an 'essay in aid of rational appropriation,' with the eventual aim—he did not know how far off it would be—of an essay on method in theology.[5] Only gradually would he come to terms with the extent to which his turn to the subject was also an overturning of the priority of metaphysics as first philosophy. As a practical matter, *Insight* embraces the turn programmatically, as enacting a kind of pedagogy of self-discovery, self-knowledge, and self-appropriation. The priority of cognitional structure is programmatic in the order of exposition, the conception of the pedagogy, and, perhaps most importantly, the conception of a metaphysical method. He had not yet, however, brought into focus all the implications of what he was up to, and in *Insight* he often gives the impression that metaphysics is still the primary problem for philosophy.[6]

In *Verbum*, Lonergan remarked that one of the significant limitations of Thomist psychology was that it was generically metaphysical and only specifically psychological. Indeed, he explained that it was a significant barrier to the construction of the *Verbum* study itself. In order to convey Thomas Aquinas's meaning, he found it expedient to reverse this order and begin from the psychological facts, even though this option was severely criticized by some.[7] This remark and the strategy adopted in *Verbum* are a first indication of the difference between metaphysical analysis of natural proportion and intentionality analysis of cognitional structure. The latter is specifically psychological and only subsequently are its metaphysical implications worked out.

5. Quote from a letter to Eric O'Connor in 1952. The full letter is reproduced in Lambert and McShane, *Bernard Lonergan*, 156.

6. See, for instance, *Insight*, 448–55. This is a limiting factor, I suspect, in Lonergan's development, in *Insight*, of his claim that the polymorphism of consciousness is the key to philosophic pluralism. See the sympathetic but trenchant criticisms of Walmsley, *Lonergan on Philosophic Pluralism*, 170–203. (I would be inclined to distinguish some of Walmsley's criticisms.)

7. *Verbum*, 222–27.

In *Insight*, although Lonergan continued to use the language of faculty psychology, he had in fact moved into a kind of intentionality analysis, although it was some time after that he appreciated this fact and its importance. (We will explain this more fully momentarily.) It may be worth noticing that Lonergan's version of intentionality analysis, however, is not a phenomenology of perception or of language and conversation, but of inquiry, whose dynamics include, of course, both perception and language. From the opening exercise—'imagine a cartwheel'—the focus of Lonergan's pedagogy in *Insight* is on the disclosure of the objects and the acts of intellectual consciousness. Although this pedagogy does eventuate in a general sketch of metaphysics, including an analysis of the unity of a human being and even the general sweep of world order, its prior goal is cognitional theory. Cognitional theory or intentionality analysis gave him a way to self-knowledge that was at once scientific and normative. As he would later point out, the scientific self-knowledge attained through a faculty analysis could not be normative, because it raised, without itself solving, questions about the priorities among the faculties. Moreover, and for the same reason, faculty psychology offered no clear way to assert the complementary normativity of both wonder and love, or, better, the normativity of love as sublating wonder.[8]

Cognitional theory is not a matter of deducing faculties from objects and acts but of verifying terms and relations that are themselves given in consciousness. As he had pointed out in *Verbum*, we know physical realities from the outside in, from their perceptible activities; but we know our mind through itself and, in knowing it, know too its proportion to its objects. In *Insight*, Lonergan schematizes the structure brought to light by intentionality analysis in terms of three 'levels' of operations:

I. Data.Perceptual Images.	Free Images.	Utterances.
II. Questions for Intelligence.	Insights.	Formulations.
III. Questions for Reflection.	Reflection.	Judgment.[9]

---

8. See Jeremy D. Wilkins, "Grace and Growth: Aquinas, Lonergan, and the Problematic of Habitual Grace," *Theological Studies* 72, no. 4 (2011): 723–749; Wilkins, "What 'Will' Won't Do: Faculty Psychology, Intentionality Analysis, and the Metaphysics of Interiority," *Heythrop Journal* 57, no. 3 (2016): 473–91.

9. *Insight*, 299.

Let me underscore the significance of this shift with a few observations. First, instead of deducing the (nonconscious) potencies in which (conscious) acts are received, we are determining a structure of interrelated levels that are present and interrelated in consciousness. Next, Thomas Aquinas had distinguished the questions *an sit* and *quid sit*, but in each case the question was operated by the light of agent intellect and the act of understanding occurred in the possible intellect. In the context of Lonergan's intentionality analysis, however, the two different types of question are two distinct operators that effect the transition from the first level to the second, and from the second to the third. In the third place, instead of distinct faculties whose relationships remain to be determined, we have a clear and exact determination of the relationship between levels. Each subsequent level presupposes and complements the prior (later he will call this relationship 'sublation').[10] Fourth, whereas the basic terms and relations of faculty psychology are attained by deductive inference, the basic terms and relations of cognitional theory are attained by grasping and verifying a structure given in consciousness. This structure, while completely open, is cognitionally basic (there is no prior structure constitutive of human knowing in the proper sense), self-assembling ("formally dynamic"), and self-regulating.

The implications of this fourth point of contrast merit further consideration. Scientific progress consists of moving from the first-for-us to the first-in-itself. The formulation of basic scientific concepts involves a kind of displacement away from the data. For instance, the basic terms and relations of physical theory are hypothetical formulations that may be verified only inasmuch as testable implications can be worked out.[11]

10. *Insight*, 299.

11. *Insight*, 94–97. There is a clear and helpful discussion of the complexity of this process in Edward MacKinnon, "Understanding According to Bernard J. F. Lonergan, S.J. - Part III," *The Thomist* 28, no. 4 (1964): 475–522, here 488–92. MacKinnon's critique of Lonergan, however, misses the mark. Its premise is that Lonergan "considers the successful laws of physics to be expressions of an intelligibility immanent in reality" (493). But this premise is involved in a vast oversimplification of Lonergan's position on the difficult problem of scientific verification. Lonergan takes verified laws to be approximations to the immanent intelligibility of physical process, converging, however, upon truth as upon a limit (*Insight*, 328; see 324–29). MacKinnon imputes ("Understanding According to Bernard J. F. Lonergan," 495) to Lonergan the Aristotelian ideal of science as certain knowledge through causes on the basis of his appeal to the Aristotelian definition (*certa per causas cognitio*) in his post-*Insight* textbook, *Divinarum Personarum*. But there is such a thing as context, and Lonergan's *Divinarum Personarum*, while certainly an expression of his views in one sense, was also a concession to the pedagogical requirements in the Roman seminary. For a much more

Whereas the general form of deductive inference[12] is

if A, then B; but A; therefore B,

scientific theory proceeds by testing implications predicted by theory, according to the form

if A, then B; but B; therefore, probably A,

where A is a hypothesis and B is some set of testable implications. Such a procedure can never yield certain results, because the testable implications B cannot exclude the possibility of some more satisfactory hypothesis A. Consequently, scientific theory is subject to paradigm shifts in which its basic terms and relations are revised.[13]

Now, like physical theory, a faculty psychology is a scientific theory whose basic terms and relations are not given but deduced. Insofar as scientific concepts name verifiable terms and relations, they are not merely hypothetical. But their systematic significance is not assured, because one cannot exclude apodictically the possibility of another, more satisfactory system of terms and relations that better accounts for the same ranges of data. Just as "any future system of mechanics will have to satisfy the data that are now covered by the notion of mass," so any alternative to faculty psychology must satisfy the data it explained through the concepts of possible and agent intellect, will, and so forth. But, again, just as "it is not necessary that every future system of mechanics will have to satisfy the same data by employing our concept of mass," so too it is not necessary that every alternative to faculty psychology would have to invoke its terms. "Further developments might lead to the introduction of a different set of ultimate concepts, [and] to a consequent reformulation of all law. . . ." Such

---

adequate account of Lonergan's views on this problem, see, for instance, Lonergan, "Aquinas Today." We may note, however, that the point on which MacKinnon assigns his disagreement with Lonergan is precisely whether the progress of scientific understanding is converging upon knowledge of reality (Lonergan) or imposing an intelligibility upon it (MacKinnon). It seems that, for MacKinnon, Lonergan is insufficiently Kantian.

12. *Insight*, 305–6.

13. *Insight*, 357–59.

revision pertains to theoretical concepts, not as verified, but as possessing a fundamental, systematic significance.

> [Theoretical] concepts as concepts are not hypothetical, for they are defined implicitly by empirically established correlations. Nonetheless, [theoretical] concepts as systematically significant, as ultimate or derived, as preferred to other concepts that might be empirically reached, do involve an element of mere supposition. For the selection of certain concepts as ultimate occurs in the work of systematization, and that work is provisional.[14]

A paradigm shift does not invalidate the verified concepts of earlier science (though it may eliminate unverified postulates, like the luminiferous aether), but it may displace them as ultimately significant, as basically explanatory, as fruitful for the progress of scientific understanding.

Although Lonergan seems not to have quite realized it at the time,[15] in *Insight* he was, in fact, effecting just such a paradigm shift with respect to faculty psychology. The shift is effected by the introduction of a new technique, intentionality analysis, and the discovery and verification of a new set of basic terms and relations, cognitional theory. What he quickly realized, however, was that cognitional theory offered a partial immunity to the prospect of a future paradigm shift. In this respect, it not only offers a scientific and normative self-knowledge but also differs from all other scientific constructions. Cognitional theory is properly scientific; that is, it proffers a set of explanatory, not primarily descriptive, terms and relations. Unlike other theory, however, the terms and relations of cognitional theory do not head away from data, from our experience. The equations of thermodynamics are explanatory but only remotely related to the experience of hot and cold and even to measurements of

---

14. *Insight*, 359.

15. See, e.g., Lonergan, "An Interview," 187–88; Lonergan, "*Insight* Revisited," 232; foreword to Tyrrell, *Bernard Lonergan's Philosophy of God*, ix. Lonergan was still reflecting on the precise character of his achievement—what exactly he had got hold of, and how—for years afterwards; see the fascinating discussions in Frederick E. Crowe, "For a Phenomenology of Rational Consciousness," in *Lonergan and the Level of Our Time*, ed. Michael Vertin (Toronto: University of Toronto Press, 2010), 77–101; Frederick E. Crowe, "The Puzzle of the Subject as Subject in Lonergan," in *Lonergan and the Level of Our Time*, ed. Michael Vertin (Toronto: University of Toronto Press, 2010), 155–79.

temperature. The terms and relations of cognitional theory, however, are themselves given in consciousness.

To say they are given in consciousness, it should be emphasized, does not mean that the events occur with labels on them. Like other sciences, cognitional theory faces an initial problem of achieving accurate description, of identifying the salient elements, of moving toward a grasp of explanatory terms and relations. Nevertheless, the successful negotiation of this challenge yields an explanatory structure whose systematic significance is directly experienced, not inferred. The basic terms and relations of that structure name elements given in consciousness itself, so that "explanation on the basis of consciousness can escape entirely the merely supposed, the merely postulated, the merely inferred."[16] Accordingly, cognitional theory enjoys an immunity from fundamental revision that distinguishes it from all other theory.

> What is the source of this peculiarity of cognitional theory? It is that other theory reaches its thing-itself by turning away from the thing as related to us by sense or by consciousness, but cognitional theory reaches its thing-itself by understanding itself and affirming itself as concrete unity in a process that is conscious empirically, intelligently, and rationally.[17]

The basic terms and relations of cognitional theory are not formulated by moving away from the immediate data, but are themselves given, discovered, and verified in the immediate data of consciousness.

Furthermore, not only are the fundamental terms and relations given, but also the unity of consciousness itself is given.[18] Without this unity, the successive, functionally interrelated operations could not coalesce into a single knowing.[19]

> Hence, if there is any judgment of fact, no matter what its content, there also is a concrete unity-identity-whole that

16. *Insight*, 358.
17. *Insight*, 362.
18. *Insight*, 350–52.
19. *Insight*, 349–50.

experiences some given, that inquires, understands, and formulates, that reflects, grasps the unconditioned, and so affirms or denies.

Note this is not the Cartesian 'cogito, ergo sum.' It is not that in thinking I am certain of my existence though I doubt the existence of the world; it is that my involvement with the world is experienced as a process with a concretely given center.

> Finally, such a concrete unity-identity-whole is a thing-itself, for it is defined by an internally related set of operations, and the relations may be experientially validated in the conscious and dynamic states (1) of inquiry leading from the given to insight, (2) of insight leading to formulation, (3) of reflection leading from formulation to grasp of the unconditioned, and (4) of that grasp leading to affirmation or denial.[20]

It is this given unity of consciousness that is the basis for the affirmation of the unity of the subject.[21] The givenness of the terms and relations as fundamental, of the dynamic states defined by the terms and relations, and of the unified consciousness in which they occur together fulfill the conditions for the self-affirmation of the knower.[22]

This represents a highly significant transition from the metaphysical analysis of natural proportion. Both begin from an analysis of acts and objects. But faculty psychology proceeds from conscious acts and objects to the deduction of active and passive potencies that are either not given in consciousness or whose status in consciousness stands in need of radical clarification (e.g., agent intellect). Only in a further step does scientific self-knowledge yield normative self-knowledge. Intentionality analysis, by contrast, proceeds from acts and objects to the identification of functional correlations among the acts and compounding in the objects. Moreover, the identification of functional correlations among conscious operations brings into focus not a set of inferred potencies whose interrelations are to be established through further analysis, but a "succession of

20. *Insight*, 362.
21. *Insight*, 362.
22. See *Triune God: Systematics*, 378, for a particularly clear statement.

enlargements of consciousness, a succession of transformations of what consciousness means,"[23] where (1) the transformations are conscious, (2) they are operated by the functionally correlated conscious operations, and (3) their normative order is itself given in consciousness. This last point means that scientific self-knowledge in the mode of intentionality analysis is also normative self-knowledge; they are not distinct steps as we found in Thomas Aquinas. Finally, metaphysical analysis determines the essence of the soul by following a chain of deductive inference and affirms the unity of nature on the basis of the objective intelligibility of natural proportion. Intentionality analysis, on the other hand, identifies and affirms a given conscious unity and verifies therein the cognitional meaning of a 'thing,' a unity, identity, whole in data. This in no way precludes a subsequent analysis that is metaphysical,[24] but it does mean that the terms and relations determined through metaphysical analysis are derived and not basic, subject to revision in light of the basic and radically unrevisable terms and relations disclosed through intentionality analysis.

Completing the Circle

Insight was finished in 1953, and the subsequent decade saw Lonergan gradually getting hold of the implications of his own project. During this period we see various attempts to state the implications of his view and relate it to the traditional scholastic assumptions. Plainly the cognitional theory of *Insight* reflected a momentous turn in Lonergan's thinking. In effect, it took him out of the orbit of scholastic faculty psychology and displaced the priority accorded metaphysics without, however, diminishing his commitment to metaphysical realism. Lonergan moved into this new territory without explicitly naming it, and it was only later that a name, 'intentionality analysis,' was supplied by his encounter with the phenomenologists in preparation for lectures in 1957, the year of *Insight*'s publication but three years after the manuscript had been completed.[25]

---

23. *Insight*, 636–37.

24. A metaphysical analysis of the development and unity of a human being is subsequently undertaken in *Insight*, 476–504, 538–44.

25. Lonergan, *Phenomenology and Logic*.

Frederick Lawrence suggests that if the Husserlian mode of intentionality analysis is a phenomenology of perception, and the hermeneutical
mode inaugurated by Heidegger and carried forward by Gadamer and
Ricouer is a phenomenology of language and conversation, then Lonergan's mode is basically a phenomenology of inquiry.[26] Now, there are
obvious affinities, insofar as both perception and language are included
in cognitional theory. Yet cognitional theory also transcends the other
approaches. For the phenomenologies of perception and of language,
being is identified as 'what appears,' and insofar as it cannot handle the
problem of judgment, "phenomenology is an inadequate method." But
Lonergan's intentionality analysis does not bog down in the precritical
morass; it brings to light that being is what is attained through correct
judgment; it is able to connect the remote issue of being in the truth,
the truth of existence, with the proximate issue of true judgment,
predicative truth.[27]

Two decades after finishing *Insight*, he would reflect back on the state
of his thinking this way:

> Without the explicit formulations that later were possible,
> metaphysics had ceased to be for me . . . the *Gesamt- und Grund-
> wissenschaft* [total and basic science]. The empirical sciences
> were allowed to work out their basic terms and relations apart
> from any consideration of metaphysics. The basic inquiry was
> cognitional theory and, while I still spoke in terms of a faculty
> psychology, in reality I had moved out of its influence and was
> conducting an intentionality analysis.[28]

Henceforth Lonergan would distinguish the 'total and basic science'
into three elements: cognitional theory, epistemology, and metaphysics.
In his use, cognitional theory means self-knowledge, knowing oneself
as a created participation of uncreated light, *potens omnia fieri et facere*.
Epistemology follows as the grasp of the proportion of the mind to

26. Lawrence, *Fragility of Consciousness*, 1–71; see Lonergan, *Phenomenology and Logic*, 260–65, for
an articulation of some differences.

27. Lonergan, *Phenomenology and Logic*, 277–78.

28. Lonergan, "*Insight* Revisited," 232. The paper was originally given in 1973; he finished
composing *Insight* in 1953, although it was not published until 1957.

reality. Metaphysics, finally, articulates the 'totality' in the basic horizon, "the whole in knowledge but not the whole of knowledge."[29]

The shift is significant. The basic science is cognitional theory. Metaphysics remains a component, the object-pole, of the 'total science.'[30] Empirical sciences are autonomous in the formation of their basic categories. A delayed sector, last in the order of discovery, is the obsolescence of faculty psychology. Gilson's warning is that one who starts in idealism ends in idealism. But Lonergan's starting point is not idealism, for idealism is a philosophic conclusion. Lonergan's first philosophy is 'know thyself.' Its precepts are self-attention, self-discovery, self-knowledge, and self-appropriation.

In the first years following *Insight*, Lonergan was wrestling with the implications of his ideas. On the one hand, he seems to have been gripped by some scholastic uneasiness at 'turning everything upside down,' and there are a few significant and perhaps subtly defensive attempts at clarification as he processed the turn his thought was taking. On the other hand, his theological writings from the Gregorian decade beginning in 1954 furnished him ample space to develop his metaphysical method and, I suspect, deepened his appreciation of the methodological priority of self-appropriation.[31] To call this priority methodological, however, is also to signal that it is not ultimate. Lonergan's transition to cognitional theory as the basis for philosophy does not preclude getting to metaphysics but rather entails it, for an articulation of the structures of inquiry that could not ground an articulation of the structures of being would be a failure. For a phenomenology of inquiry brings to light that it is being, not inquiry, that is ultimate. Hence, Lonergan remarked in his 1957 lectures on phenomenology,

---

29. *Insight*, 416.

30. At the end of a very appreciative review article of the achievement of E. Coreth, Lonergan noted that he could not, however, agree with Coreth on the priority of metaphysics as the total and basic science. The reason is that metaphysics can only be put on a scientific footing by thematizing the performance of inquiry. Lonergan, "Metaphysics as Horizon," 204; see also Frederick Crowe's editorial note l, *Collection*, CWL 4, 299.

31. Also relevant to this story are his writings on theological method during these years. See Lonergan, *Early Works on Method 1*; *Early Works on Theological Method 2*, ed. Robert M. Doran and H. Daniel Monsour, trans. Michael G. Shields, CWL 23 (2013); *Early Works on Theological Method 3*, ed. Robert M. Doran and H. Daniel Monsour, trans. Michael G. Shields, CWL 24 (2013).

Husserl's transcendental reduction to the subject is not ultimate:
the ultimate reduction is of subject and object, scientific world
and world of common sense, to being. The subject *is*, and if he
is, then he is among the beings.[32]

This remark does not represent a position Lonergan later abandoned but
a core element of his philosophy. This commitment was not called into
question by his efforts to get clear the methodical way of proceeding that
would bring the basis for metaphysics to light.

In a 1957 paper to the American Catholic Philosophical Association
(Lonergan was unable to attend and deputed the presentation to Frederick
Crowe), Lonergan situated his procedure in *Insight* within the context of
"the standard Aristotelian and Thomist distinction between what is first
quoad se and what is first *quoad nos*."[33] Aquinas had established knowledge
on metaphysical principles, while in *Insight* Lonergan had established metaphysics on cognitional principles. These represent inverse orderings, so that

the ontological and the cognitional are not incompatible alternatives but interdependent procedures. If one is assigning
ontological causes, one must begin from metaphysics; if one is
assigning cognitional reasons, one must begin from knowledge.
Nor can one assign ontological causes without having cognitional
reasons; nor can there be cognitional reasons without corresponding ontological causes.[34]

This explanation does not, of course, settle the question of methodological priority. Its main purpose seems to be to defend against two
charges: first, that by starting with the *priora quoad nos* Lonergan must
have ineluctably involved himself in some kind of subjectivism, and
second, that he had thereby made shipwreck of Aristotelian and Thomist
principles (a suggestion that may have rankled him, judging from the
extent of his attention to it in this paper).

It would be easy to take Lonergan's remarks about 'interdependent
procedures' as a kind of methodological pragmatism or neutrality. He

32. Lonergan, *Phenomenology and Logic*, 265.
33. Lonergan, "*Insight*: Preface to a Discussion," 143.
34. Ibid., 144.

does not, however, seem neutral about the methodological way forward in this paper. First, he goes on to invoke (though obliquely) the familiar isomorphism in order to generalize the interdependence of ontological and cognitional procedures. The interdependence is not restricted to the special case of knowing the soul, but "is universal from the very nature of rational and objective knowledge."[35] Thus, the ontological *actus essendi* corresponds to the cognitional judgment of existence; the ontological hylemorphism (matter and form) corresponds to the cognitional sense and insight into phantasm.[36] This correspondence, however, is rather complex, as we noted in the last chapter's discussion of the formation of the philosophic concepts of potency and form.

Furthermore, he adds, the development of metaphysics depends on the development of cognition in general and analysis of cognition in particular.

> Not only is there interdependence; it is also true that development must begin from the cognitional reasons. What began with Aristotle was, not form, but knowledge of form. What began with Aquinas was, not existence, but knowledge of existence. In like manner, any genuine development in Aristotelian and Thomist thought, if conducted on Aristotelian and Thomist principles, will originate in a development in man's understanding of the material universe; from a developed understanding of material things it will proceed to a developed understanding of human understanding; and from a developed understanding of human understanding it will reach a clearer or fuller or more methodological account of both cognitional reasons and ontological causes.[37]

This is a rather compressed statement, but I should be inclined to interpret it in line with the program Lonergan sought to realize in *Insight*. That is, a consideration of the natural sciences and their methods formed the basis for a broader inquiry into the dynamics of intelligence, and

35. Ibid.
36. Ibid.
37. Ibid., 144–45 (internal citation omitted).

the dynamics of intelligence in turn grounded a methodological approach to epistemology and metaphysics. It seems clear that what is being developed is not only the content but also the method by which the cognitional and the ontological are investigated and their interdependence articulated.

This interpretation, or at least the underlying instinct to take Lonergan's statement with reference to his program in *Insight*, finds some evidence in the sequel paragraph. There he adds that the purpose of *Insight* was to realize just such a development in a manner that meets the need of the hour. It is

> to know and to implement Aristotelian and Thomist method, to acknowledge in man's developed understanding of the material universe a principle that yields a developed understanding of understanding itself, and to use that developed understanding of human understanding to bring order and light and unity to a totality of disciplines and modes of knowledge that otherwise will remain unrelated, obscure about their foundations, and incapable of being integrated by . . . theology.[38]

Thus, a developed understanding of understanding is Lonergan's basis for the integration and grounding of the disciplines. Lonergan's invocation of the interdependence of cognitional and ontological procedures seems, therefore, not to be a declaration of methodological neutrality but an initial postulate in defense of his program.

A parallel discussion, but to a different kind of audience, occurs in Lonergan's 1958 lectures on *Insight* (subsequently edited and published as *Understanding and Being*). Here, Lonergan defends his decision to begin with cognitional self-appropriation by appealing to the metaphor of a circle to illustrate the interdependence of the cognitional and the ontological. He introduced the question of the 'starting point' in the context of a discussion of the 'problem of objectivity.'

> There is, then, a problem of objectivity, and the problem has different aspects. The first of these is the question of the starting

---

38. Ibid., 145.

point. We began from cognitional process, and we have reached a point where a notion of objectivity has been defined entirely on the basis of a study of cognitional process. As we shall see, we can proceed to a metaphysics of the object in general, of the knower, and of knowing. When we have reached that point, we will be able to give an account of knowing by positing being in terms of our metaphysics, conceiving the knower as a being, reformulating everything that has been said in terms of beings that are known and beings that know. All of the activities can be spoken of in terms of being, potency, form, act. It is just a matter of changing the language. So one may begin from knowing, arrive at objectivity, work out the metaphysics of objects and knowing, and then repeat the whole account of knowing in metaphysical terms.[39]

The notion of 'repetition' may echo something of the inverse conceptual orderings he so admired in Aquinas's treatise on the Trinity. He had shown how Aquinas treated his whole conceptual apparatus first from one side and then from the other, in a kind of analogical extrapolation of the inverse ordering of ontological causes and cognitional reasons.[40] However, Aquinas's twofold conceptual ordering was not methodologically neutral, in that the questions were sequenced according to very definite explanatory principles. Lonergan's remark about completing the circle of cognitional and metaphysical theory therefore raises the question whether what is being asserted is a kind of methodological neutrality or simply an application of the technique of metaphysical equivalence (that is, assigning the appropriate metaphysical denominators for claims about cognitional structure).

Prima facie evidence for the first interpretation is had from Lonergan's express remarks in the continuation: "In principle, it makes no difference

---

39. *Understanding and Being*, 177; "The point is to complete the circle [of cognitional theory and metaphysics]. One way to complete the circle is to begin from knowing. But one can begin with the metaphysics of the object, proceed to the metaphysical structure of the knower and to the metaphysics of knowing, and move on to complement the metaphysics of knowing with the further psychological determinations that can be had from consciousness. From those psychological determinations one can move on to objectivity and arrive at a metaphysics. One will be completing the same circle, except that one will be starting at a different point."

40. See *Verbum*, 213–22.

where one chooses to start. What is important is going around the circle."[41] He goes on to suggest the image of spiraling up and out by iterative circling: "You first do the circle in a small way, and then you do it in a bigger way. First you get the general idea of the whole way around on one [i.e., a basic] level, then you go the whole way round on a higher [i.e., more fully determined] level."[42] Since to work out a rounded philosophical view one has to complete the whole circle and indeed, complete it repeatedly, "the problem of the starting point . . . is not a material problem, a serious problem. What counts is completing the circle correctly. Start where you please, start where it best meets the exigences of your audience."[43] The exigence that settles the starting point is communication.

The interpretation seems straightforward, but it is quickly complicated by scrutiny. In the first place, the parallel with "*Insight*: Preface to a Discussion," given the previous year, composed under more controlled circumstances (i.e., because he knew he would not be able to give the paper in person, he was obliged to write it out in full rather than lecture from notes), and directed to a highly trained professional audience, suggests that the earlier paper ought to govern our reading of *Understanding and Being*. But as we have seen, Lonergan there invoked the interdependence not to rescind but rather to justify his methodological option. These factors suggest we should be cautious about taking Lonergan's remark with full generality. As Frederick Crowe put it, commenting on Lonergan's remark that "in principle, it makes no difference where one chooses to start,"

> it may make no difference 'per se, strictly in principle' (Lonergan's actual words) where we start, but that seems to regard the objective field in which cognitional and ontological are isomorphic; if our 'principles' include the more subjective field of pedagogy, development, and method, then it is clear that for Lonergan it makes a great deal of difference where we start.[44]

---

41. *Understanding and Being*, 178.
42. *Understanding and Being*, 178.
43. *Understanding and Being*, 178.
44. *Understanding and Being*, 417, editor's note j.

My own sense, as I have been suggesting, is that Lonergan had made a definite turn but was still processing its implications at this point. In fact, as I mentioned above, he tells us as much in his twenty-year retrospective, "*Insight* Revisited." The impossibility of generalizing from these statements stands out if we situate them in relation to his earlier and later stages of thought. For instance, it might be observed that Lonergan had not exactly followed his advice to "start with the exigences of your audience" in the composition of *Verbum*. It was not for the sake of his scholastically trained readership but rather because of the matter itself that he eventually decided to begin from the psychological rather than the metaphysical content of the theory. One has to take a rather broad view of the 'exigences' of the audience to justify a communications strategy virtually guaranteed not only to be misunderstood but also to provoke opposition.

On the other side, chronologically and as landmark evidence for the development of Lonergan's thought on this question, there stands "Metaphysics as Horizon," first published in *Gregorianum* in 1963. In his very appreciative essay on Coreth's *Metaphysik*—"a sound and brilliant achievement"[45]—Lonergan is nevertheless prepared to part ways explicitly on the priority of metaphysics.

> I should not equate metaphysics with the total and basic horizon. . . . Metaphysics, as about being, equates with the object pole of that horizon; but metaphysics, as science, does not equate with the subjective pole. . . . In the concrete, the subjective pole is indeed the inquirer, but incarnate, liable to mythic consciousness, in need of a critique that reveals where the counterpositions come from. The incarnate inquirer develops in a development that is social and historical. . . . The critique [of the inquirer], accordingly, has to issue in a transcendental doctrine of methods with the method of metaphysics just one among many and so considered from a total viewpoint.[46]

For Lonergan, what is 'basic' in the basic and total horizon is the subject, and self-knowledge, self-appropriation, and transcendental method are

45. Lonergan, "Metaphysics as Horizon," 204.
46. Ibid.

for him explicitly 'first philosophy.' Metaphysics remains essential as the object-pole, the totality in the total horizon. At the end of the day, metaphysics is the general semantics of "what is and could be rationally," and it is only "the rational subject, having achieved knowledge of what is and could be rationally," that is, the subject who has really taken possession of what *rationally* means, who is existentially prepared for metaphysics.[47]

The critique of the subject is, therefore, decisive. Lonergan had, in fact, made this point emphatically in *Insight*, by proposing that "the polymorphism of human consciousness is the one and only key to philosophy."[48] The plain and scandalous fact is that there are different views on every important philosophical question, starting with whether metaphysics is even possible. Insofar as these differences are oppositions, their ultimate basis is to be found in the way different patterns of consciousness mix and blend together.[49] In particular, there is the permanent tension between our animal sensorium and our intellectual nature. These are not just abstract principles; they pattern our consciousness in various manners, and until one learns to recognize the blending, mixing, and shifting, one is in Plato's cave, not yet qualified to recognize the pure intellectual pattern in which alone one is competent for metaphysics.

> It is not too surprising, then, that the philosophies have been many, contradictory, and disparate. For surprise merely expresses the mistaken assumption that the task of philosophy lies in the observation or utterance of some simple entity by some simple mind. In fact, the mind is polymorphic; it has to master its own manifold before it can determine what utterance is, or what is uttered, or what is the relation between the two; and when it does so, it finds its own complexity at the root of antithetical solutions.[50]

The mind's mastery of its own manifold is a task methodologically prior to metaphysics. It is indeed the first task of philosophy.

47. See *Method* (1972), 14, or CWL 14, 18.

48. *Insight*, 452; on this whole issue, see the penetrating study by Walmsley, *Lonergan on Philosophic Pluralism*.

49. I do not mean to exclude more proximate bases in the way philosophical conversations unfold historically.

50. *Insight*, 411.

It might not be wrong to see here the flowering of Lonergan's understanding of the interdependence of the cognitional and the ontological. Now that interdependence is expressed in terms of a differentiation of 'first philosophy' into a basic subject-pole and a derived object-pole (metaphysics) by way of epistemology. The interdependence of cognitional and ontological means that no investigation of intelligence can prescind from the objects intended, but on the other hand, the integral heuristic structure of the to-be-known cannot be erected without an analysis and critique of the knowing. It is most important to note, however, that metaphysics, in Lonergan's sense, is not an a priori affair (in the Kantian sense) but always keeps a foot in the data, as we will see more fully in chapter 7, below. This is the permanent importance of 'completing the circle': in fact, it has to be completed many times and one does not leave it. It is also important to keep in mind that the problem of the 'starting point' admits of no universal solution. In point of fact, one can only start from where one is, with the insights and questions one has; in this sense, too, the only remedy is to keep completing the circle.

Metaphysics in Practice

It seems to me a closer look at Lonergan's metaphysical practice during these years confirms this interpretation decisively. It also clarifies his method by example and shows the meaning of what he calls 'metaphysical equivalence,' the transposition of statements into ontological categories in order to clarify their exact bearing.[51] Let us begin with his characterization of metaphysical method in *Insight* and then consider three illustrations of metaphysical analysis in practice from his theology.

In *Insight*, Lonergan asserted that cognitional theory is basic and metaphysics is derived. "In any philosophy it is possible to distinguish between its cognitional theory and, on the other hand, its pronouncements on metaphysical, ethical, and theological issues. Let us name the cognitional theory the basis, and the other pronouncements the

---

51. *Insight*, 530–33; see too Jeremy D. Wilkins, "Metaphysics and/in Theology: Lonergan and Doran," *Method: Journal of Lonergan Studies*, n.s., 5, no. 1 (2014): 53–85.

expansion."[52] On the basis of cognitional structure, one is able to deduce ontological structure. Lonergan expresses the deduction formally:

> The major premise is the isomorphism that obtains between the structure of knowing and the structure of the known. If the knowing consists of a related set of acts and the known is the related set of contents of these acts, then the pattern of the relations between the acts is similar in form to the pattern of the relations between the contents of the acts. . . .
>
> The set of primary minor premises consists of a series of affirmations of concrete and recurring structures in the knowing of the self-affirming subject. The simplest of those structures is that every instance of knowing proportionate being consists of a unification of experience, understanding, and judging. It follows from the isomorphism of knowing and known that every instance of known proportionate being is a parallel unification of a content of experience, a content of understanding, and a content of judgment.[53]

These two premises provide an integrating structure. The structure, however, is developed in relation to data, so Lonergan adds that a further set of secondary minor premises are taken from reoriented science and common sense, which provide the materials to be integrated and answer the questions framed by the integrating structure.

In *Insight*, Lonergan defines "explicit metaphysics" as "the conception, affirmation, and implementation of the integral heuristic structure of proportionate being."[54] It is heuristic, "the anticipation of an unknown content," and it is a structure, "an ordered set of heuristic notions."[55] The structure is relational, so it "provides the relations by which unknown contents of [cognitional] acts can be defined heuristically."[56]

52. *Insight*, 412.
53. *Insight*, 424–25.
54. *Insight*, 416.
55. *Insight*, 417.
56. *Insight*, 420.

As conjugate forms are defined by their relations to one another, so central forms are unities differentiated by their conjugate forms; and central and conjugate potency and act stand to central and conjugate forms as experience and judgment stand to understanding. The whole structure is relational: one cannot conceive the terms without the relations nor the relations without the terms. Both terms and relations constitute a basic framework to be filled out, first, by the advance of the sciences, and secondly, by full information on concrete situations.[57]

Metaphysics is a structure because it is a nest of interrelated terms. Terms and relations are not separated so that there is one group of terms and another group of relations. Rather, the relations are the correlations that fix the meaning of the terms. In other words, potency is to form, and act is of form, in such a way that a composite reality is contained under a single definition.

Scholastic metaphysics was a notorious region of insoluble conflicts. Lonergan expected the implementation of method in metaphysics to cut through controversy.

There is much to be gained by employing the method. Aristotelian and Thomist thought has tended to be, down the centuries, a somewhat lonely island in an ocean of controversy. Because of the polymorphism of human consciousness, there are latent in science and common sense not only metaphysics but also the negation of metaphysics; and only the methodical reorientation of science and common sense puts an end, at least in principle, to this permanent source of confusion. Further, without the method it is impossible to assign with exactitude the objectives, the presuppositions, and the procedures of metaphysics. . . . Finally, the misconceptions in which metaphysics thus becomes involved may rob it of its validity and of its capacity for development.[58]

57. *Insight*, 516.
58. *Insight*, 425–26.

The developments of metaphysics Lonergan has in mind could be illustrated by many examples. Besides the significant development represented by Lonergan's method, other obvious instances might be found in his reconstruction of the Aristotelian accident as an explanatory conjugate[59] and his elimination of the Aristotelian categories (predicaments) as descriptive and therefore not basic to metaphysics.[60] There is also his solution to the problem of explanatory genera and species,[61] or his development of the notion of finality and the corresponding genetic method on the basis of the isomorphism of cognitional and ontological process.[62] For an example of theological implementation, readers familiar with the niceties of Trinitarian theory might compare Thomas Aquinas's argument, reducing the four divine relations to three, to Lonergan's treatment of the same question.[63]

It is not realistic here to give a full exposition of Lonergan's metaphysical vision. I would like to turn instead to a few examples of how Lonergan's method informs his use of metaphysical analysis as a technique. The examples are drawn from his theological practice during the Gregorian decade, the decade immediately following the composition of *Insight*. I have three goals in mind here. First, some illustrations of his practice may illuminate Lonergan's assertion that the method is a tool for cutting through metaphysical disputes. Second, it will show us how he conceived the interdependence of the ontological and the cognitional in practice, and thus further contextualize the meaning of his statements and the direction of his thought. Third, it will help us interpret his later statements about the role of metaphysics in the theological paradigm he proposed in *Method in Theology*.

Lonergan's claim, as we have seen, is that method in metaphysics promises to cut through otherwise intractable controversy. In particular, the method will eliminate empty metaphysical terms and relations and confirm valid ones. "The importance of such a critical control will be

---

59. *Insight*, 458–60, 462. Note that Lonergan's 'conjugate' is really and not only nominally different from the Aristotelian 'accident,' notwithstanding certain continuities.

60. *Insight*, 420, 520.

61. *Insight*, 463–67.

62. *Insight*, 470–76, 484–504.

63. Compare *STh* 1 q. 30 a. 1 to *Triune God: Systematics*, 246–54. Aquinas's solution is based on divine simplicity; Lonergan's is based on an analysis of relation as order.

evident to anyone" still "familiar with the vast arid wastes of theological controversy."[64] Our first two examples are instances of eliminating empty terms—the Scotist 'formal distinction on the side of the object' and the Suarezian 'mode.' Our third example will be Lonergan's argument for the real distinction between *esse* and essence.

Lonergan invoked the Scotist '*distinctio formalis a parte rei*' as an illustration of the power of his method in *Insight*.[65] It came up again for more detailed consideration in *De Deo Trino*.[66] In *Insight*, after laying out his method for the derivation of metaphysics from cognitional structure, that is, from the isomorphism of knowing and being,[67] Lonergan introduced, in a chapter called "Metaphysics as Science," a series of questions designed "to test the method and to reveal its power."[68] The first test was the problem of distinction, and it concludes with a note on the Scotist formal distinction.

> The Scotist formal distinction on the side of the object (1) presupposes the counterposition on objectivity, and (2) finds its strongest argument in the field of Trinitarian theory. God the Father is supposed to intuit himself as both God and Father; the object as prior to the intuition cannot exhibit both aspects as completely identical, for otherwise the Son could not be God without being Father. The fundamental answer is, *Ex falso sequitur quodlibet*; and the supposition of the intuition rests on a mistaken cognitional theory.[69]

In other words, Scotus urges a formal distinction between God and Father, Deity and Paternity. The question is whether this distinction is real in God or only in our reasoning about God; and the 'formal distinction on the side of the object' is an effort to straddle the difference, to say that in some way the realities (deity, divine paternity) are really identical, and

---

64. *Method* (1972), 343 or CWL 14, 317.

65. *Insight*, 513–14.

66. *Triune God: Systematics*, 298–304.

67. *Insight*, 424–25.

68. *Insight*, 512.

69. *Insight*, 514 (internal citation omitted).

in some other way they are really different.

As peculiar to Trinitarian theology, the problem is a tad recondite but might be briefly characterized in the following manner. Because God is simple, there is no distinction between the abstract and the concrete, the way we might distinguish between 'humanity' and 'this human being.' God is deity, the Father is paternity, the Son is filiation. Equally, the divine persons are, each of them, really God and not 'parts' of God, so that everything God is, the Father is, the Son is, and the Spirit is. There is, then, no distinction in being between the Father and God, or between the Son and God, or between the Spirit and God. Yet, there is a distinction between the Father and the Son, and so forth. Thus one comes up against the strangeness of saying that paternity is deity, filiation is deity, but paternity is not filiation. And, because God is simple, not composite, and not a genus or class or kind, the strangeness cannot be eliminated by dividing God into parts, or by conceiving the divine persons as participating deity, or some similar solution.

Scotus, accordingly, asks what the Father intuits when he inspects himself. The answer, according to Scotus, is that he intuits both deity and paternity; he likewise intuits that paternity is not filiation, but filiation is deity. Consequently, he intuits that deity and paternity, while really identical in himself, are nevertheless also 'formally distinct,' not only on the side of the knowing but also on the side of the object.

But what, Lonergan asks, does this 'formal distinction on the side of the object' amount to? Any distinction is drawn on the basis of a negative comparative judgment, A is not B. If the judgment means that the reality of A is not the reality of B, the distinction is real. If the judgment means only that our concept of A is not our concept of B, the distinction is notional. Notional distinctions may be further subdivided, based on the reason for the difference in our concepts. If the concepts differ because of some cause in the object—for instance, we may conceive diverse relations on the basis of a multiplicity of terms standing within a single real order—then the distinction is notional but is said to have a basis in the object. But if the cause of the diversity is solely in our way of thinking, then the distinction is merely notional (with no basis in the object).

For instance, we conceive wisdom one way and power another. But we know that in reality, divine wisdom is divine power. Because our concept of wisdom is not the same as our concept of power, we have to think of them differently. But we also know that in the reality of God, they are in fact one and the same. Thus, we distinguish God's power from God's wisdom, and both from God (as God's 'properties'), only notionally, only as a function of our way of thinking about it. But we posit them as really identical in God, even though, not knowing God by his essence in this life, we do not know how they are really identical.

On the other hand, we know that the Father is really not the Son, so divine paternity is really not divine filiation. The distinction is real. Finally, we conceive the Father's relation to the Son one way and his relation to the Spirit another. Thus, our concept of generation is not our concept of spiration. But we know that, in God, generation really is spiration, for the Father, by one and the same real ordering, utters the Word and breathes the Spirit. A multiplicity of really distinct terms does not constitute a diversity of real relations. However, it does provide a basis in the object, for distinguishing, notionally, the order of the Father to the Son, and the order of the Father to the Spirit.[70]

Lonergan, then, acknowledges real distinctions, notional distinctions with a basis in the object, and merely notional distinctions. A distinction with a basis in the object, however, is not the same as Scotus's 'formal distinction.'

> To these there cannot be added a formal distinction on the side of the object, that would formally distinguish, on the side of the object, one as formal from another as formal. For what would 'as formal' mean? Either it means the real or it does not. If it means the real, then the one as real is not the other as real, and there is a real distinction. But if it means the not-real, then one as not real is not the other as not real, and the distinction is not on the side of the object.[71]

Differences are either really in the object or only in the way we conceive the object. There is no third, 'formal' distinction that somehow posits distinct formalities on the side of the object, yet somehow also is not a

---

70. See *Triune God: Systematics*, 246–60, 732–36.
71. *Triune God: Systematics*, 302 (my translation).

real distinction. If the formalities are different in the object, the distinction is real; if they are not different in the object, then the distinction is notional, that is, of reason.

Thus, in the case of deity and divine paternity, (1) our concept of God is not our concept of paternity, (2) we know God is simple, so that whatever is really in God, is God, (3) we know deity is not opposed to paternity, and, therefore, (4) we know deity and divine paternity are not opposed, that is, really distinct, in God. While we do not understand *how* it can be the case that the Father is really identical to God, the Son is really identical to God, and yet the Father is really distinct from the Son, if we accept the revelation of the Trinity we are rationally compelled to grant these statements as true. We cannot affirm the Father to be 'formally distinct' from God 'on the side of the object,' for such an affirmation would be meaningless. Either the Father is God or is not God.

Lonergan's discussion of the Scotist formal distinction, both in *De Deo Trino* and in *Insight*, illustrates both the constructive and the critical aspects of his metaphysical method. Constructively, the validity of real and notional distinctions is elucidated from an analysis of the negative comparative judgment. If the negative comparative judgment bears on the object, the distinction is real. If it bears only on our thinking about the object, the distinction is notional. Critically, the '*distinctio formalis a parte rei*' is eliminated. It is a classic illustration of an empty metaphysical category corresponding to no cognitional intention. It cannot be derived from any meaningful prospective judgment, whether negative (X is not Y: nonidentity) or positive (X is Y: identity).

On Lonergan's analysis, the Scotist position rests on a fundamental error about cognition (inasmuch as it is involved in fundamental error, he calls it a 'counterposition'). Scotus wrongly takes knowledge to be a matter of some kind of confrontation between subject and object, in which this confrontation is achieved by a spiritual inspection or intuition. Thus he imagines the Father beholding in himself the formal nonidentity of paternity and divinity.[72] But, in cognitional fact, there is no spiritual look. Understanding is a matter of identity, not confrontation; the process by which we come to understand is identical to the process by

72. The Scotist formal distinction aims to be a kind of middle road that "acknowledged in one reality [God] formalities [divinity, paternity] that are not identical on the side of the object." *Triune God: Systematics*, 300 (my translation).

which the object comes to be understood. Because in this life there is no identity of finite intelligence with the infinite intelligible, God, our knowledge is analogical and negative. That is, it is a discursive matter of working out analogical concepts on the basis of what we *do* understand (which is not God), relating them to one another, positing them in God, but negating the limits of the way we understand them (e.g., negating that wisdom and power are different realities in God though they are conceived differently).

Clarifying the process of coming to know, then, has a twofold implication for the problem posed by Scotus. On the one hand, the 'spiritual look' is a myth, and once the myth is dispelled, the problem of God looking at himself and beholding some putative difference between deity and paternity vanishes, and so does the concocted solution, the 'formal distinction.' On the other hand, once the reality of understanding by identity comes to light, the real problem, or rather, the real mystery, comes to light with it. We do not understand the infinite intelligible, God, so we do not understand these realities as they are in God, but only as they are in finite being. But though we do not understand God, we do know God through intelligible truths: that God is simple, that paternity is really deity but is not filiation, and so forth. We hold these truths, acknowledging that they are mysterious to us but knowing also that they cannot be mysterious to God, for God *is* the simple understanding that eludes finite intellect.

Scotus is eminently logical; he is separated from Aquinas not by errors (or corrections) of inference but by a divergence of premises. Progress in philosophy will not be a matter of dropping problems into a logic machine. It will not be a matter of working out sounder, clearer definitions for the logic machine to work on. It will fundamentally be a matter of understanding exactly what we are doing so as to find the right principles. And understanding what we are doing rests on understanding ourselves. The Scotist problem can be litigated ad nauseum by logicians; it is an empty category applied to a mystery beyond the domain of proportionate being. What really lays the axe to the root of the tree is knowing in oneself what knowing is (which also helps us understand others, inasmuch as they are prone to the same kinds of basic errors as we). That achievement both eliminates the misleading notion and also indicates where the misleading notion comes from in the first place.

On the substance of the question, Lonergan takes the same position, both metaphysically and theologically, as Aquinas. What is distinctive is his explicit method; I say 'explicit,' because as we have seen, Lonergan found Aquinas to have firmly but not explicitly grounded ontology in cognitional fact. That method is the elucidation of valid metaphysical categories (real and notional distinctions) and the elimination of an empty category (the 'formal distinction') on the basis of cognitional intentionality. In this procedure, intentionality analysis is basic, and metaphysical categories are derived; the derivation cannot methodically proceed in the other direction.

> Not only is there interdependence; it is also true that develop-
> ment must begin from the cognitional reasons. What began with
> Aristotle was, not form, but knowledge of form. What began
> with Aquinas was, not existence, but knowledge of existence. . . .
> From a developed understanding of human understanding [we]
> will reach a clearer or fuller or more methodological account of
> both cognitional reasons and ontological causes.[73]

Lonergan's strategy, then, is a matter of making explicit what was incidentally going forward in the origination of Aristotelian metaphysics.

We may be briefer on our next two illustrations. The second is 'mode,' a Suarezian category invented to explain how the humanity of Christ could be a complete substance (in the Aristotelian sense) yet not be a subsistent distinct from the divine Word. Lonergan rejects 'mode' as another empty category. It does not belong to a critical metaphysics of proportionate being, since it does not correspond to any cognitional element.[74] Nor does it belong to a consideration of supernatural being, since supernatural being is conceived by analogy with proportionate being; if mode is meaningless in the case of proportionate being, it will be just as meaningless when extrapolated analogically.

The heart of his critique exactly illustrates the method of validating metaphysical categories by recourse to cognitional elements.

73. Lonergan, "*Insight*: Preface to a Discussion," 144–45 (internal citation omitted).
74. *Incarnate Word*, 376–79; *Constitution of Christ*, 62–63.

'Mode' is [in reality] nothing other than potency, form, act. . . . The proportionate object [of human knowing] is a quiddity existing in corporeal matter, where corporeal matter is known through experiencing, quiddity is known through understanding, and existence is known through true judging. But the proportion that defines potency and form is the same as the proportion between matter and quiddity, between experiencing and understanding; and the proportion that defines form and act is the same as the proportion between quiddity and existence, between understanding and judging. So, as you will gather, wherever we know by experiencing, understanding, and judging, it is possible to distinguish in the known between potency, form, and act. You will also gather that unless another, fourth essential step should be detected in our knowing, it is impossible to detect another, fourth element—namely, mode—in a proportionate object.[75]

'Mode,' then, is an empty metaphysical term, because it corresponds to no element in intentional consciousness, that is, in cognitional structure. On the other hand, the meanings of the valid terms potency, form, and act are elucidated by the conscious intention from which they are derived. For every valid ontological element, there is a corresponding cognitional element.

This analysis of Suarezian 'mode' runs parallel to the deduction of the metaphysical elements, potency, form, and act in *Insight*. The three components in the known are isomorphic to the three components in the knowing. As the cognitional elements unite into a single knowing, so the metaphysical elements coalesce in a single known. The meaning of each element is elucidated by the conscious intention from which it is derived.

'Potency' denotes the component of proportionate being to be known in fully explanatory knowledge by an intellectually patterned experience of the empirical residue. 'Form' denotes the component of proportionate being to be known . . . by

75. *Incarnate Word*, 377.

understanding [things] fully in their relation to one another. 'Act' denotes the component of proportionate being to be known by uttering the virtually unconditioned yes of reasonable judgment.[76]

The procedure followed in *Insight* to validate the metaphysical elements— the basic set of metaphysical terms and relations—is identical to the procedure followed in *De Verbo Incarnato* to eliminate the Suarezian 'mode.'

Our third and final example of metaphysics in practice is Lonergan's argument for the real distinction of finite essence from contingent *esse*.[77] Lonergan presents his argument for the real distinction in the form of a syllogism. The major premise is that where there are diverse intelligibilities, there are diverse realities. But the intelligibility of finite essence is one thing, and the intelligibility of contingent *esse* another. The simple reason is that contingent *esse* is only extrinsically intelligible, whereas finite essence is intrinsically intelligible.

> Finite essence is intrinsically intelligible; it is what becomes known by understanding. This holds not only for an essence which is identified with form alone [i.e., a separate substance], but also for an essence which is composed of potency and form, since potency is understood in form. On the other hand, contingent *esse* is not intrinsically intelligible, for contingent *esse* does not become known except in judgment; and this *esse* is not [completely] understood until it is reduced to a non-contingent extrinsic cause [God].[78]

Students of Lonergan will recognize in this last sentence an oblique reference to his claim in *Insight* that being is completely intelligible only if God exists.[79] Contingent being is not self-explanatory, and least of all is it explained by understanding finite essence.

Although the argument is somewhat undeveloped in *Constitution of Christ*, its underlying cognitional elements are familiar. There are two

76. *Insight*, 457.

77. For the sake of economy, the present discussion is confined to his treatment in *Constitution of Christ*.

78. *Constitution of Christ*, 52 (my translation).

79. *Insight*, 695–97; see 674–80.

kinds of question, two different acts of understanding, and two corresponding types of inner word. In *Insight* Lonergan distinguished the acts of understanding as direct and reflective. The direct insight grasps a possibly relevant answer to some 'what?' or 'why?' question. ('Why' or 'how' corresponds to form, how or why is this matter a house; 'what' corresponds to essence, a house is a form realized in appropriate matter.) The reflective insight grasps the relative sufficiency of the evidence for a prospective judgment. (Later he succumbed to a need for shorthand and began speaking regularly of 'insight' and 'judgment,' which tends to obscure the fact that a judgment is an inner word intelligibly emanating from a reflective insight grasping the link of a conditioned to its fulfilling conditions.)

The real distinction of finite essence and contingent *esse* is established through the familiar pattern by which any real distinction is verified: X is, Y is, X is not Y. In this case, X is a finite essence, Y is contingent existence, and X is not Y, if the real intelligibility of X is not the real intelligibility of Y. But their intelligibilities cannot be the same, for the first is grasped as the intrinsic intelligibility of some finite being, while the second is grasped by ascertaining the fulfillment of extrinsic conditions that, ultimately, are completely explained only if the formally unconditioned (God) is posited.

Many other examples might be given,[80] but these examples should suffice to indicate the sense in which Lonergan made cognitional self-appropriation methodologically basic and metaphysics methodologically derived. He operated for years in a scholastic context in which metaphysics was assumed as the basic science and provided the basic general categories for systematic theology. He found that as long as there was no more basic science than metaphysics, there also was no methodically effective way to expose vacuous categories and misleading distinctions. His solution was recourse to cognitional self-appropriation. For Lonergan, cognitional theory is the basic (though not, by itself, the total) science because it provides the basis for deriving an epistemology and a metaphysics.

Lonergan explains that "the point to making metaphysical terms and

---

80. A series of metaphysical problems are examined in *Incarnate Word*, 372–413; *Constitution of Christ*, 44–75.

relations not basic but derived is that a critical metaphysics results."[81] The resulting metaphysics are critical, because "for every [metaphysical] term and relation there will exist a corresponding element in intentional consciousness." A critical metaphysics is developed on the basis of the isomorphism of knowing and being, so that every metaphysical term and relation is derived from some element in cognitional structure—the procedure developed in *Insight* and illustrated above.

> In the measure that transcendental method is objectified, there are determined a set of basic terms and relations, namely, the terms that refer to the operations of cognitional process, and the relations that link these operations to one another. Such terms and relations are the substance of cognitional theory. They reveal the ground for epistemology. They are found to be isomorphic with the terms and relations denoting the ontological structure of any reality proportionate to human cognitional process.[82]

The ontological structure of any reality proportionate to human cognitional process pertains to metaphysics. The terms and relations of metaphysics are derived by way of the isomorphism with cognitional structure. Because of the isomorphism, all the terms and relations in a critical metaphysics (the ontological structure of proportionate being) will be grounded in corresponding terms and relations verified in cognitional structure. 'Terms and relations,' both in cognitional structure and in ontological structure, means a basic nest of correlative elements.[83]

One way to understand what Lonergan is doing here is in terms of two transitions, from symbol to metaphysics and from metaphysics to self-appropriation. Symbolic and metaphorical thinking "can draw distinctions, [but] cannot evolve and express an adequate account of

---

81. *Method* (1972), 343, or CWL 14, 317. Fuller exegesis of this contested passage in my "Metaphysics and/in Theology."

82. *Method* (1972), 21, or CWL 14, 23–24; internal references to *Insight*, 412–14; and Lonergan, "Metaphysics as Horizon."

83. The notion of a structure, that is, a set of terms defined by their correlations, is a fundamental and recurrent idea in Lonergan's thought. For instance: "For every basic insight there is a circle of terms and relations, such that the terms fix the relations, the relations fix the terms, and the insight fixes both" (*Insight*, 14); again, ". . . with the relations settled by the terms and the terms settled by the relations" (*Insight*, 417). See too *Early Works on Method 3*, 160–86.

verbal, notional, and real distinctions." The result is a symbolic articulation of the world.[84] Elements that can only remain implicit at this level are later made explicit through a fully metaphysical articulation of the world. The metaphysical articulation, because it is more explicit, offers greater control of the difference between mystery (or myth, in the positive sense) and magic, idolatry, and so forth.[85] Metaphysics sorts out the elements of affect and isolates objective warrants for truth claims. But metaphysics itself is vulnerable to obfuscation, and so a second transition makes the cognitional bases of metaphysical terms and relations themselves explicit. It thereby affords a fuller degree of control, but, because the control by its very nature resides in appropriating in oneself what cannot be adequately objectified, its implementation depends radically upon a certain form of intellectual asceticism. It is vital to note, finally, that this sequence of transpositions from symbol to metaphysics to self-appropriation is not a series of negations but a progression of controls. That progression is not a negation, because it does not eliminate or replace the surplus of meaning and affectivity proper to symbolic articulations. It does, however, resist the derailments that stem from magical thinking.

Clarification by Contrast

According to the conventional wisdom, Lonergan is a 'transcendental Thomist' who, like others of that school, "integrates Kantian epistemology into Aquinas's philosophy."[86] But, according to conventional wisdom, such an integration is impossible. Therefore, Lonergan's project must be a failure. Needless to say, this little bit of conventional wisdom has

84. *Method* (1972), 306, or CWL 14, 285–86.

85. *Method* (1972), 309, or CWL 14, 288.

86. An online philosophy quiz proposes the following associations: "Transcendental Thomism: Integrates Kantian epistemology into Aquinas' philosophy (Bernard Lonergan)." "Philosophy 201 Flashcards | Quizlet," n.d., accessed March 23, 2017. https://quizlet.com/182547159/philosophy-201-flash-cards/. For more conventional sources, see, e.g., Cornelius Ryan Fay, "Fr. Lonergan and the Participation School," *The New Scholasticism* 34, no. 4 (1960): 461–87; O'Connell, "St. Thomas and the Verbum: An Interpretation." The thoughtful discussion in MacKinnon, "Understanding According to Lonergan (III)," shows that these criticisms are both missing the point and basically unsophisticated about the problem Lonergan is dealing with. MacKinnon has criticisms of his own, orders of magnitude more thoughtful than the standard fare presented by the likes of Fay, O'Connell, or Knasas.

hardly encouraged a closer look at a project notorious both for its steep barriers to entry and for its ghettoization. The conventional wisdom is worthless. The concept of a 'transcendental Thomism' sheds no real light on Lonergan's intentions.[87] The suggestion that his intentions somehow include an integration of Aquinas and Kant, or even a fundamental reference to Kant, has nothing to do with reality. In fact, it must be said, the conventional wisdom is worse than worthless because it is not only wrong but actively prevents the corrections that would reveal it to be wrong. Lonergan is not even read because everyone 'already knows' he is a second-rate Kantian. Let me briefly catalog a few representative charges before attempting a general reply.

Lonergan claims that he is not a Kantian, not a Cartesian, not an idealist, but these protestations are widely regarded as wishful thinking. Lonergan, the critics aver, has either dogmatically renounced the conclusions properly contained in his premises, or dogmatically asserted conclusions to which they do not entitle him. So Oliva Blanchette, although thoughtful and not unsympathetic to Lonergan, cannot accredit Lonergan's 'isomorphism' of knowing and being as more than

> a *dogmatic rationalist leap* from the structure of knowing to the structure of the known. Taken in this [i.e., Lonergan's] sense, the so-called transcendental method does not yield a knowledge of the structure of being itself, but only of knowing, as Kant understood very well.[88]

To Blanchette, it seems plain that Lonergan is playing Kant's game and has not succeeded in escaping its logic.

According to William Richardson, on the other hand, the problem is less validity than soundness. That is, it is not that Lonergan does not reach his conclusions but that he is not entitled to his premises. Lonergan knew he needed another premise and flatly asserted it: "When one begins the discussion of being by simply declaring that it is the 'objective of the pure desire to know,' it does not take a very subtle analysis to infer

---

87. *Method* (1972), 13n4, or CWL 14, 17n11.
88. Blanchette, *Philosophy of Being*, 315 (emphasis added).

that being is intelligible."[89] Thus, as Richardson sees it, Lonergan's efforts to ground an ontology on his cognitional theory presume a completely arbitrary premise dressed out as an exigence of reason.

The contemporary face of idealism is 'subjectivism,' and here Lonergan seems directly implicated in error. To John Knasas, for instance, it seems plain that Lonergan selected inherently idealist, Cartesian premises; the tragic denouement is utterly predictable.[90] John O'Callaghan seems to have something like Lonergan's approach in mind when he writes that "for St. Thomas, an account of human knowing that *begins* with introspection is off target. . . . On the contrary . . . beginning with a human being immersed by his or her acts *in* the world, [Aquinas] is interested in getting *into* the soul."[91] Similarly, Mark Shiffman warns of a predilection "to interpret the vocation of reason in terms of elaborating and abiding by necessities dictated by the structure of our own thought, rather than in terms of elucidating the order of what is lovable."[92] Lonergan is not the named object of these strictures, but his project, as it is typically classified, can hardly escape them. That the typical classification of Lonergan is intellectually irresponsible has not made it any easier to dislodge.

To the accusation of arbitrariness, an answer has already been

---

89. Richardson, "Being for Lonergan: A Heideggerian View," 277.

90. See John F. X. Knasas, *The Preface to Thomistic Metaphysics*; Knasas, *Being and Some Twentieth Century Thomists* (New York: Fordham University Press, 2003); Knasas, "Why for Lonergan Knowing Cannot Consist in 'Taking a Look,'" *American Catholic Philosophical Quarterly* 78, no. 1 (2004): 131–50; Jeremy D. Wilkins, "A Dialectic of 'Thomist' Realisms: John Knasas and Bernard Lonergan," *American Catholic Philosophical Quarterly* 78, no. 1 (2004): 107–30.

91. O'Callaghan, *Thomist Realism and the Linguistic Turn*, 227. Unfortunately, it must be said that O'Callaghan does not seem overly familiar with the relevant introspective data, for he also holds that there is no *verbum mentis* as a distinct entity in the mind, verifiable apart from divine revelation. But anyone who has had the experience of forming a judgment on the basis of grasping the sufficiency of the evidence on a question is in possession of sufficient data to verify the distinction between the inner word (assent, in this case) from the act of understanding (the reflective grasp of sufficiency, in this case). See O'Callaghan, "*Verbum Mentis*: Philosophical or Theological Doctrine in Aquinas?," *American Catholic Philosophical Association Proceedings* 74, no. 1 (2001): 103–19; also "More Words on the *Verbum*: A Response to James Doig," *American Catholic Philosophical Quarterly* 77, no. 2 (2003): 257–68 (the meanings of "philosophical" and "theological" are specified at 258).

92. Mark Shiffman, "Response to Sherif Girgis," in *Subjectivity: Ancient and Modern*, ed. R. J. Snell and Steven F. McGuire (Lanham, Md.: Lexington Books, 2016), 89–94, here 93; see Shiffman, "The Eclipse of the Good in the Modern Rights Tradition," *Communio: International Catholic Review* 40, no. 4 (2013): 775–98.

presented in chapter 3.[93] If the arbitrary is the opposite of the reasonable, then they are fundamental alternatives, and Lonergan stands on the side of the reasonable. Either things and events finally have reasons, or finally they do not.[94] If finally they do, being is intelligible; if finally they do not, being is unintelligible, a brute fact without explanation. The assertion of brute facts may be logically coherent, but it is performatively incoherent: there are, by definition, no good reasons to affirm brute facts. If there were good reasons, the facts would not be brute; they would be reasonable. To affirm the complete intelligibility of being, then, far from being arbitrary, is to utterly renounce arbitrariness.

'Idealism' and 'subjectivism' are often supposed to be the inevitable or at least probable outcome of certain suppositions, of starting from the wrong end of things, or of letting subjectivity take the lead. It is not altogether clear why this should be. The purveyors of this concern assure us that knowledge is objective. From this it is plain that the knowing subject is not inherently a windowless monad; indeed, the subject is involved with the world from the outset. Yet somehow a philosophic mediation of subjectivity, far from bringing objectivity to light, is supposed to occlude it.

It is possible that such anxieties are underwritten by some reluctance to acknowledge the fragilities inherent in the process of coming to understand correctly. Correct understanding is difficult to achieve and difficult to verify, while a good hard look at the facts seems simplicity itself. As Lonergan admitted, "If you frankly acknowledge that intellect is intelligence, you discover that you have terrific problems in epistemology."[95] Given the prominence of sensation in our flow of experience, it seems easier, simpler, and irrefragably more straightforward to describe our apprehension of being as an 'intuition' on the model of simple perception.[96] This 'intuition' of being seems to me really an imprecise and

93. See above, pp. 81–93.

94. There are further distinctions to be made, of course, about the formal element of formal sin, as noted in chapter 3.

95. *Understanding and Being*, 19.

96. For instance: ". . . the pattern of all true knowledge is the intuition of the thing that I see, and that sheds its light upon me." Jacques Maritain, *Existence and the Existent*, trans. Lewis Galantiere and Gerald Phelan, Image Books ed. (New York: Image, 1956), 21. The author refers to Thomas Aquinas on the necessity of sense data for insight and for a resolution to evidence supplied by the senses for judgment, but he completely misconstrues the indispensability of sense to mean sense

frankly simplistic conflation of the mystery of wonder with the extraversion of sense. What is most obvious in knowing—taking a good look—is mistaken for what knowing obviously is. As the basis for an epistemology, such a solution could seem attractive only on a certain construal of the problem of objective knowledge. That construal assumes there is need of a 'bridge' from the prisoner 'in here' to the world 'out there.'

The problem of the 'bridge' in its modern form is generally associated with Descartes. For Descartes, the world divides into the *res cogitans* and the *res extensae*, the thoughts 'in here' and the bodies 'out there.' It follows that the problem of objective knowledge is getting from in here to the world out there, of erecting a bridge between the thoughts and the things. This bridge might be the senses, if they are truthful. The senses, however, present bodies, not thoughts. For Descartes, only the affirmation of a benevolent God could assure the possibility of objective knowledge of the sensible world: he has to know God to be certain of the world.

For Kant, our minds are immediately related to objects only through *Anschauung*, intuition. This intuition is sensitive, and accordingly everything beyond the content of the sensitive intuition—which is to say, all the categories of understanding, the regulative ideals of reason, and interior experience—is supplied by the mind. They are related to objects only by way of sensitive intuitions. Kant thus accepts the criterium of sensitive extroversion as the standard for objective knowing; accordingly, all we know 'objectively' are phenomena of sensitive experience.[97] In this paradigm, 'object' means 'out there,' and 'subject' means 'in here.' The subject as conscious is not the object of sensitive intuition and, therefore, cannot be known objectively.[98] Empiricism and positivism more or less accept this dichotomy intact. Many forms of post-Kantian phenomenology and existentialism attempt to compensate through attention to

---

is the pattern of true knowing. As Aquinas rather explicitly asserts, the proper act of intelligence, perfectly demonstrating its power, is not sense but *intelligere*, understanding. If one does not get an exact grip on what understanding is, there is no possibility of interpreting Aquinas's doctrine of cognition adequately.

97. Lonergan, "Metaphysics as Horizon," 193–94; "The Subject," 67–68; "Natural Knowledge of God," 103–5; See Sala, *Lonergan and Kant*, 41–80, esp. 45–49.

98. Lawrence, *Fragility of Consciousness*, 233–37.

the nonobjectifiable subject but without breaking from the fundamental influence of this paradigm.

For Lonergan, however, 'subject' and 'object' do not mean 'in here' and 'out there.' An object is what is intended in questions and becomes known by answering them. Questioning is not sensitive extraversion, and its objectivity is not restricted to the contents of sensitive intuition. It regards not what is 'out there' but what is: being. Thus, in questions the intention of being is immediate. Answers are not free-floating intuitions or a priori categories but responses to questions. They refer to being via the questions to which they respond, so that one has to figure out the question to understand the answer. In other words, Lonergan simply never accepted the Cartesian or Kantian construal of the problem of knowledge as a 'bridge' problem. He did not consider that the animal sensorium should provide the criterium for objective knowing. The critics who accuse him of Kantianism not only miss the point entirely but also reveal their own failure to transcend Kantian suppositions.[99]

Lonergan let himself in for comparisons to Kant by speaking of a 'critical program' and distinguishing his position as a 'critical realism.'[100] For obvious etymological and historical reasons, his 'cognitional theory' suggests a connection to Kant's program of *Erkenntnistheorie*. Kant, too, announced an intention to dethrone metaphysics and begin with 'self-knowledge.' In that game, Kant is the house and the house always wins. Thus, Lonergan's announcement of cognitional theory as first, or, as he puts it, the 'basic' element in the 'basic and total science,' is frequently taken as tantamount to a declaration of his idealism and, probably, moral relativism.[101]

The comparisons are misleading, however, because what Lonergan means by 'cognitional theory' is an exercise entirely distinct from an epistemology, a critique of reason and its limits, or an inquiry into the conditions of the possibility of knowledge. Epistemology addresses a question about the proportion of the knower to the known, or, to put it differently, about the proportion of the operations of knowing to the

---

99. Lonergan, "Metaphysics as Horizon."

100. The fundamental differences between Lonergan and Kant have been expounded perspicaciously in Sala, *Lonergan and Kant.*

101. See, for instance, our discussion of Finnis and Rowland in chapter 1.

objects they attain. The question of epistemology can be properly asked only because we do in fact know. It can be properly answered only if we bring to light the structure of this fact. It turns out that any epistemology must assume this at least tacitly, otherwise it could not be, or could not present itself as, a correct account of the status of knowledge. If, hypothetically, we did not have objective knowledge, then, *ex hypothesi*, we could not objectively know that; we could not successfully interrogate our knowledge with the questions of epistemology. So, the exercise of any epistemological inquiry has to presuppose, at least tacitly, that we can answer questions and that answering them correctly is knowing.

Kant announces his intention to begin not with the concrete knowing subject but with a consideration of the possibility of various kinds of inquiry. His consideration is abstract from the beginning. Hence, in Lonergan's judgment, Kant never did get to 'pure reason.' What he achieved was the critique of an abstraction, "the human mind as conceived by Scotus."[102] Lonergan is not interested in an abstract consideration of the intellect, or of reason, or of knowledge. He simply invites us to ask some very elementary questions—about the roundness of a cartwheel, to begin—and attend to what is going on. The 'first' in his philosophy is: first, pay attention to what you are doing when you are asking and answering questions. Pay attention to how it works; pay attention to how you might do it better. Lonergan does not start with a question about whether we know, or a question regarding the possibility of knowing. The fact of inquiry is not declared as a condition for the analysis; it is simply adverted to. By simple attention to the facts of inquiry, of the humble process of asking and answering questions, we bring to light the structure of the fact, the pattern of operations involved in asking and answering questions.

Every intentional operation attains an object, since an object is simply correlative to an intentional operation. Not every operation validates the status of its object, however; this validation is what judgment adds to the operations on the levels of sense and understanding and, in a different sense, what epistemology adds to cognitional theory. It is only after the structure of inquiry becomes the object of explicit self-knowledge that we are in a position to investigate how that structure is proportioned

102. *Verbum*, 39.

to its objects, or, in other words, why posing questions and correctly answering them is properly human knowing.

The subject that comes to light through Lonergan's first philosophy, then, is not an immanent monad struggling to get out. It is the self-transcending subject who is already related to the world not only through its sensorium but, far more importantly, through its questions (and consequently, through the answers that respond to them). Lonergan's cognitional theory is not *Erkenntnistheorie*, epistemology. It is about the performance of knowing, not the justification of knowledge. It is theory, in the precise sense that its terms and relations are explanatory, but it is not theory in the sense of moving away from phenomena, because its terms and relations are uniquely given in consciousness.

There is, then, a great difference between what Lonergan means by 'object' and the Kantian meaning, and a similarly great difference between Lonergan's project of cognitional theory and Kantian *Erkenntnistheorie*. Kant was not Lonergan's secret muse; he was not even his preoccupation. Kant was, as Lonergan put it, "an afterthought" whose presuppositions are totally different from his own.[103] The only way Lonergan can be considered a Kantian is by unthinking acceptance of conventional wisdom or an indifference to basic philosophical differences.

Kant may have been an afterthought, but as Jeffrey Allen has lately pointed out, the parallels between Lonergan and Descartes seem undeniable.[104] It was Descartes, after all, who initiated the modern philosophic turn to the subject, and Lonergan is a paying customer in good standing. Undoubtedly, there are similarities. Both loved mathematics and prized the ideal of clarity it represented. Both sought a methodical regrounding of philosophy by way of transformative exercises conducted in an experiment of consciousness that, by the nature of the case, could only be private. Both were attentive to the data of consciousness, critical of imagination's sway over intelligence, insistent in differentiating intelligence from sense. There is more than similarity, for Descartes is praised (and blamed) in *Insight*. Lonergan calls the act of insight the source of Descartes's 'clear and distinct ideas' and, lauding Descartes's insistence on starting with very small things, commences *Insight* with an illustration

103. "Kant for me was an afterthought." *Caring about Meaning*, 10.

104. See Allen, "Ignatius, Descartes, Lonergan."

of insight from geometry. He affirms the Cartesian *cogito ergo sum* as philosophically sound and compliments Descartes himself as a thinker profoundly original and of lasting importance.[105]

On the other hand, the relevant and precise question is not whether there are similarities or even whether there is an influence. The relevant and precise question regards the nature of the similarity, the character of the influence, the relation of the two philosophies. If what we have said above is correct, Kant and Descartes take for granted a primordial dualism of subject and object, which Lonergan shows does not in fact bear scrutiny. In that sense, then, the paradigm in which Descartes is operating is worlds apart from Lonergan's. For Descartes, there is a self-enclosed thinking thing doubting there is a world and looking for a reliable bridge. His turn to the subject is philosophically sound, but it is not yet a recovery of the subject as subject. It is an intuition of the indubitable, clear, distinct idea of an object, the *res cogitans*. What the Cartesian turn arrives at, it seems, is an intuition of the subject as object.[106] Lonergan's turn is not to the subject as object, as intuited. It is to the subject as subject, as inquirer and lover, open to the world in fact as *potens omnia fieri*, open in fragile achievement, open in unmerited giftedness.

The selection of a philosophic method is coincident with philosophic results.[107] The Cartesian method is universal doubt. It begins by bracketing our knowledge of the world independent of ourselves. Lonergan, on the other hand, does not bracket the world. As he points out, at the very head of his introduction to *Insight*, his "question is not whether knowledge exists but what precisely is its nature,"[108] that is, what are the activities of knowing. Lonergan holds universal doubt more foolish even than unquestioning acceptance of all propositions, for why should we not doubt the wisdom of universal doubt?[109] Nevertheless, he did admire Descartes:

> The implications of that precept [methodic doubt] fail to reveal the profound originality and enduring significance of Descartes,

105. See ibid., 18.

106. Lawrence, *Fragility of Consciousness*, 233–37, 245.

107. *Insight*, 448–55.

108. *Insight*, 11.

109. *Insight*, 435; see 433–36.

for whom universal doubt was not a school of scepticism but a philosophic program that aimed to embrace the universe, to assign a clear and precise reason for everything, to exclude the influence of unacknowledged presuppositions. For that program we have only praise, but we also believe that it should be disassociated from the method of universal doubt.[110]

The program for which Lonergan has only praise is not universal doubt, but the scrutiny of one's presuppositions, the assignment of clear and precise reasons, the embrace of the universe. Lonergan wished to scrutinize presuppositions, but he did not consider a presuppositionless inquiry possible or even desirable. Indeed, he agreed with John Henry Newman that it would be better to believe everything and let the truth gradually drive out the errors.[111]

Lonergan did not share Descartes's concern for certitude and did not consider the clarity and distinctness of ideas proof of their truth. For him, to know truth, we have to get things right, not just clear. We know we have them right through the virtually unconditioned of rational judgment, that is, sufficient evidence understood to be sufficient. For Descartes, it seems, there is a fundamental problem getting from 'in here' to the world 'out there' and only the postulate of an undeceiving God assures a reliable bridge. For Lonergan, on the other hand, this whole problem results from a mistaken juxtaposition of sensitive extraversion with intellectual self-transcendence. Descartes doubts the veracity of sense to attack the basis of his prior, unexamined certitude. The assumption that Lonergan

110. *Insight*, 436.

111. *Method* (1972), 223–24, or CWL 14, 210–11. "It was Newman who remarked, apropos of Descartes' methodic doubt, that it would be better to believe everything than to doubt everything. For universal doubt leaves one with no basis for advance, while universal belief may contain some truth that in time may gradually drive out the errors. In somewhat similar vein, I think, we must be content to allow historians to be educated, socialized, acculturated, historical beings, even though this will involve them in some error. We must allow them to write their histories in the light of all they happen to know or think they know and of all they inadvertently take for granted: they cannot do otherwise. . . . But we need not proclaim that they are writing presuppositionless history, when that is something no one can do. We have to recognize that the admission of history written in the light of preconceived ideas may result in different notions of history, different methods of historical investigation, incompatible standpoints, and irreconcilable histories. Finally, we have to seek methods that will help historians from the start to avoid incoherent assumptions and procedures, and we have to develop further methods that will serve to iron out differences once incompatible histories have been written."

somehow shared this doubt has led some to reassert, 'against Lonergan,' the reliability of sense perception.[112] But the assumption is just the mistake of an unwitting Cartesian. Lonergan's program does not originate with any doubt about the veracity of sense. It originates with a question about the structure of inquiry and learning. To suppose one could ask Lonergan's question only if one doubted the veracity of sense is already to have missed the point.[113]

Both Lonergan and Descartes propose an experiment that by its nature must somehow be private. Neither was a solipsist. But Descartes's exercise is private in a manner that might easily slide into solipsism; he asks how he could be certain there is anyone besides himself, and only the postulation of a benevolent God secures for him the existence of a universe. Lonergan's exercise, too, is private, but it is not solitary, because its focus is on the dynamics of question and answer, which relate us to the world, to others. From the beginning he is interested in how we collaborate in the achievement of understanding. He does not speak of the speculative intellect of the individual scientist, but rather he examines the procedures of inquiry and verification practiced by a scientific community. He does not speak of practical intellect but of the structure of a common sense established by a field of common and complementary experience, a common and complementary stock of insights, a community of conviction and commitment.

Descartes's God, although a conclusion, perhaps, from nontrivial principles, is self-evident to the one who grasps those principles (known per se to the wise, as Boethius might say). Knowledge of God, for him, is prior to his attainment of the external world. Lonergan, however, regards every form of the ontological argument, including Descartes's, as fallacious.[114] Lonergan does not postulate God to secure a world independent of his own mind. On the contrary, for Lonergan, the question of God is raised by the zeal of wonder regarding the splendor of a contingent order of being. It is raised by the joy of love in search of rest in the holy of holies. It is also raised by the facts of

---

112. See Knasas, *The Preface to Thomistic Metaphysics*.

113. See Wilkins, "A Dialectic of 'Thomist' Realisms."

114. See *Insight*, 692–99.

evil and decline.[115] Where Descartes postulates God to recover the world he has bracketed, Lonergan comes to God through the world of God's good creation, the love of God's self-donation, and the recoil of conscience from sin and evil.

Finally, it is suggested that Lonergan's foundational judgment, 'I am a knower,' runs parallel to Descartes's 'I am a thinking thing.'[116] There are, however, good reasons to doubt that this parallel is more than a mirage. In the first place, the Cartesian 'thinking thing' is affirmed in contradistinction to external bodies, 'extended things.' Far from clarifying the difference between the extroversion of animal sensorium and the self-transcendence of attentive observation, intelligent grasp, and rational affirmation, it simply transposes the polymorphic tension of human consciousness (as rational and animal) into a pair of coordinates that, de facto, are spatial: 'in here' and 'out there.' Furthermore, what methodic doubt yields is only the indubitability of empirical self-presence. It cannot proceed from there to scientific self-knowledge. "One can argue that before I can doubt, I must exist, but what does the conclusion mean? What is the 'I'? What is existing? What is the meaning of affirming?"[117] To these questions, one may give factually correct answers, but they do not emerge from the method of universal doubt, for rigorous application of its precept makes correct answers impossible. Universal doubt prevents analysis of the tension between sensitive extroversion on the one hand and the criteria of inquiry on the other. In the end, the Cartesian *cogito* is not an affirmation of the reasoned fact. It is just the declaration of an empirical given.

Lonergan's self-affirmation of the knower, however, is an achievement of scientific and normative self-knowledge. It requires that what is given in consciousness also be understood. It requires that what is understood be rationally affirmed. It is not accidental that the *cogito* is the first deliverance of universal doubt while the self-affirmation of the knower follows upon a long and arduous investigation of cognitional process in mathematics, natural science, and common sense.[118] Through such inves-

115. See *Method* (1972), 101–3, or CWL 14, 96–99; compare *Insight*, 709–10.

116. Allen, "Ignatius, Descartes, Lonergan," 23–24.

117. *Insight*, 434–35.

118. *Pace* Allen, who suggests that the appearance of the *cogito* only in the second meditation is comparable to the judgment of self-affirmation that occurs in chapter 11 of *Insight*. This is a

tigation, one identifies the elements in the structure of knowing to verify their occurrence, as structured, in one's own experience. Again, knowledge of the *cogito* is the affirmation of an empirical fact: I exist. Lonergan's self-affirmation of the knower, on the other hand, while factual, is not the affirmation that I exist but that I am a knower. It is the affirmation of a contingent structure of consciousness. It is not a transcendental deduction of what can only be the case; it is not the observation of an empirical given; it affirms a discovery of what happens to be the case.[119] It is true this affirmation is buttressed by a cruel retorsion the honest inquirer cannot escape. Still, the retorsion is a device for advertence to facts about knowing, not the fact that the thinking subject exists by a necessity of supposition.[120] The self-affirmation of the knower is scientific and normative self-knowledge, not the mere objectification of empirical self-awareness.

How Lonergan's turn to the subject differs from Kant's or Descartes's should not be such a mystery when he himself articulated the differences very adequately. To make it a mystery or to assume it cannot really be different is simply to beg the question of whether there is any other form a turn to the subject might take.

Conclusion

The hypothesis of this chapter is a development in Lonergan's thought on 'first philosophy.' He was raised on the scholastic assumption of metaphysics as first philosophy. In *Verbum* he made an initial break by expounding the psychology of Aquinas before the metaphysics. *Insight* marks a fundamental shift toward self-appropriation as the basic task of philosophy and self-knowledge as its basic science. The subsequent decade witnessed a series of attempts to relate his procedure to the tradition he had inherited and to implement the method he had devised. By

---

misleading comparison. Descartes explains in the fourth section of his *Discourse on Method* that the discovery of the *cogito* was immediate from the application of the method. But what Lonergan means by self-appropriation, so far from following immediately from the first exercise, responds to a question that cannot even be properly formulated at that stage. See Allen, "Ignatius, Descartes, Lonergan," 23–24.

119. *Insight*, 343–44.

120. *Insight*, 353–57.

the mid-1960s, the shift had effected a fundamental transformation, first in Lonergan's thinking about philosophy and then, as we will consider in the next chapter, in his thinking about theology.

In working out this hypothesis, I have also sought to clarify the meaning and implications of Lonergan's turn in order to dispel mistaken assumptions about what a turn to the subject can or 'must' entail. I have in mind two different kinds of critique or skepticism regarding where Lonergan's turn to the subject is coming from and where it is going. On the one side, there is the suspicion that his program of self-knowledge must originate in some kind of covert obeisance to Kantian criticism or Cartesian doubt, a suspicion that, in certain Catholic circles, amounts to guilt by association. On the other, it is supposed to involve him in the bog of subjectivism, unable to ground an epistemology, ontology, or ethics. These criticisms are not always connected explicitly, but they share a concern about the viability of a philosophical program that takes its stand on self-knowledge.

As I have argued, Lonergan's displacement of metaphysics as 'first' in philosophy was part of a larger reorientation of philosophy. Mistaken assumptions about what Lonergan is up to thrive when this larger reorientation is either missed or misconstrued so that 'first' is taken equivocally. Philosophy is an interrogation of first principles. It originated in the discovery that the antiquity and propinquity of 'our way' was no sure index of its rightness. But because they took it that the right way to live is the way in accord with the order of being, in order to answer their most practical of questions—how to live well—the philosophers were obliged to articulate the order of being.[121] It came to be that in a hierarchical arrangement of the sciences, metaphysics (the 'divine science') was first because it articulated the principles first in themselves, because by doing so it provided the architecture for all the sciences, and because its subject was noblest in itself. The scholastics had only to affirm the queenship of theology to crown the hierarchy.

At first blush, then, Lonergan's 'inversion' seems no more than a passage from the first-in-itself to the first-for-us. On this assumption, cognitional theory articulates no more than what is first-for-us, which

---

121. I say 'they took it' because, as I suggested in chapter 3, one of the distinctive features about the contemporary situation is its sense that 'nature,' i.e., the order of being, is not normative for us.

cannot be the architecture of being unless one is an idealist, and which cannot be noblest and best unless our freedom is an end in itself. Perhaps one might be tempted to say that Lonergan means no more than a pedagogical first, just as pedagogical priority was assigned to Aristotle's logical works (the 'Organon'). While this would not be wildly wrong, it does not quite get the point, either. The logical works investigate the nature and types of inference, but insight is prior to logical inference, for a valid syllogism is sound only if its premises are sound, and originally the premises are grasped in insight. Wisdom and understanding are problems prior to logic.[122] The real heart of Lonergan's interest is no system of inference but a personal discovery of the event and significance of insight. It would be to miss his point entirely to take him for clarifying rules of thought; intelligence is not the rule but the principle of all rules.

Lonergan's first philosophy is an interrogation of inquiry as such, and its basic task is to disclose the fundamental structures of inquiry. Its secondary tasks include articulating the proportion of these structures to their objects (epistemology), and working out a generalized heuristic, that is, anticipatory structure of the contents to be known (metaphysics). Cognitional theory, or, really, the practice of self-appropriation, is first in relation to an ordering of inquiry rather than an ordering of topics, fields, objects, or scientific subjects in the Aristotelian sense. Its priority is not temporal, but methodological. It is an ordering of activities rather than an ordering of contents. It does include a general ordering of contents—a metaphysics—but only by heuristic anticipation. By anticipating and relating the contents to be known through inquiry, metaphysics is also a structure for interrelating methods of inquiry. If the activities of intelligence are the characteristic activity of human beings as human, then self-appropriation also yields a fundamental anthropology.

---

122. Aristotle adverts to them in speaking, with notorious density, of the foundational *nous* (*Posterior Analytics* II.9). I find helpful the discussion in Byrne, *Analysis and Science in Aristotle*, 170–79.

CHAPTER SIX

Foundational Methodology and Theology

Since method is simply reason's explicit consciousness of the norms of its own procedures, the illumination of reason by faith implies an illumination of method by faith.[1]

BERNARD LONERGAN

T HOMAS JOSEPH WHITE illustrates the contemporary problem of theological wisdom by contrasting the historicism of Chenu with the anachronism of Garrigou-Lagrange. Chenu, as White reads him, tends toward a kind of historicism, the reduction of doctrine and faith to the expression of a spiritual experience so defined by its context as to have seemingly little transhistorical and transcultural relevance. Garrigou-Lagrange, by contrast, gives us an indistinguishable fusion of different epochs and strata of material, historical complexity unacknowledged and unexplained, "both idiosyncratic and methodologically arbitrary."[2] What is needed, White urges, is a theological wisdom able to deal with both the historical contingencies of the tradition and its permanent truth claims.

What White is after was also Lonergan's lifelong aim: to search out a new paradigm of Christian wisdom. Scholastic theology assumed the truths of faith as its first principles.[3] Doctrines, however, respond to

1. Lonergan, "Theology and Understanding," 129.

2. Thomas Joseph White, "The Precarity of Wisdom," in *Ressourcement Thomism: Sacred Doctrine, the Sacraments, and the Moral Life. Essays in Honor of Romanus Cessario, O.P.* (Washington, D.C.: The Catholic University of America Press, 2010), 92–123, here 93–97, quote at 96.

3. See Lonergan, "Theology and Understanding"; on declarative and deductive modes of scholastic

questions, and the questions have a contingent, fragile history. To believe the Gospel is to yield to mystery. But the mystery is known through statements, and the statements have a history. As theologians, we are called to give an account of this history. Theological wisdom, then, is not only concerned with discerning order in the contents of faith. It is also concerned with discerning order in the history of expressions of the faith. The ongoing development of new hermeneutical and historical techniques has brought about the fragmentation of theology into specialized and often mutually incomprehensible discourses with few common questions and no overarching conceptuality. The reconciliation of all theological claims and contents seems farther out of reach than ever. The way forward, Lonergan proposed, is a unification on the side of theological operations, an overarching framework for relating and ordering the activities of an ongoing, collaborative theology.

Rather than ask what theology knows—what its 'subject' or formal object is—Lonergan's question regards theology as an activity. That activity is an ongoing and collaborative process at the service of a church that itself is an ongoing, historically realized community. This ongoing process is cumulative and progressive, carrying forward past achievement as it develops.[4] But every theoretical integration, no matter how valid, is subject to future transformation as a science develops, and therefore cannot of itself be the basis for controlling the developmental process— even though genuine progress carries valid achievement forward. Theologians, then, must attend to ourselves and our doctrine (1 Tm 4:16). We must give an account of how a divine revelation, beyond the reach of human discovery and beyond the proportion of human reason, can make progress in the church. If we are to do so self-reflectively, we must also give some account and ordering of the forms of theological inquiry itself.

In Lonergan's opinion, paradigm shifts in natural science and historical knowledge call for a corresponding transition in theology. Lonergan distinguished three main paradigm shifts in the history of theology. The

---

theology, see Stephen F. Brown, "The Theological Role of the Fathers in Aquinas's *Super Evangelium S. Ioannis Lectura*," in *Reading John with St. Thomas Aquinas: Theological Exegesis and Speculative Theology*, ed. Michael Dauphinais and Matthew Levering (Washington, D.C.: The Catholic University of America Press, 2005), 9–22; see also Charles C. Hefling Jr., *Why Doctrines?*, 2nd ed. (Chestnut Hill, Mass.: Lonergan Institute at Boston College, 2000), 61–83.

4. See *Method* (1972), 320–24, 351–53, or CWL 14, 298–301, 324–26.

first was from the largely narrative and symbolic context of the New Testament to the propositional context of the classical dogmas. The second was from the classical context to the theology of the medieval schools. Scholastic theology was based on an explicit metaphysics and aimed for a permanent theoretical integration. The third, he envisioned, would be to a theological mode he called 'methodical,' for reasons I will explain in due course. The methodical style is appropriate to a theology that is historically self-aware, a theology that does not expect a permanent theoretical integration but nevertheless recognizes other grounds of continuity and permanance. Such grounds include the mysteries of faith, the reality of reason illumined by faith, and the existence of genuine and permanently valid intellectual achievement.

Lonergan's approach to the large problem of historicity and permanence was to break it down into a series of smaller and manageable problems. Accordingly, he distinguished theological activities into eight interrelated functions, each with its own proper methods. For Lonergan, this eightfold structure was not a merely possible ordering of theological activities (or the forms of theological inquiry) but an articulation, as Frederick Lawrence has put it, of "the ontological structure of the hermeneutic circle."[5] Method, in Lonergan's sense, is not about rules. It is about knowing what one is about, knowing how to go about it, and knowing how it relates to what others are about.

In subsequent chapters I will illustrate something of the genesis and implications of Lonergan's method by examining cases from his theological practice. The goal of the present chapter is to grasp the material significance of functional specialties in theology. To appreciate what he is up to, first we have to understand how he came to think of theology in terms of its activities and method, rather than defining it by its subject (in the Aristotelian sense) or formal object. That introduces us to the problem of theology as a science that, like other sciences, is subject to paradigm shifts in which its fundamental conceptuality may be reorganized; this is the topic of our second section. To Lonergan, this liability to reorganization meant that the unity of theology over time cannot reside in an overarching theoretical synthesis, even though the mysteries are permanent and there are other permanently valid achievements.

5. Lawrence, *Fragility of Consciousness*, xii.

Theology is fundamentally unified in the activities of reason illumined by faith and motivated by love. To this we turn in our third section. A fourth section, then, outlines the material meaning of Lonergan's proposal for functional specialties in theology. The fifth section considers a few ulterior implications of this proposal, and a sixth, finally, relates Lonergan's method to the differentiations achieved by Thomas Aquinas.

The Notion of Developing Sciences

Aquinas conceived theology as a science and, indeed, the queen of the sciences. In accord with the paradigm set forth by Aristotle in the *Posterior Analytics*, Aquinas conceived of science as knowledge of causes where, ideally, the knowledge is certain and the causes are necessary. Sciences were distinguished by what they know, their formal objects, the subjects of their predications. For his part, Lonergan never abandoned the idea that theology was the science of a reality. Nevertheless, in *Method*, he defined theology heuristically as reflection on religion and a mediation between religion and culture. That is, he thought of theology in terms of what theology *does* rather than in terms of what theology *knows*. It seems to me there are two main reasons for this. One is practical. By thinking of theology in terms of what it does, one is led to focus on the practical problem of doing that better. This cannot mean, of course, that one forgets the goal to concentrate on means. On the contrary, as Lonergan insisted, unless the goal is clearly conceived, one cannot make a good selection of means. But—and this is the second reason—it turns out that theology, like, say, politics in the classical sense, is necessarily involved in an ongoing process. The best regime is not permanent, except theoretically. Theology cannot be purely theoretical, because it has to address cultures; therefore it cannot be permanent, because cultures are not permanent. Moreover, the ongoing process of addressing the Gospel to cultures involves linking together many subordinate goals, and each of these has to be clearly envisioned so that the activities of theology may be ordered effectively.

One must not infer from this that theology, for Lonergan, is a whirligig of activity without permanent achievement and progress. He was convinced of the possibility of permanently valid achievements. But permanent validity does not constitute an end so much as a beginning for further work. What is more, the most important achievements shift the whole paradigm of a science. And it is because they do that Lonergan concluded it would not be adequate to define theology or the other sciences by their formal objects. He thought of it mainly in terms of the development, in the community of theologians, of increasingly complex and interdependent ways of knowing.

Sometime in the late 1950s, after *Insight* had been published and perhaps in preparation for his 1959 lectures on the philosophy of education, Lonergan began studying the work of educational psychologist Jean Piaget.[6] From Piaget he began to think about development in a more detailed manner and, particularly for our purposes, about the developmental history of a science. Skills, according to Piaget, develop through assimilation and adjustment. Naturally spontaneous or previously acquired operations are assimilated to new objects and tasks and gradually adjusted to the relevant differences the new tasks present. Through adjustment there comes about a gradual differentiation of operations each adapted to its proper task. The differentiation makes new combinations possible. The combinations head toward a group, the complete set of combinations of differentiated operations.[7] The group of operations is complete when every operation is matched by its reverse: addition and subtraction, multiplication and division, and so forth.[8] Successive

6. Piaget was studying the development of intelligence in children, an enterprise naturally cognate to Lonergan's interests. Lonergan reports that he had "read lots of Piaget before" his preparations for the 1959 lectures (*Caring about Meaning*, 54). As far as I know, however, Piaget is not mentioned in *Insight* or in the 1957 lectures, *Understanding and Being*; it is from 1959 forward that Piaget is regularly named and his influence becomes pronounced. The encounter seems to have catalyzed, or at least contributed to, a significant transformation in Lonergan's thought; he found Piaget's ideas fecund in ways that might have surprised Piaget. Lonergan drew on Piaget, for instance, to construct a general account of the stages of cultural development. See *Method* (1972), 27–30, or CWL 14, 28–31. The rather brisk summary in *Method* is the distillation of years of reflection evidenced in the papers and theological method institutes of the 1960s.

7. Here I am summarizing Bernard J. F. Lonergan, "Time and Meaning," in *Philosophical and Theological Papers 1958–1964*, ed. Robert C. Croken, Frederick E. Crowe, and Robert M. Doran, CWL 6 (1996), 94–121, here 109–10. There are parallel discussions.

8. Jean Piaget, *The Psychology of Intelligence*, ed. Malcolm Piercy and D. E. Berlyne, Routledge Classics (New York: Routledge, 2001), 20–55. Though the construction of a spatial field does not exhibit "reversibility" in precisely the same way as an operational field, nevertheless insofar as the subject is considered as an element within the field, changes of position are "reversible" in the sense that they can be countered by (actual or imagined) movements of one's own body; thus the complete group of (potential) displacements exhibits equilibrium. See ibid., 125.

grouping combines operations in increasingly complex paths through the hierarchical integration or sublation of lower level capacities into higher order skillsets.[9] The analysis could be extended to consider not just the grouping of groups within the performance of a single operating subject, but interlocking sets of groups. Thus, "the economy of a country [is] a grouping of groups of differentiated operations that are linked together according to certain laws, each person's skills being complemented by the skills of another."[10] Similarly, as we will see, Lonergan conceives theology as a grouping of interlocking skill and knowledge sets distributed through the community of theologians.

Parallel or perhaps isomorphic to the development of skills is an ascending hierarchy of objects. Thus, one begins by operating on sensible objects and gradually develops an ability to operate on images, words, symbols, sentences, propositions. One comes to the "final stage when one operates with respect to the operations themselves; then one is studying method or development."[11] Studying method is what Lonergan took Piaget to be doing and, in a complementary way, what he understood himself to be doing.

Lonergan and Piaget are thinking about science here as an activity or set of activities. 'Doing science' is a collaborative movement toward fuller knowledge of scientific objects. Methodology is the objectification of the operations scientists perform in order to know the realities under investigation. Scientific operations regard the objects of the various sciences, but methodology regards the operations themselves as the objects of its investigation. "The methodological viewpoint," Lonergan explained in his 1962 Regis College institute on the method of theology, "considers objects only through the operations."[12] A biologist or a theologian is interested, obviously, in understanding the realities of organic life or of God and things as ordered to God. But methodological reflection is interested in understanding the operations by which those objects are reached. Because there is a proportion between the operations and the objects, the methodological viewpoint does not exclude

9. See ibid., 165–68.

10. Lonergan, "Time and Meaning," 111.

11. Ibid., 110.

12. *Early Works on Method 1*, 19.

the objects. But its interest in the objects is indirect; when Lonergan was writing on method in theology, he was not composing a theology but reflecting on the interrelated sets of operations involved in the construction of theology.

Whether they involve themselves in this kind of reflection or not, theologians are making choices about how they go about their work. The theologians themselves are implicated in their choices. We are not only each deciding how to go about our business; we are also each deciding, explicitly or not, how we will become better at it. When we begin to reflect on method, then, there is a shift of emphasis "from objects to operations and operators."[13] As we have seen, reflection on oneself as a knower is one of the basic offices of philosophy as Lonergan reconceived it. Philosophy in this sense is 'foundational methodology.' It aims, through self-appropriation, to bring to light the different kinds of activities involved in various scientific inquiries, to scrutinize them, to reflect on their adequacy to their objects, and so forth.[14] This means, too, reflecting on the conditions for self-transcendence, on the problem of bias and the perpetual need for conversion and personal development.

For Lonergan, philosophy, too, is defined by its method, which he calls 'generalized empirical method.' It is 'generalized' in the sense that it is applied not only to the data of sense but also data of consciousness. In both cases, "it is not by sinking into some inert passivity but by positive effort and rigorous training" that one "becomes a master of the difficult art of scientific observation."[15] Knowledge of generalized empirical method is reached by articulating the fundamental structures of all inquiry; once it is reached, one has a basis for interrogating the particular methods of other sciences.[16] In the measure that it is reached, one approximates an adequate articulation of the horizon of intellectual, moral, and religious conversion.

Lonergan conceives science as an inquiry into explanatory reasons, and in that sense he places its progress in the movement from the first-for-us (description) to the first-in-itself (explanation). On the other hand, science is hypothetical, not certain; it is experimental, not demonstrated from

13. Lonergan, "Bernard Lonergan Responds (1)," 265.

14. Lonergan, "Questionnaire on Philosophy," 381.

15. *Insight*, 95–96.

16. Lonergan's basic discussion of the empirical method of the sciences is in *Insight*, 93–125.

necessary premises. Moreover, he considers the sciences autonomous in the formation of their basic categories, rather than receiving them from metaphysics. Because science achieves its goal of complete explanation of all phenomena only through successive approximations, however, the basic categories of a scientific formation are always open to further revision, on the proviso that the new categories account for all that has been so far understood, but with greater explanatory power. What provides the formal unity of science, then, is not its theoretical structure but its method.[17] If sciences are formally defined by their methods, then the basic and total science is the science of methods. The basic element in the basic and total science is cognitional theory. Derivative elements include epistemology, which articulates the adequacy of cognitional operations to their objects, and metaphysics, which articulates the heuristic structure of being as proportionate to our knowing.[18]

The idea that the sciences might be defined formally by their methods, however, seems to invite a rather obvious Aristotelian objection. If sciences are defined by their methods, then it seems physicists would be logicians because they employ logic. That is why, for the Aristotelian, sciences are defined by their subjects, and demonstrations pertain to subjects. It is one thing to use logic in demonstrating the properties of being as movable (physics) and another to investigate logic as such.[19] Lonergan knows this perfectly well, though, and one might make a facile reply on his behalf by distinguishing techniques from methods. Logic is a general technique for operating on propositions, not an activity specific to a particular science. Just as the Aristotelian natural philosopher uses logic without being a logician, so Lonergan's chemist uses logical and mathematical operations in conjunction with other operations, proper to chemistry; it is those other operations that formally define chemistry as a science. But the facile reply sheds no real light on Lonergan's meaning; it merely dodges the question for understanding raised by the objection. To meet that question—to understand what Lonergan meant—let us turn to some examples.

17. See Patrick H. Byrne, "Lonergan on the Foundations of the Theories of Relativity," in *Creativity and Method: Essays in Honor of Bernard Lonergan* (Milwaukee, Wisc.: Marquette University Press, 1981), 477–94.

18. Lonergan, "Questionnaire on Philosophy," 362–65.

19. See Wallace, *The Modeling of Nature*, 230–32.

If we were to define biology by its formal object, we might say it is the science of organic life. This definition applies equally to the biology of Aristotle and of Darwin. But if we ask how the formal object—organic life—is actually attained, we find (unsurprisingly) enormous differences between Aristotelian and Darwinian biology. "With the advent of Darwin and successive modifications of his evolutionary theory," writes William Wallace,

> a deeper significance is becoming manifest in classificatory schemes. They seem now to provide more than a static picture of the order of nature as we presently conceive it; they describe also a developmental framework in which species no longer extant but somehow preserved in the paleographical record can be located.[20]

A science, then, has a history; it is developing. What is biology? Heuristically, it is the science aiming for a complete understanding of organic life. In that sense, biology is what would be known by the scientist with a complete understanding of organic life. That is not our present understanding. Biology is under construction. Its current reality at any given stage is an assembly of differentiated operations by which the biologists understand, imperfectly, organic life. The groups of operations involved in classification of species today are vastly more differentiated and complex than the procedures of the ancient and medieval versions of biology.

The coming to light of the object is one with the coming to be of the corresponding scientific operations. Thus Wallace continues,

> the ideal that this discovery suggests is that natural classifications result not merely from the work of taxonomists but from the succession of types that originate within nature by an evolutionary process. If this is the case, then one day it will be possible to locate all naturally occurring species not merely within a hierarchy but also as branches of a phylogenetic tree—thus situating them in their dynamic and evolving relationships.[21]

20. Ibid., 78.
21. Ibid.

Even a relatively primitive biology envisaged a hierarchical ordering of life forms. But the development of methods has brought into view a set of objects that previously were not considered, namely, the dynamic relations of phylogenesis. The method and the content of the science develop in tandem. As the method develops, as practitioners develop, they become capable of asking and answering questions that previously had not been envisaged. Those questions intend objects previously unattainable. The coming to light of the objects is one with the coming to be of the science.

The difficulty represented by phylogenesis is reproduced, in a way, in the individual organism of each species. From Wallace let me turn back to Lonergan. Here is a summary of his sketch of the stages of an inquiry whose goal is to determine the immanent operator—the nature—of development and integration in an organism. It begins with the thing—a frog, let us say—as presented to our senses. We proceed to identify and label the parts, which generally requires cutting the frog open. The differentiation and description of the parts allows us to gradually develop insights into how the parts are related to the various activities and events in the life of the organism. In this way, we come to know the parts as organs. We do not know the organs just by describing the parts anatomically. We know the organs by understanding how the parts work together in the functional whole of the organism. Each organ has its own performance capacities, but none is complete without the others, so understanding the organs involves understanding the relationships of the organs to one another. It also involves understanding how the performance of each organ contributes to the life of the whole and what conditions must be fulfilled for that performance to continue. This movement from the parts as descriptively located to the parts understood as capacities-for-performance is the shift from anatomy to physiology. A third step moves from the physiology of the organs to the underlying chemical and physical processes the organs integrate and make systematic. This is rather complex. The underlying processes have to be represented for analysis, which may involve the development of quite sophisticated models transposed to equally sophisticated symbolic systems (e.g., the mathematical representation of velocity as a vector). Once the chemical and physical processes are represented, we can begin to discern the principles of the higher organic system that make these lower-order processes regular and recurrent in a way they otherwise would not be. From these principles we can go on to explain the different kinds of conditions under which the organism successfully functions with a limited range of flexibility. These flexible patterns, finally, ought to match up with the performance capacities of the different organs known through physiology.[22] Biologists, then, develop scientific understanding of the organism through a gradual displacement from descriptive into explanatory relationships.

A frog is a higher system integrating physical and chemical processes. A frog, however, has a life cycle. It is not locked into a fixed set of processes but self-assembles, so to speak, a series of processes over time. It does so in an environment that is also constantly changing, so that the self-assembly of the frog is interactive, as it were. The biologist or zoologists who asks, what is a frog?, wants to understand what makes it tick, its 'nature': the remote and immanent principle of self-assembly that integrates each stage along the way but also prepares for later stages and brings about their emergence. As long as the organism is developing, its nature—the immanent principle of its self-assembly—is performing two offices at once, which Lonergan calls integrator and operator. At each stage of its development, the self-assembling organism integrates itself into a functioning whole, a juvenile or adolescent frog, say, successfully negotiating its environment. But each stage before the final stage is transitional, and the self-assembling frog is operating its own transition by actively preparing for the next stage. I do not mean, of course, that these activities are conscious and intentional. Insofar as the process is confined to the organic level, it is not conscious and intentional. But I have left out, for sake of simplicity, everything pertaining to what might be called the psyche or sensibility of the frog, which is probably its most important specific difference from other animals.

In the frog, then, at any given stage, there is an interlocking of parts. The parts are significant because they contribute to interlocking recurrence schemes, that is, successful patterns of functioning at that stage. But besides the parts and schemes that interlock at any given stage, there is also a succession of stages which also interlock. To comprehend

---

22. *Insight*, 489; see 488–92.

the nature of a frog—its principle of self-assembly—means to grasp the principle that integrates each stage and also operates the succession of stages.[23] The operator of development has to be studied by comparing a sequence of stages.[24] It is by studying the sequence that one may discover the difference between normal and abnormal developmental processes, the difference between transitional and permanent developments, the difference between different subspecies and species, and so forth. What one is aiming to understand is how the organism at any given stage is preparing for the differences that appear in the next. The sequence of systems is the centerpiece of an understanding of the developmental principles of a frog or a flower.[25]

These examples illustrate once again what in *Verbum* Lonergan had called the logico-ontological parallel. Inasmuch as formal objects are correlative to operations, the newly attainable objects were only abstractly or implicitly included in the earlier stage of the science. I do not mean, of course, that the science is constituting or creating the reality of its objects. If the scientists succeed in transcending themselves, they are dealing objectively with reality; they are attaining or approaching what truly is so, independently of what they might wish or prefer to be so. What I do mean is that Aristotle apparently had no idea of phylogenesis as contemporary biology conceives it. It was not, for him, an object of interrogation, hypothesis, or direct or indirect verification. Abstractly, phylogenesis is included in the formal object of a science of living organisms, but concretely, it is an object of that science only when and where the proportionate operations are realized, only when and where it can actually be conceived and investigated.

In the course of its history, a science may undergo revolutionary or paradigm-shifting developments. We may conceive its formal object abstractly or concretely. Abstractly, the formal object is the object of the science simply as defined: biology is the science of organic life, theology is the science of God and things as ordered to God. The formal object in this sense is the object as correlative to the hypothetically complete

---

23. *Insight*, 491.

24. It would be worthwhile to make a careful comparison of these pages of *Insight* with the structure of Dialectic outlined in *Method* (1972), 249–50, or CWL 14, 234–235.

25. *Insight*, 491.

science, the object as it would be attained by the complete scientist through the complete group of operations proper to the perfected science. So conceived, the formal object is timeless, outside the history of the development of the science. But, so conceived, it also is not yet fully known. A concrete consideration of 'what biology is' would involve a history of biological contexts. This is more than assigning dates to its principal discoveries; it is attending to the correlation between the operations of biologists and the objects of their inquiry. It includes the formation of phylogenetic hypotheses and also the methods devised to investigate and test them. Concretely considered, then, the formal object of a science is its material object as actually attained through the operations developed at any given stage. The concrete formal object is the object of that science, not as it would be attained by the hypothetical complete scientist but as it may actually be attained by scientists operating on the level of their time.[26]

Let us turn briefly to a second example: the development of mathematics. The material object of mathematics, Lonergan suggests, is the 'empirical residue' of all sensible data, that is, what is abstracted from, and residual to, the sciences that investigate data as falling into determinate kinds. This residue includes such phenomena as "the individual, the continuum, particular places and times, and the nonsystematic divergence of actual frequency from probable expectations."[27] The empirical residue and its relevance to mathematics cannot be explored further here; whatever one might make of it, the chief point to grasp is that in Lonergan's conception, it supplies the material element in all mathematics, it is what mathematics is 'about,' what an Aristotelian might call 'mathematical matter.' But it is the formal element that is the point of the illustration.

> By mathematicians, the formal element commonly is viewed as dynamic. There is a laborious process named 'learning mathematics.' It consists in gradually acquiring the insights that are necessary to understand mathematical problems, to follow mathematical arguments, to work out mathematical solutions. This acquisition occurs in a succession of higher viewpoints. One

26. *Early Works on Method 1*, 19–23.
27. *Insight*, 336; see 50–56.

department of mathematics follows upon another. Logically, they are discontinuous, for each has its own definitions, postulates, and inferences. But intellectually they are continuous, inasmuch as the symbolic representation of operations in the lower field provides the images in which intelligence grasps the idea of the new rules that govern operations in the higher field.[28]

This process of learning mathematics is parallel to a prior, far longer, and much less efficient process, which is the discovery of mathematics. There is a history of mathematical science that is greatly telescoped by mathematical education. It is the history of an emerging and unfinished sequence of groups of operations that progressively reveal new mathematical objects. We can speak of mathematics abstractly in relation to all that would be understood by the hypothetical completion of mathematics in the hypothetically complete set of groups of mathematical operations as possessed by the perfect mathematician. Or we can speak of mathematics concretely by distinguishing a series of mathematical contexts, the context of Euclid, say, or the context of Newton.[29]

Notice that the formal element of mathematics is not a single viewpoint or system but a genetic sequence of systems. Each plateau in mathematical understanding provides new materials fermenting toward the next stage. Each department of mathematics is defined by operations governed according to certain rules. Successive departments are related to one another through the operations by which one transitions from one to the next.[30] The systematic component in mathematics, then, is not a single system but a system of systems, a genetic sequence of systematizations.

Now, as the reader will surmise, our present interest in frogs and algebra is rather limited. What we are really after is what is called the nature of theology. Like frogs and biology and mathematics, theology develops; it has stages. There is the theology of the New Testament, of the Greek or Latin Fathers, of the scholastics. But theology is self-reflective; it is operating, in part, on its own history. By operating on its past, theology is also constructing its present and, in some way, preparing its future. But

---

28. *Insight*, 336; see 334–39.
29. See *Early Works on Method 2*, 175.
30. *Insight*, 335.

who are the operators and integrators in this process? They are theologians, operating consciously and intentionally, with greater or less discernment and deliberation, possessed or not by the love of God, obedient or not to the light of faith, docile or not to the movements of the Spirit. It is they who integrate theological achievement at each stage and who prepare, advertently or not, the way for its future stages. The question of method is, do they know what they are doing?

Let us make a distinction between the theologians as the ones operating and reason illumined by faith and motivated by love as the principle by which they operate. The latter is remote, however. Proximately there are such skills as reading and construing texts, historical renarration, distinguishing gold from dross, and so forth. Lonergan's distinction of functions in theology is a way of closing in on the different kinds of capacities reason illumined by faith and motivated by love has to develop if it is to be theologically effective.

Concretely, the formal object of a science is its material object as actually attained by the operations available at some given stage in the development of the science.

> From a methodological viewpoint, then, one can define a science, its formal object, by defining the group of operations by which the object of that science is reached. In that fashion, one can define logic, mathematics, physics, chemistry, and any given science by specifying the relevant operations. That mode of division is necessary insofar as sciences are developing. As long as a science is not something *in facto esse* but *in fieri*, it is only by the succession of the developments in the groups of operations that one can say what the science is. One can assign its history.[31]

What, then, is theology? Heuristically, it is knowledge of God and all things as ordered to God. It is a progressively determinate approximation to the beatific vision. But concretely, it is under construction. To know it, we would distinguish different stages in its development and distinguish progress from deviation, regression, aberration. A development properly so-called is not just a difference; it is an enlargement of the

---

31. *Early Works on Method 1*, 121–22.

group of operations through new combinations, the introduction of new elements, the elimination perhaps of otiose procedures. Thus one speaks of the scientific context or, in theology, of the 'dogmatic-theological' context, meaning not just a context of objects but also the groups of operations by which they are attained.[32]

Imagine, for a moment, a conversation 'about the Bible' between, say, a medieval exegete and a contemporary biblical scholar. The contemporary scholar is concerned about sources, forms, redaction history, chronology, and the techniques of investigation proportionate to those questions. There is a greater differentiation of scholarly methods and a vast enlargement of the body of data to which they are applied. The conversation, then, is materially 'about the Bible,' but its formal objects, concretely considered, are coming to light together with the genesis of methods for interrogating them.

Now, one may object that the medieval exegete is more 'theological' because he apprehends the Bible not as a body of historical data on ancient Israel, Judaism, and Christianity but as a canonical whole communicating a divine revelation. No doubt the Bible—as a whole, in its parts, in its transmission—is data on the religious convictions of the people who composed and carried and adhered to it. If those convictions are true—and I do not doubt it—then the Bible expresses truths. No doubt methods appropriate to the investigation of those convictions and the communication of those truths belong to theology. But so, too, do all the methods involved in bringing the history of those convictions, their emergence and development, their expression in texts and institutions, and so forth. Finally, and most importantly, the acceptance of the Bible as communicating a divine revelation is not in itself a theological act but a personal and religious decision with theological consequences. Those consequences, of course, are enormous, for theology reflects on religious commitment and articulates its implications. But the difficulties entrained by the objection that theological exegesis has to be religious exegesis mainly illustrate the value of carefully distinguishing different kinds of questions, putting them in some practical order, and working out how to pursue them successfully—which is to say, the value of method.

32. *Early Works on Method 1*, 21. "There is the history of theology and the history of dogma. And the development is also a development in operations: further differentiations of operations, new combinations, and larger groupings of operations."

As our illustrations underscore, it is the biologists, the mathematicians, and the biblical scholars—not the philosophers—who are developing the methods and techniques proper to the problems in their fields. The methods have to be adequate to the objects and the practitioners understand best the objects they are dealing with. It is the creative tension of present achievement and unanswered questions that leavens the development of more adequate methods, which in turn resolve some problems only to bring new ones into range. "The business of the scientist is not to allege difficulties as excuses but to overcome them."[33] In this process, the modest but important office of the philosopher or methodologist is not to prescribe but to clarify through careful attendance upon the performance.

Transposing Paradigms

The development of any science is operated by questions. The development of theology is painstakingly realized by way of many and diverse steps, errors, digressions, corrections. Only the theologian who has experienced what it means to come to a systematic understanding of theology has the wherewithal to understand which elements in the historical development of theology had to be understood before others, which elements led to development in understanding and which held it back, which elements properly belong to theology and which are alien or even erroneous. Again, only through such understanding can one appreciate the emergence of genuinely new paradigms, distinguish true paradigm shifts from mere amplifications of prior achievement, and grasp how successive transformations account for all that prior theory had right while also accounting for much that had been unexplained. Just as the education of a mathematician telescopes the development of mathematics, so the development of theological intelligence mirrors, in some way, the historical development of theology itself—and it is only the theologian who has a developed understanding of the science who is competent to tell its story.

Lonergan wants to push us to think about what theology could be in this vein. The general framework that mathematics provides for the

---

33. *Insight*, 260.

natural sciences, philosophy provides for the sciences of meaning. I will say more about this in due course, but the basic idea is to understand in oneself how meaning works and how its elements may be assembled in various different manners, and therefore to have a heuristic for working one's way into the meanings of others. This in turn makes it possible, at least hypothetically, to construct a history demarking the main stage-itions in the history of human meaning. This history would be dialectical, that is, it would have to face the fact of confusion as well as clarification. As we have seen in our sketches of the development of biology and mathematics, there is a gradual, historical accumulation of insights. They are expressed with varying degrees of adequacy, and it is not always easy to discern what is correct in them. But what is correct invites development and what is incorrect invites reversal. The development of culture and education results in the emergence of new forms of expression that in turn condition the emergence and formulation of further insights.[34]

In the epilogue of *Insight*, Lonergan envisions a systematic treatise on the mystical body of Christ whose formal component would be provided by a theory of the history of meaning. "It may be asked in what department of theology the historical aspect of development might be treated, and I would like to suggest that it may possess peculiar relevance to a treatise on the mystical body of Christ." The mystical body is not a point in time but a concrete history of the communication and reception of the Gospel, not only through interior conversion "but also through the outer channels of human communication" and a consequent "transfiguration of human living." Hence, "it may be that the contemporary crisis of human living and human values demands of the theologian" a treatise on the total history of the human family "in the concrete and cumulative consequences of the acceptance or rejection of the message of the Gospel."[35]

Lonergan used the term 'transposition' to refer both to the restatement of positions in enriched contexts (transposing positions) and also to refer to the transitions from one scientific paradigm to another or one stage of meaning to another (transposing paradigms). A transposition in this broad sense affects the whole paradigm of a science and,

34. *Insight*, 609–10.

35. *Insight*, 763–64.

therefore, evokes a series of restatements in the narrower sense.[36] This narrower sense he illustrated by comparing Einsteinian relativity to Newtonian mechanics.[37] While Newtonian theory was not open to Einstein's development, Einstein's position easily integrated, and in so doing transformed, the valid elements of Newton's. The Newtonian theory of general gravitation was thus transposed to become a particular case within the context of a new and more powerful theoretic synthesis. At the same time, the transposition led to the correction of certain assumptions, previously taken for granted, about the invariance of measurements of distance and duration.[38] Thus, the transposition of positions is both genetic—there is a sequence of higher theoretical integrations—and dialectical—eliminating erroneous suppositions along the way.

Insofar as theology involves theoretical elements, it is subject to paradigm shifts in which its basic terms and relations are revised. Just as "any future system of mechanics will have to satisfy the data that are now covered by the notion of mass," so any alternative to scholastic theory must satisfy the data it explained through its concepts. But, again, just as "it is not necessary that every future system of mechanics will have to satisfy the same data by employing our concept of mass," so too it is not necessary that every alternative to scholastic theology, even one that retained its substantial achievements, would have to invoke its terms. "Further developments might lead to the introduction of a different set of ultimate concepts, [and] to a consequent reformulation of all law. . . ."[39] The important revision is not a revision of concepts as such but a reordering of concepts, a reappraisal of their scientific significance. The concepts of empirical method

> as concepts are not hypothetical, for they are defined implicitly
> by empirically established correlations. Nonetheless, its concepts
> as systematically significant, as ultimate or derived, as preferred

---

36. On some methodological problems of transposing theological positions from the scholastic to the contemporary context, see Jeremy D. Wilkins, "Metaphysics and/in Theology"; Wilkins, "Grace in the Third Stage of Meaning: Apropos Lonergan's 'Four-Point Hypothesis,'" *Lonergan Workshop* 24 (2010): 443–67. This is a major topic of Robert M. Doran, *What Is Systematic Theology?* (Toronto: University of Toronto Press, 2005). Some difficulties with Doran's position are raised in Wilkins, "Metaphysics and/in Theology."

37. Lonergan, "Horizons and Transpositions," 410.

38. *Insight*, 184–88.

39. *Insight*, 357–59.

to other concepts that might be empirically reached, do involve an element of mere supposition. For the selection of certain concepts as ultimate occurs in the work of systematization, and that work is provisional.[40]

A paradigm shift does not invalidate the verified concepts of earlier science (though it may eliminate unverified postulates, like the luminiferous aether), but it does displace them as ultimately significant, as basically explanatory, as fruitful for the progress of scientific understanding. The concepts lose not their validity but their significance "in the general sense of defining for a science 'the type of relationships to be investigated and the methods and abstractions to be regarded as legitimate within a particular problem area.'"[41]

In his important 1979 paper "Horizons and Transpositions," Lonergan distinguished three main paradigm transpositions in the history of theology: the transposition from the New Testament to the classical world, the transposition from the classical to the medieval scholastic context, and finally the transposition he sought to effect from scholasticism to a theology he styled 'methodical' (for reasons I will explain presently).[42] Let us sketch the first two of these transpositions before turning our attention to the third.

Probably Lonergan's most extensive discussion of the transition from the New Testament to the classical context occurs in the first volume (*Pars dogmatica*) of his *De Deo Trino*; we will consider it at greater length in the next chapter. For Lonergan, this transition was from one kind of clarity to another. In its own narrative and symbolic way, the New Testament clearly announces the incarnation of the Word and the repentance and faith expected of us. But that announcement raised questions (about, for instance, the divinity of the Son and the unity of God) that could not be put to rest simply by repeating the narrative. To answer them, theologians (in this case, mostly bishops) were pressed to secure the message by way of a different, propositional clarity.

40. *Insight*, 359.

41. Quoted from the editors' introduction (by Frederick Lawrence) to Lonergan, *Macroeconomic Dynamics*, lviii; internal quotation from B. J. Loasby, "Hypothesis and Paradigm in the Theory of the Firm," *The Economic Journal* 81, no. 324 (1971): 863–85, here 866.

42. Lonergan, "Horizons and Transpositions."

Lonergan distinguished four main aspects of this transposition from biblical narrative to doctrinal proposition: objective, subjective, evaluative, and hermeneutical.[43] Perhaps the most obvious of these are the hermeneutical and the evaluative aspects. The Christian bishops who formulated dogmatic confessions of faith were proposing an interpretation of the Christian messsage. That they did so by formulating their convictions in dogmatic statements implies value preferences. Those preferences were widely questioned at the time and are widely questioned, perhaps for different reasons, today. At the time, there were many who felt the language of Scripture should not be replaced by such technical terms as *homoousios*. Today, there are many for whom the transition to dogmatic formulations represented a great capitulation of Christianity to the preoccupations of Greek philosophy or was a derailment for some other reason. So a development brought about by some because they considered it necessary for the clarity of the truth was resisted by others as a novelty, an aberration, or a distortion.

Then there are the aspects Lonergan names 'subjective' and 'objective.' They are most typical of his preoccupation. First, there is a transposition of objects from a narrative to a propositional mode. What Scripture presents in a narrative and symbolic way, the dogmas present by way of propositional judgments. These judgments have a certain austerity to them; if Scripture speaks above all to the heart, the dogmas speak directly to the head. Corresponding to this transition in objects, there is a development in the subjects, the theologians. The narrative and symbolic style is, so to speak, the universal style. But the propositional style is something a person has to become capable of. The dogmas are not only propositions; they are second-order propositions, that is, statements governing other statements. To operate on propositions this way normally requires a certain educational preparation. So, in order to answer their questions, theologians had to become skillful at operating with respect to propositions, and they had to be able to order their activities toward increasingly differentiated goals while prescinding from considerations extraneous to those goals.

A second paradigm shift occurred in the transition from what is commonly described as patristic theology into scholasticism. The nature

---

43. The hermenuetical problem at this stage of Lonergan's thought is presented in *Insight*, 585–616, esp. 592–95. For discussion, see Coelho, *Hermeneutics and Method*, 49–77.

of the transposition is suggested by the relationship between Augustine and Aquinas on grace. In *Grace and Freedom*, Lonergan indicated how Thomas Aquinas transposed the Augustinian doctrine of operative grace into a scholastic context. Augustine's position (itself largely a transposition of St. Paul) developed through successive controversies that forced him to return to the biblical data and think through the implications of his presuppositions.[44] Aquinas's transposition, on the other hand, was through the gradual refinement of theoretical instruments, joined to a careful study of Augustine's anti-Pelagian writings (in the course of which Aquinas was led to acknowledge and repudiate as effectively Pelagian his own earlier views).[45] The fruits of this transposition—which was not a solitary achievement—included a theorem systematically distinguishing natural and supernatural orders, an analogical conception of God's operation in all things, a theoretical analysis of the freedom of the will, and the Aristotelian concept of habit. Together these provided a vastly richer, more theoretically differentiated context than Augustine's for the doctrine of grace as operative and cooperative.[46]

In general, the transposition into scholasticism was not a change in doctrine but a change in theory, that is, in the systematic understanding of truth claims. What I mean is that the scholastic theologians accepted as true all that the dogmas proposed. They inserted these truth claims, however, into a revamped intellectual framework. The ancient councils had created a dogmatic context for theology; the scholastics added a dependent theoretical context.[47] Think, for instance, of scholastic disputations in Trinitarian theology or Christology. Unlike the Fathers,

---

44. J. Patout Burns, *The Development of Augustine's Doctrine of Operative Grace* (Paris: Études augustiniennes, 1980); more recently and compendiously, Burns, "From Persuasion to Predestination: Augustine on Freedom in Rational Creatures," in *In Dominico Eloquio = In Lordly Eloquence: Essays on Patristic Exegesis in Honor of Robert L. Wilken* (Grand Rapids, Mich.: William B. Eerdmans, 2002), 294–316.

45. In addition to *Grace and Freedom*, see also Joseph Peter Wawrykow, *God's Grace and Human Action: Merit in the Theology of Thomas Aquinas* (Notre Dame: University of Notre Dame Press, 1995). Wawrykow provides a good example of how Lonergan's fundamental clarification of the issues involved in operative grace opens the way to understanding the related questions about the way Aquinas conceives our 'co-authoring' of our lives under grace.

46. Perhaps I should note that Lonergan was intensely interested in pointing out the theoretical criteria operating these transitions; he had little to say about the pedagogical criteria in relation, for instance, to Aquinas's work forming Dominican preachers and confessors.

47. *Method* (1972), 312–14, or CWL 14, 291–92.

who spent most of their ink trying to establish, justify, and defend these mysteries, the scholastics took them for givens. But, taking them for givens, they were able to develop further questions not about the truth of the mysteries but about how to understand them and knit them together into a coherent view of the Christian universe. I do not mean that there is none of this in the earlier period, only that the anchor points in place, the scholastics were able to focus on the subalternate questions for theological understanding in a way that had not been possible before.

The transposition of Augustine's doctrine of grace into the theoretical context of Aquinas is a case in point. It was not, fundamentally, a revision of doctrines, that is, of truth claims. It was a revision of the theoretical context in which those claims were explained. What Augustine affirmed about divine sovereignty, the infallibility of God's plan and intention, the necessity of grace, and the reality of human freedom, Aquinas accepted as true. But he inserted these claims into a theoretical context that made some of Augustine's leading questions and categories irrelevant. For example, Augustine defined freedom by way of a pair of fundamental alternatives: either servitude to sin or servitude to God. He did not work out a coherent theory of human nature as distinct from the dynamics of sin and grace. Aquinas, on the other hand, provided a properly philosophical analysis of human freedom, situated in relation to sin and vice. He was able to articulate the necessity of grace not to make us free but to ensure consistent good performance and to ground merit before God. In so doing, he also corrected some of Augustine's suppositions. Some terms were eliminated and others were assigned new meanings. So, for Augustine, prevenient grace is more or less synonymous with operative grace, and again subsequent grace is more or less synonymous with cooperative grace. But for Aquinas, each of these four terms has its own precise meaning, and none of the meanings maps exactly onto Augustine's.[48]

The significance of such developments is not always appreciated by those who bring them about. The ancient theologians (mostly bishops) had no intention of effecting a paradigm shift, but in fact they did (and we will look at it more closely in the sequel). It is generally only from the stern that the true significance of the transitions comes into

---

48. See *Grace and Freedom*, esp. 21–43, 143–49.

view. Needless to say, it is also only from within the more differentiated context, as it were, that one can judge the adequacy and fidelity of such transpositions.[49]

The context of classical and scholastic science was, in a sense, static. Science was conceived as certain knowledge through necessary explanatory causes. It was expected to be a permanent achievement that a learned person could possess as a *habitus*. Contemporary science continues to aim for the complete explanation of all phenomena, but it is not an individual habit, does not ask for certitude, and expects an ongoing succession of increasingly powerful hypotheses carrying forward what has so far been correctly understood but also correcting, qualifying, and recontextualizing it. Even the fundamental concepts of a science (e.g., mass, velocity) are open to revision. This is not to destroy all continuity, for any revision would have to be justified by its superior explanatory power and therefore has to answer the relevant questions and incorporate whatever is already explained. It does, however, mean that the ultimate foundations of a science are not in its concepts. They are in the scientists themselves, as more or less up to the job, and particularly in the way they go about their work.

All this also is true, in its own way, of theology. It is not that the mysteries of faith are in doubt, for the mysteries are held in trust from God; they are not a human discovery or invention. Yet revealed truth does not exist in a vacuum. It is given and transmitted in history. It is held in trust by historical subjects with imperfect loves and fragile minds. Theology has to deal with the articles of faith as historically articulated, imperfectly understood, and mediated into all manner of culture. This presents intellectual difficulties that have to be faced squarely, lest they mutate to religious doubts. If Christian theology mediates between the one Gospel and all peoples with their many cultures, if its matter is at once transcendent and historical, it must integrate what is permanently valid into an ongoing process. Theological investigation is collaborative and theological knowledge is distributed. Sciences rely upon their methods, and one asks whether theologians have reliable methods and know how to piece them together.

49. See, e.g., Aquinas's remark that Augustine's 'Platonic' way of speaking might conduce the unwary to error; one has to understand the realities to make good sense of the words (*STh* 2-2 q. 23 a. 2 ad 1).

As we have seen, Lonergan hypothesized two main paradigm shifts in the history of theology up to scholasticism: from a narrative and symbolic context (the New Testament) to one in which meaning was governed by propositions (dogma), and again from the dogmatic context to the elaborate theoretical superstructure of scholastic thought. The disintegration of scholasticism in the face of new historical techniques called for a third shift, comparable in scale, to a paradigm at home in the world of modern science and scholarship. Just as the earlier transpositions were cumulative, not supersessionary (except perhaps insofar as they involved the restatement of earlier positions and the revision of basic concepts), so what Lonergan envisioned entails not the end of narrative or doctrine or theory but, in some sense, their transformation. A new paradigm for theology was necessary to face explicitly the ongoing development of theology as a science, and our own responsibility for that development.

Lonergan called the paradigm he envisioned 'methodical' in contrast to the 'theoretical' paradigm of scholastic thought.[50] The scholastic paradigm sought the coherence of results by integrating them into a stable and overarching theoretical structure. But theoretical structures, however sound, reflect stages in the progress of a science. They do not of themselves introduce or guide the transition from one stage to another.

> Science does not advance by deducing new conclusions from old premises. Deduction is an operation that occurs only in the field of concepts and propositions. But the advance of science, as we have seen, is a circuit: from data to inquiry, from inquiry to insight, from insight to the formulation of premises and the deduction of their implications, from such formulation to material operations which yield fresh data and in the limit generate the new set of insights named a higher viewpoint. A basic revision, then, is a leap. At a stroke, it is a grasp of the insufficiency both of the old laws and of the old standards. At a stroke, it generates both the new laws and the new standards. Finally, by the same verification, it establishes that both the new laws and the new standards satisfy the data.[51]

50. See *Method* (1972), 288–93, or CWL 14, 270–74.
51. *Insight*, 190.

The transposition of Newtonian mechanics to Einsteinian relativity was not the result of the homogeneous expansion of Newtonian theory but rather of the tension of content and method pressing toward a new and higher theoretical synthesis.

The point here is that theology is an ongoing activity, or rather, a set of activities. Those activities yield an ever increasing body of knowledge. They can bring about basic reorganizations of the knowledge already accumulated. They are themselves transformed in the process. It is part of our task as theologians to understand the reorganizations—both of theological contents and of theological activities—that have already occurred. It falls to us to integrate the achievements of the past into the theology of the present. But we are also preparing the way for whatever the next stage will be. There have been different kinds of religious and theological meaning in the past, and we may expect an ongoing series of theoretical frameworks in the future. A decisive question for us is how to direct the process in which we are involved. That question cannot be met, Lonergan believed, by an overarching theoretical system. It has to be met, instead, by having an overarching methodical framework within which to process the inevitable pluralism of contexts, statements, and systems to bring about cumulative and progressive results. This is the meaning of Lonergan's contrast between the 'theoretical' and the 'methodical' stages of theology. "We reach the notion of method when we ask how does one effect the transition from one universe of discourse to another or, more profoundly, . . . from one level or stage in human culture to another."[52]

Foundational Methodology and the Control of Meaning

Conciliar dogma and the logical and metaphysical techniques of scholastic theology were efforts to get control of meaning, that is, to specify precisely what is meant while excluding what is not meant. If we compare (broadly) the New Testament, the dogmatic context of the ancient councils, and the metaphysical context of scholastic theology, we have a succession of increasingly differentiated controls of meaning. The context of the New Testament is basically symbolic and narrative.

---

52. Lonergan, "Questionnaire on Philosophy," 374–75.

The context of the councils is at least incipiently logical (or postlogical, in the sense that logical controls have influenced the educated strata of society), for the dogmas respond to questions raised by New Testament symbol and narrative by formulating second-order, propositional judgments (statements governing other statements); we will have more to say on this in due course.

In the context of scholastic theology the implications of Christian claims were subjected to rigorous investigation within an overarching metaphysical structure. Logic ensured the validity of arguments; metaphysics ensured the overall coherence of results. The best of scholasticism was an extraordinary achievement. Nevertheless, it occurred within a scientific paradigm that was, as we have mentioned, conceived as static. The logical arts of definition, postulation, and inference are extremely useful, provided one is already in a position to know which terms are relevant and how they are correctly and univocally to be defined. Logic, however, is no instrument for effecting or analyzing the leaps of development, for valid conclusions contain nothing not already in the premises. Moreover, to Lonergan's mind, the decay of scholasticism into intractable disputes shrouded in a fog of pseudometaphysical profundity invited the search for a new and higher principle of control—a principle that could make metaphysics itself methodical.

Lonergan was convinced that the basic problems in theology were not in the limitations of theological theories but in the limitations of theory itself as a way of directing the ongoing development of theology. Thus, as we have seen, he proposed in *Insight* a technique for discovering and verifying in oneself the metalogical principles of question and answer that are generative of logics and ground a basic semantics (metaphysics) of being as the to-be-known. This technique involves a kind of scientific attention to one's own cognitional operations, a discovery of their basic recurrent structure, and a decisive act of taking possession of them. Despite the difficulties involved in achieving adequate self-knowledge, Lonergan expected it to yield, in the long run, a reliable and versatile knife for eliminating confusion, nonsense, and obfuscation. He thought philosophy in this mode would stand to the human sciences and scholarship as mathematics to the natural sciences.[53]

---

53. For an excellent treatment, see Walmsley, *Lonergan on Philosophic Pluralism.*

Accordingly, he came to distinguish three principal stages in the control of meaning (and, therefore, in cultural development): a linguistic and literary stage, a logical and metaphysical stage, and an emerging third stage in which control is achieved through self-appropriation.[54] It is important to note that the successive stages of meaning are not supersessionary but cumulative. His strategy is to transpose logic and metaphysics into a new framework explicitly governed by self-appropriated intelligence. Logic is not a tool for discovery but a tool for clarifying what has been discovered. Metaphysics, as an integral heuristic structure for the exploration of being and an instrument for scrutinizing claims about being, is made methodical by leveraging the isomorphism of cognitional and ontological elements. What is basic, then, is self-appropriation.

Eventually, he came to call this project 'foundational methodology,' which is, in his opinion, the contemporary office of philosophy. Philosophy as foundational methodology is more than cognitional theory; it is also epistemology, metaphysics, and existential ethics (that is, a science of normative order in the soul). But in an ordering of methodological controls, first philosophy is cognitional theory: the basic science of what we are doing when we are knowing and, in that sense, the science of sciences and the root of the unity of science. It is not the office of foundational methodology to prescribe methods for the other sciences, assign their subjects, arrange them in a hierarchy, order their contents, or supply their special categories. By elucidating the structural dynamics of all inquiry, however, it does reflect on special methods, bring to light their grounds, examine their adequacy to their objects, clarify their suppositions, and demarcate their limits. Its significance is not restricted to scientific activities. It provides a basis for distinguishing and relating all the activities of inquiry, scientific and scholarly, practical ('common sense') and aesthetic, as articulately distinguished or inarticulately blending together in various degrees, and as typically derailed by bias, inattention, oversight, silliness, rationalization, ideology, and irresponsibility.

Foundational methodology itself follows an empirical method generalized to include the data of consciousness and not only, or even mainly, what is given to the senses.[55] It is not indifferent to the advances in other

54. See *Method* (1972), 85–99, or CWL 14, 82–95.
55. See *Insight*, 268–69; "Questionnaire on Philosophy," 377–78, 381; "Lectures on Religious

sciences, however, for their methods are among the objects of its inquiry.[56] Explaining and understanding particular methods would include grasping the proportion of different sets of operations (different methods) to different kinds of objects, and therefore the basic and total science expands to include an epistemology, that is, a general formulation of the adequacy of knowing to the known. It includes a basic semantics of the to-be-known (a metaphysics), not in the scholastic sense of providing categories to be filled in by the particular sciences, but in the sense of providing an overarching heuristic framework for integrating the results of the sciences and a technique for comparing propositions by analyzing the necessary and sufficient conditions for their truth.

Since the generalized empirical method takes in the data of moral as well as cognitional consciousness, foundational methodology also includes existential ethics. It cannot help but touch upon theology, since only theology deals adequately with the real dynamics of sin and grace and therefore draws up philosophy into its higher viewpoint.[57] Thus, philosophy in Lonergan's sense has a theological telos. Philosophy needs theology to round out its consideration of the human condition. Conversely, theology subsumes philosophy, for in the absence of adequate philosophical foundations, the faith itself suffers. This eliminates the separation in practice of philosophy and theology. "Once philosophy becomes existential and historical, once it asks about man, not in the abstract, not as he would be in some state of pure nature, but as in fact he is here and now in all the concreteness of his living and dying, the very possibility of the old distinction between philosophy and theology vanishes."[58] Its vanishing is not by logical unification or by negating the disproportion of natural and supernatural orders of being, but by the recovery of the unity of inquiry and of wisdom we encounter in an Aquinas.[59]

Studies and Theology (3) The Ongoing Genesis of Methods," in *A Third Collection*, CWL 16, 140–59, here 144–46.

56. The consciousness under investigation is not the infantile subjectivity of the world of immediacy but the subject as oriented in the world mediated by meaning and motivated by value. In this connection, note the importance assigned to reoriented sciences for the development of metaphysics: *Insight*, 421–26.

57. Lonergan, "Questionnaire on Philosophy," 358–59.

58. Lonergan, "Dimensions of Meaning," 245.

59. See Lonergan, "Philosophy of God, and Theology," 199–218.

Commonly it is recognized that St Thomas Aquinas took over the Aristotelian synthesis of philosophy and science to construct the larger Christian view that includes theology. But it is, perhaps, less commonly appreciated that the development of empirical human sciences has created a fundamentally new problem. For these sciences consider man in his concrete performance, and that performance is a manifestation not only of human nature but also of human sin, not only of nature and sin but also of a de facto need of divine grace, not only of a need of grace but also of its reception and of its acceptance or rejection. It follows that an empirical human science cannot analyze successfully the elements in its object without an appeal to theology. Inversely, it follows that if theology is to be queen of the sciences, not only by right but also in fact, then theologians have to take a professional interest in the human sciences and make a positive contribution to their methodology. Finally, insofar as philosophy itself becomes existentialist, it stands in the same relation to theology as the empirical human sciences.[60]

In this brief section we have drawn together some of the threads from the previous chapter and related them to Lonergan's intended transposition of theology into a methodical plane. I have tried to sketch why he thought a new kind of control of meaning is possible and desirable. Nevertheless, because this control rests on self-appropriation, it is not something that can really be communicated by a brief sketch. It involves, as I have said from the outset, a kind of long-term ascetical practice. Lonergan aimed to facilitate that practice by crafting a workbook, *Insight*. It is not a resounding success for various reasons, but I hope the reader may begin to suspect the struggle worthwhile.

Theology as Functional Collaboration

At its best, scholastic theology was united as a set of common questions and a shared conceptuality for formulating answers. It was animated by the goal of integrating all theological contents into an overarching

---

60. *Insight*, 765.

theoretical conceptuality, which proved impossible to attain. Its scientific ideals were necessity, certitude, universality, and permanence, although its ablest practitioners transcended the limits of these ideals.[61] The scientific and historical 'revolutions' put paid to these ideals.

Once we recognize the extent to which the Christian tradition and its theology have developed, we are confronted with a series of important questions. In the first place, there is the problem of understanding the character of the developments that have already occurred, and there arise treatments of, for instance, the development of dogma and attempts to understand that development in light of such principles as John Henry Newman sought to articulate. In this process, Christian theology and the Christian religion have been interdependent, for developments in theology have caused the tradition to develop, and the developing tradition has caused theology to develop.[62] Along the climb to understanding of these matters, there inevitably arise various errors. For instance, some say the development is a deductive process for which the documents of revelation supply the premises. Others counter that the Scriptures supply no such premises and therefore conclude either that the development is illegitimate or perhaps that it represents some kind of ongoing revelation in the church.

An even bigger problem arises if we shift our attention from the past to the future. For the fact is that theology is under construction still, and we are its constructors. The quality of our work will inevitably shape the future of the church. When, therefore, Lonergan raises the question of method, he is not only trying to understand how theology has already developed. He is trying to face explicitly the problem of how it will develop in the future. And, while our control is inevitably rough, it can at least be improved by proceeding methodically in accord with a method adequate to the task. The prevalence of mistaken notions adds greater urgency. "Knowledge of method becomes a necessity when false notions of method are current and more or less disastrous."[63] The repudiation of dogma, of metaphysics, of the possibility of religious truth

---

61. See Bernard J. F. Lonergan, "Isomorphism of Thomist and Scientific Thought," in *Collection*, CWL 4, 133–41.

62. For a helpful discussion, see Ben F. Meyer, *The Church in Three Tenses* (Garden City, N.Y: Doubleday, 1971).

63. Lonergan, "Questionnaire on Philosophy," 374.

claims: disorientation of this kind is disastrous for Christianity. It is, unfortunately, also common. For Lonergan, then, theological method is practical in the same way philosophy as self-appropriation is practical; it is practical as an exercise of responsibility and, indeed, an attempt to exercise responsibility collectively.

Means are ordered to an end, and method, which orders operations to an end, begins by envisioning the goal to be achieved. The overarching goal of Christian theology, for Lonergan, is the mediation of the Gospel into diverse cultures. The activities of theology, then, are mediating the Gospel into present cultural situations. Obviously, conceived this way, theology cannot achieve its goal once and for all, nor can it achieve it through a single activity, but only by assembling the results of many coordinated activities. Each of these activities, in turn, has its own proper, subordinate goal, and each proceeds according to the methods and criteria appropriate to its goal. Hence, distinguishing the activities is for the sake of ensuring each its appropriate autonomy and resisting the intrusion of alien criteria. Distinguishing the activities of theology, however, is also for the sake of coordinating them. The activities are coordinated so that the practitioners can envisage how their work is related to a larger goal and to the other activities likewise ordered to that goal—without expecting each theologian to master every skill set, comprehend every procedure, or personally assimilate all the results.

Once this is grasped, the central question becomes how to identify, distinguish, and relate the tasks. Our present concern is Lonergan's eventual proposal in *Method in Theology*, but it will be helpful to offer a few signposts along the path of his development to that point. His initial division of theological tasks was on the basis of the Aristotelian and Thomist procedures of analysis and synthesis, the way of discovery and the way of explanation, recast as the dogmatic and the systematic ways in theology. The systematic way—for Lonergan the signal illustration was always Aquinas's treatise on the Trinity—presupposed the articulation of the mysteries and in that sense was subordinate to the dogmatic way. He quickly realized, however, that way of discovery required further distinctions. The positive part of theology had to be distinguished from the dogmatic, for it is one thing to apprehend the particular in its particularity—the theology of Paul as distinct from John—and another to bring to light the universal in the particular—Paul and John as witnesses to a common faith. But he also realized that the witnesses had to be dialectically scrutinized to disclose the limitations of their thought—the materialist assumptions of a Tertullian, for instance— and that a statement of the one faith, a properly dogmatic statement, could emerge only after dialectical scrutiny had effected a preliminary purification of theological categories. Practically, then, by the early 1960s Lonergan had distinguished positive, dialectical, doctrinal, and systematic functions of theology. We will say more about these issues in the next chapter, because it represents the stage of his thinking at the time his Trinity manuals were finalized, but already, we will see, the river was overflowing the banks.

In February 1965, Lonergan made a decisive breakthrough in his understanding of how the tasks of theology should be distinguished and coordinated. This breakthrough is expressed in the architecture of eight functional specialties that is the central proposal of *Method in Theology*. Lonergan realized that the structure of theology as a functional unity was grounded in fact on the prior functional unity of consciousness itself as a conversational structure. The functions of theology could be distinguished and related by a kind of isomorphism to the conversational structure of consciousness.

Lonergan was hardly unique in conceiving theology as conversational, that is, as a matter of 'hearing' and 'saying,' as he put it in his original formulation of functional specialties in theology.[64] Lonergan's proposal is distinctive because the differentiation is through *functional* specialization rather than the common field or subject specializations, and the differentiation of functions is grounded in the normative operational structure of consciousness. The operational structure of consciousness unfolds normatively through (1) attention to what is presented in experience, (2) interrogation and discovery of intelligible order or, perhaps, "of hitherto unnoticed or unrealized possibilities,"[65] (3) reflective assessment of evidence and rational assent, and (4) discerning values and taking responsibility. This operational structure is a functional whole; the

---

64. See the so-called 'Discovery Page,' Lonergan's handwritten notes, from 1964, outlining the original conception of functional specialties in theology (47200D0E060).

65. *Method* (1972), 53, or CWL 14, 52.

operations unfold not in a strict linear sequence but in functional inter-dependence with one another. The higher order operations sublate—that is, presuppose and integrate—the lower. Inquiry presupposes data given in experience. Reflective appraisal construes evidence in relation to a possibly relevant intelligibility reached through inquiry. Responsible agency incorporates a reflective, rational grasp of what already is the case and what might be realized by our choices. Choices set the stage for new experiences to be attentively processed. The whole assembly is a wheel or arc of functionally interdependent activities.

Any scientific activity will, in some sense, be a particular implementa-tion of this structure. The natural and human sciences already distinguish, for instance, 'pure' from 'applied' functions, data collection, experiment, or fieldwork from theory, ethics from policy, the interpretation of texts from the history of polities, societies, and cultures, and so forth.[66] They involve, furthermore, responsible decisions regarding the questions to be pursued and the most efficacious means of pursuing them. To be efficacious, the work has to be shared, and the results have to be coor-dinated. Lonergan likened this interdependence of practitioners to the relationship of theoretical to experimental physicists:

> Experimental physicists alone have the knowledge and skills needed to handle a cyclotron. But only theoretical physicists are able to tell what experiments are worth trying and, when they are tried, what is the significance of the results. Once more a

---

66. I do not claim that these functions are adequately distinguished in most current discussions of method but that they are distinct functions in fact. Consider the difficulties entrained by Paul J. Griffiths's 2014 plenary address to the Catholic Theological Society of America. In my opinion Griffiths is working with an insufficiently differentiated conception of theology in terms of three functions only, Discovery, Interpretation, and Speculation; the critical functions of Dialectic and Foundations get short shrift, and the solution is provided by proposing some claims as metatheo-logical, foundations in the sense of first propositions. These first propositions, however, are theolog-ically specific truth claims about the meaning of conversion; they are properly internal to theology as a topic for theological investigation, dispute, and reflection. By contrast, Lonergan's method, precisely because it settles not the content of theology but the procedures by which the content is to be handled, anticipates theological disagreements and provides for them to be handled through processes internal to theology. Paul J. Griffiths, "Theological Disagreement: What It Is, and How to Do It," ABC, Aug. 26, 2014, http://www.abc.net.au/religion/articles/2014/08/26/4074627.htm. Compare Griffiths, *The Practice of Catholic Theology: A Modest Proposal* (Washington, D.C.: The Catholic University of America Press, 2016), esp. 33–40, 129–34; it does not appear the problems have really been resolved.

single process of investigation is divided into successive stages,
and each stage becomes a distinct specialty.[67]

Theology is relatively more complicated than other zones of inquiry,
because it is involved with a multifaceted reality (including nature,
which is proportionate to our intelligence; sin, which is objectively irrational; and the supernatural order, which exceeds the proportion of our
intelligence) and is also involved in the construction or mediation of
that reality. In other words, theology is both coming to terms with the
Christian tradition and its message and also, by communicating that
message across many cultures, contributing to the present and future
reality of the church. As we might expect, this calls for a relatively
differentiated method.

Theology, like faith itself, starts with receiving an address with a
listening that promotes conversion. It culminates in a speaking, in a
communication of the word. Lonergan's first architectonic distinction,
then, is between two phases we might describe as *ressourcement* (mediating the past) and *aggiornamento* (addressing the future). Lonergan
himself described them as mediating and mediated, by which he meant
that, in the first phase, theological activities are mediating an encounter
with the whole Christ, head and members, and in the second, theology
mediates knowledge of Christ and thereby supports the mutual self-
mediation of head and members, the historical self-mediation of Christ
in his body.[68] Theology comes to grips with the problem of transposition
(from one culture to another or one stage of development to another) by
methodically differentiating and ordering the various functions involved
in encountering the past and determining its relevance to the present.

A distinction of functions corresponds to a distinction of proximate
objects and goals, and theology, which regards the whole Christ, head
and members, in its concrete past and present becoming, must deal variously with texts, their meanings, historical processes, conflicts and the
principles of their resolution, the mysteries of faith, faith seeking understanding, and pastoral implementation. Theology, then, is a functional
unity of distinct, coordinated activities, in which each activity is ordered

67. *Method* (1972), 126, or CWL 14, 122.
68. See *Method* (1972), 135, 363–64, or CWL 14, 129–30, 334–36.

to an objective corresponding to one of the principal operations in the structure of human consciousness. Because that structure has four main levels of activity, and theology moves in two phases, Lonergan distinguishes eight functions in all—the four principal operations as they operate in the two phases. The activities of the first phase move from data to understanding to judgment to evaluation; the activities of the second phase move inversely from evaluation to judgment to understanding to presentations. I will henceforth capitalize the eight functions: Research, Interpretation (or exegesis), History, Dialectic, Foundations, Doctrines, Systematics, and Communications. Lonergan's discussions of each are not detailed prescriptions but, as it were, foundational reorientations.

The functions of the first phase mediate an encounter with the tradition, but they do so by distinguishing different elements entering into that encounter. For instance, what Paul wrote is its own question. What Lonergan means by Research, then, has its proper goal, to establish the text, the data of Paul's writings, and it unfolds according to the criteria and procedures appropriate to that goal. If what Paul wrote is one question, what he meant in writing it is another.

Interpretation, then, has its own criteria and procedures. It also has its own finality: to understand what was meant, the meaning immanent in the data, the texts. Obviously, moreover, establishing the texts in Research and understanding them in Interpretation are interdependent procedures. The dependence of Interpretation upon Research seems fairly obvious, but it is also true that Research cannot be isolated from Interpretation, because (among other reasons) there are variants in the manuscript tradition settled by internal indications and programs of Research motivated by exegetical questions.

While what Paul meant is complicated enough by itself, his role in the formation and rise of early Christianity is another and perhaps still more difficult question. The functional specialty History, then, has its own criteria, its own procedures, and its own finality to a determination of just how Paul contributed to a historical process. Once again, the interdependence of functions should be obvious. History depends on data (Research) and the interpretation of meanings (Interpretation). In turn, it provides a larger context for those activities and influences their selection of relevant questions. History, though, is more than an aggregation of evidence or of interpretations. It responds to a distinct question of its own: not just what traces were left or what was meant by the tracers, but what really happened and what was the shape of the movement.

Inevitably, establishing Paul's writings, interpreting his meaning, and judging his role in the emergence of Christianity invite further questions of evaluation that regard not only Paul but also the interpreters and the historians. For different exegetes propose different, and sometimes conflicting, interpretations of Paul's gospel. Different historians reach different, and sometimes opposed, judgments of his role in the rise of Christianity. Moreover, there is the question of Paul himself and his gospel. As it turns out, not everyone likes Paul or is sympathetic to his gospel. Not everyone considers him a reliable interpreter of Jesus, or a reliable witness to Pharisaism, or what have you. Paul was himself party to conflict, and we cannot study the conflicts without at some point finding ourselves taking sides. But taking sides in a serious way involves sorting out the relative importance of differences, for not every difference is an opposition. It involves assigning the real grounds for differences and clarifying the bases for preferring one side or another. These activities pertain to the specialty, Dialectic. Dialectic, then, has its own distinct criteria, procedures, and finality to evaluation and to decisions about which side we are to take.

The distinction of functions ensures their due autonomy. But the autonomy is not unaccountable. Autonomous exegesis may be secularist exegesis if one's presuppositions are secularist.[69] But the function of Dialectic is evaluative. It regards not only the texts but also the researchers, not only interpretations but also exegetes, not only histories but also historians; it regards Paul himself but also all the practitioners involved in the mediating process. Its point is to face the conflicts squarely and trace out their roots. It is to scrutinize the relative adequacy and influence of such presuppositions as a secularist, a positivist, a reductionist might bring to the table, in such a way as to promote the clarity of one's own fundamental principles.[70]

69. See *Method* (1972), 317–18, or CWL 14, 295–96. In the epilogue to *Insight*, Lonergan laments that "we live in the midst of a sensate culture, in which very many men, insofar as they acknowledge any hegemony of truth, give their allegiance not to a divine revelation, nor to a theology, nor to a philosophy, nor even to an intellectualist science, but to science interpreted in a positivistic and pragmatic fashion" (766).

70. The relationship between the dialectical function in theology and what, in *Insight*, Lonergan conceived as the "universal viewpoint" is rather complex: see *Method* (1972), 153n1, or CWL 14,

These, then, are the activities of the first, mediating phase of theology: Research, Interpretation, History, and Dialectic. Encounter with the past occurs through an assembly of functionally interrelated activities: determining what Paul actually wrote (Research), determining what Paul meant (Interpretation), determining Paul's place in the formation of primitive Christianity (History), and evaluating Paul's gospel (Dialectic). The first phase of theology is indirect discourse. It is coming to terms with others: what they said and did, what they meant in saying and doing it, what they achieved for good or ill, and whether the achievement was worthwhile and why. It culminates in personal encounter through Dialectic.

The cumulative sifting of the first phase prepares and invites the theologian to take a personal stand. The second phase of theology begins, as it were, where the first, mediating phase leaves off: personal encounter. Encountering others, one is invited to take sides. Taking sides, one finds oneself. The two phases, then, move in inverse directions. The first phase rises from the presentations of the witnesses to exegesis, from exegesis to the predicative truth of history, and through predicative truth to the encounter with historical persons in the truth and untruth of their existence. The sequence of functions follows an arc ascending from the maximal particularity of data through a progression of universalizing operations to the maximal universality of fundamental options and principles (Dialectic and Foundations), to descend again through a series of mediating operations to the maximal particularity of Communications.

Response to personal encounter marks the transition from the phase of listening to the phase of speaking. Involvement in Dialectic requires taking sides, and taking sides urges a basic clarification of principles. The radical principles are not extrinsic. One speaks out of the truth or untruth of one's own existence in Christ. Of course it is true that one also listens and reports this way, for nothing is heard except in the manner of the hearer. Nevertheless, it is in the second phase that one moves from reporting on others to speaking for oneself.

Dialogue with the tradition, then, provides the materials for self-discovery. It does not, of course, ensure it. The conversion of the theologian is decisive for theology, but it is not a theological operation. It is a

---

146n2. This whole matter is given a thorough investigation by Ivo Coelho; see his *Hermeneutics and Method*, esp. 200–203.

religious and personal reality, precarious and imperfect, ever a turn from existential untruth and toward the light. It is a reality that in its religious, moral, and intellectual dimensions is inevitably at play from the outset. It is the reality that is coming to light in what the theologian admires in the tradition and what he or she finds repugnant; what he or she deems progress and what derailment; what he or she is prepared to believe or reject. Before ever one's criteria are objectified and subjected to scrutiny, they are operative, not as a fixed point but as a reality under construction. The activities of theological listening do not ensure conversion, but they invite and dispose. They nudge the inadequacies of one's present reality into the open, if not for one's own recognition, then often enough for others'. In the office of Foundations, Lonergan proposes we lay down our markers with such clarity and amplitude as we can muster.

Foundations, in turn, ground the other specialties of the second phase. It is the truth of one's existence that not only founds but also radically qualifies one's assent to the mysteries in the judgments articulated in Doctrines. It is the truth of one's existence that settles the devotion, sobriety, and diligence by which one seeks an obscure but fruitful understanding of the mysteries achieved in Systematics. And only the truth of existence vivifies the proclamation of the Gospel, as affirmed and more or less understood, to all the world in Communications.

Perhaps it is curious that Lonergan situates the function of Doctrines within the direct discourse phase of theology. This is because assent to doctrine—not as a report about others but as a personal act—presupposes a foundational stand. Consequently, the theological articulation of doctrine—not only its content but, perhaps even more, its relation to reality—inevitably is conditioned by the quality of the theologian. The finality of Doctrines is to a statement of Christian truths, in the ordinary sense of truth as true predication. This, of course, presupposes that Christianity has truths, a question on which theologians have significant differences for philosophical, theological, and religious reasons.[71] Different theologians take different stands, to be sorted through another turn of the wheel round to Dialectic.

71. For instance, Guarino, *Foundations of Systematic Theology*, 1–39, and Matthew Levering, *Scripture and Metaphysics: Aquinas and the Renewal of Trinitarian Theology*, Challenges in Contemporary Theology (Malden, Mass.: Blackwell, 2004), 23–46, both argue that Christian doctrine presupposes a particular notion of truth.

Lonergan's own stand was that theology is not merely the exegesis of religious experience (this is how he characterized 'modernism'[72]) but the intellectual mediation of religious realities; it is not a science of propositions but a science of reality. That reality is God and God's involvement in history.[73] God's involvement is historical in a twofold sense. Christianity, like any tradition, has a history and is still making for itself a history. It is doing so in conversation with God. But the basis of that conversation is not only God's prior, unmediated word, the word of the indwelling Spirit; it is also the personal entrance of God into history, the historical life of the Word incarnate.[74] Christians, then, not only walk in the light of God's supernal love; they also walk in the light of belief in supernatural mysteries revealed by the Word incarnate.[75] Inevitably, to be Christian is to be involved not only with a religious grammar but with truth claims and, therefore, with the realities those claims mediate.

For Lonergan, then, involvement with God's word in history entails a realism—not, indeed, just any form of realism, but a realism mediated by true judgments: *praestet fides supplementum / sensuum defectui*.[76] The history of Christian doctrine is not only the history of a community expressing its self-understanding or articulating its convictions; it is the history of the progressive clarification of what God has revealed. Christian theology, then, is not basically an articulation of the historical forms of Christian religious experience, but basically an articulation of the Christian message, its meaning and value, role and significance. For this reason, Lonergan's conception of methodical theology includes Doctrines and yet, in the functional subalternation of Doctrines to Foundations, makes explicit the dependence of predicative upon existential truth.

About Systematics and its relation to Doctrines, we will also have much more to say in the chapters to come. Lonergan conceives the function of Systematics primarily as explanatory of the mysteries received in faith. It takes its proximate start from the truths settled in

---

72. *Triune God: Doctrines*, 262–63.

73. See Lonergan, "Theology and Understanding," 117.

74. *Method* (1972), 118–19, or CWL 14, 114–16; compare "Horizons," in *Philosophical and Theological Papers 1965–1980*, CWL 17, 10–29, here 21.

75. See Lawrence, *Fragility of Consciousness*, 384–404.

76. "Faith provides what the senses lack": a verset from Thomas Aquinas's well-known hymn for Corpus Christi, *Pange lingua*.

Doctrines. Its relationship to the data of Scripture and tradition, then—and whatever other data theologians come to regard as germane to their enterprise—is mediated by the series of prior activities sketched in the paragraphs above. This conception, as we shall see most fully in chapter 8, frees Systematics to order questions for theological understanding in accordance with its own internal objectives and criteria, without prejudice to the order found in the documents of revelation.

The function of Communications, finally, completes the arc of theological offices in a return to the same maximal particularity and concreteness characteristic of Research. All of theology has an ulterior finality to the universal witness of the church. But Communications is the function in which that finality comes to its practical fruition. It is the pastoral presentation of the Gospel to persons of every age, culture, and educational attainment. This includes the communication of theologians with their colleagues in other sciences. Because, however, it is maximally concrete, it is also the domain of *phronesis* more than of theory. The better one understands, the freer one is in communication. But that understanding is two-sided. One has to know theology to communicate it, but one has to know one's audience to know what kind of communication will render them genuine service. Pastoral agency and encounter, finally, alters facts on the ground. Those changed situations are part of the universe of Christian experience directly relevant to theological listening.

In summary, Lonergan's proposal distinguishes theology into two phases, listening and speaking. It distinguishes the activities of each phase on the basis of a series of proximate goals, thereby breaking down the large problem of 'hermeneutics' and 'evangelization' into a series of more manageable problems. The activities of the first phase are Research (what Paul said), Interpretation (what Paul meant), History (what Paul achieved), and Dialectic (evaluation of Paul's gospel). The activities of the second phase are Foundations (basic principles), Doctrines (truth and value claims), Systematics (theological understanding), and Communications. Explicitly distinguishing them ensures the appropriate level of autonomy for each in working out its procedures and criteria. It promotes coordination without confusion. The activities are ordered together as a functional whole with an ulterior finality to Christian witness, the mediation of the Gospel into every culture.

Specialties and Specialists

Functional specialization is not a system of theology but a framework for theological collaboration, an architectonic clarification of theological activities.[77] It envisages a dynamic structure of tasks. Its explanatory basis is not a distinction of specialists but a distinction of specialties.

> The eight functional specialties are a set of self-regulative, ongoing, interdependent processes. They're not stages such that you do one and then you do the next. Rather, you have different people at all eight and interacting. And the interaction is not logical. It's attentive, intelligent, reasonable, responsible, and religious. . . . Doing method fundamentally is distinguishing different tasks, and thereby eliminating totalitarian ambitions. Systematic theologians for a couple of centuries thought they were the only ones who were theologians, then positive theologians thought they were the only ones. . . . What I want is eight different tasks distinguished. One extraordinary person might very well do all eight—but he's doing eight different things, not just one and the same thing over and over again.[78]

The unity of theology in this mode is not on the side of the contents, which are under construction, but on the side of the activities involved in the construction. It is a functional unity to which properly belongs each step in the process from data to results. It moves in an arc, beginning from the concrete and particular to ascend to the level of universal principle only to return to the concrete. There results a transposition of the classical functions of wisdom and prudence into a new wisdom that is neither purely speculative, in the ancient sense of dealing with the universal and necessary, nor purely practical as a matter of what is to be said and done, but also a matter of judging what is contingently true about ourselves and about the world of our involvement, which is also the world of God's involvement.

---

77. See Frederick E. Crowe, *Christ and History: The Christology of Bernard Lonergan from 1935 to 1982* (Ottawa: Novalis Press, 2005), 183 (Lonergan presents "not so much a system of theology as a system for doing theology"). It is not exactly a system, either.

78. Lonergan, "An Interview," 178–79.

Functional specialties distinguish and coordinate theological operations; they do not dictate a division of theologians into particular specialties.[79] Lonergan's purpose was to help theologians clarify the different, interrelated kinds of operations they are in fact performing. Theology is an ongoing collaboration involving many different, interrelated skill and knowledge sets distributed in the community of theologians. Nevertheless, while the distinction of specialists is not the basis for functional specialization and is not required by it, something like it may gradually come to pass. Widespread adoption of functional specialization would, presumably, induce theologians to rethink their activities in relation to the differentiation of functions, methods, and skill sets rather than content areas. It would be surprising if this did not result, over the long run, in some redistribution of specialists along the lines suggested by functions rather than, as now, into fields. On the other hand, the implications this would have for the organization of institutions and of education are not wholly straightforward. The framework of functional specialties is not directly a blueprint for the reorganization of theological departments, curricula, or textbooks.

A functional conception of theology deconstructs the conventional categories of theological field specialization. Rather than asking, for instance, what historical theology is, a theology that is methodical in Lonergan's sense asks, what are the functions that mediate the Christian past in theology, and how are they related to the functions creative of the Christian present and future? In a sense, all theology—that is, the whole coordinated set of activities—is, or should be, historical, for theology mediates a tradition into a culture, which it cannot do without incorporating the activities that bring the tradition to light. But the conception of functional specialties also acknowledges that every activity pertaining to the mediation of the Gospel into cultures is, or can be, properly theological. Distinction and coordination, then, are of equal moment, for each task in the assembly has its own proper goals, and each is theological to the extent that it enters into the functional unity of an ongoing mediation—which is also the constitution—of the church.

In a functionally specialized theology, the conventional field and subject divisions lose their methodical significance for the coordination of theological activities. They do not, however, lose their whole significance.

---

79. *Method* (1972), 136–38, 141–42, or CWL 14, 130–31, 134–35.

Inasmuch as the activities of the first, listening phase of theology involve the acquisition of a common sense specialized to particular places and times, the specialists will have to choose, for example, which languages to acquire and which cultures, at which periods, to immerse themselves in; so field specialization will remain a relevant subdivision of the materials for the first phase. And inasmuch as theological knowledge is to be communicated, organization by topic or subject will remain a useful way of presenting the results. On the other hand, it seems likely that, in a functional context, the training of theologians would take not the distribution-requirements approach but rather the study of problems as a way into both the constitutive questions of the tradition and the special methods of theological activity.[80] All of this is to say that the portents of functional specialization for the way theology is studied and the way it is communicated are somewhat multiform.

Transformation and Continuity in Theological Method

Some inchoate differentiation has always been part of theology, not only in its practiced reality but in its self-reflection. Irenaeus carefully distinguished theology from the Gospel: the latter is a public teaching for everyone, no matter how untutored; the former is an inquiry into its rhyme and reason.[81] Augustine's *crede ut intelligas*, Anselm's *fides quaerens intellectum*, and, above all, Thomas Aquinas's articulation of theology as a science subalternate to the knowledge of God and the blessed effectively transposed this distinction of truth and inquiry. Aquinas implemented two fundamental breakthroughs: the distinction of judgment from understanding[82] (implicit in Irenaeus's defense of the unlearned, whose faith was true though their understanding primitive) and the theorematic differentiation of grace as entitatively disproportionate to nature.[83] By distinguishing judgment from understanding, Aquinas

80. On field and subject specialization, see *Method* (1972), 125–26, 136–145, 167–73, or CWL 14, 121–22, 130–38.

81. Irenaeus, *Adversus Haereses* 1, 10; 3, 4. English translation in Cyril C. Richardson, ed., *Early Christian Fathers* (Philadelphia: Westminster Press, 1953), 360–61, 354–75.

82. E.g., *De veritate* q. 14, a. 1c.

83. A theorem is not new data but the introduction of a set of intellectual coordinates for organizing the known data. See *Grace and Freedom*, 14–20.

grounded the distinction of the level of truth (*quia, an sit*) from the level of understanding (*quomodo, quid sit*). The theorem of the supernatural, furthermore, provided a technical instrument for expressing the superiority of the light of faith to the light of human intelligence. Aquinas was thus able to elucidate the goal of theology in its speculative function as an imperfect, analogical *intelligentia fidei*. The way was opened to a formulation of the different kinds of procedures to be used in relation to different kinds of questions.

This achievement is embedded in the architecture of the *Summa contra gentiles*. A twofold mode of truth distinguishes mysteries too high for us from truths proportionate to our reason. With regard to the latter, we give demonstrative reasons even if we can understand the realities only analogically (for instance, the existence and attributes of God). The mysteries, however, are held in faith; to establish them, we rely on authorities. Because they are too high for us, our understanding is obscure, imperfect, analogical.[84] By distinguishing, in effect, these different offices or functions of reason, Aquinas was able to work out refined procedures for establishing philosophical and theological truth claims (*demonstratio quia, determinatio fidei*) and for giving an intelligent account of them.

Lonergan carried these achievements forward, but he transposed them in various manners. Where Aquinas conceived *sacra doctrina* as a subalternated science on the model set forth in Aristotle's *Posterior Analytics*, Lonergan conceives theology as a functional assembly of tasks severally and cumulatively implementing the general structure of inquiry.[85] The speculative function, Systematics, retains its subalternation to the articles of faith affirmed in Doctrines, but theology as a functional whole is subalternated not to doctrines but to conversion and faith. Note, therefore, that the functional subalternation of Systematics to Doctrines is not the only or even the most important manner in which Lonergan's method transposes Aquinas's conception of *sacra*

84. See Thomas Aquinas, *Quodlibet* 4 q. 9 a. 3, in *Quaestiones de quolibet*, vol. 2, 2 vols., Opera Omnia 25, Leonine ed. (Paris: Editions du Cerf, 1996), 339–40; *STh* 1 q. 1 a. 8. See also *Method* (1972), 337, or CWL 14, 312; *Triune God: Systematics*, 6–11.

85. The method is 'transcendental' both in the sense of not being restricted to some genera of inquiry and also in the sense of articulating the conditions—necessary though not sufficient—for the possibility of inquiry. It is 'generalized' as expanded to attend to data given in consciousness as well as the data of senses.

doctrina as a subalternated wisdom. He effects, we might say, a two-fold transposition, functionally in the subalternation of Systematics to Doctrines and existentially in the subalternation (as it were) of all of theology to conversion.

By asserting that the existential foundation of theology is the wisdom, more or less adequate, of the theologian, Lonergan transposed Aquinas's notion of *sacra doctrina* as a wisdom inasmuch as it is faith in contact with reason. For Lonergan, theology is authentically theological only in the measure that theologians themselves are truly wise both by the infused wisdom of self-surrender and by the achieved wisdom of self-knowledge.[86] Indeed, Lonergan's insistence on the existential priority of conversion means that the achievement of theological learning is actually wisdom only inasmuch as it is grounded in and at the service of the higher wisdom of self-surrender, docility to the Spirit. For Lonergan, the basis of transhistorical and transcultural normativity is not in permanent formulations but in the measure to which theologians actually are adequate to their vocations, that is, are more or less thoroughly converted, responsive to the Gospel, at home in prayer, in theory, in interiority. Methods and procedures, sources and results, and theologians themselves are all subject to dialectical critique.

The transposition was also a transformation, inasmuch as it also displaced the Thomist subalternation of theology to the truths of faith into the system of functional specialties. The result is "a greatly enlarged notion of theology" conceived now not in terms of its material and formal objects but as a mediation of the Gospel into a culture.[87] All the mediating operations that once were regarded as merely adjunct to theology are now explicitly conceived as pertaining to theology as an ongoing process from data to results, parts of a functional whole. In this process the data pertain to the whole Christ, head and members; the results are the building up of that same body.

Lonergan is more explicit than Aquinas in basing the differentiation of theological functions on the finality of cognitional operations, just as Lonergan's philosophy is more explicit than Aquinas's in articulating the recurrent structures of conscious intentionality. Lonergan takes his stand

---

86. Lonergan, "Bernard Lonergan Responds (1)," 265.

87. Ibid.

on the fact that "theologies are produced by theologians, that theologians have minds and use them, that their doing so should not be ignored or passed over but explicitly acknowledged in itself and in its implications."[88] Thus, he is not inventing procedures *ex nihilo* but ordering and methodically prosecuting tasks that, on examination, turn out to bear more than a family resemblance to successful procedures of the past. Where Aquinas distinguishes the *determinatio fidei* (a doctrinal function on the level of judgment) from *intelligentia fidei* (a speculative or systematic function on the level of understanding), Lonergan expands the structure in both directions and reduplicates the structure into the two phases of receiving the tradition and taking responsibility for it. Thus there is an ascending movement from data to evaluation and a descending movement from decision to presentation. The functional priority he assigns to activities such as establishing texts (Research), exegesis (Interpretation), and determining what happened (History) together fulfill, approximately, the positive function of *lectio* in the scholastic context. The classification and analysis of conflicts (Dialectic) and the articulation of fundamental principles for settling them (Foundations) correspond, approximately, to the tasks of scholastic disputation. Doctrines and Systematics correspond, approximately, to Aquinas's distinction between the *determinatio fidei* by appeal to authorities and the quest for fruitful understanding through analogical reasons in the *via doctrinae*. The function of Communications generalizes preaching and pastoral theology.

While preserving the functional subalternation of the systematic or speculative function of theology—theology as faith seeking understanding—to the truths held in faith, Lonergan also recognized that doctrines, as appropriated, were proper to the 'speaking' (and not just the hearing/reporting) phase of theology: 'I believe.' On the one side, doctrines have a historical context and that context has to be reconstructed if their meaning is to be retrieved. On the other side, doctrines are not only meanings retrieved by theologians operating in more or less adequate horizons; they are also affirmations of truth and value made in light of personal commitment, actively related to a subsequent history of doctrinal development and situated within an analogy of faith.[89] For better and

88. *Method* (1972), 24, or CWL 14, 26.
89. See *Method* (1972), 312–14, or CWL 14, 291–92.

worse, truth, as the correspondence of mind to reality, is not "so objective as to get along without minds."[90] The problem is not eliminated by deference, however laudable, to the participated wisdom of the magisterium,[91] for, as nothing is received except in the manner of the recipient,[92] only wisdom receives aright what the church proposes.[93] The normativity of doctrine, then, is derivative; what is basic is putting on the mind of Christ, so that doctrines are received and handed on with the church's authentic meaning (*"in eodem sensu, eademque sententia"*).[94]

It has been pointed out that the structure of functional specialization is not, in itself, specifically theological. Lonergan concurred that his structure would be relevant to any discipline confronting the future out of the past.[95] The wider relevance of functional specialization should not be too surprising. Method is a framework for handling questions in an orderly way; it does not predetermine which questions may arise and be permitted a serious hearing. What makes it theological is its use to mediate religious meanings and values into a cultural matrix. What makes it authentically theological is the wisdom, the adequacy of the theologian, the responsible preparation of reason informed by faith, motivated by love, and docile to the Spirit. The method foresees that theologians may fail to measure up to the tradition. It assigns to Dialectic the task of sifting through the variable contributions and taking sides. It assigns to Foundations the task of articulating the basis for making one's own claims. It does not assume a doctrine of grace as such, but it does assume a reality of grace, a reality of conversion. It is this reality that makes religion 'religious' and theology theological. Finally, in the functional subalternation of Systematics to Doctrines, it preserves the traditional conception of speculative theology as *intelligentia fidei*,

---

90. Lonergan, "The Subject," 62. Note that 'truth' in its ontological aspect is convertible with being, but in its cognitional aspect is a relation of knowing to being: see *Insight*, 575–76.

91. See *Early Works on Method 1*, 105–6; *Triune God: Systematics*, 58; compare *Method* (1972), 320–26, or CWL 14, 298–303.

92. *Quidquid recipitur ad modum recipientis recipitur.* Basically a metaphysical axiom for Aquinas (see, e.g., *STh* 1 q. 75 a. 5; compare 1 q. 12 a. 4c.; 1 q. 14 a. 1 ad 3; *ScG* bk. 2, chap. 79, no. 7; *De Veritate* q. 2 a. 3c.), for Lonergan it has an existential significance (see, e.g., *Triune God: Systematics*, 25).

93. A similar point is made by Joseph Ratzinger, *The Nature and Mission of Theology: Essays to Orient Theology in Today's Debates*, trans. Adrian Walker (San Francisco: Ignatius Press, 1995), 50–58.

94. Fuller discussion in the next chapter. See 1 Cor 1:10 (Vulgate).

95. Lonergan, "An Interview," 210.

without determining, at the methodological level, the content of faith
or of theology. Which authorities are to be accepted or what doctrines
are to be believed are theological questions to be handled by theologians,
preferably methodically.[96]

Conclusion

When he placed the material 'starting point' of theology not in truths
but in data, Lonergan was signaling the priority of listening to saying
and of questions to answers. By affirming the priority of data, Lonergan
affirms the priority of questions and refuses to predetermine what
questions and sources may count as theological, that is, prove relevant to
the mediation of the Gospel into a culture. It is not for the methodologist
but for the theologians to make that determination.

That determination can only belong to an ongoing conversation.
Theology is conversational and collaborative because learning is not like
looking. Learning is through the gradual development of understanding.
Its operator is the question, and questions usually arise and are refined
and explored in conversation. It is not achieved by some kind of spiritual
inspection, some mythical intuition of being prior to inquiry, as would
be well suited to the solitary. Learning circles round and out in a spiral
ascent through attention, wonder, discovery, formulation, construal and
appraisal of evidence, revision and correction and iteration. Coming to
know reality is a matter of hitting upon fruitful questions and gradually working out correct answers to them. The answers are known to
be correct not through an intuition of being but through a grasp of
the evidence on a question. The whole process is conversational; it is in
conversation that questions arise and are refined, data is brought to our
attention, the implications of ideas are worked out, tests are devised, and
evidence is produced or uncovered. By contrast, the counterpositional
stand on knowledge as looking is a matter of comparing concepts and
deducing the true conclusions contained in true premises. Unless one is

96. De facto, Lonergan's own practice in the Doctrinal function reflects the influence of Melchior
Cano's *De locis theologicis* and commonly accepted scholastic conventions about theological
arguments from authority. But these practices are internal to Doctrines, and, indeed, to Doctrines
within a particular articulation of a Catholic horizon—hence, to Doctrines as a theological function subalternated to Foundations, which explicates the implications of conversion.

a deficient logician, conversation is just a distraction. Knowing as looking begins and ends with the animal sense of reality 'out there.' Lonergan considered this position to overlook intelligence almost entirely. Computation—the application of rules—can be safely delegated to a machine, but posing questions, discovering rules, achieving synthesis, appraising evidence, these belong to the light of the mind. The distinction of functions in theology is the distinction of interrelated goals in a collaborative, conversational process of discovery and learning.

In a deductive process, controls may be objectified as rules for validity. In a process of learning, however, the basic event is not deduction but discovery. There are transitions in theology—for instance, from the largely narrative order of the Scriptures to the propositional order of the dogmas, or again, from Augustine's initial discovery of operative grace to Aquinas's reformulation in a fully theoretical context—that are not deductions but transpositions. Such nonlogical (but not illogical) transitions raise questions of a different kind of validity. There arises a problem of internal control—how the transitions are to be validated—which cannot be met automatically or by the application of rules. Validity in this sense can only be judged by wisdom.

Functional specialization faces this problem explicitly by recognizing that the real control, the judicial function of wisdom, is a result of theologians measuring up as hearers and doers of the word, thoroughly converted and at home in prayer and theory, scholarship and self-attention. Apart from self-appropriation and the concomitant grasp of the possibility of differentiations of consciousness, there is no adequate resolution of the questions of validity, criteria, and preference endemic to theology, nor could there be a way to meet—not to say surmount—the permanent problem of disagreement.[97] That control is explicitly applied in the functions of Dialectic and Foundations. Lonergan fixes the relation of the positive functions—Research, Interpretation, and History—to the Doctrinal, speculative (Systematics), and pastoral (Communications) functions through the explicit control of Dialectic and Foundations. It

97. To the extent that the problem admits of a solution, Lonergan sketched its structure in *Method* (1972), 250, or CWL 14, 234–35. An underlying issue regarding the adequacy of theologians is lack of differentiation in themselves: "Less differentiated consciousness finds more differentiated consciousness beyond its horizon and, in self-defence, may tend to regard the more differentiated with . . . ressentiment" (273; 256).

is a strategy for bringing problems and conflicts into the full light of day where they can be faced squarely.

Because it aims to get a handle on the conversational structure of historical existence, Lonergan's differentiation of functions in theology addresses how unprepared we may really be for collective responsibility, for listening and saying in a way that is historically serious—responsible to the history that has made us and responsible to the history we are making. In Lonergan's analogical structure of hearing and saying, 'hearing' is cumulative involvement with the given, with meaning, with truth, with others and Another. The consummation of 'hearing,' in theology as in life, is personal encounter: *cor ad cor loquitur*. As 'hearing' culminates in personal encounter, so one's 'saying' emerges from and discloses one's stance in the world, one's 'readiness' ("God called to Abraham. 'Ready,' he replied."):[98] what one is ready to do, approve, or censure; believe, affirm, or deny; understand, ask, or even notice. Thus, in Lonergan's proposal, Foundations follows functionally upon Dialectic because the coming to light of one's deepest commitments is one with the personal encounter. One 'finds oneself' admiring others. "The being of the subject is becoming,"[99] and the becoming is conversational.

One starts, then, where one already is, which means as a Christian and a theologian already struggling to reach up to the tradition, honor its best achievements, and let them enlarge and transform one's horizon. Theology, like faith itself, starts with receiving an address, with conversion from hearing. In its prior, listening phase, theology is both a measuring up and a being measured. In its second, speaking phase, theology is a mediated knowledge of Christ, head and members, through the foundational, doctrinal, systematic, and pastoral articulations of the theologian.

98. Gen 22:1, New American Bible (1970).

99. Bernard J. F. Lonergan, "Existenz and Aggiornamento," in *Collection*, 222–31, here 223; see *Insight*, 649.

Entr'acte

THE OFFICE OF WISDOM is to order and to judge. For five chapters we have tracked Lonergan's distinctive approach to wisdom as a problem of ordering inquiry to be fundamentally resolved through self-appropriation. This itinerary culminated, in the most recent chapter, in a preliminary and rather descriptive overview of his proposal for ordering activities in theology. Its predecessor had presented, in much the same manner, his proposal for method in philosophy. Along the way, we have not been unconcerned with wisdom's objects, the knowledge wisdom is to order, for we have wanted to understand what Lonergan says by watching what he does. Nevertheless, our focus has been on wisdom as a reality in the subject who does the ordering. It is the reality of wisdom, ever precarious and never to be taken for granted, that addresses the problem before truth.

Now the focus of our attention shifts, however, from the activities of ordering wisdom to the knowledge wisdom orders. In the three chapters to follow, we make a series of strategic visits to Lonergan's workshop. Method is reflection on performance, and Lonergan worked out his ideas on method in theology in the course of his efforts to practice theology under "impossible conditions."[100] By watching him at work, we hope to move from a notional to a real apprehension of the portent of his method. Our selection of problems cannot be omnivorous, however. Already we have seen some strategic instances of Lonergan's work, notably his interpretation of Thomas Aquinas and some samples of metaphysical analysis. Now we take three forays into what seems to be the distinctive heart of Lonergan's theological practice.

In the next chapter we will see Lonergan at work on a complex of problems connected to doctrine, its development, and its significance.

100. Lonergan, "Philosophy of God, and Theology," 174.

His efforts to come to terms with these issues in his Latin manuals of the 1960s refined his conception of Dialectic as a distinctive specialty in theology, conceived in relation to the prior, positive functions of exegesis and history and the posterior functions of dogmatic and speculative theology. In the sequel, we will practice a dialectic of our own by comparing methodological alternatives in Trinitarian systematics. Our question shall be why Lonergan regarded the treatise on the Trinity in Aquinas's *Summa theologiae* the apex of theological speculation on its topic, while Karl Rahner judged it a disaster. In the last chapter, we return to the theme of wisdom as gift by a meditation on the wisdom of Christ. This affords us a twofold opportunity to collect the threads of Lonergan's achievement. On the one side, we see how he thought through a problem for theological understanding in continuity and development of the tradition. On the other, we get a glimpse of something more foundational for him: his personal adherence to Christ, wisdom incarnate.

PART 2

Wisdom as Object

CHAPTER SEVEN

Doctrine and Meaning

As believers, we accept statements; and we accept statements not
as acceptable modes of speech or obligatory modes of speech but
as having a meaning. When a philosophy eliminates the possible
meaning of fundamental elements in our statements, it can eliminate
fundamental elements from our faith . . . for the simple reason
that Christian doctrine is doctrine; it is a message.[1]

BERNARD LONERGAN

LONERGAN DID NOT ATTEMPT an overarching theory of doctrinal development. His position was that developments are always concrete, so that one has to study particular developments to understand the factors at work. He had in *Insight*, however, attempted to work out some general considerations on the kinds of factors affecting the development of doctrine, as well as an instrument of analysis he called 'Dialectic.'[2] This would serve, according to one of his favorite metaphors, as the 'upper blade' of an analysis of development. The 'lower blade' could only be supplied by the evidence uncovered through research and understood and appraised through exegetical and historical studies. Already conceived as a technique, however,

---

1. Bernard J. F. Lonergan, "The Origins of Christian Realism (1961)," in *Philosophical and Theological Papers 1958–1964*, CWL 6, 80–93, here 266–67.

2. *Insight*, 553–617; for Lonergan's development on this topic in the period under consideration in this chapter, see Coelho, *Hermeneutics and Method*, 101–12.

Dialectic was not yet situated as a functional specialty within an over-arching methodological framework.[3]

Probably Lonergan's most important theological experiment in Dialectic was conducted in the context of his Gregorian University course on the Triune God. There, over a decade before *Method in Theology*, he attempted to implement the strategy devised in *Insight*. If there is little doubt his grip on method deepened considerably in the interval, the theological dialectic Lonergan conducted in his Trinity course is nevertheless the most fulsome illustration of his purpose. I propose, therefore, to explore his method by an examination of this effort. The result, unfortunately, is only a snapshot of Lonergan's practice up to 1964, but the alternative is to forsake our immediate interest in his performance to plunge instead into a wide-ranging study of his developing account of method.[4]

As for that performance, it leaves much to be desired. At the Gregorian he was assigned the tracts on Trinity and Christology. Lonergan knew from his long apprenticeship to Thomas Aquinas what the climb of scholarship entails. He had neither the time nor the preparation to achieve the kind of scholarly proficiency in the New Testament or in patristic theology that would truly qualify him for his assigned tasks. He regarded the division of labor then in force in Catholic theologates as imposing impossible obligations upon professors of dogma, obligations that could be properly handled only by a team of specialists. He did not have a team, so he did what he could.[5] Despite the constraints, he attempted a dialectical analysis of the formation of Trinitarian and Christological dogma. The progress of exegetical and historical studies in the interim allows one to hope the analysis may someday be repeated on a richer basis.

Lonergan tended to deprecate his Latin textbooks as "practical

---

3. See *Method* (1972), 235–66, or CWL 14, 220–49; brief discussion in Donna Teevan, *Lonergan, Hermeneutics & Theological Method*, Marquette Studies in Theology 45 (Milwaukee, Wisc.: Marquette University Press, 2005), 146–49.

4. Coelho, *Hermeneutics and Method*, and Walmsley, *Lonergan on Philosophic Pluralism*, are excellent studies of Lonergan's development on some of the most relevant issues. Older but still useful for understanding Lonergan's development to 1970 is Tracy, *The Achievement of Bernard Lonergan*.

5. Lonergan, "An Interview," 178–79; summarized by Conn O'Donovan in his translator's preface to Bernard J. F. Lonergan, *The Way to Nicea: The Dialectical Development of Trinitarian Theology*, trans. Conn O'Donovan (Philadelphia: Westminster, 1976), xxiv–xxvii.

chores." A textbook by its nature has to face many issues to which the author has little new to add, and in Lonergan's textbooks one finds a certain amount of standard fare. He granted, however, that they contained some "permanently valid chunks."[6] His dialectical analysis was among the bits that pleased him, despite its limits, and seemingly it was Alois Grillmeier, eminent historian of dogma, who encouraged him to think he was on to something. So it came about that in 1976 he permitted an English translation of his dialectical exercise—shorn even of its cursory preamble—by Conn O'Donovan.[7] Then and now, many felt it would have been better left buried in Latin.[8] No doubt Lonergan did too little to properly contextualize the truncated presentation of an already terse exposition. O'Donovan provided a useful introduction to its place in the context of Lonergan's overall trajectory, but neither he nor Lonergan had made an effort to connect it to other work in the field.[9]

The reader who expects a history will be disappointed; the professional historian may well be pained. Lonergan attempts here very little in the way of a narrative such as one might find in a good historical study; his aim is something different. It is better revealed by the titles of several subsequent reprises of his analysis: "The Origins of Christian Realism" (a title used more than once), "Theology as Christian Phenomenon," and the late paper "Horizons and Transpositions."[10] Partly his aim was to show the subterranean influence of unexamined philosophical assumptions in the achievement of a realism adequate to the truth claims of the Christian word. Partly it was to sort out how Christian theology had become involved in a basic shift into a new stage of meaning, a stage marked by logical control and a movement toward systematic terms and

6. Lonergan, "An Interview," 178.

7. The detail about Grillmeier's influence was related to me in personal conversation by Frederick Lawrence. The translation is Lonergan, *Way to Nicea*. Judging from the reviews, which are very largely uncomprehending, it may have been a mistake.

8. For example, see Mark Santer, review of *The Way to Nicea: The Dialectical Development of Trinitarian Theology*, by Bernard J. F. Lonergan, *The Journal of Theological Studies* 29, no. 1 (1978): 224–26; more recently Barter Moulaison, "Missteps on The Way to Nicea." It cannot be said that either of them took Lonergan's point.

9. So complained Nicholas Lash, review of *The Way to Nicea: The Dialectical Development of Trinitarian Theology*, by Bernard J. F. Lonergan, *New Blackfriars* 58, no. 682 (1977): 150–51.

10. Lonergan, "Origins of Christian Realism (1961)"; "The Origins of Christian Realism (1972)," in *A Second Collection*, CWL 13, 202–20; "Theology as Christian Phenomenon," in *Philosophical and Theological Papers 1958–1964*, CWL 6, 244–72; "Horizons and Transpositions."

relations. On both counts it was also to illumine how statements from different stages in the process might be related to one another.[11]

Rather than recount the details of his analysis, it will be more profitable to examine its structural features. The chapter falls into six parts. Three treat different aspects of meaning: narrative, propositional, and systematic meaning. A fourth addresses the truth of dogma, a fifth deals with dialectic as a process of development and a form of analysis, and a final section approaches the problem of dogma as received in the church.

Narrative and Symbolic Meaning

Lonergan sharply distinguished the process of revelation from the formation of doctrine. Each is a development, but the developments are of somewhat different kinds. Each has a clear meaning, but the clarity is of different kinds. These differences of process and of the resulting clarity are due to different stages in the control of meaning. The New Testament witness is expressed (mostly) in a narrative and symbolic mode of meaning. The doctrinal formulations are expressed (mostly) in a propositional and logical mode. The latter attempt to get a handle on the precise meaning of the former through the application of logical and incipiently metaphysical techniques; in that sense, the doctrines pertain to a subsequent stage in the control of meaning.

Lonergan's most sustained treatment of the divinity of Christ in the New Testament appears not in *De Deo Trino* but, unsurprisingly, in his Christology textbook, *De Verbo Incarnato*. That text is subdivided into parts, of which the first concerns the New Testament announcement and consists of a sole thesis, running to about eighty pages. He called that first part "The Doctrine of the Hypostatic Union in the New Testament." Doubtless most biblical scholars today would be surprised to learn that the New Testament has a doctrine of the hypostatic union, and in a sense they would be justified. The seeming anachronism of Lonergan's title prompted Robert Doran to remark, in his editor's preface to the Collected Works edition, that "'Biblical Bases of Christological Dogma'

---

11. On this whole topic, see the clear and insightful study, somewhat dated but still valuable, by Charles C. Hefling Jr., *Lonergan on Development: "The Way to Nicea" in Light of His More Recent Methodology* (Ann Arbor, Mich.: UMI, 1983).

would perhaps have been a more accurate title."[12] Concepts formulate answers to questions; they have dates, and Lonergan knew that the concept of the hypostatic union was not entertained by any New Testament author. Why, then, did he choose this curious title?

The answer emerges from the thesis and argument itself. Theology is not a science of concepts but a science of reality. At issue is the New Testament doctrine, that is, the reality attested by the New Testament witness. That reality is the personal union of human and divine in the one Son, which Lonergan designates by the familiar 'hypostatic union.' The argument of the thesis is that the New Testament witnesses to this reality. It does so, however, in its own way, which differs from the manner employed by the councils. In speaking of the New Testament's doctrine of the hypostatic union, then, Lonergan knew what he was doing. The truth attested by the New Testament is not different from the truth attested by the councils. But the mode in which that truth is asserted is different. These are the two basic claims of the thesis. The title of this part seems like a marginal point, but it is actually central to Lonergan's understanding of the relationship between the New Testament and the dogmas. Lonergan was after "an explanatory interpretation of a non-explanatory meaning."[13]

Lonergan was well aware that the New Testament collects a variety of texts from different authors and periods. Nevertheless, his concern in this work was primarily doctrinal rather than precisely exegetical. No doubt this seems like an odd thing to say, but it has to do with Lonergan's conception of the way different theological activities are interrelated. As we have seen, the function of Interpretation regards the particular as particular: the thought of Paul or of John, say. But Doctrines regard the one faith of the many witnesses. These are obviously not strictly separable, but they are distinct. Lonergan's conception of Functional Specialties relates them via a series of intermediary functions. The interpretation of Paul and John enters into a History of Christianity in the first and early second centuries. Different interpretations and different accounts of the history are subjected to comparison and scrutiny in Dialectic. One takes sides and, in Foundations, spells out one's criteria for doing

12. *Incarnate Word,* xxvi.
13. *Insight,* 610.

so. Depending on the side one takes, one lays down one's markers in Doctrines. All of this was not worked out at the time Lonergan composed his great Latin treatises, but it does shed some retrospective light on his procedure. The New Testament authors are regarded as witnesses to the one faith. Although each testifies in his own way, the question of the thesis, the question for Doctrines, is to determine that one faith and, later, to show that the one faith attested in the New Testament is the same as the faith attested by the councils.

The different witnesses have different idioms, and, moreover, their witness as a whole developed. The development is not only discernible from a comparison of different strata of documentation but also more or less explicitly signaled by the writers themselves, who narrate in various ways their initial confusion and gradual understanding, as well as their disputes and their uneasy resolution. Lonergan referred to this process as 'progressive revelation.' It was, he argued, just what one should expect. For the mystery of Christ could only be apprehended through a gradually deepening conversion. Moreover, Christ upended the antecedent expectations Jews had about the Messiah, and Gentiles had to be initiated to a whole tradition before they could grasp how it was fulfilled and transformed by the Christ. Nor was there an existing language ready to hand in which the first believers might name a mystery that so radically reconfigured their monotheism. What cannot be named can hardly be proclaimed, and even had a more adequate language been ready to hand, the mystery itself defies comprehension. It was a matter to be pondered in the heart, for which every possible image and expression would be insufficient. It entailed new meanings and values demanding enculturation, in one way for the Jews and another for the Greeks.[14]

Despite the diversity of authors, idioms, and contexts, Lonergan maintained that the one faith of the New Testament witnesses was clearly announced. The manner of that announcement was not the propositional clarity of later dogmatic formulations, but rather the clarity proper to a narrative and symbolic mode of meaning. To this extent, Lonergan's point is of a piece with arguments more recently set forth by the likes of Martin Hengel, Richard Bauckham, and Larry Hurtado. Here is Bauckham's contention:

14. *Incarnate Word*, 38–53.

Once we understand Jewish monotheism properly, we can see that the New Testament writers are clearly, in a deliberate and sophisticated way, expressing a fully divine Christology by including Jesus in the unique identity of God as defined by Second Temple Judaism. Once we recognize the theological categories with which they are working, it is clear that there is nothing embryonic or tentative about this. In its own terms, it is an adequate expression of a fully divine Christology.[15]

Now, there are obviously many further questions here, and I cannot go into them at once. What is useful to notice for the present is that Bauckham, too, claims a kind of clarity proper to the New Testament's announcement. This similarity hardly erases other differences between Lonergan's argument and those of the others I have mentioned. Whatever their weaknesses, they are surely equipped with fuller historical knowledge than was Lonergan; he was very frank about the limitations of his learning on that score. Lonergan has his own point to make, as they have theirs, yet on this point there is a certain synergy between their historical reconstruction and his dialectical analysis. But what Lonergan especially wanted to show—not because it is the only important point but because it was given to him to make it—is the relevance of different realms of meaning and the stages of their development to

---

15. Richard Bauckham, *Jesus and the God of Israel: God Crucified and Other Studies on the New Testament's Christology of Divine Identity* (Grand Rapids, Mich.: William B. Eerdmans, 2008), 58. The classic in this line seems to be Martin Hengel, *The Son of God: The Origin of Christology and the History of Jewish-Hellenistic Religion*, 1st American ed. (Philadelphia: Fortress Press, 1976). Similar or allied arguments are made, inter alia, by Sigurd Grindheim, *God's Equal: What Can We Know About Jesus' Self-Understanding in the Synoptic Gospels?* (London: T&T Clark International, 2011); Larry W. Hurtado, *Lord Jesus Christ: Devotion to Jesus in Earliest Christianity* (Grand Rapids, Mich.: William B. Eerdmans, 2003); Hurtado, *One God, One Lord: Early Christian Devotion and Ancient Jewish Monotheism*, 3rd ed., Cornerstones (London: Bloomsbury T&T Clark, 2015); and Chris Tilling, *Paul's Divine Christology* (Grand Rapids, Mich.: William B. Eerdmans, 2012). My main point in mentioning these works—none of which is invulnerable to critique—is merely that the *kind* of argument Lonergan is making is not beyond the scholarly pale. His argument, however, simply assumes the material context of the New Testament canon. It obviously raises many historical questions he was not able to face. For a rather astringent critique of Hurtado, especially his construal of Jewish monotheism, see Paula Fredriksen, review of *Lord Jesus Christ: Devotion to Jesus in Earliest Christianity*, by Larry W. Hurtado, *Journal of Early Christian Studies* 12, no. 4 (2004): 537–41. Whatever may be said about the historical difficulties of reconstructing ancient Jewish monotheism, it seems to me one can appraise its symbols aptly only with a certain religious sensitivity, and in that respect, Hurtado has a winning point.

an understanding of the development of dogma and theology and the relationship among its stages.

The New Testament, then, belongs to a stage in which the divinity of the Son is announced mainly through narrative and symbol rather than through propositional judgments of a second order. To the Son are ascribed the prerogatives, activities, and symbols proper to God alone.[16] Thus he is said to bear the name above all names (and other divine titles), to be worthy of worship and supreme love, to share the throne and judgment of God, to pardon sins and govern the Sabbath, to participate in the creation and ordering of the universe, and so forth.[17] The symbolic and narrative style of the Bible is laden with feeling, employing "parable and aphorism and apocalyptic to shift thought and meaning from [our] everyday world to the world of religious meaning."[18]

Lonergan was impressed with the way Alois Grillmeier had used the patterns *Logos-sarx* (Word-flesh) and *Logos-anthrōpos* (Word-human) to analyze the development of patristic Christology.[19] In his own analysis of the New Testament, he sought to organize the data by identifying typical patterns in which the mystery of Christ was initially apprehended and expressed.[20] Each pattern draws together titles and images from the prior tradition and from the life of Jesus in order to elicit a deeper understanding and assent to the mystery. Though differently verified in different cases, such common schemes of apprehension and presentation indicate the New Testament's basic unity of faith.

Lonergan identified four main patterns. A first pattern, typical of the synoptic Gospels, begins from the earthly life and looks forward to the exaltation of the Son of Man, who must suffer and so enter into his

16. The thesis itself runs: "Ex doctrina Novi Testamenti constat unum eundemque Iesum Nazarenum et (1) verum hominem esse, et (2) multipliciter divina participare, et (3) verum esse Deum." *Incarnate Word*, 2; see 4–5.

17. *Incarnate Word*, 70–115.

18. Lonergan, "Questionnaire on Philosophy," 363.

19. *Incarnate Word*, 46–47, 204–9; "Christology Today," 87–88.

20. *Incarnate Word*, 42–45. The term Lonergan uses in his Latin works is *schemata*. His English expressions varied. In a 1964 lecture, he referred to the same New Testament patterns as "schemes or modes of apprehension" ("Theology as Christian Phenomenon," 247–50). In a 1975 lecture, he spoke of the same New Testament patterns, and also of Grillmeier's types, as "patterns or models or schemata," with a tendency to prefer 'pattern' ("Christology Today," 87–88). In a 1979 lecture, he referred to them as "schemata" and "models" ("Horizons and Transpositions," 432).

glory at the right hand of God. A second pattern, more typical of Paul, begins from the present exaltation and looks back over the earthly life to the very foundation of the world. So the Lord, the Christ, the Son of God, the second Adam, now enthroned in power and majesty, came into this world but existed before it and was present at its creation. A third pattern begins with the Son, in the beginning with the Father, sent from the Father into this world, exalted to the right hand of the Father to reign forever: he was in the form of God (Phil 2:6–11), the Word with God (Jn 1), the Son whom God appointed heir of all things and through whom God made the universe (Heb 1). Each of these three patterns has a kind of temporal or sequential narrative structure to it, linking different and mutually exclusive attributes to one and the same Son: rich and poor, Creator and created, Lord and servant. They express one and the same Jesus Christ as both divine and human in a symbolically invested narrative.[21]

The fourth pattern is somewhat different; Lonergan calls it Paul's 'synthetic' pattern, but we might call it the pattern of symbolic interchange. This pattern does not rely upon a narrative of stages but rather symbolizes the relationship between Christ and us. We receive by grace, adoption, conversion, and baptism a share in the Sonship, the image, the glory that is Christ's by nature and right; there are two solidarities, one with Adam in death, another with Christ in life; there are two patterns to which we may be conformed, the pattern of this world and the pattern of Christ; there is the headship of Christ who fills his members and is being formed in them.[22] The first three patterns present the conjunction of what is human with what is divine by way of a sequence. This last presents it by way of an exchange—his becomes ours and ours becomes his—and by a symbolic conjunction of Christ and Adam.

Now, these schemes are not interpretations of any particular passage, nor a substitute for careful study of particular passages. They are, rather, general schemes of apprehension and expression verified in different ways across ranges of passages, and they may be helpful when it comes to noticing structural features and similarities.[23] To the extent the patterns

21. *Incarnate Word*, 42–53.

22. *Incarnate Word*, 52–65; see 114–133; "Christology Today," 84–85.

23. See *Method* (1972), 227–28, 284–85, or CWL 14, 214–15, 266–67.

are in fact verified in the pages of the New Testament, they indicate some
of the ways the mystery of the incarnate Son was able to be expressed by
those to whom it was first entrusted. Later, there would develop different
manners of conception in response to the questions arising in subsequent
ages and different cultural contexts. But, as we noted, the New Testament
itself is already involved in the problem of cultural difference. Its writings
are, in a sense, the first exercises in the transposition of the Christian
message from 'those of the circumcision' to the wider Hellenistic world,
and therefore we find in it both Hebrew and Hellenistic elements
marshaled to express the mystery of the Son.

The New Testament's narrative and symbolic expression of the
mystery would raise, in the event, questions for understanding and
judgment that would bring about the development of Trinitarian and
Christological dogma. Fundamentally, the operative question was, who
is this Son of God announced in Scripture, one with us but one also
with his Father? To protect the integrity and truth of their narrative
from various forms of debasement and corruption, Christians found
it necessary to pursue the question 'who is the Son?' into a precise and
technical territory. This question established the heuristic structure for
the development of Trinitarian and Christological dogma; the process
of development occurred in order to secure a precise determination
of this question, not in the narrative mode of Scriptural meaning but
in the propositional mode of logical and, as we shall see, incipiently
systematic meaning.

Propositional Meaning

Lonergan's most extensive treatment of the transposition of the Gospel
into the non-Jewish world of classical antiquity was in the preliminary
section of his Trinitarian textbook *De Deo Trino*. Lonergan divided this
work—the last edition appeared in 1964—into two volumes, *Pars
dogmatica* and *Pars systematica*. What O'Donovan translated as *The Way
to Nicea: The Dialectical Development of Trinitarian Theology* was just a
sliver—approximately the first third—of the *Pars dogmatica*. The bulk of
that first volume consisted of five dogmatic theses affirming the consubstantiality of the Son with the Father, of the Spirit with both, distinction

by relation, the order of the processions, and the transcendence of the mystery beyond the capacity of any finite intelligence. These theses were prefaced by a long section Lonergan called 'Praemittenda,' the section O'Donovan translated.

O'Donovan translated only what Lonergan permitted. His translation begins abruptly with Lonergan's discussion of dogmatic development. Lonergan, having just published *Method* in 1972, was willing to present his analysis to an English readership, but he was evidently reluctant to allow his terse Latin notes to represent his mature views on method. Unfortunately omitted, therefore, are the three short prefatory paragraphs in which Lonergan frames the question he is attempting to answer by means of his dialectical analysis. O'Donovan obviously recognized the misfortune, for he summarizes those paragraphs in his translator's introduction. He writes:

> In a short preliminary note Lonergan indicates the question that inspires this ten-stage inquiry and guides its progress: how is it that the ancient Christian writers not only did not anticipate the Nicene and subsequent conciliar decrees, but even appear at times to have held the opposite of what was later defined as dogma? With that question answered, he says, the dogmatic theses will become clearer and easier to understand.[24]

O'Donovan's summary is in fact virtually an abridged translation of one of Lonergan's paragraphs.[25]

Lonergan states the difficulty by reference to Petavius (Denis Pétau), a seventeenth-century theologian and historian whose "great glory," according to Joseph de Ghellinck, "is due to his patristic works and his importance in the history of dogma. With good reason he may be styled the 'Father of the History of Dogma.'"[26] After Nicaea, Lonergan says, a

---

24. O'Donovan, translator's introduction, *Way to Nicea*, xi–xii.

25. *Triune God: Doctrines*, 28 (". . . inde a Petavio, quaeri solet cur antiquissimi scriptores christiani adeo decreta Nicaena aliaque subsequentia non praeviderint ut opposita interdum sensisse videantur. . . . Hac enim quaestione expedita atque amota, non solum clariora et faciliora redduntur argumenta patristica postea in thesibus exponenda. . . .").

26. Joseph de Ghellinck, "Denis Pétau," in *The Catholic Encyclopedia* (New York: Robert Appleton, 1911), accessed September 11, 2015, http://www.newadvent.org/cathen/11743a.htm.

dogmatic systematization emerged "almost by itself."[27] In its retrospective light, the ante-Nicene authors seem almost uniformly heretical. If we frankly admit that dogma has a history and the history is contingent, there arises a problem of how the faith can be ever the same. And if the ante-Nicene authors possessed the selfsame faith as the later, how could they have said so much that on its face is incompatible with the Nicene dogma?

The problem of this long section of Praemittenda, then, is to help students of Lonergan grasp how the doctrine developed so that they may understand why the ante-Nicene authors could have said the kinds of things they did. The two opposed methodological errors he calls 'anachronism'—reading later developments into earlier stages—and 'archaism'—reading the developments as corruptions that originate, he says, in a nonunderstanding ("non-intelligentia") of doctrinal development.[28] Anachronism and archaism, in Lonergan's judgment, share a common root in the tendency to assign ultimacy to deductive logic. Anachronism would validate the later forms by reducing them to the earlier as to logical premises. Archaism would invalidate the later forms because they are not logically deducible from the earlier. This same tendency underwrites historicism, too. The historicist, noticing that the transition from one world of discourse to another or one cultural stage to another is not deductive, leaps to the conclusion that the transitions represent either a new revelation or a sequence of expressions each so bound to its original context as to be meaningless in any other.[29] The Collected Works translation (but not O'Donovan's) regrettably mistakes Lonergan to say that the post-Nicene systematization of Trinitarian and Christological dogma makes it easier for us to understand the ante-Nicene authors, when in fact Lonergan's whole argument presupposes the contrary.[30] Our later, systematic clarity obscures the difficulties presented to earlier authors. The radical basis for resolving all these problems—anachronism, archaism, historicism, and our inclination to apply such unhelpful labels as 'subordinationist'—is to clarify the dynamics of intellectual and cultural development.[31]

27. *Triune God: Doctrines*, 254 ("fere sponte proflueret").

28. *Triune God: Doctrines*, 268.

29. Lonergan, "Questionnaire on Philosophy," 374–75.

30. Discussed in Jeremy D. Wilkins, "Traduce Not the Inner Word: On Reading and Rendering Lonergan's Latin," *Method: Journal of Lonergan Studies*, n.s., 5, no. 2 (2014): 87–107, here 98–102.

31. *Incarnate Word*, 27; *Method* (1972), 305–18, or CWL 14, 285–96; "Doctrinal Pluralism."

The Collected Works edition and translation of Lonergan's *Pars dogmatica* was called, by his editors, *The Triune God: Doctrines*. As the foregoing makes plain, however, it is not exclusively an exercise in what he later called the theological function, Doctrines. The part of it Lonergan evidently thought most significant was an experiment in theological Dialectic. In his author's preface to O'Donovan's translation, Lonergan describes Dialectic as an X-ray to bring the subterranean issues into view, in this case, the unexamined philosophical suppositions funding conflicting accounts of the divinity of the Son.[32] Dialectic traces the conflicts to their hidden roots and thus effects a preliminary purification of theological concepts.[33] Implicitly mediating between the Dialectic and the five dogmatic theses are Lonergan's own foundational principles, which he had largely worked out in *Insight*, but this mediation would only be articulated functionally after his breakthrough, in 1965, to the framework of Functional Specialties.

In the previous chapter we briefly observed that Lonergan distinguished four aspects of the process of doctrinal development, which he called objective, subjective, evaluative, and hermeneutical.[34] They merit a longer consideration here.

The 'objective' aspect is the transposition of the message from one mode of expression to another. As we have noted, Lonergan maintained that this transposition was not from obscurity to clarity but from one kind of clarity to another.[35] The mystery expressed in a compact, narrative, symbolic mode in the New Testament was transposed to the differentiated, propositional mode of the patristic controversial writings and professions of faith. This shift was enriching, in the sense that it responded to the kinds of questions an educated Hellenistic audience might raise about the claims of the Gospel. That is, it was enriching in something like the sense in which, Lonergan explains, abstraction is enriching.[36] When we abstract, we are intelligently disregarding whatever is not relevant to the question we are asking. This intelligent disregard

32. *Way to Nicea*, vii–viii; reproduced as an appendix in *Triune God: Doctrines*, 735–36.

33. *Method* (1972), 292, or CWL 14, 273–74.

34. See *Triune God: Doctrines*, 30–54.

35. *Triune God: Doctrines*, 48–51. In the same place, he explains that the development of the *ratio* of dogma itself was a movement from obscurity to clarity.

36. *Insight*, 111–12.

of the irrelevant is enriching in the sense that it brings into focus just what is relevant to the question at hand. But, at the same time, it also leaves something behind, and what is left behind may have its own kind of richness. Thus, the message of the New Testament is addressed to the whole person: heart, head, and sensibility. But the doctrines articulate only one dimension of this richness, its intelligible truth claim.

This transition in the manner of expression requires a corresponding development in the subjects, the Christians, who are doing the expressing. The transition to a new way of articulating their convictions is not only a change in the expressions of faith but also a development in the capacities of the persons doing the expressing. Now, in the event, the transition was from one style of meaning to another, and the second style was proper to a later stage in cultural development or the control of meaning.[37] That is, in the later stage, meaning is controlled by the application of logical and metaphysical techniques unknown to the previous stage. For this transition to occur, the Christian writers not only have to learn the new techniques and become at home in the new style, but they also have to be able to order their operations toward increasingly differentiated goals while prescinding from considerations extraneous to those goals. The development of doctrine, in other words, was not only a momentous development in the history of the Christian message; it was also a momentous development in the history of the church as a process of self-constitution.[38]

The objective and the subjective aspects of the development are two sides of the same coin: a development in the expression of the Christian message and, by the same stroke, an intellectual development within (a portion of) the Christian community. This development, in fact, involved the church in a new, propositional stage in the control of meaning. It also involved them in an explanatory realm of meaning. It was, at risk of oversimplification, a shift from apprehending the mysteries mainly in relation to ourselves to apprehending them in relation to one another. But it was more than that: it was also a shift from apprehending the mysteries in a global, compact fashion addressed to the whole person, ordered above all to a decisive personal decision, to a specific differentiation of

37. See *Method* (1972), 85–99, or CWL 14, 82–95.
38. See *Method* (1972), 363–64, or CWL 14, 334–36.

their cognitive truth-intention. It was thus concomitant with a transition into a new stage of meaning, a stage in which the cognitive meaning of true predications would be controlled by logical and, later, metaphysical techniques. This does not mean the prior stage is 'left behind,' but that the original, compact mode of symbolic and narrative meaning now lives alongside another, differentiated mode of logical proposition. In this sense, the stages are cumulative, and what marks the second stage is the occurrence of two modes side by side. Moreover, not everyone makes the leap, so to speak. So there remain many for whom the logical and propositional is just ivory-tower stuff, while others have questions that can only be answered adequately through recourse to such procedures. Luminous apprehension of these differences is rare, however, and if Lonergan hoped theologians today might envision and set out to attain it, he was not under the illusion that the ancient Christian writers were very clear about what they were doing. They emerged into a new stage rather by providential accident.[39]

In addition to this development in the object of Christian affirmation and in the subjects who are doing the affirming, Lonergan also notes an evaluative and a hermeneutical aspect of the process from the New Testament to the doctrines. The development involves an evaluation: the questions are important and worth addressing, even if addressing them involves going beyond the symbolic and narrative context of the New Testament. Notice that archaism (for instance)—the valorization of the primitive just because it is primitive—also rests on a value judgment. For the archaist, change is not only difference but aberration, distortion, or pernicious invention.

Finally, the development involves a hermeneutical aspect; it is an interpretation of the Christian message. The development of dogma was not an effort to elaborate Christian consciousness but an effort to

---

39. As we have seen, Lonergan would later characterize this not only by way of comparing common sense and theoretical modes of meaning, but by distinguishing at least four realms of meaning at play. "When the realms of common sense, of theory, of interiority, and of transcendence are distinguished and related, one easily understands the diversity of religious utterance. For its source and core is in the experience of the mystery of love and awe, and that pertains to the realm of transcendence. Its foundations, its basic terms and relationships, its method are derived from the realm of interiority. Its technical unfolding is in the realm of theory. Its preaching and teaching are in the realm of common sense." *Method* (1972), 114, or CWL 14, 110.

elaborate the Christian message.[40] It was not an exegesis of any particular testimony as such. It involved, rather, an interpretation of the one faith in the many witnesses, an articulation of the hermeneutical principles, as it were, on the basis of which the testimonies of scripture were to be read as a whole.[41] To achieve it, the ancient Christian authors had to grasp both the meaning of the New Testament and how to express that meaning in a manner that would speak to the questions and concerns of their own later context. Largely, they did so in a style Lonergan described as 'classical' exegesis.[42] That is, they were relatively innocent of the historical and cultural differences that loom large for us. They took for granted the veracity of the biblical witness. Their procedure was to work out the conditions of the possibility of that truth attested by the New Testament on the assumption that its statements were true. This they pursued by defining terms, eliminating the obviously mythological elements, working out properties and implications. The whole enterprise is in the mode of rational discourse.[43] Despite its limitations, the validity of classical exegesis rests on the possibility of expressing the same truth in many different ways. Classical exegesis did not attempt to recreate the cultural context of the New Testament, but it did succeed in bringing into focus the central truth claims entailed by the biblical witness. It made explicit what in the narrative and symbols of the New Testament is implicit.[44] The implication in question, however, is not precisely logical implication. It is worked out by grasping, as we shall presently see, the synthetic principles underlying the narrative and symbolic expression.

The transition from the New Testament to the doctrinal confessions of the ancient councils was basically the result of questions. Both contexts are concerned about the identity of Jesus, but in different ways. When the Lord in the New Testament asks his disciples who they understand him to be, the answer is given in terms of the symbols and story of Israel: Elijah, Jeremiah, the prophets, John the Baptist, the Messiah; the one

---

40. Lonergan, "The Dehellenization of Dogma," 21.

41. For a helpful discussion, see Khaled Anatolios, *Retrieving Nicea: The Development and Meaning of Trinitarian Doctrine* (Grand Rapids, Mich.: Baker Academic, 2011), 108–27.

42. Bernard J. F. Lonergan, "Exegesis and Dogma," in *Philosophical and Theological Papers 1958–1964*, CWL 6, 142–59.

43. See "Exegesis and Dogma," 148–49.

44. "Exegesis and Dogma," 150.

who shares the throne of God, receives the name above all names, judges and forgives, binds and looses, masters wind and waves, is fittingly worshiped. But the answer is also given in a way that invites conversion; the paramount issue is not just assent but consent, commitment, decision. The question behind the question is, what are you to do?

The councils were also concerned with questions, and in some way with the same question: Who is the Son? But they put the question in a manner that prescinded from all other considerations to focus exclusively on the truth claim entailed. Thus, the question at Nicaea (325) was whether Jesus was truly God. The question at Ephesus (431) was whether one and the same was both God and a human being. The question at Chalcedon (451) was whether one and the same Son, God and human, possessed two natures, human and divine, and two corresponding sets of properties. And in the seventh century (Constantinople III, 680–81) the further implication was drawn that he therefore willed with a human will and with a divine will, operated in a human way and in a divine way. All along the line, the questions are 'ontological' in the sense that they are concerned about the truth-intention of Scripture and its implications.[45]

As we will detail more fully below, this doctrinal transposition had the effect of casting the truth-intention of the Gospels in the very different form of a discourse that is 'second-order' in the sense that it makes statements about statements. To this end, the Christian writers borrowed a Greek technique.[46] When Athanasius backed into the observation that what is said of the Father is said of the Son except the name Father, he was backing into a second-order judgment. His assertion does not specify the content of true statements about the Father and the Son, although he arrived at it by canvasing the statements he found in the Bible. It does not depend on an imaginable divine substance they both share. It simply asserts that whatever the true statements are, they are equally true of both Father and Son—except when they are directly connected to the relational names Father and Son.

Similarly, to deal with the unity and distinction in Christ, a general exegetical framework was developed whose main lines may be found in

45. *Incarnate Word*, 360–65.

46. Lonergan, "The Dehellenization of Dogma," 21–23.

numerous Catholic authors of the fourth and fifth centuries, though the details vary as does the interpretation of particular texts. The framework comes down to a set of judgments embodied in rules for predications about Christ. All true statements of Christ refer to one and the same person, one and the same subject. But they refer to him either in his divinity or in his humanity. Statements about Christ in his divinity may be further subdivided: they refer to him insofar as he is equal to the Father, or insofar as he is from the Father. Similarly, statements about Christ in his humanity can refer to him as an individual, or as head of the body. Thus by referring all true statements to one and the same subject, the unity of person was secured, while by distinguishing the statements according to nature, the integrity of two natures was preserved.

In general the ancient and medieval authors applied such rules as if the New Testament were itself a propositional text. They were mostly unaware of the cultural and historical gulf separating them from the originating context and unaware of the extent to which their problems were mainly historical rather than logical. Still, they were responding to the 'dogmatic' character of the New Testament, that is, they correctly recognized that the New Testament makes truth claims and therefore involves believers in an implicit realism mediated by true judgments.

Systematic Meaning

Lonergan argues that there was a twofold development on the way to Nicaea, and that only one aspect of this twofold development was intended by its historical authors. What was intended was the resolution of a Christological controversy, and the result of this intention was the doctrine of consubstantiality. What was not intended and in some way remained unnoticed was the emergence of what, in *De Deo Trino*, Lonergan calls the *ratio* of dogma itself.[47] He regards the Nicene *homoousion* as the first achievement of dogma in this precise sense.

In his preface to that work, Lonergan explains that while the task of the 'positive part' of theology is to understand the particular as particular—the mind of Paul, say, or of Athanasius—the task of the 'dogmatic part' is to grasp the universal in the particular, the one faith in the many

---

47. *Triune God: Doctrines*, 46–53, 736.

witnesses.[48] He notes that dogma results from a process of synthesizing the truth claims of the New Testament narrative in order to give a kind of precise, technical formulation of their principle or foundation.[49] Subsequently, in *Method in Theology*, he explains that what begins at Nicaea is the use of "systematic meaning in church doctrine."[50] The *ratio* of 'dogma,' then, in Lonergan's precise sense, is connected to the use of systematic meaning to articulate the mysteries of faith.

Lonergan first arrived at the notion of what he came to call different 'realms of meaning' by reflecting on the Aristotelian distinction between the 'first-for-us' and 'first-in-itself.' In *Insight*, Lonergan formulated this distinction in terms of descriptive and explanatory meaning. His later interaction with Piaget led him to conceive distinct realms of meaning in terms of groups of operations that do not group together; in this light he distinguished (descriptive) common sense and (explanatory) theory, transcendence and interiority.[51] In *Method in Theology*, he suggested each of the differentiations after common sense emerges in answer to a particular exigence: theory in response to the systematic exigence, interiority to meet the criteriological problem, and transcendence from the demand for ultimacy.[52] For the present, however, let us confine our attention to the contrast between descriptive and explanatory meaning.

Descriptive meaning is the distinctive mode of 'common sense' or practical intelligence. By 'common sense' Lonergan means the specialization of intelligence in the practical and dramatic business of everyday life.[53] This notion differs from the Thomist concept of 'practical reason' in that, for Lonergan, common sense is always relative to some particular cultural context; every time and place has its own common sense, its own distinctive body of practical insights into 'how things work.' Once one has acquired some particular common sense, one understands how to deal with the typical situations of that time and place; successful performance requires only the further insight that identifies the situation at hand.

48. *Triune God: Doctrines*, 2–27; also *Triune God: Systematics*, 66–101.

49. *Triune God: Doctrines*, 30–33.

50. *Method* (1972), 307, or CWL 14, 286.

51. See *Early Works on Method 1*, 42–55.

52. *Method* (1972), 81–85, or CWL 14, 78–82.

53. *Insight*, 296–204.

Because it is a specialization in the practical, common sense cannot be generalized or formulated into principles and rules. A person of common sense knows his or her practical affairs perfectly well but, as Socrates discovered in Athens, is generally quite unable to provide explanatory definitions and commonly is disinterested in further investigation that is not obviously practical. Common sense has no use for theory. Common sense is with Cephalus, who escapes Socrates's interrogation about justice to attend to the practical business of pious living (*Republic* 328C–331D). It is with Thomas á Kempis in excluding disputation because only faith is needful (*Imitation of Christ* IV.18). It may know nothing of Special Relativity but heeds the voice of its GPS. It is sure to want this year's flu shot, though it may regard evolution as far-fetched. Common sense meaning is 'cultural-linguistic' in the sense that for practical purposes, it is quite enough to know how to use the language and get things done and quite a waste of time to define all one's terms. None of these observations is meant to denigrate common sense. It is highly intelligent, and no one can get by without it. But common sense has limits to its interests and to its capacities for analysis.

By contrast to the descriptive, practical orientation of common sense, however, systematic thought opts for explanatory meaning. It "develops technical terms, assigns them their interrelations, constructs models, and adjusts them until there is reached some well-ordered and explanatory view."[54] It is a "style and mode of thought in which controls are constantly and explicitly applied. Terms are defined, assumptions are expressed and acknowledged, hypotheses are formulated and verified, and conclusions are drawn in accord with logical paradigms."[55] Where common sense meaning regards things as related to us, as relevant to us and our daily lives, systematic meaning regards things—including ourselves—in their explanatory relations to one another. The bath, the morning coffee, the gazpacho may all be too hot or too cold, but what that means differs in each case, because the reference is to one's own sensibility. But we compare them to one another by comparing them to a common standard: temperature. Physicists conceive heat not as warming

---

54. *Method* (1972), 304, or CWL 14, 283.

55. Bernard J. F. Lonergan, "Merging Horizons: System, Common Sense, Scholarship," in *Philosophical and Theological Papers 1965–1980*, CWL 17, 49–69, here 49.

my body but as molecular kinetic energy. When one correlates temperature, pressure, and volume to formulate, say, the ideal gas law, one has left the world of common sense, the world of things as related to us, to explore the relations of things to one another. One begins to develop a set of explanatory relations.

Of course, it is perfectly possible for a person to move back and forth, to acquire a smattering of scientific understanding and apply it to the tasks of everyday life. Scientists, too, live in an everyday world. In contrasting description and explanation this way, we are not constructing hermetically sealed boxes but explanatory notions, contrasting orientations of intelligence. Nevertheless, once these realms are differentiated within consciousness, its initial unity is shattered. There arises the question of how these new and different worlds—the 'academic' world of theory, the 'religious' world of one's prayer and worship, the 'philosophic' world of the hermeneutics of interiority—fit together with the 'real' world of everyday practical life. One's consciousness is apt to be troubled by this fragmentation until a second unification is achieved through "the self-knowledge that understands the different realms and knows how to shift from any one to any other."[56]

Any kind of scientific meaning will be systematic. It is true that a systematic language, as a set of conventional signs, depends on a community of practitioners and in that sense is 'cultural': to enter the scientific community is to learn its language. But it is also to learn the explanatory correlations to which that language refers. Hence, in the measure that it names explanatory relationships of things to one another, systematic meaning achieves a kind of universality. The meaning of its basic terms is fixed by their verified correlations. Pisa and Dubai may be worlds apart culturally, but there is not one law of falling bodies valid at the Leaning Tower of Pisa and another at the Burj Khalifa. And though theology is not physics, still there is not one relationship between God the Father and God the Son valid at Nicaea in the fourth century and another at Yale Divinity School in the twentieth.

Systematic expression begins from what is first and most intelligible in itself, and moves toward explaining the more obvious to us. So, for instance, instruction in chemistry begins with the correlation of the

---

56. *Method* (1972), 84, or CWL 14, 81.

elements in the periodic table. But there is a certain equivocation in the concept of what is more obvious, or first, for us.[57] We are not all the same; indeed, we are in some sense different even from our past and future selves, for we are constantly changing, and our world is changing with us.[58] What may seem perfectly obvious to one generation or in one culture is not perfectly obvious in another. Thomas Jefferson and the Continental Congress declared it a truth self-evident that "all men are created equal," but it hardly seemed self-evident to Plato, and he has not been alone. 'More obvious to us' is a moving target. If, then, the Gospel is to be preached to all the nations, theology must include a communicative or enculturating function that specializes in expressing the Gospel in the particular varieties of common sense available to different places and times, cultures and educational levels. But if the Gospel to be preached is one and the same (Gal 1:8; 2 Cor 11:4), if Christians are not to be "blown about by every wind of doctrine" (Eph 4:14) and "carried away by all kinds of strange teachings" (Heb 13:9), then the communicative function of theology presupposes and complements other functions whose aim is to determine the one faith in the many witnesses (a universalizing function) and seek an imperfect but illuminating understanding of its mysteries (a systematizing function). Such, in part, was Lonergan's proposal in *Method in Theology*, and, in part, the significance of the Nicene *homoousios* lies within the universalizing and systematizing functions of theology.[59]

Lonergan contends that the movement from the New Testament to the Nicene *homoousios* was, de facto and unintentionally, a shift toward systematic meaning in the formulation of Christian teaching. The

---

57. See *Triune God: Systematics*, 82–87.

58. *Insight*, 232–37.

59. *Triune God: Systematics*, 88–91. There is an interesting progression in Lonergan's thought on this matter. In the Latin manuals, Lonergan was thinking of doctrines in the 'ascending' phase, i.e., the movement from the particular to the universal. In his 1962 Institute on Method, the pivot is dialectic: "Dialectical analysis, insofar as it introduces a normative element, effects the transition from the history of the doctrine to the doctrine itself. This is a fundamental point in theological method, namely, the possibility of a transition from the history of a doctrine to the doctrine itself, the transition from positive to systematic theology" (*Early Works on Method 1*, 27). In the context of *Method in Theology*, the functional specialty, Doctrines, pertains to the 'descending' movement from the most universal principles, established in Dialectic and Foundations, to the particularities of Christian witness in Communications. Nevertheless, for present purposes it is enough to observe that it pertains to the universalizing arc of theology, that is, the process by which the original message is transposed from one cultural context to a multiplicity of others.

Gospels possess the kind of clarity that belongs to everyday life and relates things to us. Their form is mainly narrative and symbolic. The doctrine of the Trinity began as a narrative that, as distilled by St. Paul, tells about the Father sending his Son in the fullness of time to redeem us, that we might receive adoption as children, wherefore God has sent the Spirit of his Son into our hearts, crying out, "Abba, Father!" (Gal 4:4–7). Through this Spirit, one is to acknowledge the Lordship of Jesus, to love him with one's whole heart and mind and strength, to order one's life to him as completely and unreservedly as to the God of Abraham, because, indeed, love and obedience to Jesus is the same as love and obedience to God. The existential issue is unmistakable.[60] This existential clarity can be worked into an orderly worldview expressing a Christian perspective and orientation. So we find it in Irenaeus's description of the Son and the Spirit as the 'two hands' of God at work in the world. Here the Father, Son, and Holy Spirit are identified by the different functions each one has in relation to us and our world.[61]

In comparison to the prior formulae on which it draws, the specific difference of the Nicene creed consists in the addition of certain technical expressions to an underlying narrative profession, to wit, the Son is "from the Father's substance, God from God . . . consubstantial (*homoousios*) with the Father."[62] At Nicaea, the fateful decision was taken to incorporate the unscriptural term *homoousios* into the profession of faith. Both then and now, the decision has had its share of detractors. Though Lonergan is hardly among them, like them he thinks Nicaea was a turning point. The significance of the turn, however, is not that *homoousios* is unscriptural. It is that its meaning is systematic. One need not consider Nicaea the last word nor even subscribe to its doctrine to recognize the plain fact that Nicaea uses technical terms to make a systematic statement, and, given that statement, the intent of the teaching is undeniable. It relates the Father and the Son not to us but to each other. It does so by implying a rule that elsewhere was explicitly formulated by Athanasius: what is said of the

---

60. *Triune God: Doctrines*, 34–37.

61. *Triune God: Doctrines*, 334/5, 338/9–340/1, 414/5.

62. Council of Nicaea I, *Profession of Faith* (AD 325), in Tanner et al., *Decrees of the Ecumenical Councils*, 1:5 (translation altered).

Father is said of the Son, except the name Father. The Father is light and the Son is light; the Father is God and the Son is God; but there are not two lights, two Gods.

Lonergan reads the ante-Nicene writers as representing various steps, so to say, along the way to a satisfactory determination of the explanatory relations. Obviously, this is not how they could possibly have understood themselves. To understand a process, one has to know where it is going, as they did not. What the heresies exposed, what the Catholic authors gradually recognized were, in part, the limitations of thinking of the divine persons only in relation to us and our world. The personal properties of the Father, Son, and Spirit are revealed by their distinct functions in the economy of creation and grace. But if we focus only on the functions and never proceed to a consideration of the persons, we come up against a considerable danger. The danger is that we come to identify the persons with their functions, or even to suppose that the different functions mean different natures. This is precisely what happened in the Arian crisis. It was a danger that could not be definitively overcome without articulating the relations the divine persons have not to us but to one another. To do this, however, is to introduce systematic meaning into the formulation of ecclesiastical doctrine.

This use of systematic meaning is not simply a matter of a more compendious retelling of the New Testament story. There is an important difference. The difference is not that the New Testament proposes one thing, and the dogma proposes something else. It is rather that what the New Testament proposes in terms of the everyday religious meanings of first-century Palestinian Jewish and Greco-Roman life, the dogma proposes in the form of a synthetic and, in a way, explanatory principle. The Father, Son, and Spirit, whom the New Testament presents mainly in relation to us, the dogma declares in their relations to one another. To ask if such a turn was necessary or desirable is to raise again the controversy that so vexed Athanasius in the aftermath of Nicaea. The intention of the Council was not the development of systematic meaning in theology but the exclusion of Arian heresy. Yet a shift that was neither intended nor quite understood was nevertheless accidentally achieved en route to that other goal.

Dogma and Truth

It is certain that the fourth-century partisans of the *homoousios* deemed it a matter of exceeding urgency and moment. But if we ask why they did, we will come to a deeper issue implied in the foregoing but not yet raised explicitly. That deeper issue is the realism entailed by the Christian message. Before Athanasius denounced the Arians, Tertullian wrote against Praxeas, Dionysius against Sabellius, Hippolytus against Noetus, and Irenaeus against the Gnostics, and Justin Martyr added blood to ink in defense not only of the Christian way of life but of the truth of the Christian faith.

Lindbeck, as I understand him, claims the function of doctrine is to provide a kind of grammar of the faith; directly, doctrines govern the way Christians tell and celebrate their story, and thereby, indirectly, they shape the kind of persons Christians become and the kind of communities they build.[63] There is much to be said for the insight, because the Gospel is not simply a disclosure of truths to be known about God and salvation. Obedience to the Gospel constitutes the identity of Christian community and personality, or, as Lonergan would later put it, the meaning of the Gospel is constitutive and effective and not only cognitive.[64] Nevertheless, Lonergan insisted that the Gospel involves us in ontological truth claims that doctrines articulate. The meaning of doctrine is not only constitutive and effective; it is also cognitive. We know the real through the true, and the doctrines are true.

Consider a problem of interpretation from the celebrated *Oresteia* trilogy of Aeschylus. The protagonist Orestes, having avenged his murdered father upon his hated mother, is terrorized by the Furies. They are, he is assured, inventions of his febrile agitation, but to Orestes "they are clear, / and real, and here; the bloodhounds of my mother's hate."[65] The narrative order is as clear to us as the Furies were to Orestes. But what do the symbols and the drama mean? That, as the critics attest, is no simple question. The Furies are in the soul, but they are also in the world. They represent,

---

63. See Hefling Jr., "Turning Liberalism Inside Out," 57.

64. *Method* (1972), 76–77, or CWL 14, 74–75.

65. Aeschylus, *The Libation Bearers*, in *Oresteia*, trans. Richmond Lattimore, The Complete Greek Tragedies, ed. Richmond Lattimore and David Grene (Chicago: University of Chicago Press, 1953), 91–131, here 131, lines 1053–56.

as Fagles and Stanford point out, superhuman powers, but also personify our powers. Would Aeschylus disenchant the world, as E. R. Dodds submits? Is his *Oresteia* "a grand parable of progress," as Lattimore reads it, from tribal passion to the magnificent order of Hellenic culture? Might it not as easily be read, as Neil ten Kortenaar suggests, as a tale of domestication, "The Pacification of the Primitive Tribes of the Lower Peloponnesus"?[66]

Obviously, our present interest in Aeschylus is rather limited. If the commentators are all on to something, it is because the symbolic style is connotative, evocative, polysemous, rather than denotative, precise, univocal. The symbolic style is universally accessible, laden with feelings and implications for action. But the very compactness that yields such impressive advantages has an opportunity cost. Connotation and polysemy are wonderful, unless one's aim is to be exact. Yet my point is not even that literary hermeneutics are complex, although they are. It is that symbolic literature, precisely because it is rich in meaning, raises questions about reality. To inquire into that reality is to discover the insufficiency of mere renarration, distilled to whatever proof. The commentators are not writing tragedies; they are writing essays.

The New Testament expresses the Christian horizon in a style that, like Aeschylus's, is symbolic and narrative. Like Aeschylus, the New Testament makes claims about reality. Yet the central claims of the Gospel are of a fundamentally different genus from the central claims of the *Oresteia*. Whatever Aeschylus intended by his Furies, whatever his ancient or his modern audiences may make of them, we are not meant to affirm them as real hypostases. They are figures in a play that evoke some other, more diffuse reality, existentially vital in its way but not inviting the all-important question, 'Who do you say I am?' But when we turn to Mark and Luke, John and Paul, we find something altogether different and urgent at stake. Like Aeschylus's, their writings are imbued with symbolic meaning. But at the heart of their symbolism stands a historical figure who, they would assert, is no mere symbol but the only Son of the

---

66. Robert Fagles and W. B. Stanford, "The Serpent and the Eagle," in Aeschylus: The Oresteia, trans. Fagles (New York: Penguin, 1977), 13–97, here 89; E. R. Dodds, *The Greeks and the Irrational* (Berkeley: University of California Press, 1951), 40; Lattimore, in his translation of *Oresteia*, 31; Neil ten Kortenaar, "Chinua Achebe and the Question of Modern African Tragedy," *Philosophia Africana* 9, no. 2 (2006): 83–100, here 90.

one true God. Unfortunately, as Christians quickly learned, the devil is an exegete. If they were not prepared to lay down some markers about the meaning of their story, someone else would do it for them.

The question of religious truth may be uncomfortable in our culture, but it is not recondite. We make and dispute truth claims with surprising regularity, and today there is no shortage of would-be prophets prepared to tell Christians the real meaning of their convictions. Freud, to take just one example, had his own take both on the symbolism of Greek tragedy and on the meaning of Christian faith. He diagnosed the latter as a case of infantile wish fulfillment. I am not out to refute him here; he may be on to something, if not about the Gospel at least about what commonly is called 'faith,' to judge from the phenomenon Robert Bellah and his colleagues named 'Sheilaism':

> Sheila Larson is a young nurse who has received a good deal of therapy and describes her faith as 'Sheilaism.'. . . . 'I believe in God,' Sheila says. 'I am not a religious fanatic. I can't remember the last time I went to church. My faith has carried me a long way. It's Sheilaism. Just my own little voice.'[67]

Sheila has a story and it works just fine for her. She hastens to assure us that she is not a fanatic for believing it. But what is there to be fanatical about? "Just my own little voice": is that God's voice or hers? It seems obvious what Freud would say. What, then, will Christians say about their own religious claims? If we are merely expressing our experience, a therapist can always be found to tell us what that experience "really" means.

The truth of the Gospel is an issue that Christian theologians cannot responsibly burke. Who is this Son whom God has sent—who is he, not merely for me, but in himself, in his relation the Father? To raise such a question is to invite a development from the compact, evocative clarity

---

67. Robert N. Bellah, ed., *Habits of the Heart: Individualism and Commitment in American Life* (Berkeley: University of California Press, 2008), 221; the therapeutic phenomenon in American religion is documented more recently and fully in Christian Smith and Melinda Lundquist Denton, *Soul Searching: The Religious and Spiritual Lives of American Teenagers* (New York: Oxford University Press, 2005). See too the discussion of deviated transcendence in Rosenberg, *The Givenness of Desire*, 184–205.

of the symbol to the precise, technical clarity of systematic meaning. It is to invite such a development, not for the sake of intellectual exercise, but for the sake of the Gospel itself. In the fourth century it became all too clear that renarration was a rearguard action; Catholics became involved in systematic meaning in the service of Gospel truth. The judgment expressed in the Nicene decree and its attendant anathema is that the Son is from the substance of the Father; that he is begotten not made; that he is *homoousios*, consubstantial with the Father; and that those who say there was when he was not or that he came to be from another substance are anathema. Athanasius made his celebrated defense of this decree by distinguishing two senses of the name Son (*De decretis*, chap. 3), vindicating the Catholic sense as applied to Christ (chap. 4), defending the conciliar *homoousion* (chap. 5), and repudiating the Arian interpretation of 'unoriginate' (chap. 7).

The decree of Nicaea and its defense by Athanasius leave no doubt, first, that the proximate context of *homoousios* is dogmatic and theological and, second, that its meaning is ontological, that is, it makes a claim about what is so, quite apart from what anyone happens to believe or accept. The claim is warranted because the meaning of the Christian word is not only constitutive and effective but also cognitive. These are not exclusive alternatives, but different functions of the selfsame word. The word has a constitutive function, for it defines us as Christians. It has an effective function, for it assigns our goals, directs our decisions, informs our plans. And the same word has a cognitive function, for by it we know who it is that has loved us to the end. The debates of the fourth century may seem abstruse, but they have a point. Is God's love proved to us in the brutal death of a Galilean rabbi or the self-surrender of God's own beloved Son? Contrary answers to this question define quite different religions and bear quite different implications. The constitutive and effective functions of the word cannot be separated from its cognitive function.

The Gospel refers to realities beyond the New Testament and beyond the Christian community, and the development of Trinitarian and Christological dogma was largely driven by a need to come to grips with the cognitive meaning of the kerygma.[68] If the Christians had not been persuaded that the New Testament has a cognitive meaning, they would

68. *Triune God: Doctrines*, 378–81.

not have universally acknowledged a certain and manifest rule of faith, which rule they regularly distinguished from their own opinions; they would not have determined a canon of books to be received and others to be excluded on the basis of their orthodox testimony; they would not have articulated their faith in propositional creeds; they would not have excluded heretics from communion; and they would not have argued so energetically against heretical interpretations of the Gospel. Above all, they would hardly have shed their blood bearing witness not merely to the Christian way of life but also to the truth of Christian doctrine.[69]

For Lonergan, 'realism' means that "a truth acknowledged in the mind corresponds to reality."[70] Realism is implicit in Scripture which presents itself as the word of God, adjures truthfulness, and anathematizes any other Gospel. This realism, as Christians gradually apprehended it, is 'dogmatic' in the sense that it pertains to the *ratio* of dogmatic judgments. But it is also 'dogmatic' in the sense that its assertion was not the fruit of philosophic reflection but the accidental and only dimly grasped outcome of a process whose proximate object was not the articulation of a Christian philosophy but of the mystery of the Word incarnate. Whether Christian realism can be philosophically grounded is a further matter; the Christian fathers, by and large, did not try. Lonergan's contention is that anyone who denies knowing reality through true judgments is hopelessly involved in performative self-contradiction.[71]

Dialectic: Process and Analysis

Lonergan's dialectic names both a process and an analysis of the process. Readers expecting a history of Christian professions of faith, their narrative forms, and uses in worship, preaching, and teaching are apt to be disappointed and probably puzzled by Lonergan's account of the 'dialectical development of Trinitarian theology.'[72] What he has to offer here is not original research, detailed interpretation of authors, or a

---

69. *Triune God: Doctrines*, 292–99.

70. *Triune God: Doctrines*, 243.

71. *Insight*, 343–71; *Method* (1972), 3–25, or CWL 14, 7–27.

72. See, e.g., Anatolios, *Retrieving Nicea*; Lewis Ayres, *Nicaea and Its Legacy: An Approach to Fourth-Century Trinitarian Theology* (New York: Oxford University Press, 2004); John Behr, *The Way to Nicaea*, The Formation of Christian Theology 1 (Crestwood, N.Y.: St. Vladimir's Seminary Press, 2001).

history of movements, ideas, institutions, or practices. In fact, far from replacing such investigations, Lonergan's purpose presupposes them. What, then, is it? As a first approximation, consider Christopher Stead's distinction between exposition and criticism. Exposition would remain "within the writer's circle of ideas," while criticism would "appreciate their achievements and explain their mistakes" in light of clearly conceived philosophical criteria.[73] Lonergan's dialectical analysis is, roughly, along the lines of Stead's criticism rather than his exposition. Its function is to detect the influence of implicit philosophical presuppositions on early attempts to articulate the mystery of Christ.

As I mentioned, Lonergan compares dialectical analysis to an X-ray that brings into view the issue behind the issues.[74] It may be helpful to begin with an illustration not from theology but from philosophy. According to Thomas Aquinas, Plato posited a separate genus of immaterial ideas in which corporeal realities participate. But, Aquinas urges, the falsity of this position appears from two considerations. First, because Plato's ideas are separated from matter and from movement, it would be impossible through them to know matter and movement. But in fact, movement and material causality are intelligible to us. The second reason is that knowledge of separate ideas would not allow us to make judgments about the things manifest to our senses.[75] Now, we are not concerned with whether Aquinas has Plato just right; we are interested in his mode of analysis. What Aquinas is pointing out is an objective contradiction: the theory of separate ideas is incompatible with the facts it was evolved to explain. Moreover, Aquinas reduces this objective contradiction to its root. Plato correctly grasped that we understand through intelligible similitudes. But he mistakenly supposed that these similitudes must be in the knower in the same way that they are in the things known. Because they are in the knower as universal, immaterial, and immovable, he inferred that the objects we understand must themselves exist the same way. Aquinas's reduction of the contradiction to its roots exemplifies dialectical analysis. The

---

73. G. Christopher Stead, "The Concept of Divine Substance," *Vigiliae Christianae* 29, no. 1 (1975): 1–14, here 2–3.

74. *Triune God: Doctrines*, 736.

75. *STh* 1, q. 84, a. 1c.

error is eliminated at its roots, and the genuine discovery—namely, that we know reality through intelligible species—is brought forward. Note, finally, that Aquinas selects Plato because he affords a clear illustration of a tendency. The same tendency might be detected in others who know nothing of Plato. It is one thing, then, to determine an author's ideas (Interpretation), another to explain the historical genesis and consequences of those ideas (History), and another still to detect hidden suppositions and trace them to their roots (Dialectic).

If the dialectical analysis seeks to bring to light the radical bases for conflicts, the objective dialectical process results from the concrete interaction of the operative principles in tension. On the philosophic level, there is conceived a bipolar dialectic as a function of the conjunction and opposition between (1) the attachment and partiality of sensitivity and intersubjectivity, and (2) the detachment and disinterest (impartiality) of the pure and unrestricted desire to know. Lonergan distinguishes the dialectical process into material and formal elements. First, the material element in the dialectical process is an objective contradiction, which may be implicit or explicit. Second, the formal element is the spirit of critical inquiry, which sooner or later brings the contradiction to light and seeks to eliminate it.

In purely philosophic matters, reason alone suffices for the formal principle. But when the matter at hand is revealed mystery, reason operates beyond its competence if it does not acknowledge mystery as mystery and submit to the rule of faith. In *Insight*, Lonergan described how the introduction of divine grace and mystery transforms the dialectical process. On the supposition of supernatural revelation, merely human perfection itself becomes a limit to be transcended: "the supernatural solution involves a transcendence of humanism," a yielding to a mystery not for us to understand in this life.[76] Revelation, then, exacerbates the tension between attachment and detachment by requiring us to go beyond our humanity if we would save it. The result is a tripolar dialectic that is objectified "in the dialectical succession of human situations."[77] Its poles (in matters of revealed mystery) are reason, imagination, and

76. *Insight*, 748.
77. *Insight*, 749.

faith.[78] When the matter in question is a divinely revealed mystery, reason may eliminate the contradiction by submitting to the rule of faith or by eliminating the mystery. The dialectical process is a de facto historical collaboration in which different authors probe the possibilities until, gradually, a satisfactory resolution is achieved.

Let us consider how this plays out in Lonergan's analysis of the way to Nicaea. Khaled Anatolios has argued that the doctrinal struggles of the fourth century represent a collision of two different ways of accounting for the unity of Father and Son: unity of will and unity of being.[79] The conflict came into the open because a newly deepened sense of divine transcendence challenged traditional ways of conceiving and expressing the primacy of Christ: "We can locate the central point of this agitation in the newly developing break between [the church's] allegiance to the primacy of Christ and its newfound clarity on what constitutes divine primacy as such ... being uncaused, absolutely and unqualifiedly prior."[80] The new questions revealed the inadequacy of old answers and stimulated a period of intensely creative theological activity.

Lonergan's dialectical analysis is functionally subalternate to some such historical hypothesis as Anatolios presents. Arguments over the unity of divine being reflect divergent working assumptions about what is meant by 'being' and 'to be.' These divergences were moving in and through the conflict, but none of the participants had them directly in view. The immediate object of their questions was the identity and divinity of the Son of God. Underneath was the problem of achieving a realism adequate to the truth claims of the word of God while remaining faithful to those claims. In order to get to a satisfactory statement of the mysteries of Trinity and incarnation, Christians had to grope their way, implicitly, to an adequate realism; dialectical method aims to bring that underlying confusion, which accounts in part for the diversity of positions, into view.

Consider the problem of 'substance.' Christopher Stead distinguished 28 distinct possible meanings to be found in ancient Christian authors

78. *Insight*, 242–43, 267–69.

79. See Anatolios, *Retrieving Nicea*, 30–31, for a summary statement.

80. Ibid., 41.

and warned that the actual uses of particular authors may not fall cleanly into any of them.[81] Many of these are more linguistic than real differences, but beyond mere misunderstandings there are genuine conflicts. Lonergan traces the roots of the genuinely philosophic differences to a radical tension between the autonomous norms of reason and the spontaneous tendency to picture-think.[82] This underlying problem arises because of the ineluctable duality in human nature, which, as animal, is subject to spontaneous biological extroversion but, as rational, is governed by autonomous criteria of rational judgment.[83] These two opposed principles give rise to two radically opposed tendencies. One tendency is to imagine substance as a kind of spiritual 'stuff.' The other is to conceive substance as what is known through rational affirmation. These two opposed possibilities do not exclude such halfway houses as idealism, which knows substance is not imagined but understood, yet fails to break through to rational judgment.

The Trinity, however, is not a philosophical problem; it is a mystery of faith. The mystery presents a further and specifically theological ambiguity.[84] Consubstantiality in creatures means specific but not numerical unity. In this sense the Council of Chalcedon asserts that Christ is consubstantial with us in his humanity. But if, as the Nicene decree presupposes, there is only one God, then logically consubstantiality in the Trinity must mean the divine substance is one not merely specifically but numerically.[85] Naturally enough, this is a source of confusion. The philosophical and theological ambiguities can combine in various ways with each other and with merely linguistic differences to account for the riot of possible meanings of and objections to *homoousios* (and other terms) found in ancient (and modern) authors.[86]

---

81. Stead, "The Concept of Divine Substance," 11–13.

82. *Triune God: Doctrines*, 170/1–176/7; 322/3–324/5.

83. *Insight*, 22–23; 275–79.

84. *Triune God: Doctrines*, 176–81.

85. *Triune God: Doctrines*, 180–85.

86. *Triune God: Doctrines*, 170–99; see Ayres, *Nicaea and Its Legacy*, 92–100, 278–301; Anatolios, *Retrieving Nicea*, 127–33; Pier Franco Beatrice, "The Word 'Homoousios' from Hellenism to Christianity," *Church History* 71, no. 2 (2002): 243–72; G. Christopher Stead, *Divine Substance* (Oxford: Clarendon Press, 1977), 190–222.

The dialectical development of Trinitarian doctrine, then, exhibits the tripolar tension of faith, reason, and imagination, which may be illustrated by three examples. Please note that the examples are just that: examples of an underlying problem largely unnoticed by the antagonists. It is in no way a complete telling of the story.

According to Tertullian, (1) the Son is God as the Father is God, and (2) the Son is temporal, subordinate, and less than the Father.[87] In these assertions there is an objective contradiction, for if the Son is God, he is not less than the Father, and if he is less than the Father, he is not God. Its roots in Tertullian's thought seem to lie in his failure to break from imaginative extroversion as the criterion of the 'real': Father and Son are both God, if they are made of the same divine stuff. On Tertullian's supposition that divinity is a kind of stuff, it is perfectly coherent for the Son to be composed of divine stuff and so be God, and yet be later and less than the Father.[88] Dialectical analysis reduces the objective contradiction in Tertullian's thought to its roots in Tertullian's 'naive realism': the presupposition, which Tertullian did not examine, that the 'real' is what is 'already out there now,' some kind of material object lying in the field of experience rather than what is truly affirmed. But Tertullian, because he is rational, cannot escape so easily. Alongside this sensate conception of substance as 'stuff,' there is implicitly operative in his thought another, rational conception of substance as what is known through true judgments, and "when the rule of faith is stated in true propositions, sooner or later the rational and true conception is bound to drive out the one overly attached to images."[89] Now, the present point is not that Tertullian's writings exercised a decisive influence on later debates over *homoousios*;[90] it is that Tertullian exemplifies a philosophic error that infected (and still infects) theology.

If Tertullian represents an unexamined thrall to imagination, Origen represents an incomplete breakthrough to intelligible truth. Origen's theology contains an objective contradiction, for he considered the Son to be God by participation but, objectively, a participation in the divine

---

87. *Triune God: Doctrines*, 94–105.

88. *Triune God: Doctrines*, 94–105, 322–27.

89. *Triune God: Doctrines*, 324–5 (translation altered).

90. For later debates on *homoousios*, see Lewis Ayres, "Athanasius' Initial Defense of the Term *Homoousios*: Rereading the *De Decretis*," *Journal of Early Christian Studies* 12, no. 3 (2004): 62–84, 183.

nature can only be a created participation.[91] Still, it would be anachronistic to infer from this objective contradiction that Origen conceived the Son to be a creature.[92] Such a conception presupposes a clear and exact distinction between uncreated and created being, which was only attained in the fourth century. According to Lonergan, the concept of 'subordinationism' itself is anachronistic.[93] We should "speak not of subordinationism but rather of a dialectical process whereby the word of God, revealed and firmly believed, gradually eliminated less exact conceptions and prepared the way for the theology that followed."[94] In point of fact, the earlier authors had not grasped the conclusions of later theology, because they had not yet clearly conceived the questions. Thus, it is anachronistic to thrust Origen into the Arian controversy and anachronistic to interpret him in light of the later, more clearly articulated disjunction between God and creatures.[95]

In Athanasius and the Nicene *homoousion*, however, we have a push toward emancipation from imagination and toward a context in which the meaning of Trinitarian unity is governed not by any theory of participation or of substance but by a nest of true judgments.[96] Father and Son are correlative terms included within the dynamic unity of God, and *homoousios* denotes their unity: what is true of the Father as God is true of the Son as God, and vice versa, excepting only their relational distinction. If the Father is eternal and immutable, so too is the Son. This point has been made, in ways that are different but complementary to Lonergan's, by Lewis Ayres and Khaled Anatolios. According to Ayres (in effect), for Athanasius the term *homoousios* was shorthand for a nest of truth claims discerned in Scripture; its meaning was to be settled heuristically from theological considerations and not from sampling its uses in other discourses.[97] Similarly, Anatolios's interpretation is quite consistent with Lonergan's point; Anatolios explains,

---

91. *Triune God: Doctrines*, 130–33.

92. *Triune God: Doctrines*, 268–71, 360–63, 378–81, 492–501, 598–601.

93. *Triune God: Doctrines*, 90–95.

94. *Triune God: Doctrines*, 95.

95. *Triune God: Doctrines*, 132–37.

96. *Triune God: Doctrines*, 188–99, 470–71; compare Anatolios, *Retrieving Nicea*, 110–33.

97. Ayres, "Athanasius' Initial Defense of the Term *Homoousios*," 337–59.

Neither the council fathers of Nicea nor Athanasius himself were working with any determinate technical sense of *ousia* or *homoousios*. Moreover, they were not attempting to signify the divine essence by directly invoking an objective referent, whether the being of God or some creaturely analogue. The meaning of *homoousios* thus resides not in its inherent capacity to invoke an objective referent on its own, but rather in its assigned function of regulating how scriptural language as a whole refers to God and Christ. To say this is not to deny that the doctrine, in thus regulating scriptural language, successfully refers to God. In Athanasius's understanding, such reference succeeds when the Nicene *homoousios* is understood to regulate the reference of the whole nexus of scriptural *paradeigmata* [titles] in the direction of the radical ontological correlativity of Father and Son.... The regulation of scriptural language provided by the *homoousios* arises *from within* the scriptural language and narrative considered as a whole.[98]

What Anatolios is describing here is just what Lonergan means in characterizing the *homoousion* as a second-order statement governing other statements, expressing a kind of synthetic rule derived from a consideration of the narrative and symbolic patterns exhibited in Scripture itself and articulating a true, heuristic judgment about God without picture-thinking and without recourse to a theory of participation. Although Athanasius did not articulate an account of Christian realism, performatively he attained knowledge of reality through true judgment. This is the *ratio* of dogma, which, Lonergan argues, was achieved beyond the intention of any of the participants.

Still, the theological dialectic is tripolar; it involves a mystery of faith, and the mystery may be lost or renounced. To put it a different way, everything depends on locating the element of mystery. Here again is Anatolios, contrasting Arius with his bishop Alexander, the latter a defender of community of substance:

Perhaps every theology must ultimately invoke the ineffability of the divine mystery. But theologies, as well as the experiences

98. Anatolios, *Retrieving Nicea*, 128.

they inculcate, are crucially determined by where the mystery is located. For Arius, the ultimate mystery is the supremely ineffable reality of the one Unbegotten, and this way of specifying the location of the ultimate divine mystery remains a consistent tenet of the trajectory of trinitarian unity of will. Alexander, however, clearly and persistently attempts to present the mystery of the Unbegotten as mutually coordinate with the mystery of the Only-begotten, such that they are really two aspects of the same mystery.[99]

For Arius, the Creator-creation relationship is the heart of the mystery. Because God is absolutely prior, the Only-begotten cannot share God's being in the proper sense, but rather is produced by God's will.[100] For Alexander, the mystery is not only divine transcendence, which grounds the radical distinction of Creator and creation; it is also the relational mutuality of Father and Son within the unity of divine being.

The tripolar dialectic presents fundamental alternatives at both the philosophic and the theological levels. Philosophically opposed are the imaginal orientation to the focal points of biological extroversion and the rational orientation to intelligible truth. Theologically and, indeed, religiously opposed are the alternative conceptions of the Son. To a contemporary audience uncomfortable with religious truth claims, the doctrinal controversies of the ancient church can seem like the derailment of authentic religion into pedantic nitpickery. But the theological alternatives specify opposed conceptions of God and God's condescension to us. Both may be philosophically superior to Tertullian's materialism, but only one of them is a genuine development in Christian theology.[101] On the one side is a monadic God who voluntarily produces a Word as his instrument; God's condescension consists in sending his most exalted creature to the doom of the cross. On the other is a God intrinsically relational, whose condescension is the kenosis of the only-begotten Son;

---

99. Ibid., 82.

100. Arius exhibits some of the participation language we find in Origen, but for Arius participation is not continuous with the substance of God. The heightened sense of God's primacy has created for him the impossibility of affirming that a participated deity is God in the strictest sense, or conversely, that one begotten can be the first principle. See ibid., 46–47.

101. *Triune God: Doctrines*, 106.

it is gratuitous to the uttermost.[102] At the end of the day, these are opposed religious commitments.[103] To locate the mystery on the wrong side of the divide between God and creatures is finally to make shipwreck of faith in the self-emptying Word. As tripolar, then, the theological dialectic involves a philosophic moment but is ultimately governed by faith in "the word of God, revealed and firmly believed."[104]

It must be emphasized that what Lonergan intends (and what I have too briskly illustrated) is not a complete telling of the history in all its rich detail, but an analysis of a decisive underlying issue: realism. Tertullian and Origen are merely exempla of, on the one hand, a tendency to 'naive realism' and, on the other, a kind of idealism that results from an unconsummated breakthrough to intelligible truth—unconsummated in that it does not go all the way to rational judgment as the criterion of the real. These are recurring problems in theology. It is easy to imagine no one makes Tertullian's mistake today, but as far as I can tell, varieties of social Trinitarianism (because they burke the problem of individuation) and varieties of process theism (because they subject God to conditions of time) both, in their ways, result from the intrusion of imaginative criteria.

Dialectical analysis aims to understand the roots of conflicts and so distinguish differences that are Church-dividing from differences that are not. Within the ambit of Christian faith there is a necessary unity and a legitimate pluralism. The necessary unity is brought about by charity and by the authority of the Word of God as true and infallibly proposed by the Church. The legitimate pluralism is a function of complementary or genetically linked ways of meaning the same reality. There are different varieties of common sense and so different enculturations of the Gospel. Moreover, though not every Christian is obliged to be at home in the rarified air of theory, or scholarship, or mystical prayer, or philosophic self-knowledge, still some come to be so. These differentiations of consciousness may be combined in various ways in different persons, and the result is a further legitimate ground

---

102. See Anatolios, *Retrieving Nicea*, 100–108.

103. On the difference between theological and religious apprehensions of doctrine, see *Method* (1972), 333, or CWL 14, 309.

104. *Triune God: Doctrines*, 95.

of pluralism. But there is also a pluralism that is destructive of the unity of faith, and its ground is some defect of conversion. The dialectical process, then, is governed by love for the truth of God's word and a spirit of fraternal correction.[105]

Doctrine in Ongoing Contexts

The formal context for interpreting a text like the Nicene decree is the set of interwoven questions and answers that reveal its original meaning. Needless to say, this formal context is reached through careful study and investigation that brings to light the significant questions to which the formulation was proposed as a response. Besides that formal context, however, there is an ongoing context. "Ongoing context arises when a succession of texts express the mind of a single historical community."[106] Such a context was created by the stream of interrelated conciliar formulations that emerged in the centuries after the council of 325. Understanding that ongoing context does not determine the originally intended meaning of the Nicene decree, but it does indicate what in fact became, for Catholic theology, the context in which the meaning of the decree was to be understood.[107]

Here I propose to illustrate this through a brief example. About a decade ago, Sarah Coakley presented a celebrated paper on the meaning of Chalcedon.[108] Her aim was to determine the nature of the Christological *horos*, or definition, proposed by the Council, as a presupposition for its correct interpretation. She began with a thoughtful and fair critique of three streams of interpretation: a Lindbeckian 'grammatical' interpretation, John Hick's 'metaphorical' interpretation, and recent Anglo-American analytic interpretations. This was followed by her own hypothesis: the *horos* establishes a

---

105. See Dorothea Wendebourg, "Chalcedon in Ecumenical Discourse," *Pro Ecclesia* 7, no. 3 (1998): 307–32, here 316–18, 325–27. Wendebourg describes the fecundity of a certain kind of perspectivism deliberately adopted by Catholic and Reformed dialogues with the Oriental and Assyrian traditions. To some extent, as Wendebourg shows, something similar was also adopted in the Orthodox-Oriental dialogues but was freighted, it seems to me, with some rather unfortunate baggage.

106. *Method* (1972), 313, or CWL 14, 291.

107. *Method* (1972), 312–314; compare 320–26, or CWL 14, 291–92, 298–303.

108. Sarah Coakley, "What Does Chalcedon Solve and What Does It Not? Some Reflections on the Status and Meaning of the Chalcedonian 'Definition,'" in *The Incarnation: An Interdisciplinary Symposium on the Incarnation of the Son of God* (New York: Oxford University Press, 2002), 143–63.

kind of apophatic horizon for Christology. Coakley proceeded to list nine summary conclusions about questions left undetermined by the decree. Many of these conclusions seem indisputable, but two of them run counter to Lonergan's and therefore provide a useful point of contrast. On Coakley's reading, the Chalcedonian definition (1) does not expressly identify the one hypostasis in Christ as the hypostasis of the Word, and (2) does not say clearly that hypostasis means the same in Christology as in Trinity. She also mentions a further conclusion from John Hick: (3) the decree does not mean to propose that the two natures are contradictory.

For Lonergan, the constitutive question for Christology is, who is the Son? In the Nicene symbol, that question is answered by applying two mutually exclusive sets of predicates to one and the same subject. The Son is born of the Father before all ages and born of the Virgin in time. Begotten not made, the one through whom all things were made, he is nevertheless also among the things made as incarnate of the Virgin. It seems impossible to avoid the conclusion that the predicates (not made, made) are contradictory. It seems equally impossible to avoid the conclusion that the person in question is divine person, the Son begotten of the Father.[109]

The Nicene symbol presents a structure that the Chalcedonian definition later elaborates. In Chalcedon, we read explicitly and repeatedly of "one and the same Jesus Christ our Lord." To him are applied two distinct sets of predicates, divine and human, without changing or confusing the predicates, nor separating or dividing them from the one. Chalcedon's one selfsame subject is not 'one' in the predicamental sense, an imaginable, countable, material individual. He is not 'one' in the sense of intelligible wholeness, since there are in him two complete natures. He is of 'one' at the level of judgment: one and the same, to whom all the predicates of both complete natures apply.

---

109. Coakley, however, is far from alone. Karl Rahner, for one, also doubts that 'person' in Christology means just what it means in Trinity: ". . . 'Person,' wenn dieser Begriff in der Christologie verwendet wird, *einfachhin* dasselbe wie in der Trinität meine." Rahner, "Der dreifaltige Gott als transzendenter Urgrungd der Heilsgeschichte," in *Mysterium Salutis. Grundriß heilsgeschichtlicher Dogmatik*, ed. Johannes Feiner and Magnus Löhrer, Mysterium Salutis 2, Die Heilsgeschichte vor Christus (Einsiedeln: Benziger, 1967), 317–401, here 331. Joseph Donceel's translation of this paragraph is completely inattentive to the technical meanings of terms; Rahner's 'Eigenart' is rendered variously "peculiar nature," "peculiarity," and "proper nature," but it corresponds to the Latin 'proprium' and so, in the context of Trinitarian theology, ought to be rendered 'property' and never conflated with 'nature.' Rahner, *The Trinity*, trans. Joseph Donceel (New York: Crossroad Publishing, 1997), 27.

The problem of the *communicatio idiomatum* arises because Christ is two at the level of intelligible unity, since he has two natures, distinct and unconfused. The problem can be resolved adequately only by affirming an identity, one and the same, who is both. The solution to the problem of the *communicatio* is formulated in second-order, heuristic statements that govern other statements. Thus the one selfsame Word is all that it means to be the divine Word and all that it is to be human, except sin. What is true of him in virtue of being human, though, is not confused with what is true of him in virtue of being God. In this way, the definition of Chalcedon represents the ascent to intelligible truth demanded by the mystery. It recognizes two at the level of natural intelligibility and one at the level of identity, one and the same.

Chalcedon's 'one and the same' in two complete natures achieves for Christology what *homoousios*, in the Athanasian and Nicene sense, achieved for Trinitarian dogma.[110] It does so, moreover, in a way that incorporates and extends Nicaea's heuristic use of *homoousios*, for Christ is said to be *homoousios* with the Father in his divinity and *homoousios* with us in his humanity. What is true of the Father, then, is true of the Son, except the name Father, and what is true of us is likewise true of the Son in his humanity, except sin.

Both the Nicene and the Chalcedonian decrees illustrate the cognitive function of dogma. First, like the Nicene, so the Chalcedonian decree introduces technical terms: *hypostasis, homoousios*. It is very easy to get bogged down in an exegesis of those terms. Yet the conflict of interpretations, in the fourth century and in our own, should not be allowed to make mysterious what in the decree itself is perfectly clear, albeit heuristic. The question is: Who is the Son? And the answer is: He is the eternal Son of the Father, born of the Virgin in time. Likewise, the dogmatic meaning of the Nicene *homoousion* is heuristic: whatever is true of the Father is true of the Son, except the name Father. Furthermore, the numerical unity of the divine substance is logically implied by the supposition that there is only one God. It may be observed that understood thus, the judgment is not only heuristic but also apophatic. It is not a claim to comprehend all that may be said of God; it does not pretend to know God's substance; it affirms only that God's substance is to be

---

110. Lonergan, "Origins of Christian Realism (1972)"; Lonergan, "Christology Today."

known through intelligible truth, so that what is said of the Father is to be said of the Son, except the name Father.

Next, the *horos* is not literal in the sense of univocal, nor is it metaphorical, but it is analogical, because the meaning of the terms varies systematically with the differences in the objects to which they refer. So, to take the most important example, the precise meaning of 'consubstantial' varies as a function of the differences between God's substance and ours. In God, person and substance are really identical. Three divine persons are numerically one God. In us, person and substance (second substance, i.e., essence) are really (though inadequately) distinct. Three human beings share a common species but not a single *esse*.

Because it is analogical and heuristic, the dogma is also apophatic, in the sense that it acknowledges the intelligible truth of revealed mystery without claiming to understand it. 'Apophatic' adds to 'heuristic' the acknowledgement of a mystery that cannot be plumbed to its depths by us. Inasmuch as the structure intends a mystery, the meaning of its terms cannot be filled in except analogically and by remotion. Since the divine substance is *ipsum esse subsistens*, since a divine hypostasis is identical with the divine substance, it is impossible to know what God is without being God. In the next life we may understand without comprehension; here below, we do not even understand except through comparison to another with an ever greater dissimilarity.

Furthermore, as we have already explained, the dogma is synthetic, an achievement of systematic meaning, both in the sense that its terms and relations are implicitly defined in a structure and in the sense that it formulates synthetic explanatory principles rather than descriptions of things in relation to us. So, for instance, 'consubstantial' is shorthand for a kind of synthetic and explanatory principle or rule governing attributions. It functions not by describing or listing attributes—although examples are listed—but by affirming an underlying principle that governs attribution. Because Christ is consubstantial with us, what is true of us as human is true of him as human, except sin. Because he is consubstantial with the Father, what is true of the Father is true of him as God, except the relative property signified by 'Father.'

'Hypostasis' functions heuristically in both the Nicene and the Chalcedonian decrees, and, indeed, has the same heuristic function in both: what is three in God and one in Christ. In the Nicene decree, the one selfsame Son is the subject of the two sets of predicates. In the Chalcedonian decree, one and the same, our Lord Jesus Christ, is the subject of the two natures. If Chalcedon's one hypostasis is the Logos, it is antecedently probable that hypostasis in Chalcedon is the same as hypostasis in Nicaea. The later heuristic structure expands upon the first to affirm in the Son one hypostasis and a twofold consubstantiality. The use of the Nicene 'consubstantial' in this new context implies that the Nicene heuristic structure is being enlarged, not replaced by a different, unrelated structure in which all the terms have a different, unrelated meaning. The meaning of hypostasis and consubstantial are not fully determined, but they are structurally interrelated.

The dogmas, taken heuristically, are more than regulations about what Christians can say or ought to say. They are not merely patterns of linked images, such as *logos-sarx*, ascending-descending, or the narrative and symbolic patterns Lonergan discerned in the New Testament.[111] They present, rather, a structure of judgments about the truth claim intended by such patterns. As a structure of judgments, the definitions are ontological in the sense of making ontological truth claims, not merely grammatical regulations. They articulate the Church's infallible judgment about the truth-intention of divine revelation, though the affirmation is heuristic and not a univocal determination.

The achievement realized by the Councils was not brought about by a single author or a single generation of authors. It was brought about by a de facto theological collaboration over hundreds of years. Although the original achievement was difficult, still it is not arcane. It is simply a more mature apprehension of the faith. Anyone able to operate on propositions can grasp what it means to say that the glory and eternity of the Father are likewise the glory and eternity of the Son and the Holy Spirit. To proceed from understanding to assent, of course, is a further step, which no one can take without the Holy Spirit (1 Cor 12:3).

---

111. Lonergan, "Christology Today," 86–88.

CHAPTER EIGHT

Systematics and Systematicians

One who seeks understanding may safely ignore the multitude and listen to the most wise; wherefore, holy mother church proposes as guide for our studies neither all theologians equally nor even the most common opinions, but only St Thomas.[1]

BERNARD LONERGAN

NOTHING SEEMS MORE PASSÉ in Trinitarian theology than the 'psychological analogy.' It is still widely taken for granted that the psychological analogy represents a moribund strain of Latin Trinitarianism. If Augustine is the villain of this story as the originator of Latin 'essentialism,' Thomas Aquinas is generally considered to have perfected the type in his *Summa theologiae*. Lonergan's monumental *De Deo Trino*, whose systematic part represents a major development in this line, can hardly merit more than a footnote observing the last gasps of a moribund project.

Lonergan, however, regarded Aquinas's treatise in *via doctrinae* "a masterpiece of theology as a science and the apex of Trinitarian speculation,"[2] a "genuine achievement of the human spirit" with "a permanence of its own. . . . Unless its substance is incorporated into subsequent work, the subsequent work will be a substantially poorer affair."[3] There are two excellent reasons to take Trinitarian theology as our first case

1. *Triune God: Systematics*, 72 (my translation).
2. *Verbum*, 218.
3. *Method* (1972), 352, or CWL 14, 325.

study for method in the Systematic function of theology. The first is that Lonergan conducted, in *Verbum*, a study of Aquinas's achievement on this point that, as we have seen, marked him indelibly. The second is that Lonergan's own systematic treatise on the Trinity was probably the most refined of his Latin treatises. It provides, therefore, a vivid illustration of the theologian at work.

Our present interest is less with the content than with the method and criteria of Lonergan's systematic theology. I do not propose, therefore, to expound the cumulative and progressive results Lonergan attained by building on the foundation Aquinas skillfully laid, which I have attempted to sketch elsewhere.[4] Rather, our procedure shall be dialectical. The significance of Lonergan's options comes to light by comparing them to the more influential criticisms of his illustrious contemporary, Karl Rahner. The dialectic is merely preliminary, however, because I have no aspirations to the detailed study of Rahner that a complete analysis would require. For our limited purpose, it will suffice to consider Rahner's explicit and well-known criticisms of the psychological analogy. Because I do not wish to present a simulacrum of Rahner as Lonergan's foil, I will let him speak for himself as much as possible.

The chapter is divided into six sections. First, by way of an overview of Rahner's critique, we show how it converts Régnon's typology into an evaluative judgment. This brings to light three different problems of order in which Rahner's critique is involved, which are outlined in the second section. One of these is the problem internal to systematic theology, to which we turn in the third section. Systematic theology, however, is subaltern to the truths of faith and itself proceeds hypothetically. This raises peculiar problems for verification, which are discussed in the fourth section. Our fifth and sixth sections treat, respectively, the role of analogy and the notion of fittingness in systematic theology.

Rahner's Critique and Its Context

The opposed evaluations of the psychological analogy reflect more than a difference in theoretical views. To illumine the extent to which the

---

4. I have sought to do this elsewhere, though only in overview: Jeremy D. Wilkins, "Why Two Divine Missions? Development in Augustine, Aquinas, and Lonergan," *Irish Theological Quarterly* 77, no. 1 (2012): 37–66.

differences are involved in deeper questions of order and method in theology generally, let us begin with a little history.

The well-known typology that divides Trinitarian theology into Latin 'essentialism' and Greek 'personalism' has its origins in the monumental work of the Jesuit historian of doctrine Théodore de Régnon, *Études de théologie positive sur la sainte Trinité*.[5] Régnon discerned a turning point connected with the Arian, Sabellian, and Macedonian crises, when, in order to safeguard the revealed mystery, the Fathers formulated the Trinitarian dogma in terms of person and nature.[6] He systematized this insight into an analytic scheme for understanding the historical development of Trinitarian theology. Since the dogma of the Trinity affirms three who are distinct as persons but identical in nature, the concepts of 'nature' and 'person' provide two ways into a synthetic account of the mystery, variously realized as the concepts are variously ordered.[7]

> Latin philosophy first contemplates the nature in itself, and proceeds to the supposit; Greek philosophy first contemplates the supposit, and then penetrates it to find therein the nature. The Latin sees personality as a mode of nature; the Greek sees nature as the content of the person. There are here two opposed designs, which project conceptions of the same reality onto different backdrops.[8]

According to Régnon, on the Latin starting point, one conceives "la nature *in recto* et la personne *in obliquo*." On the Greek starting point, conversely, one conceives "la personne *in recto* et la nature *in obliquo*."[9]

---

5. Théodore de Régnon, *Études de théologie positive sur la sainte Trinité*, 4 vols. (Paris: Victor Retaux, 1892). Ralf Stolina, "»Ökonomische« und »immanente« Trinität? Zur Problematik einer trinitätstheologischen Denkfigur," *Zeitschrift für Theologie und Kirche* 105, no. 2 (2008): 170–216, traces the history of the economic-immanent distinction in eighteenth- and nineteenth-century German theology.

6. Régnon, *Études de théologie positive*, 1:117–244, esp. 117–128, where he frames the problem.

7. Ibid., 1:250–51.

8. "La philosophie latine envisage d'abord la nature en elle-même et poursuit jusqu'au suppôt; la philosophie grecque envisage d'abord le suppôt et y pénètre ensuite pour y trouver la nature. Le Latin considère la personalité comme un mode de la nature, le Grec considère la nature comme le contenu de la personne. Ce sont là des visées contraires, qui projettent les concepts de la même réalité sur des fonds différents" (ibid., 1:433–34). Translations are my own unless otherwise indicated.

9. Ibid., 1:251–2.

Now since *in recto* and *in obliquo* refer to conceptual orderings, the adequacy of the typology clearly depends on the actual execution of any given author. In other words, Régnon's model may have its uses as an ideal type, but it is not itself a description of anyone's actual theology.

The expectation fostered by this scheme is that Thomas Aquinas will be typical of the Latin pattern. In fact, Régnon does not hesitate to say that Latin scholasticism in general exhibits this pattern,[10] and he specifically applies it to Aquinas: "At the starting point of St. Thomas's Trinitarian theory, we meet a God who is single, subsistent, possessing a spiritual nature, a God who is perfect and presents all the characteristics of a 'personal' God, of a Person-God."[11] Effectively, he thinks, this means God the Father, which he tentatively approves as fitting the ancient pattern, "for during the first centuries of the Church's life, the name 'God,' unmodified, preeminently meant God the Father, source of divinity."[12] We leave to one side the fact that this is certainly not how Aquinas understood the matter, since for him the Father or Speaker in God can only be conceived relationally. (I return to this below.)

Régnon insisted that his typology was not meant to be evaluative in itself. For him, the two patterns are of equal value and equal adequacy, though they follow different routes, though they be like two paintings of the same mountain from two quite different perspectives.[13] His project and purposes were different from those of later scholars who adopted his scheme—often without acknowledging him—and applied it to their own ends.[14] The reception of his typology into contemporary Trinitarian theology has had far-reaching, if unintended, consequences. It has become very widely taken for granted not merely as a possibly relevant set of ideal types but as an actual description of the theology of Augustine, Aquinas, or the Latin tradition generally. In the process, it

10. Ibid., 1:252.

11. "Au point de départ de la théorie trinitaire de saint Thomas, on rencontre un Dieu unique, subsistant, possédant une nature spirituelle, Dieu parfait et présentant tous les caractères d'un Dieu 'personnel', d'une Personne-Dieu" (ibid., 2:212).

12. ". . . car pendant les premiers siècles de l'Église, le mot 'Dieu' prononcé seul, signifiait plus spécialement Dieu le Père, source de la divinité . . ." (ibid., 2:213; see 1:491–99).

13. See, e.g., ibid., 1:252, 433–35. Nevertheless, it has an evaluative feel to it, and it is not difficult to sense Régnon's dislike for scholastic theology.

14. See Kristin Hennessy, "An Answer to de Régnon's Accusers: Why We Should Not Speak of 'His' Paradigm," *Harvard Theological Review* 100, no. 2 (2007): 179–97.

has also become an evaluation. Personalism is good, and essentialism is bad. The psychological analogy is supposed to exacerbate this badness. It begins from the consciousness of a single person. Therefore, it cannot really get to three persons. Its protestations to the contrary are arbitrary. A unipersonal analogy cannot illumine a tripersonal God. (One recalls Harnack's quip that Augustine escaped modalism only by repeatedly insisting on it.)

Yves Congar, surveying Régnon's historiography and its influence,[15] accepts that there is a basic difference between Greek and Latin approaches and credits Régnon with revitalizing interest in the historical study of the distinctiveness of the Greek Fathers. "At the same time, however, de Régnon simplified the difference between the [Greek and Latin] theologies, with the result that many theologians, especially Orthodox scholars, have since taken his most clear-cut formulae as they stand."[16] Thus when Régnon's hypothesis is linked, as it usually is, to the assumption that Augustine marks the point at which Latin theology parted ways with a more ancient, more authentic, personalist tradition of Trinitarian theology, it is used to justify a negative judgment on Augustine specifically and the Latin tradition after him generally. (This was not, it bears noting, Régnon's own take on the matter; for him the parting of the ways antedates Augustine and even Nicaea.)

In these contexts, it is often implied or asserted that Augustine departed from the sounder biblical and patristic tradition, and other traditional authorities are positively evaluated on the basis of their putative differences from Augustine.[17] For Orthodox authors with an apologetic or controversial purpose, and for Catholic and Protestant authors reacting to the real or imagined evils of scholastic or neoscholastic theology, the conversion of Régnon's model to an evaluative discrimen presents an attractive and convenient prospect. The whole tradition stemming from Augustine can be condemned as a derailment. To some

15. Yves Congar, *I Believe in the Holy Spirit*, trans. David Smith, rev. ed., 3 vols. (New York: Crossroad Publishing, 1983), 3:xv–xxi.

16. Ibid., 1:xvi. Numerous examples are given.

17. See, e.g., my discussion of various interpretations of Gregory Palamas: Jeremy D. Wilkins, "'The Image of This Highest Love': The Trinitarian Analogy in Gregory Palamas's *Capita 150*," *Saint Vladimir's Theological Quarterly* 47, no. 3–4 (2003): 385–414. Neil Ormerod, *The Trinity: Retrieving the Western Tradition* (Milwaukee, Wisc.: Marquette University Press, 2005), is a vigorous brief, strongly influenced by Lonergan, for the Augustinian tradition.

authors, that means virtually the whole experience of Latin Christianity.[18] But conventional wisdom about Augustine, Aquinas, or the Latin tradition in general can and often does stand in the way of serious engagement with the constitutive questions and goals of that tradition.

Karl Rahner's little treatise *Der dreifaltige Gott* was likely the most influential mediator of Régnon's typology into Catholic systematic theology. His criticisms of Aquinas (and more broadly of the 'Augustinian-Latin' conception) convert Régnon's categories into theological value judgments. Rahner regarded Aquinas and Lonergan as exemplars par excellence of a derailment of Trinitarian theology, a tendency to privilege divine unity over the persons and to isolate the Trinity not only from the rest of theology but from Christian life itself.

According to Rahner, the psychological approach to Trinitarian theology closes the Trinity in upon itself so that it loses touch with its sources on the one hand and the realities of religious commitment on the other.

The treatise on the Holy Trinity occupies a rather isolated position in the total dogmatic structure. To put it bluntly (and naturally with some exaggeration and generalization): When this dogmatic treatise is concluded, the subject never comes up again. Its function in the whole dogmatic structure is only dimly seen. This mystery seems to have been communicated only for its own sake. Even after its communication, *as a reality* it remains locked within itself.[19]

---

18. For fuller discussion, see Lewis Ayres, "'Remember That You Are Catholic' (Serm. 52.2): Augustine on the Unity of the Triune God," *Journal of Early Christian Studies* 8, no. 1 (2000): 39–82; Michel René Barnes, "De Régnon Reconsidered," *Augustinian Studies* 26, no. 2 (1995): 51–79; Michel René Barnes, "Augustine in Contemporary Trinitarian Theology," *Theological Studies* 56, no. 2 (1995): 237–50; Gilles Emery, "Essentialisme ou personalisme dans le traité de Dieu chez saint Thomas d'Aquin?," *Revue Thomiste* 98, no. 1 (1998): 5–38; Emery, *Trinity in Aquinas*, trans. Matthew Levering and Teresa Bede (Naples, Fla.: Sapientia Press of Ave Maria University, 2003), 165–208; André de Halleux, "Personnalisme ou essentialisme trinitaire chez les Pères cappadociens," in *Patrologie et Œcuménisme: Recueil d'Études* (Louvain: Leuven University Press, 1990), 215–68; Stolina, "»Ökonomische« und »immanente« Trinität?"

19. "Der Traktat über die Heilige Dreifaltigkeit im Gefüge der ganzen Dogmatik ziemlich isoliert dasteht. Einmal grob (und natürlich übertreibend und verallgemeinernd) gesagt: Wenn dieser Traktat in der Dogmatik einmal abgehandelt ist, kommt er später dann auch nicht mehr vor. Man sieht seine Funktion im Ganzen der Dogmatik nur undeutlich. Dieses Geheimnis scheint nur um seiner selbst willen mitgeteilt zu sein. Es bleibt, auch nach seiner Mitteilung, *als Wirklichkeit* in sich selbst verschlossen." Rahner, "Der dreifaltige Gott," 322 (emphasis in original). Rahner's

[In St. Thomas] the treatment begins not from God the Father as the unoriginate origin in the Godhead and the reality of the world, but from the nature common to all three persons. . . . In this way the treatise on the Trinity is ever more placed in a 'splendid isolation,' through which it comes very seriously in danger of being felt a matter of no interest for religious *Existenz*. It looks as though everything about God that matters to us had already been said in the treatise *De Deo uno*. . . .[20]

If one starts from the basic Augustinian-Western conception, an a-Trinitarian treatise *De Deo uno* comes as a matter of course before the treatise on the Trinity. In this way, however, the theology of the Trinity must all the more arouse the impression that only absolutely formal statements can be made about the divine persons (with help from the concepts of the two processions and the relations), and even these only concern a Trinity absolutely enclosed, not outwardly open in its reality (and of which we who are shut out know something only by a curious paradox).[21]

---

essay is available in English as *The Trinity*, here 14. The Donceel translation is not very precise and sometimes misleading, especially on technical matters. Unfortunately, the selection of English idioms and the frequent use of emphatic typesetting in the Crossroad edition tend to exaggerate Rahner's criticisms compared to the original German.

20. "Hier [bei Thomas] wird nicht zuerst von Gott dem Vater als dem ursprunglosen Ursprung in der Gottheit und der Weltwirklichkeit, sondern zuerst von der allen drei Personen gemeinsamen Natur gehandelt. . . . Auf diese Weise gerät der Trinitätstraktat noch mehr in eine « splendid isolation », durch die er sehr stark in Gefahr kommt, also für die religiose Existenz uninteressant empfunden zu werden: Es sieht so aus, als ob alles, was für uns selbst an Gott wichtig ist, schon vorher im Traktat De Deo uno gesagt worden wäre." "Der dreifaltige Gott," 324 (internal citation omitted). Donceel's translation (pp. 16–17) of this passage leaves much to be desired; where Rahner contrasts the Father as starting point with the essence as starting point, Donceel's rendering contrasts the Father as source with the Father as essence. Note that Rahner's reading of Aquinas on this point, whatever its problems, is more accurate than Régnon's. The latter had taken the reference of *De Deo Uno* to be the Father as a matter of course.

21. "Geht man aber von der augustinisch-abendländischen Grundkonzeption aus, liegt ein a-trinitarischer Traktat De Deo uno wie selbstverständlich vor dem Trinitätstraktat. Dadurch aber muss die Trinitätstheologie erst recht den Eindruck erwecken, es könne in ihr von den göttlichen Personen nur absolute Formales (mit Hilfe des Begriffs der zwei Prozessionen und der Relationen) gesagt werden, und selbst dieses betreffe nur eine absolute in sich geschlossene und in ihrer Wirklichkeit nicht nach aussen geöffnete Dreifaltigkeit (von der wir, die Ausgeschlossenen, nur in einem seltsamen Paradox doch etwas wüssten)." "Der dreifaltige Gott," 325; *The Trinity*, 18.

To help overcome this forgetfulness, Rahner urges a return to the biblical and Greek understanding of God as a proper name for the Father.[22] It is a proposal in which he has been widely joined.[23]

Rahner exercised an enormous influence on Trinitarian theology. Congar, notwithstanding his own trenchant criticisms of Rahner's project (largely consonant with those ventured here), considered Rahner's "the most original contemporary contribution to the theology of the Trinity."[24] Originality may be said in many ways, but Rahner's sharp criticisms and enormous influence have perhaps done more than anything else to create the impression, at least in Anglo-Atlantic theology, that the psychological analogy is a dead end. Rahner's criticisms are forcefully presented and frequently echoed. Still, there are good reasons to doubt that Rahner grasped the strategy and structure of Aquinas's mature treatise on God. He acknowledged that he did not understand why, in the *Summa theologiae*, Aquinas "separated" (*scheiden*) his treatment into a series of questions on what belongs to the divine unity, followed by a series on what belongs to the plurality of persons, or, as Rahner put it, into two separate treatises.[25] It seems quite reasonable to suppose that the real source of Rahner's neuralgia is not Aquinas but the neoscholastic curriculum that divided the material into separate tracts and separate courses. Aquinas, for his part, revised his presentation of the Trinity several times, and we might have a better understanding of his mature options if we understood his reasons for making them.

Rahner's alternative program receives its basic formulation in his famous axiom (*Grundthese*): "The 'economic' Trinity *is* the 'immanent'

22. "Der dreifaltige Gott," 323–24; *The Trinity*, 16; also Karl Rahner, "*Theos* in the New Testament," in *Theological Investigations*, vol. 1, trans. Cornelius Ernst (New York: Crossroad Publishing, 1982), 79–148, here esp. 145–47.

23. See e.g. Walter Kasper, *The God of Jesus Christ*, trans. Matthew J. O'Connell (New York: Crossroad Publishing, 1984), 299 ("The doctrine of the Trinity must start with the Father and understand him as origin, source, and inner ground of unity in the Trinity"). Compare Colin Gunton, *The Promise of Trinitarian Theology* (Edinburgh: T&T Clark International, 1991); Catherine Mowry LaCugna, *God for Us: The Trinity and Christian Life* (San Francisco: Harper, 1991); John D. Zizioulas, *Being as Communion: Studies in Personhood and the Church* (Crestwood, N.Y.: St. Vladimir's Seminary Press, 1985).

24. Congar, *I Believe in the Holy Spirit*, 3:11; see 3:11–18.

25. Rahner, "Der dreifaltige Gott," 323–24; *The Trinity*, 15–16.

Trinity, and vice-versa."[26] Rahner did not himself execute a full-scale Trinitarian theology along the lines of this proposal. He did, however, sketch out its main lines in explicit contradistinction to the theology of Aquinas and, in the footnotes, to Lonergan's textbook *De Deo Trino.*[27]

Three Problems of Order

Wisdom in theology means, in part, distinguishing and relating different tasks, and grasping clearly what one is doing in each of them. A functionally differentiated theology parses out issues that otherwise tend to remain somewhat obscure.[28]

According to Rahner, the approach to Trinitarian systematics through the psychological analogy has forgotten the economy of salvation from the outset.

> The classical psychological theory of the Trinity also suffers from another methodological deficiency. Its speculation does not include knowledge about the origin of the dogmas concerning the 'immanent' Trinity. As it begins to develop its ideas, it has, in a way, forgotten about the 'economic' Trinity.[29]

26. "Die 'ökonomische' Trinität *ist* die 'immanente' Trinität und umgekehrt." Karl Rahner, "Bemerkungen zum dogmatischen Traktat »De Trinitate«," in *Schriften zur Theologie*, Bd. 4, *Neuere Schriften* (Einsiedeln: Benziger, 1967), 103–33, here 115 (emphasis in original); an identical statement occurs in "Der dreifaltige Gott," 328; *The Trinity*, 22. For the meaning of the terms, see "Der dreifaltige Gott," 328; *The Trinity*, 21–24.

27. Frederick Lawrence informs me, however, that the author of the footnotes was not Rahner himself but his then-assistant, Karl Lehmann.

28. According to Frederick Lawrence, Lonergan remarked that Rahner tried to go straight from Foundations to Communications.

29. "Die klassische psychologische Trinitätstheorie leidet auch unter einem anderen methodologischen Mangel. Sie setzt in ihrer Spekulation das Wissen um die Herkunft des Dogmas von der 'immanenten' Trinität nicht ein. Wenn sie anfängt, ihre Ideen zu entwickeln, hat sie gewissermaßen die 'ökonomische' Trinität vergessen." "Der dreifaltige Gott," 396; *The Trinity*, 119 ("The classical psychological doctrine of the Trinity suffers also from another methodological weakness. In its speculations it does not refer to what we know about the origin of the dogma of the 'immanent' Trinity. When developing its ideas it has, as it were, *forgotten about the 'economic' Trinity*" [Donceel's emphasis].) The footnote adds, "Genau diesen Eindruck bietet z.B. das große zweibändige, schon mehrfach erwähnte Werk *De Deo Trino* von B. Lonergan." Similar charges about the psychological analogy are made in Karl Rahner, *Grundkurs des Glaubens: Studien zum Begriff des Christentums*, ed. N. Schwerftfeger and A. Raffelt, Karl Rahner Sämtliche Werke 26 (Zürich: Benziger, 1999), 134;

The criticism seems to bring three different problems into view, but without putting any of them into clear focus: (1) the relationship between systematic theology and the documents of revelation, (2) the relationship between systematic theology and doctrines, and (3) the problem of order within systematic theology itself.

In the first place, there is the problem of relating the documents of revelation to systematic theology. For Aquinas, that relationship was mediated in a sense through the establishment of articles of faith from the documents of revelation. That is, the documents of revelation supplied authorities for establishing the articles. The articles supplied the first principles for theology as a subalternate science. These procedures are briskly outlined in his response to a *quodlibetal* question: should the teacher (*magister*) resolve theological questions by giving authorities or by giving reasons?[30] These alternatives correspond, respectively, to two different goals: removing doubt and error as to what is so, on the one hand, and leading students to an understanding of the truth, on the other. To achieve the former, one appeals to authorities and, indeed, such authorities as the hearers already acknowledge. To achieve the latter, however, one seeks the roots in order to understand how the articles are true: "facientibus scire quomodo sit verum quod dicitur" (alluding to the Aristotelian scientific syllogism, *syllogismus faciens scire* in Aquinas's Latin[31]). To fail in this latter, properly systematic or speculative task is to

---

Foundations of Christian Faith: An Introduction to the Idea of Christianity, trans. William Dych (New York: Seabury Press, 1978), 135.

30. Thomas Aquinas, *Quodlibet* 4, q. 9, a. 3. "Respondeo. Dicendum, quod quilibet actus exequendus est secundum quod convenit ad suum finem. Disputatio autem ad duplicem finem potest ordinari. Quaedam enim disputatio ordinatur ad removendum dubitationem an ita sit; et in tali disputatione theologica maxime utendum est auctoritatibus, quas recipiunt illi cum quibus disputatur; puta, si cum Iudaeis disputatur, oportet inducere auctoritates veteris testamenti: si cum Manichaeis, qui vetus testamentum respuunt, oportet uti solum auctoritatibus novi testamenti: si autem cum schismaticis, qui recipiunt vetus et novum testamentum, non autem doctrinam sanctorum nostrorum, sicut sunt Graeci, oportet cum eis disputare ex auctoritatibus novi vel veteris testamenti, et illorum doctorum quod ipsi recipiunt. Si autem nullam auctoritatem recipiunt, oportet ad eos convincendos, ad rationes naturales confugere. Quaedam vero disputatio est magistralis in scholis non ad removendum errorem, sed ad instruendum auditores ut inducantur ad intellectum veritatis quam intendit: et tunc oportet rationibus inniti investigantibus veritatis radicem, et facientibus scire quomodo sit verum quod dicitur: alioquin si nudis auctoritatibus magister quaestionem determinet, certificabitur quidem auditor quod ita est, sed nihil scientiae vel intellectus acquiret et vacuus abscedet."

31. See Thomas Aquinas, *Expositio Posteriorum*, lib. 2 lect. 9 n. 2.

send the hearers away empty of scientific understanding, knowledge of the 'reasoned fact.' Theology as scientific understanding of 'the reasoned fact' might be applied to illumine the documents, as we find in the biblical commentaries, or again, it might be confirmed by showing its power to explain the documents.

This process from the documents of revelation to theological science and back again was largely uncomplicated by the encumbrances of historical criticism. Today it is vastly more complicated by our historical awareness of the cultural and historical contingencies affecting the formation of the New Testament documents (individually and as a canon) and the path from the New Testament to the dogmas of the Church. For Aquinas, as long as the documents of revelation were interpreted within the analogy of faith, they were immediately applicable to systematic theology. Today, we have to contend with a series of mediating operations between the Bible and systematic theology. We know too well the distance that separates us from the New Testament authors. It is not the psychological analogy that threatens to separate us from the 'economy.' For the later scholastics it was the preference for commenting on the theologians rather than commenting on the Scriptures, and for us it is the "impenetrable wall" of scholarship between the systematic theologian and the sources.[32]

Next, there is the role of the articles of faith in systematic theology. For Aquinas, the articles of faith (doctrines) are the principles of theological science, the starting point in the quest for theological understanding; conversely, the goal of *sacra doctrina* in the *via disciplinae* is a fruitful understanding of the mysteries.[33] Today we know a great deal more than did Aquinas or any of his contemporaries about the "origin of the dogmas concerning the 'immanent' Trinity," if by this is meant the historical process from the New Testament to the reception of the conciliar dogmas of the fourth century. We are much more acutely aware not only of the fact that doctrine develops, but also that its development is conditioned by corresponding developments from a symbolic and

32. See *Method* (1972), 276, or CWL 14, 258.

33. The fundamental idea—though not, of course, in the differentiated Aristotelian sense in which Aquinas understands it—goes back to the very beginnings of the theological tradition, when Irenaeus proposed that the aim of theology is to understand the articles of faith that it takes as its principles.

narrative mode of discourse to a propositional and logical mode, and later into an explicitly metaphysical mode. As we take note of its development there arise for us questions about the transitions, the continuity between stages or orderings of doctrine, the criteria for preferring one ordering to another, and the shift toward increasingly systematic orderings which inevitably are further removed from the largely narrative order of the sources.[34]

As we have seen, it seems to be the case, de facto, that the process from the New Testament to the Nicene *homoousion* moves from the first-for-us to the first-in-itself, that is, from the relations of Father, Son, and Spirit to us, to the relations they have amongst themselves. The historical process arrived at a new ordering of doctrine, expressed incipiently in the Athanasian "whatever is said of the Father is said of the Son, except the name Father," and somewhat more systematically in the Cappadocian distinction between 'common' and 'proper' names in God. This terminus became the starting point for Augustine in his *De Trinitate*, which begins not from the divine essence, but from the equality of the divine persons, and flowers in the various scholastic formulae to the effect that in God all is one where there is no opposed relation. The question raised by Rahner's criticism is whether these transitions are valid. Still more fundamentally, the question regards the criteria for judging the validity of transitions from one ordering of doctrine to another.

The problem, as we have taken pains to indicate, is deeper and different than Rahner's criticisms let on. It may be that the fourth-century *homoousion* is not an authentic starting point for a subsequent stage of doctrinal and theological development, but then one has to formulate criteria for discriminating between inauthentic and authentic developments. It is radically insufficient to assert merely that the stage from Augustine forward is removed from the sources, for the *homoousion* itself is removed from the sources (as its fourth-century critics were delighted to observe). If Aquinas did not deal with these questions—which were not up in the thirteenth century—it may be said in his defense that he took the articles of faith as the starting point of his investigation of *sacra doctrina* in the *via disciplinae*. As we have seen, Lonergan's solution to

---

34. See *Early Works on Method 2*, 37–80; Crowe, "Lonergan's Search for Foundations, 1940–1959," 185.

these problems is to differentiate functions in theology. He does not treat them as if they were all the same problem, nor does he attempt to treat them all as pertaining to the systematic function of theology. The basic problem of order is getting clear on what one is doing, when. By distinguishing and relating the systematic function of theology to its other tasks, Lonergan also retains doctrine as the proximate and proper norm for systematic theology, without having to assume that the doctrines are simply unproblematic.

If it is granted that the articles of faith, formulated in ecclesial and theological doctrines, may authentically serve as the starting point for systematic theology, there is a still further question about the internal ordering of questions within systematic theology itself. Aquinas met the problem of order in part with a distinction between the way of discovery and the way of teaching, which he took over from Aristotle.[35] The way of discovery begins from what is first-for-us—the given in the sensible order—and proceeds to what is first-in-itself. The way of teaching is explanatory. It proceeds from a grasp of the reasoned fact to an explanation of the phenomena.[36] Aquinas generalized this strategy and applied it analogically to *sacra doctrina*. The goal of the first movement is certitude, the removal of doubt, and in matters theological one proceeds to this end by appeal to recognized authorities. The goal of the second is to understand not *whether* but *how* the truth is true, and to attain this goal one has to find the reasons that go to the root of the matter, though in theology these are grasped only analogically.[37]

It is on the basis of this distinction that Aquinas conceived and organized the *Summa theologiae* "secundum ordinem disciplinae" (as he says in the prologue). At the beginning of the questions on the Trinity, he observes that "secundum ordinem doctrinae," the first question regards the origins, then the relations of origin, and then the persons in God.[38] "Now this arrangement," Lonergan observes,

35. In Aristotle, see *Posterior Analytics*, i.13, 75a 14; *Metaphysics* i.1, 981a 30; *Nicomachean Ethics* iii.3 1112b 18–20 (the first link in the chain of causes is the last in the order of discovery). In *Basic Works of Aristotle*, trans. Richard McKeon (New York: Modern Library, 2001).

36. See Byrne, *Analysis and Science in Aristotle*, 201–4.

37. *Quodlibet* 4 q. 9 a. 3.

38. *STh* 1 q. 27 prol.

is strikingly different not only from the magnificent disorder of the *Scriptum super Sententias* but also from the conspicuous order of the *Contra Gentiles* and from the still different order of the *De potentia*. It would seem that Aquinas had conducted a rather elaborate experiment in theological method.[39]

The *Summa theologiae* thus became for Aquinas the occasion to restructure the entire treatise on God.[40] It is this very structure which Rahner finds so perplexing and unsatisfactory.

For Aquinas, at least, the *ordo disciplinae* or *via doctrinae* is determined by a pedagogical judgment. If the issue were a proof of the divine processions, Lonergan suggests, the most efficacious procedure would be to begin from the consubstantiality of the persons and show that their real distinction must be based on relations because it cannot be based on absolute perfections. The relations cannot presuppose the distinctions they ground and therefore must be relations of origin. Such relations of origin must be based on processions, and thus the question arises how we might possibly conceive processions in God. Since God is infinite spiritual consciousness, and since any processions must be open to the most perfect identity of principle and term compatible with real distinction, the only processions we can conceive in God are based on the analogy of consciousness as intellectual, as rational, as moral, as in the throe of love. This path of demonstration follows the order not of explanation but of discovery.

Yet its terminal point sets up the inverse order of explanation. "Inversely, if one aims at generating in pupils the limited understanding of mystery that can be attained in this life," Lonergan explains, then

> one directs one's attention not to demonstrations of existence but to the synthetic or constructive procedure in which human intelligence forms and develops concepts. First, one works out in detail the notion of God without asking any Trinitarian questions. Then one inquires, not whether the Son proceeds from the

---

39. Lonergan, "Theology and Understanding," 121 (internal citations omitted); a sketch of the successive attempts is offered in *Verbum*, 206–15.

40. See *Verbum*, 213–22.

Father (which would be to presuppose the notion of person), but whether there are processions in God. Though this question is not *quid sit* but *utrum sit*, still it involves one in the necessity of determining in what sense we can speak of processions in God; and such a clarification is all that we can attain, for as we do not understand God himself, so we do not understand the processions identical with God. Next, the clarification of the notion of the divine processions leads to a clarification of the divine subsistent relations. Finally, from three mutually opposed subsistent relations we can advance to some understanding of the truth that there are three really distinct yet consubstantial persons.[41]

Determining in what sense we can speak of processions in God presupposes we have some notion of God.

Note, however, that this pedagogical judgment is not a judgment about the intrinsic connections among the realities under consideration and, in fact, cannot be.

It cannot claim to be based on any *priora quoad se*, for in the Blessed Trinity nothing is prior or posterior. But it is the order of the genesis in our minds of our imperfect *intelligentia mysteriorum*; and by identity it is the order of Aquinas' *scientia subalternata* presented in the *ordo doctrinae*.[42]

This may seem counterintuitive, since in the previous paragraphs I suggested that the movement from the symbolic and narrative world of the New Testament to the cool, propositional world of the Nicene *homoousion* was also a movement from the first-for-us to the first-in-itself. Since in the way of discovery the missions reveal the persons, the persons reveal the relations, and the relations disclose the originating processions affirmed in the Nicene Creed, it might seem that the processions are intrinsically prior to the relations and persons in God. From this vantage point the structure of Aquinas's treatise might be easily

41. Lonergan, "Theology and Understanding," 122.
42. Ibid.

misunderstood as expressing a judgment about the intrinsic priority of essence to processions to relations to persons in God; the persons are somehow an afterthought.

This, however, is to confuse different kinds of order that Lonergan's differentiation of functions clarifies. There is the functional order in which doctrines—the articles of faith—precede systematic understanding, and Aquinas expressed this order in terms of the subalternation of *sacra doctrina* to the knowledge of God and the blessed. There is the order of discovery in which we arrive at the conclusion that the Trinity is an infinite, spiritual order of giving and receiving. Since the adequate explanatory principle of that order is the divine essence, which in this life we cannot know, there is, finally, the order of explanation that proceeds not from the divine essence, in which there is neither priority nor posteriority, but from a fruitful principle for the development and ordering of analogical concepts.[43] Thus, the functional priority of doctrines to theological understanding is quite distinct from the question of pedagogical order, which is internal to systematic theology itself. *Sacra doctrina secundum ordinem disciplinae* may presuppose doctrines as determining its basic problems for understanding, but its own internal ordering is governed by the considerations of pedagogical efficacy, the most effective way to develop explanatory concepts. Questions are ordered so that earlier questions presuppose the least and later questions build upon the earlier. In this way the learner is brought to a fruitful and transformative understanding of the mysteries even though the realities in themselves are not understood directly in this life.

Systematic Order

The fundamental problem for understanding in Trinitarian theology, according to Lonergan,

> lies in the following facts: (1) the Son is both *a se*, from himself, and not *a se*, not from himself; (2) the Holy Spirit is both *a se*, from himself, and not *a se*, not from himself; (3) the way in

---

43. Note that it is the concepts that are analogical. Directly, what is understood is the analogate. On the basis of the analogate, which is understood, we develop analogical concepts of the reality that is not directly understood.

which the Son is not *a se*, not from himself, is different from
the way in which the Holy Spirit is not *a se*, not from himself.[44]

This problem is distinctively theological; it arises from the conjunction of
divine simplicity with an order of distinct persons. That is, because God
is simple, God is *a se*; because the Son and Spirit are God, each is *a se*;
but they are also 'from another' each in a different way. The problem for
systematic understanding is not merely a logical reconciliation of three
with one. It is to give an account of an order in God that is not repugnant
to divine simplicity but also sheds positive light on the revealed truths
about the relationships among the divine persons.

Obviously, unless there is a prior clarification of what is meant by
'God,' the problem cannot even be formulated, let alone faced. Thus,
Aquinas's decision to handle the questions on the divine being and operations before dealing with the distinction of persons is pedagogical and
scientific, in the sense that it is an ordering of scientific ideas. A learner
who has not radically clarified the meaning of 'God' through the kind
of process Aquinas initiates in question 2 cannot come to grips with
the fundamental Trinitarian problem, nor appreciate why the key to the
problem is discovering a fruitful analogy for the divine processions, nor
grasp the importance of opposed relations of origin for personal identity
in God. The ordering of these questions does not reflect some judgment
about the priority of the divine essence vis-à-vis the divine persons, nor
does it reflect a bias toward essence rather than person. It is a function of
a judgment about the most expedient way to communicate the material
synthetically to learners.

The only real intrinsic order in God is the order of the divine persons.
The order in which we work out our concepts is not identical to the order
of the realities they mediate, because God is simple but our knowing
develops discursively.[45] Hence though God is without priority or posteriority, still we arrive at a mediated understanding of this by developing
our concepts cumulatively. Because the critics are usually rather vague
about the relationship between developing understanding and knowledge
of the real, they easily convert Régnon's typology into an evaluative

44. *Triune God: Systematics*, 126–27.
45. See Aquinas, *Super Ioannem*, chap. 1, lectio 1.

judgment. If Aquinas or Lonergan considers the essence of God before he considers persons in God, he must think there is some real priority of essence to person, etc. What is at stake here, however, is not the order intrinsic to the realities—Aquinas acknowledges no real order in God other than the order of the persons, and even there he denies every semblance of priority, even to the Father[46]—but rather the order efficacious for developing understanding.

Such pedagogical discipline is not at all a matter of "forgetting about the economic Trinity." It is rather a reversal of the movement of the way of discovery: as the way of discovery moves from the historical missions to the affirmation of the mysteries to the elimination of incoherencies, or again from the consubstantiality of the persons to their relations to their origins to the discovery of an analogue, so the way of teaching unfolds the questions in an ordered series so that prior questions do not presuppose but shed light on later questions. What is at stake is not a deductive chain but a process of developing understanding. In the order of discovery, it grasps that the intelligibility of the missions is founded on the identity of the persons; that the identity of the persons is a function of the relations; that the intelligibility of the relations flows from and presupposes the conception of the processions; that the conception of the processions flows from and presupposes—in our thinking—the divine nature. And, in the way of teaching, it follows an inverse ordering of questions.[47]

This is the task of the wise pedagogue: to find the problem that presupposes the least and illumines the most so as to proceed in an orderly way through the connected problems. In this way are avoided the multiplication of useless questions, the occasional and haphazard mode of proceeding, and the frequent repetition the Angelic Doctor laments in the prologue to the *Summa theologiae*.

Aquinas, one hardly needs to add, did not conceive the *via disciplinae* as the whole of theology. He presupposes the practices of *lectio* and *praedicatio* (conducted, as it were, in the *via inventionis*) that were the staples of theological study in his time and in fact constituted his main

46. See *STh* 1 q. 33 a. 1; q. 40 a. 3c.; a. 4 esp. ad 1; and q. 42 a. 3.
47. See *Triune God: Systematics*, 58–67.

work.[48] As we find it in Aquinas, then, theological exposition *secundum ordinem doctrinae* is one moment in a larger project, albeit a moment of particular significance in terms of the conception of *sacra doctrina* as a science (in the Aristotelian sense). If he says that *sacra doctrina* is ultimately more speculative than practical, it is because its ultimate finality is to the vision of God, and for this very reason it also has a practical, we should say pastoral, finality.[49] It is also because there are exercises of intelligence that need not be justified by their ulterior 'results,' and the contemplation of divine mystery is among them.

Lonergan, as we have seen, transposed this whole arrangement into his functional conception of theology. The distinction between discovery and explanation may recur in different ways in different functions of theology. Thus, for instance, in a critical history there is a first inquiry that evaluates information to establish the facts and a second inquiry that uses the established facts to construct an account of historical processes. It is one thing to verify the facts and another to verify the dependent hypothesis.[50] Similarly, in Trinitarian doctrine there is the process of discovery that moves from missions to persons to relations to origins, and the process of synthesis that defines the mystery on the basis of the consubstantiality of the person to formulate some such statement as the 'Athanasian' creed. In Trinitarian systematics, there is the process of discovery that moves from the consubstantiality of the persons to the discovery of a principle for conceiving them analogically, and the inverse process that constructs a theoretical articulation on the basis of that principle.

Since, as Lonergan conceives it, theology has not one but eight recurring functions, the distinction of two ways, discovery and explanation, has to be complexified by insertion into a structure that distinguishes theological functions, each with its own proper goal and procedures, and relates the functions to one another. It has to be complemented by a clarification of different kinds of meaning so that we can relate the symbolic and narrative mode of New Testament discourse to the propositional

---

48. Gilles Mongeau, *Embracing Wisdom: The* Summa Theologiae *as Spiritual Pedagogy* (Toronto: Pontifical Institute of Medieval Studies, 2015), 91–117.

49. *STh* 1 q. 1 a. 4c.

50. *Method* (1972), 201–3, or CWL 14, 198–90.

mode of the doctrines and relate both to the realities of cognitional and moral interiority and to the distinct realm of transcendent experience.

The *via disciplinae* in systematic theology fulfills an exigence of faith seeking understanding, without supposing that this is the whole exigence of faith or that systematics is the whole of theology. This means the goal of systematic understanding in theology can be pursued without prejudice to the legitimate and necessary goals of research, exegesis, history, dialectical analysis of conflicts, the articulation of adequate foundations, the appropriation of doctrines, and pastoral communication. The psychological analogy is not a forgetfulness of religious *Existenz*, if theological pedagogy may be a method of intellectual and spiritual transformation in preparation for the vision of God. It is not a forgetfulness of the religious origins and aims of theology in a theological method that makes conversion foundational, a method oriented to God as utterly transcendent mystery, a method that does not operate under the illusion that anything it might possibly say could "exhaust or even do justice to that meaning."[51] It is not a forgetfulness of the sources, if it is legitimate to complement the *via inventionis* with a *via disciplinae*. It is not forgetfulness of the 'economic' Trinity, if the development of doctrine sets the basic problem for theological understanding and if the *via disciplinae* results in an enriched, fruitful, and profound understanding of the 'economy' in light of the 'theology.' It is not a forgetfulness of pastoral purpose, if one must have some understanding of the mystery to be proclaimed.

Hypothesis and Verification

Verification in systematic theology is different from verification in doctrines. Doctrines are truth claims held in trust. To them one assents unconditionally. The goal of systematics, however, is an imperfect, analogical, fruitful understanding of the mysteries affirmed in doctrines. Systematics begins with truths and ends with understanding.

Karl Rahner points out that the *intelligentia fidei* yielded by the psychological analogy is only hypothetical:

51. *Method* (1972), 350, or CWL 14, 323.

That is where, in fact, the difficulties of the classic psychological speculations about the Trinity set in. They have no evident model *from* human psychology *for* the doctrine of the Trinity (a model known already before the doctrine of the Trinity), to explain why divine knowledge, as absolute primordial self-presence, necessarily means the distinct manner of subsisting of that which is 'uttered.' Or even why divine knowledge means an *utterance*, and not simply original self-presence in absolute identity. Rather it postulates *from* the doctrine of the Trinity a model of human knowledge and love, which either remains questionable, or about which it is not clear that it can be more than a *model* of human knowledge precisely as *finite*. And this model it applies to God. In other words, we are not told why in God knowledge and love demand a *processio ad modum operati* (as Word or as 'the beloved in the lover'). . . . Then it becomes clear too that such a psychological theory of the Trinity has the character of what the other sciences call an 'hypothesis.'[52]

What are we to make of these remarkable statements? Does Rahner mean to suggest that the rational psychology underlying the analogy is somehow contrived—he calls the reasoning circular—or only to point out the contingent fact that the psychological analysis was developed in connection with theological questions? And why does he underscore its hypothetical character? Does he think its hypothetical status tells against

---

52. Rahner, "Der dreifaltige Gott," 395 (internal citations omitted; emphasis in original); *The Trinity*, 117–18 (the translation given above). ("Hier beginnen nun tatsächlich die Schwierigkeiten der klassischen psychologischen Trinitätspekulation. Sie hat kein [vor der Trinitätslehre schon gewußtes] einleuchtendes Modell *aus* der menschlichen Psychologie *für* die Trinitätslehre, um verständlich zu machen, warum göttliche Erkenntnis also absolutes ursprüngliches Beisichsein notwendig die distinkte Subsistenzweise des 'Ausgesagten' bedeute oder überhaupt göttliche Erkenntnis Aussage und nicht blosses ursprüngliches Beisichsein in absoluter Identität besagt, sondern postuliert eher von der Trinitätslehre her ein Modell des menschlichen Erkennens gerade als eines *endlichen*, und wendet dieses Modell dann wieder auf Gott an. Es wird, anders ausgedrückt, nicht verständlich gemacht, warum Erkennen und Lieben in Gott auch eine 'processio ad modum operati' [als Verbum oder als 'amatum in amante'] fordern. . . . Dann wird auch deutlich, daß diese psychologische Trinitätstheorie den Charakter dessen hat, was man in der sonstigen Wissenschaft eine 'Hypothese' nennt.") The footnote adds, "Vgl. z. B. die Aussagen von B. Lonergan, *De Deo Trino* . . . die zuletzt auch nur auf eine 'Hypothese' hinauslaufen." ("Compare, for example, the statements of B. Lonergan, *De Deo Trino* . . . they too, finally, amount only to a hypothesis.")

it, or does he wish merely to remind us that no hypothesis can have a special claim on our allegiance? Is it that the psychological analogy is not modest enough, that through it theologians try to know too much without adequately adverting to the merely hypothetical character of their instrument of analysis?

Aquinas's distinction between the two theological ends of determining the truth and developing understanding, each with its corresponding procedure, was transposed by Lonergan into the doctrinal and systematic functions of theology, as prepared by a series of prior operations. I would not wish to be apodictic about Karl Rahner, but it seems that only a failure to distinguish the respective goals and methods of these two different tasks could lead to a critique of systematic theology for its hypothetical character. The alternative, it seems, would be semirationalism, the proposition that necessary reasons can be discovered for revealed mysteries.

In these two distinct functions there occur two instances of truth and two instances of understanding. The goal of the doctrinal function of theology is a clear and distinct confession of the mysteries hidden in God and revealed to faith. That is, the articles of faith propose truths that we cannot understand in this life. Understanding is not the basis for our assent; rather, we assent in trust of God who reveals. In formulating doctrines, then, our concern for understanding is restricted to a clear and distinct announcement of the mystery.

On the other hand, systematic theology is an explanatory function. We hold revealed mystery though we do not understand, but we hold a theory in the measure it helps us understand. In most matters of any scientific complexity this understanding is, at most, hypothetical. It is systematic, but the system is not static; it is constantly developing toward ever more adequate explanation. When the matter to understand is transcendent mystery revealed by God, then our theoretical understanding is also necessarily analogical, imperfect, and often no more than probable, but nevertheless highly fruitful.[53] Indeed, a hypothesis is all the more probable the more questions it is capable of resolving in a single view and the more alternative hypotheses are excluded as unsatisfactory.[54] In this light, the appropriate question is

53. *Method* (1972), 348–50, or CWL 14, 321–23; *Triune God: Systematics*, 30–59.
54. *Triune God: Systematics*, 42–43, 48–53.

not whether systematic theological understanding is certain or 'merely hypothetical'; short of the beatific vision, it could never be more than an illuminating theory. The relevant question is whether, and to what extent, the theory illumines and is confirmed by the facts.[55]

To speak in terms of hypothesis and verification, of course, is to leave the idiom of Thomas Aquinas and accept the idiom of a later science. Of itself, that fact tells us nothing of the legitimacy of this development, which has its foundation in the twofold act of the mind. Nevertheless, Aquinas did proceed in this way. He explained that the role of theology in its doctrinal office was to establish the *credenda*, while its speculative office was to formulate a congruent theory that might give an account of the mysteries.[56] Such theory might regard the mystery of God, necessary in itself, or it might seek to account for contingent mysteries like the incarnation, whose fittingness is hidden in divine wisdom. Since in this life we do not know God except by his effects, we do not understand the Trinity and we do not grasp, except imperfectly, the fittingness of God's works. For a perfect understanding of these mysteries, the one sufficient principle is the divine essence, which in this life we cannot know.[57]

The development of theological method between the twelfth and thirteenth centuries effectively brought to light the importance of this structure in the investigation of the mysteries of faith. Aristotle had conceived science as true and certain knowledge of things through their causes. Even so, the conception of *sacra doctrina* as a science in the Aristotelian sense had to be expanded to make room for the Augustinian *crede ut intelligas* for the simple reason that reasons proportionate to supernatural mysteries are not proportionate to human intelligence in this life.[58] If modern science understands itself to be no more than a succession of hypothetical approximations, indirectly verified, Thomist *sacra doctrina* at least acknowledges that the mystery of God has no cause

55. Lonergan expressly stresses the hypothetical character of the analogy: see *Verbum*, 213–22; but he also presents compelling reasons to deem it the best available hypothesis: see *Triune God: Systematics*, 168–81; *Triune God: Doctrines*, 638–84; and Philip McShane, "The Hypothesis of Intelligible Emanations in God," *Theological Studies* 23, no. 4 (1962): 545–568.

56. *STh* 1 q. 32 a. 1 ad 2.

57. Lonergan, "Theology and Understanding."

58. *Verbum*, 213–22.

and that the contingent mysteries of creation and salvation have their sufficient cause in divine wisdom and goodness.[59]

It does not follow either that theological hypotheses cannot be verified or that we must expect an endless series of alternatives with no real progress in understanding. To the problem of verification we will return in a moment; first, a word on the problem of continuity. In the first place, the mysteries of faith do not change, which means the fundamental problems for theological understanding will continually recur despite changes in cultural and scientific context. In the second, God's grace is not going away, and in the third, theologians have always had minds and will continue to use them. Theologians may sometimes forget their questions, but they cannot stop asking them. Furthermore, scientific progress or even a scientific reorganization, as distinct from scientific derailment, does not throw out genuine achievement, though it may recontextualize or build on it further.[60] Unfortunately, this presumes a continuity of problems and method that theology, at present, does not have. Unmethodical theology is unclear about its proper criteria.

Trinitarian theology has, in consequence, come to an awkward pass. The fundamental problem for understanding has been obscured, and its solution has not been understood. The problem has been obscured, partly because inadequate philosophies propose as true that propositional truth is meaningless, partly because historical difficulties are mistaken for religious doubts, partly because these questions are not methodically distinguished from the problem proper to systematic theology as functionally subsequent to doctrines, and partly because unmethodical theology does not have clear criteria in light of which to conceive its problems. The solution has not been understood, partly because the average manualist and the average commentator never did understand what intelligible emanation really meant, partly because most theologians do not either, and partly because the prevailing narrative discourages figuring it out. But there is another, more justifiable reason, and it is that theologians have been busy navigating the many difficulties attendant upon the profound cultural transformations we are rather belatedly facing. As far as this last goes, the wheat and chaff are mixed. There are

---

59. Lonergan, "Isomorphism of Thomist and Scientific Thought."
60. *Method* (1972), 351–53, or CWL 14, 324–26.

real new questions and it is not too surprising that they should occupy the attention of theologians, even if the neglect of traditional doctrinal topics is unfortunate; on the other hand, there are also many distractions.

Nevertheless, despite the overwhelming acceptance in contemporary theology of the verdict condemning the psychological analogy to the dustbin of history, sooner or later the true notion of God will drive out the currently fashionable mistaken notions. Sooner or later the fundamental problem for understanding the Trinity will come back into focus. Then it will be as clear as ever that the key to solving those problems in an orderly manner is an analogy of spiritual emanation. That analogy may be enriched and deepened. It was enriched by Aquinas's transposition of Augustine's insight into a more adequate theoretical context. It was deepened considerably by Lonergan's hermeneutics of consciousness. But it is not forward progress to set aside what is not understood, nor to sidestep the fundamental problem of Trinitarian theology to involve oneself in speculations with ulterior criteria supplied by political or ethical or other concerns (however valid and pressing in their own right those concerns may be), and without an adequate handle on the relationship of symbolic to explanatory meaning.

Perhaps I may note in passing that the critics who reject the psychological analogy because it supposedly privileges divine unity are missing the point. It is true that the analogy begins with intelligible emanations within a unified field of consciousness. But it does so to conceive that perfect communion of mind and heart for which we ourselves pray: "the three Persons are the perfect community, not two in one flesh, but three subjects of a single, dynamic, existential consciousness."[61] It is, ironically, Karl Rahner who posits God as Absolute Subject.[62] For Lonergan, the divine persons are each subjects, distinct centers of conscious identity within a single blaze of infinite, true love.[63]

Let us return to the problem of verification. The absence of method results in a criteriological vacuum. The distinction of functions results in a criteriological clarification. Theology deals with many different kinds

61. Lonergan, "The Dehellenization of Dogma," 24.

62. See Rahner, *Grundkurs*, 122, 132, 133–34, 202, 207, 289 (= *Foundations*, 122, 133, 134–35, 209, 215, 304); Rahner, "Der dreifaltige Gott," 364–66, 385–93 (= Donceel, trans., *The Trinity*, 75–76, 103–15).

63. *Triune God: Systematics*, 376–421.

of questions, but the goal of systematic theology is understanding the mysteries. Its criteria, accordingly, are those proper to understanding. A theological hypothesis, like hypotheses in any other discipline, is verified indirectly by working out its implications and testing them against the relevant facts. Thus we may ask of a hypothesis whether it sheds light on the fundamental problem, whether it does so in a synthetic and orderly manner, whether it subsumes ranges of data under a single coherent perspective, and whether there are viable alternatives that may handle the questions in a more satisfactory manner. On all these counts, the psychological analogy seems uniquely adequate.[64]

The mysteries are received in faith though we do not understand them, but a hypothesis in systematic theology is accepted precisely because it is understood and its explanatory power appreciated. Where the criteria are set by the desire to understand, then what is wanted is an account that addresses the fundamental problem for understanding and that opens up a synthetic perspective on a range of connected problems. There are, of course, competing desires, and where they are allowed to set the criteria, political utility or cleverness or some value other than explanatory power will determine the success or failure of theological hypotheses. I do not mean values are excluded altogether. Devotion to getting things right, to understanding matters on their own terms without colonizing them for ulterior purposes, is a commitment to a value that will not be realized by an abstraction called speculative intellect, but only by deliberate self-discipline.

Lonergan pulled no punches about the standards to which systematic theology ought to aspire. "Mathematics, science, scholarship, philosophy" are all difficult, he wrote.

> But the difficulty is worth meeting. If one does not attain, on the level of one's age, an understanding of the religious realities in which one believes, one will be simply at the mercy of the psychologists, the sociologists, the philosophers, that will not hesitate to tell believers what it really is in which they believe.[65]

64. *Triune God: Doctrines*, 144–81; see too Wilkins, "Why Two Divine Missions?"
65. *Method* (1972), 351, or CWL 14, 324.

He might have added the historians to his list, and there would have been no need to stop there. But the point is that Christianity's cultural position and vitality depend partly on the intellectual seriousness and rigor of its intellectual apostolate. As the speculative function of theology, systematics bears a special burden in this regard. It is also exposed to a special risk. Disciplinary standards tend to be both clearer and stronger for the scholarly functions of theology (Research, Interpretation, and History in particular), because it is easier to appreciate that success is related to getting texts and authors and movements right on their own terms. The criteria for success in Systematics are more readily contested, particularly when, as often happens, it is effectively subsumed into the ethical concerns of Foundations or the pastoral concerns of Communications.

Necessity and Analogy

We cannot here give a full explication of the psychological analogy, which is really an analogy from spiritual consciousness. Its main lines have at least been sketched in our earlier chapters, for the heart of the analogy is the notion of intelligible emanation, which was the central question animating Lonergan's *Verbum* investigation. Intelligible emanation, or what he later sometimes called spiritual autonomy, is exemplified by the conscious dependence of conception upon understanding, of judgment upon a grasp of the sufficiency of the evidence, of rational love upon moral judgment.[66] Lonergan's mature view was that the analogy had to take its stand on a spiritual consciousness suffused with love. The eyes of love discern value, the discernment grounds rational affirmation, and the rational affirmation grounds devotion.[67] The divine processions are not conceived on the general analogy of efficient causality but on the precise analogy of the *because* within consciousness: the yes is consciously *because* of the discernment, and the devotion is consciously *because* of the inwardly uttered yes.[68] What we ourselves experience as the rational and moral necessity of true judgment and rightly ordered love is in God

---

66. *Triune God: Systematics*, 174–81.
67. Lonergan, "Christology Today," 91–92.
68. *Triune God: Systematics*, 164–65.

an absolute necessity that, we know from revelation, also is dynamically ordered to speak a Word that breathes Love.

Critics seldom have an exact grasp of these facts, in my experience. Karl Rahner, regrettably, is no exception. He continues the passage introduced above:

> The difficulty grows because we cannot say that the actual divine knowledge or love, insofar as either is the Father's as such (already given with his divine essence) are formally constituted by the Word. We cannot say, therefore, that the Father knows *through* the Word; rather he says the Word because he knows. If human psychology can demand an *operatum* (an object of the act of knowing), it can do so only because and insofar as otherwise spiritual knowledge would not exist.[69]

To Karl Rahner, it appears a grave defect that the hypothesis of intelligible emanations does not explain what it is supposed to explain: the necessity (*Notwendigkeit*) of immanent *processiones operatorum* in God. As he remarks in his *Foundations of Christian Faith*:

> Ultimately they [the speculations of the psychological theory] are not really all that helpful. A 'psychological theory of the Trinity'. . . in the end does not explain precisely what it is supposed to explain, namely, why the Father expresses himself in a Word, and with the Logos breathes a Spirit which is different from him. For such an explanation must already presuppose the Father as knowing and loving himself, and cannot allow him to be constituted as knowing and loving in the first place by the expression of the Logos and the spiration of the Spirit.[70]

---

69. Rahner, "Der dreifaltige Gott," 395 (emphasis in original); *The Trinity*, 118 (the translation given above). ("Die Schwerigkeit wächst, weil ja nicht gesagt werden kann, daß die aktuelle göttliche Erkenntnis oder Liebe, insofern sie die des Vaters als solchen ist [und schon gegeben ist mit dem göttlichen Wesen des Vaters], formal konstituiert sei durch das Verbum, der Vater also *durch* das Wort erkenne [er sagt vielmehr das Wort, weil er erkennt]. Wenn aber eine menschliche Psychologie ein 'operatum' fordern kann, dann gerade nur deshalb, weil und insofern sonst die geistige Erkenntnis also solche nicht gegeben wäre.")

70. Rahner, *Grundkurs des Glaubens*, 134; *Foundations of Christian Faith*, 135 (the translation given above). ("[Die Spekulationen einer 'psychologischen Trinitätslehre'] . . . im letzten Grunde doch

As Rahner understands it, the analogy of intelligible emanations takes for granted the prior constitution of the Father as unoriginated possessor of the divine essence and does not explain why he must speak or why the Speaking should spirate love.

Now, Bonaventure was prepared to conceive the Father as in some way distinct prior to the generation of the Son: the Father is the unbegotten instance of 'habens deitatem,' and his primal fecundity suffices to identify him even apart from the relation of paternity. Insofar as the Gentile conceives God as a self-sufficient person, he or she knows the Father.[71] For Aquinas, however, it is otherwise. Each of the divine persons is conceived relationally and none can be conceived apart from the structure of relations.[72] For Aquinas, when non-Christian monotheists conceive God as personal and one, they do not conceive the Father, because they do not ask whether there are distinct subsistents in God, only whether God is distinct, intellectual, and subsistent. The conception of God the Father pertains to a context in which it is known that there are three distinct subsistents in God; since non-Christians do not know this, their conception is not properly of any distinct subsistent in God, but rather of the divine substance itself as subsistent, apart from any knowledge of the real relations in God. To say this is in no way to posit some kind of fourth reality in God apart from the divine persons who are really identical with the divine substance, for we are making not an assertion about some reality in God, but an assertion about an imperfection in the non-Christian conception of God, which does not advert to the relational distinction of persons in God.

The point is twofold. Both the analogy and the treatise are structures, not parts in isolation. The analogy is a structure; it does not explain the persons in isolation but as consciously interrelated. The

---

nicht sehr hilfreich sind. Eine 'psychologische Trinitätslehre'. . . erklärt am Ende gerade das nicht, was sie erklären will, nämlich warum der Vater sich im Wort aussage und mit dem Logos ein von ihm verschiedenes Pneuma hauche. Denn eine solche Erklärung muss den Vater als sich erkennend und liebend schon voraussetzen und darf ihn nicht durch die Aussage des Logos und die Hauchung des Pneumas erst als erkennend und liebend konstituiert sein lassen.") These remarks do not suggest an exact grasp of the underlying psychological facts.

71. Bonaventure, *Commentaria in Librum Primum Sententiarum*, d. 27 pars 1 a. 1 q. 2 ad 1; ad 3. In *Doctoris Seraphici S. Bonaventurae Opera Omnia*, vol. 1 (Ad Claras Aquas [Quaracchi]: Ex typographia Collegii S. Bonaventurae, 1882).

72. *STh* 1 q. 40 a. 3c.

Speaker is the 'because' of the Word; the speaking is the 'because' of the proceeding Love.[73]

> Father, Son, and Spirit are eternal; their consciousness is not in time but timeless; their subjectivity is not becoming but ever itself; and each in his own distinct manner is subject of the infinite act that God is, the Father as originating love, the Son as judgment of value expressing that love, and the Spirit as originated loving.[74]

In this structure and in the reality it conceives, however imperfectly, there is no question of conceiving any of the divine persons apart from the others.[75]

The treatise, too, is a structure. There is the order of our concepts in development, and then we first conceive processions in God; the processions yield relations, and the relations as subsistent are the persons. Once these concepts are deployed, the order is reversed: we consider the persons in general, individually, and as compared to the divine essence; the relations are revisited as personal properties; and the processions are revisited as notional acts. The processions and the notional acts are really identical but conceptually distinct; we conceive the former in order to posit relations and persons; we conceive the latter in order to think about the processions in terms of personal operations.

> In this presentation the starting point is not God the Father but God; the first question is not whether there is a procession from God the Father but whether there is a procession in God.... The *Summa's* structure ... implies a twofold ordering of our Trinitarian concepts. There is the order of our concepts *in fieri*, and then processions precede relations and relations precede persons. There is the order of our concepts *in facto esse*, and then there are the persons as persons, the persons considered individually, the persons

---

73. See *Verbum*, 46–48, 204–8. See too Frederick E. Crowe, "For Inserting a New Question (26A) in the Pars Prima," in *Developing the Lonergan Legacy: Historical, Theoretical, and Existential Themes*, ed. Michael Vertin (Toronto: University of Toronto Press, 2004), 332–46; McShane, "The Hypothesis of Intelligible Emanations in God."

74. Lonergan, "Christology Today," 92.

75. This should be qualified by noting that it is possible, while developing concepts, to conceive Speaker and Word without yet adverting to the procession of Love. But then one is not yet at the full conception of the speaking.

compared to the divine essence, to the relations, to the notional acts. Now these two orders are inverse. The processions and the notional acts are the same realities. But the processions are in God prior, in the first order of our concepts, to the constitution of the persons. On the other hand, the notional acts are acts of the persons and consequent to the persons conceived as constitute.[76]

By way of this twofold ordering of concepts, Aquinas eliminates "even the semblance of a logical fiction of a becoming in God."[77]

Moreover, the structure of the treatise illustrates where the analogy from the *imago Trinitatis* enters the scene and where it surrenders to the mystery. It shows where the analogy enters the scene, for there is a careful development of the notion of God by conceiving pure perfections and attributing them to God by way of affirmation, negation, and eminence. Reason, illumined to be sure by faith but operating within its own proper ambit, conceives God as infinite being, understanding, truth, love. But it is only faith that knows God is a breathing of Love from the speaking of Truth, and so the analogy of the *imago*, of intelligible emanations, prolongs the insights of natural theology. The analogy itself is unfolded in two, inverse conceptual orders, and these "stand on different levels of thought. As long as our concepts are in development, the psychological analogy commands the situation. But once our concepts reach their term, the analogy is transcended and we are confronted with the mystery."[78]

Comprehensive understanding of the mystery is beyond us in this life. "No system we can construct will encompass or plumb or master the mystery by which we are held."[79] It is even, in a sense, beyond us in the next, though we hold fast to the promise to know as we are known (1 Cor 13:12). Hence, Lonergan warns, "Do not think that Aquinas allows the psychological analogy to take the place of the divine essence as the one sufficient principle of explanation. The psychological analogy is just the side door through which we enter for an imperfect look."[80]

76. *Verbum*, 213–14.
77. *Verbum*, 213.
78. *Verbum*, 215.
79. *Method* (1972), 341, or CWL 14, 315.
80. *Verbum*, 216.

It is not, then, a bug but a feature of the analogy that it does not pretend to explain what in this life we cannot understand: the intrinsic and absolute necessity of Trinitarian relations in God. There is no doubt about that necessity, since God is the sufficiency beyond all conditions. Yet to pretend to explain it would be the error of rationalism or semirationalism. In this life we know the divine Trinity only by revelation and can conceive it only analogically.[81]

Contingency and Fittingness

The *Grundthese* of Karl Rahner's proposal for a project in Trinitarian theology is the axiomatic identity of the Trinity *in se* and in the world: "the 'economic' Trinity is the 'immanent' Trinity, and vice versa."[82] The proposal is correct in a sense but too compact in another. It is correct in its fundamental intention, for the divine missions reveal the divine persons by giving them to us, so that we receive by grace what God is by nature. This reception, however, is a created and contingent order, grounded indeed in divine wisdom, but nevertheless with an immanent intelligibility of its own. To put it differently: God, the all-sufficient, has no conditions; we, on the other hand, are radically conditioned, and it is precisely God's self-communication to us that fulfills the conditions for us to receive it.

The point is, those conditions have an intelligibility of their own, which is distinct from the necessary and infinite intelligibility of God; it is a finite and conditioned intelligibility, immanent in the contingent order of God's self-communication. That intelligibility is *conveniens*, fitting.[83] Lonergan defines it this way: "Fittingness is a proper intelligibility, necessary neither in its existence nor in its essence, and which in theological matters cannot be perfectly grasped by us in this life."[84] To say

---

81. *Triune God: Doctrines*, 576–639.

82. On the conditions for the missions, see Rahner, "Der dreifaltige Gott," 382–83; *The Trinity*, 100–101. Compare *STh* 1 q. 13 a. 7; q. 43 aa. 1–3; Lonergan, *Triune God: Systematics*, 436–43.

83. Compare Gilbert Narcisse, *Les raisons de Dieu: argument de convenance et esthétique théologique selon saint Thomas d'Aquin et Hans Urs von Balthasar*, Studia Friburgensia 83 (Fribourg, Suisse: Éditions universitaires, 1997), esp. 101–113. Narcisse's sympathy to von Balthasar sometimes unbalances his work so that the epistemological validity of *rationes convenientiae* in theology is not adequately assessed.

84. Bernard J. F. Lonergan, "De Ratione Convenientiae: Methodus Theologica Ad Finem Incarnationem Applicata/The Notion of Fittingness: The Application of Theological Method to the

it is a proper intelligibility is to say that it may be understood directly, not only inversely (as we may conceive nothingness, or again sin, on the basis of an inverse insight grasping the absence of an expected intelligibility). Again, an intelligibility is not a concept, for a single intelligibility may be expressed through a multiplicity of concepts, for instance, the sequence of positive integers or the concepts of center, radius, and perimeter. What is not absolutely necessary, finally, is contingent, conditional.[85]

The concrete intelligibility of the actual order of divine self-communication, then, is its fittingness. Its root is divine wisdom, and if divine wisdom were our wisdom, we would understand how all things fit together in a single view. In this life, however, divine wisdom is not our wisdom, so we have to be content to enumerate many different aspects and connect them as best we can.[86] One thing we know for certain, though it is not highly intelligible to us, is that the contingency of divine self-communication is no more a change in God than the creation of the world is a change in God.[87]

When it comes to contingent mysteries, the mysteries of God's self-communication, an understanding of fittingness is the proper goal for systematic theology. Such an understanding is subalternate to the mysteries. It is in progress. Its achievement is hypothetical, analogical, and obscure, but nevertheless highly fruitful. It is not a grasp of necessity and impossibility but of a possibility wisely conceived and lovingly chosen by God apart from any obligation. It is an understanding that proceeds by analogy with what is naturally known and by the interconnections the mysteries have among themselves and with our last end.[88]

The importance of these differentiations in theological method comes to light over against the relative compactness of Rahner's axiom. Rahner's critique of the hypothesis of intelligible emanations leaves the

Question of the Purpose of the Incarnation," in *Early Latin Theology*, CWL 19, 482–533, here 482 (my translation).

85. Lonergan, "De Ratione Convenientiae," 484–89.

86. Ibid., 490–95.

87. *Constitution of Christ*, 80–99.

88. *Triune God: Systematics*, 10–19. Lonergan expounds his position as an implementation of Vatican I's teaching on theological understanding: see Vatican Council I, *Dei Filius*, chap. 4; in Tanner et al., *Decrees of the Ecumenical Councils*, 2:808; also *Method* (1972), 336, or CWL 14, 311.

impression that an insight into fittingness is no understanding at all. First, he rejects the notion that any divine person might have become incarnate as destructive of our understanding of the mystery.

> Starting from Augustine, and as opposed to the older tradition, it has been among theologians a more or less foregone conclusion that each of the divine persons (if God freely so decided) could have become man, so that the incarnation of precisely this person can tell us nothing about the property of *this* person within the divinity.[89]

> If we admit that *every* divine person might assume a hypostatic union with a created reality, then the fact of the incarnation of the Logos "reveals" properly nothing about the Logos *himself*, that is, about his own relative property within the divinity.[90]

Elsewhere, he adds that the Son should be understood as God's *ability* to manifest himself.

> If by three persons, or, more precisely, by the formalities which form the 'person' and distinguish the 'person,' we understand three modes of subsistence in the one God, and the second of these is exactly identical with God's *ability* to express himself [*Aussagbarkeit*] in history, which ability precisely as such belongs immanently and essentially to God and is inner-Trinitarian, then we can and also have to speak of a preexistence of the subject who expresses himself in Jesus Christ.[91]

89. Rahner, "Der dreifaltige Gott," 320 (internal citation omitted; emphasis in original); *The Trinity*, 11 (translation altered). ("Es ist ja unter den Theologen seit Augustinus [gegen die ihm vorausgehende Tradition] eine mehr oder weniger ausgemachte Sache, daß jede der göttlichen Personen [wenn es von Gott nur frei gewollt werde] Mensch werden könne und somit die Menschwerdung gerade dieser bestimmten Person über die innergöttliche Eigentümlichkeit gerade *dieser* Person nichts aussage.")

90. "Der dreifaltige Gott," 332 (emphasis in original); *The Trinity*, 28 (translation altered). ("Wenn man annimmt, daß *jede* göttliche Person eine hypostatische Union mit einer geschöpflichen Wirklichkeit eingehen könnte, so 'enthüllt' die Tatsache der Incarnation des Logos von ihm *selbst*, das heißt von seiner innergöttlichen eigenen relativen Eigentümlichkeit eigentlich nichts.")

91. Rahner, *Grundkurs des Glaubens*, 289 (emphasis in original); *Foundations of Christian Faith*, 304

It is not claimed that divine self-communication is necessary. It is claimed, however, that if there is to be a divine self-communication, it must be through the Word.[92] Negatively, this claim excludes the possibility of another divine person's becoming incarnate; positively, it means to protect the direct intelligibility of divine self-communication through the Word.

As is well known, in asserting that any divine person might have become incarnate, Augustine was refuting an older assumption that linked the revelatory office of the Word to frankly subordinationist views. Rahner has no interest in repristinating the older tradition in this regard. He conceives God as Absolute Subject subsisting in three modes (*Subsistenzweisen*).[93] One of these modes is God's *Aussagbarkeit* and so, necessarily, that is the mode in which God would communicate. We know this because the economic Trinity is the immanent Trinity. The alternative supposition would be destructive of our knowledge of the immanent Trinity and of our understanding of the economy. There is, then, a contingency to divine self-communication but not to the office of the Word.

For Aquinas, on the other hand, there are not three modes of subsistence but rather three who subsist; they are not personal modes but persons. By recovering the meaning of 'intelligible emanation' and restating the position within a much more explicit account of interiority, Lonergan makes fully explicit what in Aquinas is implicit but ineluctable: three persons means three conscious subjects; one nature means one infinite consciousness.[94]

(translation given above). ("Versteht man unter den drei Personen, d. h. genauer unter den 'Person'-bildenden und 'Person'-unterscheidenden Formalitäten drei Subsistenzweisen des einen Gottes, von denen die zweite gerade identisch ist mit der geschichtlichen Aussag*barkeit* [sic] Gottes, die gerade so, Gott immanent und wesentlich zugehörig, immanent-trinitarisch ist, dann kann und muss von einer Präexistenz des sich selbst in Jesus Christus aussagenden Subjekts gesprochen werden.") (emphasis in original). Compare "Der dreifaltige Gott," 330–32; *The Trinity*, 24–28.

92. "Der dreifaltige Gott," 333; *The Trinity*, 29. "Eine Offenbarung des Vaters ohne den Logos und seine Inkarnation dasselbe wie ein Reden ohne Wort wäre" ("A revelation of the Father without the Logos and his incarnation would be like speaking without words").

93. See Rahner, *Grundkurs des Glaubens*, 122, 132–34, 202, 207, 289; *Foundations of Christian Faith*, 122, 133–35, 209, 215, 304; "Der dreifaltige Gott," 364–66, 385–93; *The Trinity*, 75–76, 103–15.

94. Bernard J. F. Lonergan, "Consciousness and the Trinity," in *Philosophical and Theological Papers 1958–1964*, CWL 6, 122–41.

It is abstractly possible that any of these subjects, or all three at once, might be incarnate.[95] The peremptory reason is that each is God, God is infinite, and the infinite is not subject to any conditions whatsoever. The possibility of divine revelation in history has its sole sufficient condition in the infinite wisdom, goodness, and power of God. It has its consequent term in history. That is, God revealing or not revealing involves a difference not in God but in history.

Concretely, on the other hand, the actual economy features the incarnation of the Word, the gift of the Spirit, the promise of the Father. None is necessary; all are fitting. We are presented, so to speak, with not one but two contingencies: the fact and the manner of divine self-communication. Concretely, of course, they are one, but they may be sufficiently distinguished to ask why it was fitting that God be incarnate, and again why it was fitting that the Word be incarnate (to say nothing of the further questions one might ask about the gift of the Spirit, and so forth).[96]

Apropos the incarnation, then, the question for theological understanding is not why it had to be the Word. The question is why it fittingly was the Word. The multiplicity of this fittingness and the complexity of its involvement with the surd of sin make it impossible for us to reduce the fittingness of the incarnation to a single synthetic perspective.[97] That perspective is divine wisdom, which, in this life, we do not have. Yet even in divine wisdom, sin does not reduce to a synthesis, because it is absurd; sin is known and judged by God, but it is not explained by God.

Other questions arise. One wonders if it is sufficient to conceive the divine persons as modes of subsistence, or to assign 'expressibility' (*Aussagbarkeit*) as the property of a divine person, or if a mode of subsistence can possibly be the center of identity in Christ if God is Absolute Subject. This is not the place to pursue them, however, because our purpose is not directly an understanding or critique of Rahner but an

---

95. *STh* 3 q. 3 aa. 1–6.

96. *STh* 3 q. 1 and q. 3 a. 8. On the fittingness of the gift of the Spirit, Aquinas is more diffuse: see Jeremy D. Wilkins, "Trinitarian Missions and the Order of Grace According to Thomas Aquinas," in *Philosophy and Theology in the Long Middle Ages: A Tribute to Stephen F. Brown*, ed. Kent Emery et al., Studien und Texte zur Geistesgeschichte des Mittelalters, Bd. 105 (Boston: Brill, 2011), 689–708.

97. Bernard J. F. Lonergan, "The Redemption," in *Philosophical and Theological Papers 1958–1964*, CWL 6, 6–28.

understanding of the role of fittingness in systematic theology. It is, in a sense, not untrue to say that the immanent Trinity is the economic Trinity. It is somewhat more difficult and more important to ask how the contingent, immanent intelligibility of the economy is related to the immanent intelligibility of the divine persons, which, in this life, we conceive only by distant analogy. The whole gratuity, the wild prodigality of divine self-communication to us resides in its contingency.

Conclusion

Fundamentally different conceptions of the goal of theological understanding result in corresponding differences in the conception of how the goal should be achieved and how it should be presented. Systematic theology is not the whole of theology, and the differences of method are not all within systematic theology. They extend to how clearly the different tasks of theology are distinguished and related and how the systematic task of theology is understood to be related to other tasks. Without an adequately differentiated method, problems of quite different kinds tend to merge and lend each other confusion.

In a functionally differentiated theology the distinction between two inverse orders, analysis and synthesis or discovery and explanation, recurs variously in different functions. The analysis/synthesis distinction is therefore not the complete solution to the methodological problems facing systematic theology, but it plays an important role within the systematic function. Because systematics is subalternate to doctrines, it takes the articles of faith as its proximate norm and as determining its basic problems for understanding. Nevertheless, it has its own analytic procedures to determine appropriate synthetic principles for the development of its analogical concepts. Analysis of the fundamental Trinitarian problem demonstrates an exigence for a wholly spiritual analogy. The hypothesis of intelligible emanations thus provides the analogical principle for conceiving the divine persons.

The use of hypothetical, analogical, and fitting intelligibilities in systematic theology raises special problems of verification. The mysteries of faith, as articulated in doctrines, are truths antecedent to systematic theology. But theological hypotheses are verified indirectly by their explanatory power and the exclusion of alternatives. Such hypotheses regard not necessity and impossibility but rather concretely verified possibilities. This hypothetical character does not preclude the possibility of cumulative and progressive results, as we see in the successive transpositions from Augustine to Aquinas to Lonergan.[98] Just as the development of Trinitarian dogma was not merely linear or accretive, neither is progress in systematic understanding. At each stage a developing tradition is received and transformed to form a dynamic, open, and expansive *theologia perennis* of the mystery of the Trinity.

Analogy and fittingness are the modes of understanding attainable by us in this life. Yet even were we beholders contemplating the eternal splendor of divine wisdom, we should grasp in the economy not a necessity but a realized possibility, a contingently chosen value brought about in the sovereign freedom of divine love. Karl Rahner remarks that Aquinas's Trinity "seems to have been communicated for its own sake." Quite so. May "our love . . . pass over into him, that as God willed all things to be for his own sake, so too we may wish neither ourselves nor anything else to have been or to be, except equally for his sake, on account of his will alone and not our pleasure."[99]

---

98. On Aquinas's differentiation of Augustine's theology of grace and freedom, see Lonergan, *Grace and Freedom*, 14–20, 181–91.

99. St. Bernard of Clairvaux, *De diligendo Deo*, X, 28; P.L. 182, 990D–991A ("Oportet proinde in eumdem nos affectum quandocunque transire: ut quomodo Deus omnia esse voluit propter semetipsum, sic nos quoque nec nosipsos, nec aliud aliquid fuisse, vel esse velimus, nisi aeque propter ipsum, ob solam videlicet ipsius voluntatem, non nostram voluptatem"). The translation is my own. The passage is quoted and discussed in Étienne Gilson, *The Mystical Theology of Saint Bernard*, trans. A. H. C. Downes (New York: Sheed & Ward, 1940), 131.

CHAPTER NINE

Wisdom Incarnate

*[Christ's] is the love of a man with an incomprehensible, an
incommunicable secret. How can a man announce that he is God?*[1]

BERNARD LONERGAN

INCARNATE MEANING IS "the meaning of a [person's] life, or the
meaning of a decisive gesture in a person's life. The meaning resides
in the person, in everything he has done leading up to this moment."[2]
Personal identity, in the narrative sense, is constituted by meaning: who
I am is determined by the meanings I live for, the meaning of my story.
What I love and live for is not separate from whom I love and live for,
whom I would wish to be like. It is also unfinished and ambiguous and
sometimes tragic business. To be a Christian is to live for Christ and to
live into him. To be Christ was to live for us and to live into the history
of human meanings. Christ is the meaning of God, incarnate. He is the
entry of divine self-meaning into the history of human self-meaning. He
is the wisdom and power of God expressed in the fragility of a human
frame, conditioned by a time and a place in human history, confronting
the malice of the human heart and the suffering it entrains. He lived for
us, each and all, and he meant it.

I do not mean only that God meant in Christ to reconcile the world
to himself. I mean that the human being Christ Jesus, a Jew of ancient
Galilee, knew and loved me, even as his enemy dead in sin, and gave

1. Bernard J. F. Lonergan, "The Mystical Body of Christ," in *Shorter Papers*, CWL 20, 106–11,
here 108.
2. Lonergan, "Time and Meaning," 101 (emphasis in original).

himself up for me. I mean that with his human heart he loved and with his human mind he knew God's love, God's judgment on sin, God's compassion for sinners, and purposefully meant to make these known. He knew not only that God meant to love us into loving God, but also that his human life would be sign and instrument of this divine loving. A Jew of Galilee, living a human and historical life on the basis of his human mind and heart, still Christ was more than a prophet, more than a messenger to whom the word comes, more than a bearer of the word; he was the Word, in the beginning with God, in space and time with us. Naturally one asks how that is even possible in the intended sense, or if one does not, one has not yet grasped the intended sense. The question is how he could know—not as God but as a human being, a Jew of Galilee—what he was doing.

There are several excellent reasons to take Lonergan's answer to this question as our final illustration of his theology. In the first place, the problem itself illustrates the ongoing interdependence of doctrinal and systematic contexts, inasmuch as advances in doctrinal clarity evoked progress in systematic theology and, conversely, the advances in systematic theology contributed to the progressive clarification of the doctrinal issues. Furthermore, Lonergan's own contributions to the problem for theological understanding—the systematic problem—illustrated the kind of cumulative and progressive results he expected a methodical theology to yield. Third, of its nature, the problem of Christ's human consciousness and knowledge occasions a salutary reprise of some fundamental elements in Lonergan's philosophy. Fourth, as my remarks above suggest, the proximate issue may be doctrinal and systematic, but behind it lies a question about one's foundational stance as a Christian believer. Lonergan's doctrinal conviction and systematic hypothesis about the wisdom of Christ was also an expression of his personal faith and discipleship. In this connection, finally, it seems fitting to conclude a book on Lonergan's quest for a wisdom for today by returning to the theme of the wisdom from above. That wisdom is not only an inner gift; it is also a divine message and the personal entrance of the eternal Word into the history of human meaning: Christ's human and historical life.

The chapter unfolds in seven steps. A first clarifies the question. Next, I very briefly situate the testimony of the tradition within the context of the development of theological understanding. Third, I review how historical criticism and existentialist concerns have made the older consensus problematic and led to the formulation of alternative accounts. In the fourth step, there is urged a qualified reaffirmation of the traditional view: both immediate knowledge of God and knowledge acquired through experience were essential to Christ's work as revealer. In the subsequent three sections I unfold Lonergan's hypothesis regarding the nature of immediate knowledge of God, its similarities and dissimilarities to other natural and supernatural realities, and its role in Christ's human development.

The Question

Ever since the question came into focus in the ninth century, a virtually unanimous consensus affirmed that the basis of Christ's human living was an immediate knowledge of God. That is, he knew God in this life even as the glorified angels and saints behold God face-to-face in that Jerusalem where there is need of neither lamp nor sun nor looking glass. That consensus lasted nearly up to the present day. Now, however, by all appearances, another has taken its place. It considers the old consensus implausible, mythological, and even—so incompatible do the exalted claims of tradition seem with the true humanity of one like us in all things—implicitly erroneous. To affirm such knowledge in Christ is to remove him from history, to make him an abstraction.

Lonergan, however, preferred rather to solve the objections than to jettison the old consensus. It was for him, in the first instance, a matter of personal faith. Christ incarnated the highest wisdom not only because he was a divine person but also because, in his humanity, he knew God face-to-face. This was the foundation of Christ's revelatory work and the reasonable basis for our assent to him in faith. Lonergan was well aware, nevertheless, of the difficulties we have believing what seems utterly implausible. He thus sought theological hypothesis that could bring traditional concerns about Christ's competence as revealer together with recent concerns about his genuine human historicity and development.

He asserted, indeed, that both immediate knowledge of God and genuine human and historical development were necessary conditions of

Christ's work. Far from excluding or preventing his human development, Christ's immediate knowledge of God both required and enabled him to make of his human life the definitive word, in history, of divine wisdom and love in the face of sin. Lonergan made a remarkable contribution to this question when, in the third (1964) edition of his textbook *De Verbo Incarnato*, he pointed out that immediate knowledge of God would be strictly incommunicable, whereas the vocation of Christ was to make it communicable.[3]

Let me forestall misapprehension by adding two brief words about my purpose. First, the present issues lie within the doctrinal and the systematic functions of theology. There is a traditional doctrine; it is not defined, but for many centuries it enjoyed, for good reason, moral unanimity. But it also is not without reason that the doctrine has become unintelligible and, therefore, appears incredible. Lonergan's originality on this question lies largely within the systematic function of theology; it is his analogical hypothesis regarding the compatibility of Christ's immediate knowledge of God and his authentic human and historical path of development. That hypothesis is not in itself a hypothesis about the meaning of Matthew or Mark, Paul or John; it is not a historical reconstruction of the 'psychology' of Jesus; it is not an interpretation of ecclesiastical doctrine. It may be relevant to all of these as a hypothesis about 'how it might have been,' but that relevance remains to be determined. If in expounding it I regularly employ the indicative mood to describe the experience of Christ, it is for the sake of straightforward exposition and not because I have ESP.

Second, the topic is not Christ insofar as he is God but Christ insofar as he is a human being. Unless this is clearly grasped, the entire point of the chapter will be missed. About Christ's knowledge as God, I have

---

3. Others have expounded or sought to develop this suggestion in various ways, notably: Frederick E. Crowe, "Eschaton and Worldly Mission in the Mind and Heart of Christ," in *Appropriating the Lonergan Idea*, ed. Michael Vertin (Washington, D.C.: The Catholic University of America Press, 1989), 193–234; Charles C. Hefling Jr., "Another Perhaps Permanently Valid Achievement: Lonergan on Christ's (Self-) Knowledge," *Lonergan Workshop* 20 (2008): 127–64; Hefling Jr., "Revelation and/as Insight," in *The Importance of Insight: Essays in Honour of Michael Vertin*, ed. David S. Liptay and John J. Liptay (Toronto: University of Toronto Press, 2007), 97–115; Guy Mansini, "Understanding St. Thomas on Christ's Immediate Knowledge of God," *The Thomist* 59, no. 1 (1995): 91–124; Gilles Mongeau, "The Human and Divine Knowing of the Incarnate Word," *Josephinum Journal of Theology* 12, no. 1 (2005): 30–42.

nothing whatever to add to what others have amply explained,[4] except
to point out the obvious. Divine understanding is simple, eternal, unrestricted, and the cause of the whole order of contingent realities. Quite
obviously, therefore, on the basis of his divine act of understanding, the
Word is the transcendent Creator of his own human and historical life.
But insofar as he assumes a created, human nature, he is also the subject
of created acts of understanding and all the other contingent acts that
constitute his human and historical life.[5] It is to those created acts and
their created principles that all our present interest is directed. Now, this
may seem to divide Christ in two, but in fact it is the revealed mystery
proposed by the church: "one and the same Son, our Lord Jesus Christ
. . . consubstantial with the Father in his divinity, the same consubstantial
with us in his humanity . . . acknowledged in two natures, without
confusion or change, without division or separation,"[6] having "two
natural volitions or wills and two natural principles of action, without
division, without change, without separation, without confusion."[7] If the
natures are distinct, unconfused, and unchanged by the union, then the
operative principles and acts of each can be considered in their integrity,
without, of course, forgetting that one and the same Word is the subject
of both. The Word as God is unchanged by the incarnation—that is the
church's confession and not merely an opinion of the scholastics—so
what may be said about his divinity belongs in a treatise on God. But

---

4. *Insight*, 667–74; Bernard J. F. Lonergan, "De Scientia Atque Voluntate Dei/God's Knowledge
and Will," in *Early Latin Theology*, CWL 19, 262–411. Much needless confusion is introduced into
the present problem by failure to seriously come to grips with the eternity of divine knowledge and
will and of the difference between temporal and eternal subjectivity. Divine knowledge creates and
contains all times, including the totality of Christ's temporal subjectivity. See *Triune God: Systematics*,
398–413; *Incarnate Word*, 726–61.

5. What it might mean for one and the same person to be the psychological subject of both an
eternal, divine subjectivity and a temporal, human subjectivity is an obvious further question, but
for the moment it is sufficient to acknowledge the revealed mystery. Lonergan argued that one
person in two natures with two natural operations transposes into a single subject of an eternal and
a temporal subjectivity (*Constitution of Christ*, 190–285; *Incarnate Word*, 464–539; "Christ as Subject"). Lonergan's hypothesis about the psychological constitution of Christ is an important presupposition for his hypothesis about Christ's human knowledge, but we cannot go through it here.

6. Council of Chalcedon, *Definitio fidei* (AD 451) (translation altered), in Tanner et al., *Decrees of
the Ecumenical Councils*, 1:86.

7. Council of Constantinople III, *Exposition of Faith* (September 16, 681), in Tanner et al., *Decrees of
the Ecumenical Councils*, 1:128 (translation altered). Nature is *principium quo* of operation; see *STh*
3 q. 19 a. 1 ad 4; *Incarnate Word*, 358–61.

the Word became a Jew of Galilee; he "worked with human hands; he thought with a human mind. He acted with a human will, and with a human heart he loved."[8] In short, as he lives his divine life on the basis of a divine principle of operation, so Christ lives his human and historical life by the light and love accorded him in his human nature and by grace. To respect the distinction of natures, it became customary in theology to speak of *Christus ut Deus, Christus ut homo*. The concern of these pages is with the created principles of Christ's human living. Here, therefore, "Christ" always means *Christus ut homo*, Christ in his human and historical life, unless otherwise indicated.

Doctrine and Theory: Interdependent Contexts

It seems that no one before the ninth century explicitly affirmed that Christ enjoyed immediate vision of God in his earthly life. However, only with some consideration of the nature and development of theological understanding can we understand why this doctrine is not an abstruse scholastic novelty, nor simply a deduction, but a "fuller understanding of divinely revealed truths."[9] The question presupposes the clarification of prior questions regarding (1) the ontological constitution of Christ, (2) the relationship between nature and grace, and (3) the analogical conception of divine, beatific, angelic, and human knowing. The patristic writers neither expressly affirmed nor expressly denied what they had not yet clearly conceived. There prevailed a global and largely undifferentiated sensibility that Christ surely knew God because he was God.

Prior to the fourth century, when a satisfactory statement of the mysteries of the Trinity and the Incarnation was still forthcoming, it is not hard to find orthodox authors prepared to attribute some ignorance to Christ. St. Irenaeus, for example, appealed to Christ's ignorance of the eschaton in order to refute Gnostic pretensions to divine knowledge.[10]

---

8. Vatican Council II, Pastoral Constitution *Gaudium et Spes*, no. 22 (December 7, 1965), in Tanner et al., *Decrees of the Ecumenical Councils*, 2:1082 (translation altered).

9. *Incarnate Word*, 602–661, especially 602–13; quoting from 679. Raymond Moloney, *The Knowledge of Christ*, Problems in Theology (New York: Continuum, 1999), is heavily influenced by Lonergan. For a contrary reading of the tradition, see Jean Galot, "Le Christ terrestre et la vision," *Gregorianum* 67, no. 3 (1986): 429–50, here 429n3.

10. Irenaeus, *Adversus Haereses*, II, 28, 6, quoted in *Incarnate Word*, 612–13.

Origen, on the other hand, denied that Christ ever asked questions out of ignorance.[11] From the fourth century onward, it became standard to dismiss Christ's apparent ignorance, either by attributing it to his pedagogy (e.g., St. Cyril of Alexandria) or by resorting to exegetical devices (e.g., Ss. Basil, Gregory of Nazianzus, Augustine).[12] By the sixth century (at the latest), attributing ignorance to Christ, even in his humanity, came to be regarded as Nestorian.[13]

This consensus could not, of course, be formulated in terms of immediate knowledge until many exact distinctions were carefully drawn, some by the Fathers but others only by the scholastics. First, what is meant is immediate knowledge of God in a created intellect.[14] Such knowledge could not be affirmed in Christ until the powers of his human soul were clearly and precisely conceived. Second, such knowledge is strictly supernatural. Until the scholastics attained, in the twelfth century, an explanatory differentiation of the orders of natural and supernatural being, they could not exactly investigate the supernatural principles of Christ's created knowledge of God. Finally, such knowledge is conceived by us only by analogy, and until the scholastics had analyzed the nature of knowing sufficiently to distinguish and relate different kinds of knowing, they could not precisely explore whether Christ, in his earthly life, had immediate knowledge of God. These achievements did not spring forth full-grown one day like Athena from the brow of Zeus, but gradually the scholastics assembled the instruments to undertake a vastly more differentiated investigation of Christ's human knowledge, thereby receiving and enriching the ancient Catholic consensus.[15]

It became standard among the scholastics to distinguish four kinds of knowing: divine, beatific (immediate), angelic (infused), and acquired.[16] According to Aquinas, Christ as man knew God immediately by beatific vision; through this same vision he knew all other things in a mediated

11. Origen, *In Matthaeum commentarii*, 10, 14, quoted in *Incarnate Word*, 614–15.

12. See *Incarnate Word*, 606–7.

13. *Incarnate Word*, 597–99. See too Alois Grillmeier, *Christ in Christian Tradition*, vol. 2–2, *From the Council of Chalcedon (451) to Gregory the Great (590–604)*, trans. John Cawte and Pauline Allen, 3 vols. (Louisville, Ky: Westminster John Knox Press, 1995), 362–82.

14. See Lonergan's explanation of terms, *Incarnate Word*, 574–85.

15. *Incarnate Word*, 602–5. See too Moloney, *Knowledge of Christ*, 53–68.

16. *Incarnate Word*, 608–11.

way; and through infused species, he also had an immediate knowledge of all things.[17] Initially, Aquinas denied that Christ learned anything through experience, but he later expressly repudiated this position, becoming, it seems, the first scholastic theologian to posit acquired (in addition to beatific and infused) knowledge in the human soul of Christ.[18] This would eventually become the scholastic consensus, though expounded in different ways by different theologians.

The doctrine that Christ enjoyed immediate knowledge of God was never itself formally defined but exercised a strong influence on the formulations of the ecclesiastical magisterium in the modern period.[19] Vatican II spoke from a settled Catholic sensibility when it asserted that Christ, the mediator and the fullness of revelation (§2), explains the inmost things of God (*intima Dei enarraret*) (§3). The Council did not say how Christ came to know the inmost things of God, but this last text cites John 1:1–18. It is difficult not to see in the conciliar *intima Dei enarraret* an echo of John 1:18 in the Vulgate: *Deum nemo vidit umquam unigenitus Filius, qui est in sinu Patris, ipse enarravit.* J. A. Riestra has shown that virtually all of the bishops who spoke on the matter during the Council took the traditional doctrine for granted as a matter of faith or at least theologically certain.[20] The *Catechism of the Catholic Church* attributes to Christ both an immediate knowledge of God and an acquired knowledge.[21] On the other hand, the International Theological Commission, eschewing "philosophical terminology," is content

17. See *STh* 3, qq. 9–11.

18. *Incarnate Word*, 710–11. See too Jean-Pierre Torrell, "Le savoir acquis du Christ selon les théologiens médiévaux: Thomas d'Aquin et ses prédécesseurs," *Revue Thomiste* 101, no. 3 (2001): 355–408; Augustin Sépinski, *La psychologie du Christ chez saint Bonaventure* (Paris: Librairie philosophique J. Vrin, 1948), esp. 98. In the Parisian *Scriptum* Aquinas denied acquired knowledge in Christ (*In III Sent.*, d. 14, a. 3, sol. 5 ad 3m; d. 18, a. 3 ad 5m). Later he affirmed that Christ had acquired knowledge, expressly repudiating his earlier position (*STh* 3 q. 9 a. 4; q. 12 a. 2). Since then theologians have commonly taught Aquinas's later doctrine, understood in various ways.

19. Lonergan, *Incarnate Word*, 598–99; see too Moloney, *Knowledge of Christ*, 118–25. See, e.g., Holy Office Decree *De scientia animae Christi* (1918), DS § 3645–47; Pius XII, *Mystici Corporis*, Encyclical Letter (1943), DS § 3812; John Paul II, Address (May 4, 1980), in *Insegnamenti*, III–1 (1980), 1128.

20. J. A. Riestra, "La scienza di Cristo nel Concilio Vaticano II: Ebrei 4, 15 nella costituzione *Dei Verbum*," *Annales theologici* 2, no. 1 (1988): 99–119.

21. *Catechism of the Catholic Church*, 2nd ed. (Washington, D.C.: United States Catholic Conference, 2000), nos. 472–474.

to affirm only that Christ was "conscious" of his divine filiation, knew his mission, intended to found the Church, and, in some way, personally loved those for whom he laid down his life.[22] (In the absence of philosophical elaboration, of course, 'conscious' says about as little or as much as one wishes.)

Lonergan, for his part, was quite struck by the historical emergence of this "concrete judgment delivered by the Catholic sense," because in its own way it seemed contrary to a testimony of the word.

> When we speak of a solidly grounded consensus, therefore, we are not speaking of a question exactly conceived, we are not speaking of scriptural texts effectively brought to bear, and we are not saying that extraneous or erroneous influences were always ruled out. We are, however, speaking of a Catholic sense which read in scripture that the Son knew not, and yet believed not, marveled, doubted, explained, and taught the contrary. But we are also acknowledging, further, the first cause of this Catholic sense: the very special divine providence which, in this matter as in others, directed God's church to the place where God foresaw and willed that it would arrive.[23]

The church found it could not accept without qualification the imputation of ignorance to Christ. So we arrive at a consensus that, in one sense, was contrary to scripture and, at the same time, "also determined by the scriptures," which declare Christ in his human life to be the revelation of God and attribute to him "the wisdom, the knowledge, and the fullness of truth which were required for the proper carrying out of his work."[24]

Winds of Change

"For many, however, it now seems that what once was received and handed on without difficulty is swarming with very obscure or even

---

22. "The Consciousness of Christ Concerning Himself and His Mission (1985)," in *International Theological Commission: Texts and Documents*, ed. Michael Sharkey (San Francisco: Ignatius Press, 1989), 305–16, here 307.

23. *Incarnate Word*, 680 (translation altered).

24. *Incarnate Word*, 681–83.

insoluble problems."[25] From the beginning of the nineteenth century, old objections got a new lease on life.[26] Beatific knowledge seemed to exclude what Scripture plainly attests: that Christ was ignorant and grew in wisdom, that he was free, subject to temptation, and his obedience was meritorious.[27] A far more fundamental challenge was posed by the application of historical-critical methods to the New Testament, which ushered in a paradigm shift for the theological use of Scripture. The new methods raised new questions about the composition of the Gospels, the development of their theology, and the historical figure standing "behind" their testimony. The problems put forth by the exegetes were compounded by the marginalization of scholastic philosophy and the ascendancy of existentialism, phenomenology, and personalism. Theologians lost interest in the habits, acts, and objects of Christ's human intellect; they became interested in the historical subject, his authenticity and *praxis*, his projects and self-understanding, his psychological unity. An earlier age, it is felt, could treat Jesus as a timeless abstraction, but theologians today must apprehend the first-century Jew.[28]

These winds have been blowing for over two hundred years. The neo-scholastics, for the most part, strove to batten down the hatches, but "the gale was upon the increase, if anything, blowing indeed a complete hurricane."[29] Amidst the wreckage, the received tradition seems to many like a fairy tale. Karl Rahner voiced a widespread sentiment when he implied that the traditional assertions about the scope of Jesus' human

---

25. *Incarnate Word*, 605.

26. See *Incarnate Word*, 610–11.

27. *Incarnate Word*, 610–11. See Mk 13:32 (the Son knows not the day); Mk 12:36 (attributes Ps. 110 to David); Lk 2:40 (grows in wisdom); Heb 5:7–10 (learned obedience through suffering); Heb 4:15, Mk 1:13 and par. (was tempted); Jn 10:18 (freely lays down his life); Phil 2:8–9 (merits the name above all names). No doubt these objections factored into the reticence of Vatican II: see Riestra, "La scienza di Cristo nel Concilio Vaticano II." The objections are traditional: see *STh* 3 q. 10 a. 2 esp. ad 1; q. 18 a. 4; q. 19 a. 3, esp. ad 1; q. 20 a. 1; q. 46 a. 8.

28. Lonergan, "Theology as Christian Phenomenon," 271; *Incarnate Word*, 610–11. Here are two brief indices of the problematic: Raymond E. Brown, "'And the Lord Said?' Biblical Reflections on Scripture as the Word of God," *Theological Studies* 42, no. 1 (1981): 3–19; John P. Meier, "The Present State of the 'Third Quest' for the Historical Jesus: Loss and Gain," *Biblica* 80, no. 4 (1999): 459–487. For an attempt to meet it from a Thomist perspective, see Gaine, *Did the Saviour See the Father?*

29. Edgar Allan Poe, "Narrative of Arthur Gordon Pym of Nantucket," in *Complete Works of Edgar Allan Poe*, vol. 3, 3 vols. (New York: G. B. Putnam's Sons, 1902), here 3:26.

knowledge betray a cryptic docetism: they "sound almost mythological today . . . they seem to be contrary to the real humanity and historical nature of our Lord."[30] Others, too, judge the traditional view a casualty of the storm but assign different (and, it would seem, mutually exclusive) causes of death: Jean Galot and John Meier suspect a tendency to mono-physitism,[31] while Thomas Weinandy catches a whiff of Nestorianism.[32] The coroner's report is pending, but the old consensus has passed away.

The new consensus, such as it is, is unified mainly in its explicit break from the old. I would say the break is open-eyed, but that might imply the merits of the old doctrine, and the ramifications of laying it aside, had been weighed on the scales and found wanting. I am not sure that was ever widely true, but I am fairly confident that today very few understand what was and is at stake in this question. The present variety of opinions include some kind of unobjectified 'filial consciousness' (K. Rahner,[33] Kereszty,[34] Weinandy,[35] and perhaps the International Theological Commission[36]), a 'missional consciousness' (von Balthasar[37]), infused enlightenment together

30. Karl Rahner, "Dogmatic Reflections on the Knowledge and Self-Consciousness of Christ," in *Theological Investigations*, vol. 5, trans. Karl-H. Kruger (Baltimore: Helicon, 1966), 193–215, here 194–95.

31. Galot, "Le Christ terrestre et la vision," 432; Meier, "The Present State of the 'Third Quest,'" 487.

32. Thomas G. Weinandy, "Jesus' Filial Vision of the Father," *Pro Ecclesia* 13, no. 2 (2004): 189–201.

33. Rahner, "Dogmatic Reflections on the Knowledge and Self-Consciousness of Christ," 206, 208. For Rahner, the "ontological self-communication of God is . . . a factor in the self-consciousness of the human subjectivity of Christ" and "the really existing direct vision of God is nothing other than the original unobjectified consciousness of divine sonship, which is present by the mere fact that there is a Hypostatic Union." See Raymond Moloney, "The Mind of Christ in Transcendental Theology: Rahner, Lonergan and Crowe," *Heythrop Journal* 25, no. 3 (1984): 288–300.

34. Roch Kereszty, *Jesus Christ: Fundamentals of Christology*, 2nd ed. (Staten Island, N.Y.: Alba House, 2002), 390–93.

35. Weinandy, "Jesus' Filial Vision of the Father"; see Thomas G. Weinandy, *Jesus the Christ* (Huntington, Ind.: Our Sunday Visitor, 2003), 94.

36. International Theological Commission, "The Consciousness of Christ Concerning Himself and His Mission (1985)."

37. Hans Urs von Balthasar, *Theo-Drama: Theological Dramatic Theory*, vol. 3, *The Dramatis Personae: The Person in Christ*, trans. Graham Harrison, 5 vols. (San Francisco: Ignatius Press, 1993), 191–202. See the recent attempt by Robert Doran to bring von Balthasar's position into conversation with Lonergan's: Robert Doran, "Are There Two Consciousnesses in Christ? Transposing the Secondary Act of Existence," *Irish Theological Quarterly* 82, no. 2 (2017): 148–68. Doran's article would have been altogether more satisfactory had it included a dialectical reorientation of von Balthasar on consciousness, rather than tacit acceptance of consciousness as a kind of self-perception.

with "an authentic human discovery of the Father" (Galot[38]), an 'abba experience' (Schillebeeckx[39]). Even the Thomist luminary, Jean-Pierre Torrell, has his reservations about the *lumen gloriae*, proposing instead a *lumen christicum* analogous to the *lumen propheticum*, only higher.[40] If the bishops at Vatican II took the traditional doctrine quite for granted, theologians today are not apt to give it much credence, and the question, once central to Christology, seems to have dropped off many a radar screen. It is not hard to find Christology textbooks that do not even broach the question. A recent undergraduate text explains that Jesus learned about God from his parents and the village elders.[41] Most radical of all, perhaps, is the approach of a Roger Haight: the important thing is not what Jesus himself understood or intended but what he symbolizes for us—it is what we see in Jesus, not what he saw in God, that counts.[42]

Here and there, briefs are entered on behalf of the older tradition, particularly from Thomists.[43] Simon Gaine, attempting to face the historical and theoretical problems squarely, bids us grasp the fundamental issue: Christ's competence to lead us to the vision.[44] Thomas Joseph White holds that only the beatific vision ensures the personal continuity of Christ's human activity with his identity as the Word.[45] As we shall

---

38. Jean Galot, *Who Is Christ? A Theology of the Incarnation* (Rome: Gregorian University Press, 1980), 358–59; see 353–59 and the discussion of Christ's consciousness, 319–43.

39. Edward Schillebeeckx, *Jesus: An Experiment in Christology*, trans. Hubert Hoskins (New York: Seabury Press, 1979), 256–67.

40. Jean-Pierre Torrell, "Saint Thomas d'Aquin et la science du Christ: une relecture des Questions 9–12 de la *Tertia Pars* de la Somme de théologie," in *Recherches thomasiennes: Études revues et augmentées* (Paris: Librairie philosophique J. Vrin, 2000), 198–213.

41. Thomas P. Rausch, *I Believe in God: A Reflection on the Apostles' Creed* (Collegeville, Minn.: Liturgical Press, 2008), 45, 53.

42. Roger Haight, *Jesus, Symbol of God* (Maryknoll, N.Y.: Orbis Books, 1999), 38–39, 288–97, 357–61. The Catholic Press Association's 'Book of the Year' in 2000, it was censured by the Congregation for the Doctrine of the Faith in 2004: from any standpoint a rather sad commentary on the state of affairs in the erstwhile *regina scientiarum*.

43. See, e.g., Mansini, "Understanding St. Thomas on Christ's Immediate Knowledge of God" (heavily influenced by Lonergan); Romanus Cessario, "Incarnate Wisdom and the Immediacy of Christ's Salvific Knowledge," in *Problema theologici alla luce dell'Aquinate*, vol. 44:5, Studi Tomistici (Vatican City: Libreria editrice Vaticana, 1991), 334–40.

44. Gaine, *Did the Saviour See the Father?*

45. White, *The Incarnate Lord*, 236–74. For Lonergan, the issue is rather that without the beatific vision, Christ would be a believer not essentially outside the class of prophets, which runs contrary to the mystery declared in the New Testament.

see, what Lonergan has to offer that is most distinctive is an explanatory hypothesis about the relationship of Christ's acquired knowledge and his immediate knowledge of God.

This is not the place to explore or appraise these various projects. I invoke them to illustrate the somewhat fragmented, somewhat forgetful state of current opinion. That so many can have forgotten the question or not grasp its significance only goes to show how implausible the former consensus now seems. Immediate knowledge of God, it is widely felt, makes Christ an ahistorical abstraction. It seems to preclude the limitations, the personal growth, the historical and cultural conditioning, the social interdependency involved in the making of a human and historical life and thus implicitly denies that Christ was 'like us in all things but sin.'

Presently we shall turn to Lonergan's proposal. Let us pause, however, to register a curious fact. The prevailing sentiment is that the traditional doctrine is unacceptable because it is, in one way or another, ahistorical. According to Lonergan, however, the radical problem is not historical but philosophical. It is not historical because it was not the naïveté of later believers that led them to such exalted claims for Jesus but rather their acceptance of the testimony of the first believers. For it is from the very first that Christians worshiped Jesus and announced him as the definitive revelation of God. Now, it is not as a historian but as a believer that one confesses Jesus as Lord. Still, it is as a historian that one explains, or explains away, the historical fact that the most astounding claims for Jesus are not the invention of ahistorical scholasticism but the testimony of the original believers. Naturally there arises the question of whether that attestation, as John Meier put it, "goes back to the historical Jesus and his actions or whether instead it is an example of the faith and missionary propaganda of the early church retrojected onto the historical Jesus."[46] Here, at least, is Ben Meyer's verdict:

> As a teacher, then, no less than as a proclaimer, Jesus was not a rabbi but a prophet and, like John, 'more than a prophet.' He was the unique revealer of the full final measure of God's will. Only on the hypothesis that such was the understanding and

46. Meier, "The Present State of the 'Third Quest,'" 480.

self-understanding of Jesus are the traits of his teaching fully intelligible. Among these traits we take three to be decisive: that his teaching strictly correlated with his proclamation of the reign of God; that it regularly transcended the Mosaic economy; and that its authority was personal rather than exegetical.[47]

Historical criticism is legitimately interested in the concrete and historical Jesus, not an atemporal abstraction. But the route from Jesus to the worship and testimony of the early church is also concrete and historical, and historians have to account for it.

The radical issue, then, is not the historical evidence but the plausibility structures in light of which the historian appraises it. The fact is that "the historian operates in the light of his whole personal development, and that development does not admit complete and explicit formulation and acknowledgement" in the manner of mathematical axioms.[48] Lonergan put the dialectical issue with respect to the analogous question of miracles.

> Can miracles happen? If the historian has constructed his world on the view that miracles are impossible, what is he going to do about witnesses testifying to miracles as matters of fact? Obviously, either he has to go back and reconstruct his world along new lines, or else has to find those witnesses either incompetent or dishonest or self-deceived.[49]

The disqualification even of a great cloud of witnesses is far easier than the reconstruction of one's world. Now, the wisdom claimed for Christ in the Gospels is somewhat of a miraculous wisdom, and the real question is whether an educated, historically minded, modern subject can admit it.

This is not a question to be handled in the systematic function of theology but in dialectic and foundations. Yet it explains why Lonergan opined that the radical problem today is the same as ever: the nature

---

47. Ben F. Meyer, *The Aims of Jesus*, Princeton Theological Monograph Series 48 (San Jose, Calif.: Pickwick Publications, 2002), 151.

48. *Method* (1972), 223, or CWL 14, 210.

49. *Method* (1972), 222, or CWL 14, 209. "Evidently, the scientific case against miracles has weakened" (213; 226).

of knowing. What we do not understand easily seems incredible to us. But without an understanding of our own knowing, we have no basis to clearly and distinctly conceive the doctrine of Christ's knowing. Unless the doctrine itself is clearly conceived, it cannot be analogically understood. Unless it is in some way understood, it remains in the zone of implausibility, especially when it seems to conflict with what seems most evident to us, the historicity of Christ's human life. Hence, the radical problem:

> It is from one's own experience that knowing of human knowing may be drawn. Those who do not achieve this successfully have neither the beginning nor the foundation from which they can proceed analogically to think clearly and distinctly about other kinds of knowing. Absent an analogy . . . [the distinctions needed for this problem] will merge into one big hazy fog. And from the fog a wailing is heard: "This is a hard thesis, and who can understand it?"[50]

Contemplata aliis tradere: The Vocation of Christ

"One who wishes to reveal himself by the word of his heart clothes it, as it were, in letters or voice; so too, God, wishing to make himself known to us, clothes in historical flesh his Word conceived from all eternity."[51] In describing the apostolic ideal of his Dominican order, St. Thomas Aquinas envisioned someone who hands on to others what he himself contemplates; such was the life Christ chose.[52] Lonergan was convinced, as a matter of faith seeking understanding, that Christ, throughout his

---

50. *Incarnate Word*, 605.

51. "Et sicut homo volens revelare se verbo cordis, quod profert ore, induit quodammodo ipsum verbum litteris vel voce, ita Deus, volens se manifestare hominibus, verbum suum conceptum ab aeterno, carne induit in tempore" (Thomas Aquinas, *Super Ioannem*, chap. 14, lectio 2). My translation is free rather than literal. I rendered *in tempore* as "in history" rather than "in time" to capture the sense of both time (duration) and a historical context. The best edition is *Super Evangelium S. Ioannis Lectura*, ed. Rafael Cai, 6th ed. (Turin: Marietti, 1972); see *Commentary on the Gospel of John*, trans. Fabian R. Larcher, Thomas Aquinas in Translation (Washington, D.C.: The Catholic University of America Press, 2010), no. 1847.

52. *STh* 1–2, q. 188 a. 6c.; 3 q. 40, a. 1 ad 2. See Mary Ann Fatula, "*Contemplata Aliis Tradere*: Spirituality and Thomas Aquinas, the Preacher," *Spirituality Today* 43, no. 1 (1991): 19–35.

human life, contemplated divine wisdom and love in the light of glory proper to the heavenly Jerusalem. Thus, he preferred to meet the questions of the present day without "thereby retreating from the doctrine received in the church." Meeting them would involve "that serious labor which aims at perfecting and enlarging old things with new."[53]

Lonergan's commitment to the old doctrine was not simply unthinking traditionalism or deference to authority. It was because he himself shared the 'Catholic sense.' That is, he believed that Christ's contemplation of God was the heart of his mystery. "The whole mystery of Christ . . . is nothing else than this: all Christ's sensible words and works incarnately manifest and reveal the divine mystery to us . . . not in ignorance of the divine mystery, but knowing it immediately."[54] "The mystery of Christ demands both ineffable and effable knowledge: ineffable, for Christ the man to know divine mystery; effable, for him to reveal, manifest, and communicate divine mystery in an incarnate way."[55] "For what we believe through Christ, Christ himself did not believe: he knew with ineffable knowledge what he said or did with effable knowledge."[56] What is said here is that Christ contemplated God in a manner strictly ineffable, that is, inexpressible through any sensible or imaginable image. Nevertheless, Christ's vocation was to express it, to render the ineffable effable, and for this he had to develop and discover and, in a certain sense, even learn from others.[57]

In itself, this is not a hypothesis but a doctrine, a declaration of mystery. For Lonergan, systematic theology is subaltern to doctrines, and his systematic-theological hypothesis about the relationship between Christ's contemplation and his communication presupposes this doctrine. It will be helpful to articulate the doctrine as precisely as possible:

(1) Christ enjoyed the highest kind of contemplative knowledge of God, namely, immediate knowledge of the divine essence, so that he might immediately understand the divine wisdom and love, the divine filiation, he came to mediate to others.[58]

---

53. *Incarnate Word*, 605.

54. *Incarnate Word*, 673.

55. *Incarnate Word*, 577.

56. *Incarnate Word*, 597; compare 674–75.

57. *Incarnate Word*, 590–91.

58. *Incarnate Word*, 576–79.

(2) Christ acquired effable knowledge through experience and inquiry, discovery and judgment, not merely because it was fitting for him to do so, but because doing so was as intrinsic to his work as knowledge of two languages is to the work of a translator, or the composition of poetry to the work of St. John of the Cross. As a translator must invent the English idiom for what was first known through Spanish, as St. John of the Cross had to invent the poetic expression for what was first known through mystical theology, so Christ had to discover how to live in conformity to his contemplative knowledge and how to express it to us.[59]

(3) Christ probably had infused knowledge (that is, in finite species) of certain details pertaining to his work, but Lonergan judges this less relevant to the contemporary problematic.[60]

In brief, Christ was both beholder and pilgrim. As beholder, his contemplation of God was immediate and constant. He knew divine love and wisdom in that direct and intimate way enjoyed by the saints in glory. But as a pilgrim, it was the task of his life to discern, in some sense invent, and enact what this supernal knowledge concretely required of him and how it might be communicated to others.[61] This enactment was his human and historical life. He made of himself, for us, the phantasm, the constellation of data, in which we might grasp how divine wisdom and love convert evil to good. As every preacher gives from what is above for the good of the whole,[62] so Christ, whose very life was his proclamation, lived out of an ineffable light of glory. He is the very paradigm of development 'from above' under the light of grace.

The Silence of Eternity

A first step toward systematic understanding lies in a consideration of the nature of immediate knowledge of God, and there are two main aspects for our present purpose: first, its object, which is God essentially; second, its manner, which is ineffable.

---

59. *Incarnate Word*, 586–95.

60. *Incarnate Word*, 597, 708–15.

61. For the interplay between this immediate beatific knowledge and the effable and acquired knowledge, see *Incarnate Word*, 692–95.

62. Thomas Aquinas, *De perfectione spiritualis vitae*, Opera Omnia 41, B, Leonine ed. (Rome: Ad Sanctae Sabinae, 1969), chap. 17, p. 89.

First, immediate knowledge of God is the perfection of contemplative knowledge. Although lower kinds of contemplation may have as their objects the works of God, as conducing to knowledge of God, this kind of contemplation has the divine essence itself as its object.[63] Note, therefore, that although it is the summit of contemplative knowledge, it is also radically discontinuous from all other knowledge of God. All other knowledge of God is through a finite intelligible species and is analogical: knowledge of difference as well as similarity. This knowledge is through God himself, the infinite intelligible. Once this is clear, it is also clear that had Christ known God only analogously, his revelatory work would differ from that of the prophets not in kind but only in degree. On the other hand, the contemplation of the saints in glory is different from that of Christ the man only in degree; they receive by grace what he has by right.

This immediate knowledge of God is absolutely supernatural. It is proper to no creature whatever, because it regards an infinite intelligible and no creature is actually infinite.

> Proper knowledge is an act of understanding in virtue of a form proportionate to the object; hence proper knowledge of God must be in virtue of an infinite form, in virtue of God himself; such knowledge is beyond the natural proportion of any possible finite substance and so is strictly supernatural; it is what Aquinas called 'videre Deum per essentiam' and is identical with the act commonly named the beatific vision. . . . A philosopher operating solely in the light of natural reason could not conceive that we might understand God properly; for understanding God properly is somehow being God; and somehow being God is somehow being infinite.[64]

Immediate knowledge of God, accordingly, is not comprehensive. An infinite intelligible cannot be comprehended by a finite mind, however excellent. Although Christ and the saints in glory know God essentially and not analogically, still not even Christ the man knows God

---

63. *Incarnate Word*, 578–79. *STh* 2-2 q. 180 a. 4c. and ad 3; 1, q 12, aa. 1–2.

64. Lonergan, "Natural Knowledge of God," 83.

comprehensively, although, on account of the greatness of his love, his contemplative understanding exceeds all others.[65] Just as one can grasp a principle without immediately grasping all that the principle implies, so too one can have immediate knowledge of God without comprehending everything to which divine wisdom, freedom, and power extend. Thus Aquinas says that even the angels, who gaze upon the face of God, do not comprehend divine providence; hence they do not have a clear knowledge of future contingents, though they can conjecture about them with greater clarity and distinctness than we.[66]

Immediate knowledge of God is the communication of divinity itself. God, the all-sufficient, is not conditioned in his self-donation; rather, his self-donation is creative of the appropriate conditions in those who receive it. Just as God's indwelling love creates the loveliness of the saints, so God's self-insertion into a finite mind illumines created consciousness with the light of glory.[67] Just as the supernatural loveliness of those whom God specially loves does not destroy their humanity but perfects and sublates it, so the supernatural clarity of Christ's glorified consciousness does not destroy his humanity but perfects and sublates it.

Nevertheless, the seeming antinomy between such exalted knowledge and a genuine human and historical life is overwhelming and, indeed, has quickly overwhelmed a consensus of longstanding. What caused a wholesale revision of Lonergan's treatment of this question was a realization that the antimony could be resolved by conceiving the ineffable character of immediate knowledge of God. To appreciate why, we have to understand why immediate knowledge of God is ineffable.

In this context, ineffable and effable are used not rhetorically but technically. Ineffable knowledge is strictly apart from all words, images, or sensible experience of any kind. It therefore does not depend upon sense or imagination in any way, and insofar as a person exercises only this kind of knowing, sense and imagination are neither needed nor used.

> To the extent that one exercises ineffable knowledge *and this alone*, one neither needs nor uses one's senses; without these, one

---

65. *Incarnate Word*, 686–87; *STh* 1, q. 12, aa. 7–8; 3, q. 10, a. 3; q. 10, a. 4 ad 2.

66. *STh* 1 q. 57 a. 3; cf. q. 86 a. 4; 2–2 q. 95 a. 1; *De veritate* q. 8 a. 12.

67. *Incarnate Word*, 576–77; *STh* 1, q. 12, aa. 4–5.

exercises no human action composed of body, sense, intellect, and will. . . . Thus, just as it is not in any human way that one learns ineffable knowledge, or expresses it in words, or manifests in works, so too it is not in any human way that one lives by it.[68]

This way of knowing takes one, as it were, beyond the state of this present life, and therefore normally results in the rapture of the senses.[69] This rapture is not a necessary consequence, however; precisely because ineffable knowledge is essentially apart from sense and phantasm, it does not preclude or contradict the use of the senses and can coexist with normal operations.[70]

For the same reason, ineffable knowledge cannot be expressed. There is no imaginable or sensible presentation from which it was originally derived and no presentation to which it can be made to correspond.[71] Consequently, there is no imaginable or sensible presentation to which another person could be referred in which the intelligibility might be directly grasped.[72] This has two important implications for this question. It means that Christ could not articulate this knowledge to us, because our normal human way of knowing is by insight into phantasm. But it also means he could not articulate it even to himself. There can be no proportionate articulation.

Perhaps we may call upon John of the Cross for a more concrete description of an experience similar in respect of its ineffability. He reports a kind of infused contemplation in which God conveys an ineffable knowledge beyond the senses and without even an extrinsic relation to sense or phantasm:

68. *Incarnate Word*, 575; see 574–577.

69. *Incarnate Word*, 578–79. Compare *STh* 2–2 q. 180 a. 5c.

70. *Incarnate Word*, 578–79. Aquinas denies that anyone can see God in this life but admits transitory visions to Paul and Moses as special cases (*STh* 1 q. 12, a. 11 ad 2; 2–2 q. 175 a. 3 ad 1; q. 180 a. 5c.), each time referring to Augustine, *De Gen. ad litt. 12*, who explains that alienation from the senses is a kind of departure from this present life. Christ's beatific knowledge, like Paul's, did not redound fully through his senses, but unlike Paul's, it did not withdraw him from his senses and was permanent rather than transitory (*STh* 3 q. 14 a. 1 ad 2; q. 15 a. 5 ad 3; a. 6; see 2–2 q. 175 a. 4 ad 2). This is evident in lower forms of infused contemplation, which essentially are the contemplation of intelligible truth but incidentally make use of phantasm (*STh* 2–2 q. 180 a. 5 ad 2).

71. See *Incarnate Word*, 574–77.

72. Aquinas understood Paul's rapture to be knowledge of this kind (*STh* 2–2 q. 175 a. 4).

It is called night, because contemplation is dim; and that is the
reason why it is also called mystical theology—that is, the secret
or hidden wisdom of God, where, without the sound of words,
or the intervention of any bodily or spiritual sense, as it were in
silence and in repose, in the darkness of sense and nature, God
teaches the soul—and the soul knows not how—in a most secret
and hidden way. Some spiritual writers call this "understanding
without understanding," because it does not take place in what
philosophers call the active understanding, which is conversant
with the forms, imaginations, and apprehensions of the bodily
powers, but occurs in the understanding as it is possible and
passive, which, without receiving such forms, etc., receives only
passively the substantial understanding of them, stripped of
imagery. This occurs without effort or exertion on its part.[73]

This is not an immediate knowledge of God, and John goes on to observe
that in comparison to immediate knowledge it is dark. Indeed, in the
paradoxical sense of 'darkness' that pertains to infused contemplation, we
might expect beatific knowledge to be, as it were, the darkest of all. It
is ineffable, given by grace, apart from any human effort. Because it has
no relation to sense or phantasm, it is in itself incommunicable by us.
The soul neither understands how it is so taught, nor can it adequately
express its understanding so as to teach others.[74]

Ineffable knowledge, because it is un-worded and un-imaged, also
cannot be discursive or successive. It is all at once.[75] It is not attained
by inquiry and insight into phantasm, and it is not confirmed by any
reflective review and assessment of the evidence. It is the simple grasp

---

73. John of the Cross, *Cantico Espiritual* (B), 39.12; *Obras Completas de San Juan de la Cruz*, ed.
José Vicente Rodriguez and Federico Ruiz Salvador (Madrid: Biblioteca de Autores Cristianos,
1982), 727; *Collected Works of St. John of the Cross*, trans. Kieran Kavanaugh and Otilio Rodriguez
(Garden City, N.Y.: Doubleday, 1964), 561; *A Spiritual Canticle of the Soul and the Bridegroom
Christ*, trans. David Lewis and Benedict Zimmerman (Grand Rapids, Mich.: William B. Eerdmans,
2000), 151.

74. Note that for John of the Cross, the daily bread of Christian discipleship comes through the
nakedness and austerity of faith, not extraordinary phenomena. If his remarks upon infused contemplation can help us better understand the nature of ineffable knowledge, we should not suppose
they yield a complete view of his theology. See Karol Wojtyla, *Faith According to St. John of the Cross*,
trans. Jordan Aumann (San Francisco: Ignatius Press, 1981).

75. *STh* 1 q. 12 a. 10.

of an indemonstrable first principle and, indeed, the very first of all principles. It is not reached through reasoning, but it may be the principle for subsequent processes. And, in Christ's life, it was.

We develop our understanding by raising and answering questions in the light of a capacity for wonder oriented to all of being. This same capacity for wonder heads us beyond the world of our experience to ask about God whether he is, and what. Christ's way is converse to ours. Our end is his beginning. From the immediate knowledge of God, he progressed not only to effable knowledge but to its expression for us in his human life.[76] Any teacher is moving from insight to the construction of suitable phantasms for the pupils.[77] But in other cases, the teacher first learned by insight into phantasm; the matter to be taught is not ineffable. Christ, however, "did not live in order to know: he knew in order to live and give life. Beginning from the divine Word he knew immediately, he proceeded to reveal, to manifest, to communicate the divine Word to us in his every sensible word and deed."[78] Thus he moved absolutely from the inexpressible to the expressible, a progression which Charles Hefling has aptly called 'converse insight.'[79] What he knew ineffably in the Word, he had to come to know discursively in words.[80]

Perhaps we are now in a position to clear away a few misunderstandings. Ineffable knowledge is not like looking at a picture or a map. If one supposes that understanding is just like looking, or forgets that ineffable knowledge does not require the faculties of sense or imagination, then one will be hard-pressed to grasp how Christ could unceasingly contemplate divine wisdom and love, yet avoid the fate of Thales who, gazing at the stars, fell into a well.

Ineffable knowledge does not resemble a computer database, an instruction book, or a series of If-Then-Else commands. It is not like a storehouse of data that one summons forth as needed. Data are

---

76. *Incarnate Word*, 578–81.

77. Here I am using 'phantasm' in an extended sense; precisely, the phantasm is the problem as imaginatively represented. I will trust the intelligence of the reader to take my meaning.

78. *Incarnate Word*, 700 (translation on 701, altered).

79. Hefling Jr., "Revelation and/as Insight."

80. I am grateful to Gordon Rixon for suggesting this apposition in his paper, "Understanding in the Word" (presented at the West Coast Methods Institute, Loyola Marymount University, Los Angeles, Calif., April 2017).

imaginable or sensible presentations, in which understanding grasps intelligibility, but ineffable knowledge is insight apart from any imaginable or sensible presentation; there are no 'data' that could be 'retrieved.' It follows that ineffable knowledge is not like having the Bible memorized. The Bible is a text, a phantasm, a set of signs that are per se communicable. To be familiar with the text as such, one must read or hear it.

On the other hand, one who has the light of glory is an infallible judge of the divine intention,[81] so Christ was a sure judge of the things of his experience. He knew that the prophecies applied to himself and also that it was his to freely determine how they should be fulfilled.[82] Infallible judgment is not the same as comprehensive knowledge, and Christ's knowledge of the order of divine effects was not fully determinate. Future contingents, even those pertaining to himself and his work, even those foretold in Scripture, he discerned only obliquely, globally, and by conjecture, unless in a particular case some specific revelation was given to him.[83] What was yet to be, he had to discern and freely bring about under the light of glory, "all his human abilities and powers straining, as if to fill a void, effably to render that which was possessed, ineffably, within the same consciousness."[84]

It is not that Christ knew the end but had to discover the means. In an obscure, global, and ineffable way, he grasped in divine mercy that he himself was to be the means, that divine love renders not evil for evil,

81. See *STh* 1 q. 12 a. 11 ad 3.

82. *Incarnate Word*, 750–52.

83. Lonergan suggests such episodes as the Lord's reply to his mother at Cana ("My hour has not yet come") and his declaration that he did not intend to go to the feast may be possible to understand "in terms of the transition from ineffable to effable knowledge" (*Incarnate Word*, 705; see 708–15). This may help explain the obscurity of his eschatological statements; see Ben F. Meyer, *The Aims of Jesus*, 202–9, 242–49; *Christus Faber: The Master Builder and the House of God*, Princeton Theological Monograph Series 29 (Allison Park, Penna.: Pickwick Publications, 1992), 41–58. Aquinas says that in the vision, Christ clearly grasped temporally present realities and the principles of things (*STh* 1 q. 56 a. 3 ad 1) but also that he knew future contingents only conjecturally (*STh* 1 q. 57 a. 3). But I am a little unsure how to take Aquinas's affirmation that as beatific knowledge confers on its possessor an understanding of all things pertaining to himself, Christ the judge of all knew in the Word all actual deeds, words, and thoughts pertaining to whatever time, past, present, and future, in addition to knowing all that lies within human power (*STh* 3 q. 10 a. 2; see 3 q. 46 a. 6 ad 4). Aquinas also says even the angels know the contingent future only conjecturally through the beatific vision; no created intellect can know the future in itself (1 q. 57 a. 3), and he is prepared to grant other ways the full effects of the vision were withheld from Christ (see *STh* 3 q. 14 a. 1 ad 2; q. 15 a. 5 ad 3; a. 6c.; q. 46 a. 6c.).

84. *Incarnate Word*, 701 (translation altered).

that divine wisdom orders all things sweetly to bring good even from the consequences of sin. But how, concretely, this would unfold he had to discover and choose, in such a way as to knowingly, freely, and deliberately compose his life. Again, it is not that Christ knew God in act but that he knew things in God only habitually. His ineffable contemplation was always in act, both with respect to its primary object, God, and its secondary objects, things in God.[85] But as Christ's immediate knowledge was not comprehensive and, moreover, was ineffable, it did not preclude or replace acquired knowledge of creatures.

Finally, because this kind of contemplation is unrelated, even extrinsically, to sense or phantasm, it also is not conditioned by space or time. It does not in any way depend, therefore, upon the freshness of the psyche. In Christ, ineffable contemplation was permanent, not in the manner of a habit, but in the manner of continuous operation. Hence Aquinas says that Christ enjoyed beatific knowledge from the first moment of his conception.[86] If today this seems the most incredible assertion of all, it only serves to highlight how inclined we are to misconstrue the nature of this knowledge and give free rein to the spontaneous trespass of imagination upon intelligence. Ineffable insight is not achieved through the process of question and answer. It presupposes no material organ. It is an operation of the mind that does not make use of the brain, even extrinsically.[87] Where the organs of the body are in no way involved, there is no question of weariness. It is precisely this disengagement of the lower faculties that gives this kind of contemplation its oft-remarked character of 'unknowing.'

Development from Above

To say that Christ's human life is the definitive word of divine love, justice, and wisdom is to say something about the meaning of his life. But it is not always easy to say what someone's life means. For human beings live

---

85. *Incarnate Word*, 686–87. See *STh* 3 q. 11 a. 5 ad 1.

86. *STh* 3 q. 34 a. 4. See *Incarnate Word*, 672–73.

87. Here the basic issue is the per se immateriality of intellectual knowing, which requires an organ per accidens insofar as it takes the form of insight into phantasm. The beatific vision is not insight into phantasm but pure understanding and, therefore, *ex hypothesi*, presupposes no material organ.

spontaneously long before—if ever—they deliberately begin to order their lives toward some definite purpose or goal. And even when they do, that ordering is never fully efficacious. It is invariably disfigured by sin.[88] At best, one turns from sin and yields to a love and a mystery that takes one quite beyond one's own powers,

> *. . . something given*
> *And taken, in a lifetime's death in love,*
> *Ardour and selflessness and self-surrender.*[89]

Giving, taking, and self-surrender are all the more efficacious the better they are known, the more freely they are embraced, the more deliberately they are carried out. And not only more efficacious; they are also more fully human. For it is proper to human beings to govern themselves, to order their own lives, to make of themselves incarnate meaning.

Yet where other human lives are imperfectly deliberate and ambiguous words, the human life of the Word of God is unambiguously a word of divine love for sinners, divine judgment on sin, divine wisdom converting evil to good.[90] Though there was spontaneous development in him, still, from the beginning of his human life he knowingly, freely, deliberately ordered his words and deeds to manifest his intended meaning. And in that knowing, free, deliberate unfolding of his life, Christ was most fully human, not only in nature but also in deed.[91] In this way the life of Christ expressed the eternal Image of God in human terms and displayed the perfection of the created image. This meaning, part of the divine plan and intention from all eternity, was deliberately brought about by Christ, so that what God meant with his

---

88. Invariably, that is, except in the case of our Lady.

89. T. S. Eliot, "The Dry Salvages," V, 203–205, in *Four Quartets* (New York: Harcourt Brace Jovanovich, 1971), 44.

90. See *ScG* bk. 4, chap. 54. This is a major theme in the last three theses of Bernard J. F. Lonergan, *De Verbo incarnato* (Rome: Gregorian University Press, 1964), as well as a set of unpublished Latin notes on the redemption. These materials are now presented, with interleaf translation, in Bernard J. F. Lonergan, *The Redemption*, ed. Robert M. Doran, H. Daniel Monsour, and Jeremy D. Wilkins, trans. Michael G. Shields, CWL 9 (2018). For discussion, see Charles C. Hefling Jr., "A Perhaps Permanently Valid Achievement: Lonergan on Christ's Satisfaction," *Method: Journal of Lonergan Studies* 10, no. 1 (1992): 51–76; Loewe, *Lex Crucis*, 283–368.

91. *Incarnate Word*, 702–3.

life, Christ too not only intended but also properly understood, though without fully comprehending it.[92]

Fundamentally, this is a thesis about grace, about divine love at work in Christ and, through him, vouchsafed to us. Divine love and the wisdom entrusted to that love were the first principles in the development of his conscious life; he developed 'from above.' Though Christ is not a pure case of development from above, as if there were in him no development 'from below,' still he is the paradigm of all such development. Like us in all things but sin, he is also the cause of our being made like him in grace.

Although there are gifts of grace that take us beyond history, still the gift of divine love is not, in principle, opposed to the integrity of human and historical living, whether in us or in Christ. Grace does not destroy nature; on the contrary, it heals human nature and confers on us a share in a higher order of being. Divine grace at work in the life of Christ no more vitiates his authentic humanity than it does ours. Rather, in him no less than in us, its effect was to create new exigencies, confer new capacities, and bring about his development as an authentic human being. Thus, the development of Christ the pilgrim, moved by an unutterable love, walking by an ineffable light of glory, is a singular instance of the general development of human beings under the influence of grace. As grace in us in no way prevents but rather invites, enables, and obliges our development, so divine grace working in him invited, enabled, and obliged the development of Christ the pilgrim.[93] As our lives concretely develop within the compound dialectic of sin and nature and grace, so Christ developed his human life in fulfillment of the exigencies of human nature, elevated by grace, in response to sin (not his own, but the sin of others).[94] By grace our minds are governed by the higher light of faith by which we behold the human life of Christ as a mirror of divine glory. By grace Christ's human mind was governed by the light of glory by which he knew God face-to-face so that he might express the mystery in his life for us. By grace our hearts are enlarged with the inexpressible

---

92. Thomas Joseph White argues that only if Christ as human knew and intended all that Christ as God knew and intended for his life can we say that his human words and deeds were the personal acts of the divine Word (*The Incarnate Lord*, 236–74).

93. *Incarnate Word*, 694–705.

94. *Incarnate Word*, 688–91.

sweetness of divine love, and by grace he loved even his enemies, dead in sin, and laid down his life for them.

Each of us—Christ, too—lives out of ineffable mystery. A husband's love for his wife, a father's love for his children: these are ineffable. Such love might shape a life, but there is no sensible or imaginable phantasm in which it might be directly understood in itself. Not understanding the love that moves them, even the most conscientious and deliberate husbands or fathers, wives or mothers frequently fail to grasp its requirements. Again, the wonder of the scientist, of the philosopher, of the poet, of plain common sense: this, too, is ineffable, a created participation of uncreated light.[95]

Wonder is radically open-ended. There are many determinate questions, but the font of them all, wonder itself, cannot be nailed down. Out of these ineffable mysteries of light and love, we all move toward personal discovery and toward the one and only composition of our lives. What is true on the level of nature is certainly no less true when supernal light suffuses our minds and divine love floods our hearts.

These ineffable forces shape our conscious living in a way that not only is fully compatible with our human development but in fact enables, obliges, and directs it. Nor would it be otherwise if they were better known to us, as sometimes happens in cases of rare spiritual insight. Beatrice evoked such insight in Dante. She was for him an epiphany of divine love, summoning forth

> . . . the sigh that issues from my heart
> a new intelligence, which Love,
> weeping, places in him, draws him ever upward.[96]

To express the meaning of this love, he directed all the power of his extraordinary imagination under the government of the 'new intelligence' it brought forth in him. Yet he did not comprehend and could not adequately express the reality of this ineffable love: "But my wings had

---

95. *Incarnate Word*, 578–81, 698–701.

96. Dante Alighieri, *Vita Nuova*, trans. Dino S. Cervigni and Edward Vasta (Notre Dame, Ind.: University of Notre Dame Press, 1995), 143.

not sufficed for that."[97] He understood less than he felt and could say less than he understood, and such understanding as he achieved was by way of conversion to phantasm under the direction of love.[98]

In each of these cases, ineffable mystery exercises a deep and pervasive influence. It functions as an operator and integrator of development from above, flowering forth in new perceptiveness, fresh insights and judgments of value, new and lasting commitments. It can effectively dominate a life, though it be scarcely understood. In these cases, insight into this dark mystery is attained, if at all, through conversion to phantasm, inquiry into such data as there may be. To be sure, the inquiry may be prompted and sustained by a love from on high. It may proceed under the light of faith and be guided by supernatural instincts of understanding and wisdom, instincts themselves ineffable and given from above.[99] It may take as its object realities of the supernatural order. In all these respects it is knowledge from above, though it moves along the course of inquiry, discovery, and verification.

To be sure, Christ presents a major exception even in comparison to the mystics. His understanding was 'from above' in the ultimate sense. St. Teresa testifies that infused contemplation in the saints is intermittent, lest the tension and distraction become unbearable,[100] but Christ's was lifelong. Aquinas concurs that ordinarily, in this life, immediate contemplation of God excludes the normal operation of the lower faculties of the mind. The general rule is that no one can see God in this life. Aquinas admits a partial exception for St. Paul and Moses, who were withdrawn from this world in rapture and, in a sense, suspended for a time between this life and the next. But Christ's contemplation was continuous, without the suspension of his lower faculties or the exclusion of finite species. He was able to be fully present to the next life and fully present to this. While living in this life, he was already in the next.

---

97. Dante Alighieri, *Paradiso*, trans. Robert Hollander and Jean Hollander, First Anchor Books ed. (New York: Anchor Books, 2008), 916/917 (canto 33, line 139).

98. Cf. *STh* 2–2 q. 180 a. 5 ad 2.

99. Cf. *STh* 2–2 q. 8; q. 45.

100. Teresa of Avila, *Interior Castle*, vol. 7, in *Obras Completas*, ed. Efrén De la Madre de Dios and Otger Steggink, 8th manual ed. (Madrid: Biblioteca de Autores Cristianos, 1986), 569; Teresa of Avila, *Collected Works of Teresa of Avila*, trans. Otilio Rodriguez and Kieran Kavanaugh, 3 vols. (Washington, D.C.: Institute for Carmelite Studies, 1980), 2:431.

Christ, then, lived his human life out of a supernal love matched by a transcendent vision. There is a sense in which it did place him above history, though without removing him from the flux of his time.

> He knows nothing of the rules and limitations of contemporary vision; he is not dependent on the manner of seeing current in his century; he is dependent on nothing but the object of his contemplation. It is an eminently mystical attitude: penetrated by it, flooded with it, submerged in it . . . [he] submits himself to it . . .[101]

These lines were penned about a little sketch of the Crucified by St. John of the Cross. Should it be very remarkable that they might be said of the Crucified himself?

On the other hand, though we affirm in Christ an exceptional contemplation of God, still we should emphasize the sense in which Christ was not exceptional. Ineffable grace is a factor in the concrete unfolding of each of our lives. Living out his life under the direction and influence of divine grace did not make Christ fundamentally dissimilar to us. Those who belong to Christ are, like him, borne along by an ineffable love. This love is a principle of development, in Christ no less than in us. What distinguishes Christ from his members is that we live toward the end, while he lived out of the end. We live out of a mystery that grasps us; he lived out of a mystery that he grasped. We walk by the faint light of faith; he walked by the resplendent light of glory, tasting the hidden manna and making it his daily bread. He was given to understand divine wisdom, love, filiation, that he might interpret them for us.[102]

---

101. R. Huyghe, quoted in the introduction to John of the Cross, *Collected Works of St. John of the Cross*, 40.

102. See *Incarnate Word*, 580–81, 696–703. How love and light were ordered in Christ, and whether that order differs from other cases of infused contemplation in this life, is too vast a question to be properly considered here. Some considerations are suggested by Crowe, "Eschaton and Worldly Mission," 223. The light of glory is bright in proportion as charity is great (*STh* 1 q. 12 a. 6; see 2–2 q. 45; 1–2 q. 28 a. 2).

Interpreted by Love

Christ did not have to discover God, from his parents, the rabbis or the village elders, from Moses or Isaiah or anyone else.[103] On the contrary: it is in him that we discover God. He made himself, his very life, the presentation, the phantasm, the constellation of data, in which we are invited to learn how divine wisdom and love respond to the malice of sin. This he did freely and deliberately, subordinating the whole power of his passions, his sense, and his imagination to the love of God poured into his heart through the Holy Spirit and directing them by the light of glory by which he grasped the very nature of that love. The insight that governed his life was not insight *into* phantasm, but insight utterly apart from phantasm and directing the composition of phantasm: his life, the phantasm of divine love.

With St. Luke we acknowledge that Christ grew in wisdom, age, and grace. In wisdom, for what God taught him by way of secret, wordless contemplation, he had to bring about in his human life, and so share with others, by way of discovery, reflection, and deliberate decision. In grace—the effect of divine love in us—because the schemes of recurrence by which divine love effectively dominates the life of a child become vastly more complex in the life of an adult. In age, not merely in terms of his physical stature, but above all in that maturation of psychic, affective, and imaginative life and its harmonious coordination with intellectual, moral, and religious development, which is presupposed as the matter of his growth in wisdom and grace.[104]

His contemplation did not suspend the operation of his senses or confer on him an invulnerable psyche. If anything, all the normal problems of somatic, psychic, intellectual, and religious integration were compounded for him, both because the purity of his heart and vision complicated his relations with others and because ineffable knowledge poses special challenges for the integration of the sensitive psyche with

---

103. See *Incarnate Word*, 702–7.

104. See *Incarnate Word*, 591–94, 694–97. Compare *STh* 1–2 q. 113 a. 2c.; 2–2 q. 24 a. 4 ad 3. Aquinas tends to think in terms of the completed habit, so that the disjunction between sin and grace is in the foreground, and the prospect of development in grace, for which he does not really have an adequate heuristic structure, remains in the background. See also C. Journet, cited in Jacques Maritain, *On the Grace and Humanity of Jesus*, trans. J. Evans (New York: Herder and Herder, 1969), 78n24.

the higher part of the mind.[105] The laws of psychic development, though uncomplicated by the entailments of original and actual sin, though directed by a higher light, still applied. The problem of internal communication between the sensory and imaginal world of the psyche and the intelligible world of the mind was not eliminated but in some ways magnified by the intensity of his contemplation.

Then, too, contemplation of this kind creates its own dynamic of psychological frustration. Operations of the psyche and the lower faculties that normally accompany the process of knowing in this life are excluded from this 'unknowing' and its consolations. At the same time, contemplation introduces a peace, joy, and fulfillment the present life cannot begin to contain. The tension this produces can be, according to the mystics, nearly unendurable. For Christ, his natural powers uncompromised by the Fall, his contemplation more intense and more prolonged than theirs, it was heightened to the uttermost. "Who could suffer this for a lifetime if even the greatest mystics feel like they will die after even a few minutes of contemplation?"[106]

> Be shellèd, eyes, with double dark
> And find the uncreated light:
> This ruck and reel which you remark
> Coils, keeps, and teases simple sight.[107]

It was not in solitary contemplation, however, but through his experience of the world and his interaction with others, that his imagination was shaped, his human subjectivity refined, his capacity for expression cultivated and enlarged. Christ, like others, followed a way of development in wisdom, age, and grace. His vocation was to make God known, to discover and freely bring about its concrete realization, to lovingly

105. *Incarnate Word*, 700–701. Lonergan says that Christ was straining to render effable what he possessed ineffably in the same human consciousness.

106. Anthony Lilles, personal correspondence, June 21, 2009 (punctuation altered). Intense in the extreme, still this suffering could not be mistaken for the suffering of the lost or the damned, because the suffering of the damned is from the inability to love, whose offspring are fear, resentment, and mistrust of the outstretched hand of Christ. His suffering, on the other hand, was from the very breadth and depth of his love.

107. Gerard Manley Hopkins, "The Habit of Perfection," in *Poems and Prose*, ed. W. H. Gardner (New York: Penguin, 1985), 6.

express the silence of eternity in the medium of his own life. This required of him an enormous development—"to hammer and to hearken day and night"[108]—in his capacities for relating to and communicating with other human beings. Christ's deliberate entry into the human world of meaning was also the process by which he made himself. He unfolded his life in conversation with others, and there is a sense in which he received from them.[109]

Christ was not exempted from the general law that roots human communication in the body. Like others, he entered into the long and complex process of living into the community of interests and concerns that constituted the Jewish world of his time and place, learning to communicate and adapting himself to a way of life. Herbert McCabe puts it helpfully:

> In order to learn the language of a wholly strange people it is necessary to live with them, to share their efforts and disappointments and pleasures, their daily way of life. Then by imitation we come to use their language appropriately, we discover the use of their various sounds. We learn by our mistakes, recognizing a mistake by the fact that it makes a barrier between ourselves and the community, impeding our conformity to their way of life. . . . Insofar as a people differed from us in, for example, the things that gave them pleasure or saddened them, still more if they differed altogether in the bodily expression of such emotions, we should find it hard to live into their community.[110]

Christ traveled the road of mutual assimilation and adjustment to others, of mirroring (in some measure) in childhood their responses, experiencing, we might surmise, bafflement and sadness where sin and resentment and mimetic concupiscence distorted the affects of those around him. He experienced more keenly than others how sin divides us from one another and distorts the spontaneity of body language and intersubjectivity. He

---

108. Rainer Maria Rilke, *Letters to a Young Poet*, trans. Stephen Mitchell (New York: Vintage, 1986), 70 (letter 7, May 14, 1904).

109. *Incarnate Word*, 591–94.

110. Herbert McCabe, *Law, Love and Language* (New York: Sheed & Ward, 1968), 80–81.

had to learn to read humor, irony, and sarcasm, though he recoiled from the cruelty that so often inflects them. Undoubtedly Christ found this a lonely road, but by its very nature it could not have been a solitary one. Not for nothing did divine providence make Mary his first teacher of human feeling and his first model of human maturity, and Joseph his first model of manhood.

His exceptional love and contemplation united him to others and divided him from them.[111] Suffused by a great love, he had a human sympathy deep beyond measure. He was intimately bound to others, sharing their joys and hopes, grief and anxieties. Yet the very magnitude of his love, and the bright clarity with which he understood its demands, also separated him from those around him, from the common pleasures and aims of this world. To have his purity of heart and clarity of vision would be to find the whole world of human smallness, brokenness, and malice sad, pitiful, and ugly. "[I]f you saw people's sins as I do, you would marvel much more at my patience, and sorrow much more at people's sin, than you do."[112] He was strange to this world, and it was strange to him. "It is indeed hard upon a man to find himself a lost stranger, helpless, incomprehensible, and of a mysterious origin, in some obscure corner of the earth." So writes Joseph Conrad of his shipwrecked migrant Yanko, washed up on the alien shore of Kent, "innocent of heart, and full of goodwill, which nobody wanted," ignorant of the language and mores, roundly feared and reviled on account of his strangeness.[113] So we might imagine Christ, at home in the language but never quite in the culture, deeply misunderstood and so mistrusted, an unsettling and, to many, a reproachful figure, and the object of enormous resentment. He was, in this too, truly the Man of Sorrows: *Vigilavi et factus sum sicut passer solitarius in tecto.*[114]

One who does not comprehend the total order of divine providence in this world is far from being able to judge its goodness by comparison

---

111. This is beautifully evoked by Georges Bernanos, *The Diary of a Country Priest*, trans. Pamela Morris (New York: Carroll & Graf Publishers, 2002), esp. 211–16, 295.

112. Words attributed to Jesus in Margery Kempe, *The Book of Margery Kempe*, trans. Barry Windeatt, 1st ed. (New York: Penguin Classics, 2000), 83.

113. Joseph Conrad, "Amy Foster," in *"Typhoon" and Other Tales*, ed. Cedric Watts, rev. ed. (New York: Oxford University Press, 2009), 201–40, here 211, 230.

114. Ps 101:8 (Vulgate); see Teresa of Avila, *Life*, 20.10 (*Obras Completas*, 111; *Collected Works of Teresa of Avila*, 1:132).

to other possible orders. Christ did not know why God had preferred to bring about this order, in which the power of darkness was to have its hour and he was to take the part of the Suffering Servant.[115] Even though he grasped that his clean oblation was to be the supreme instrument of divine mercy, the height and depth of divine wisdom remained in some sense inscrutable to him. He had, then, a kind of trust in God. His trust was not blind, for he knew that God was trustworthy. Still, in the supreme moment of his self-donation, he entrusted himself to the mercy of God, in (as von Balthasar puts it) a "fundamental, genuinely human act of trusting self-abandonment to a future that is not at one's own disposal."[116]

He would go apart to a quiet place, not merely to set an example for his disciples, but also to refresh the rhythms of his psyche, frayed by the constant pressure of crowds and critics. He would review the images and experiences of the day and judge them in light of his ineffable contemplation. He would plan his future course, imagine and conceive, judge and elect the next steps. All of this was necessarily discursive; it required the acquisition of effable knowledge, and so it was dependent upon the psyche. Though he never ceased to contemplate God, Christ knelt in prayer for many of the same reasons we do: to recollect his faculties, to remember and reflect upon the events of the day, to discern and plan, and perhaps above all to find a moment's respite from the conflicts, the relentless misunderstanding, the painful rejection of divine love.

> *O Sabbath rest by Galilee,*
> *O calm of hills above,*
> *where Jesus knelt to share with thee,*
> *the silence of eternity, interpreted by love.*[117]

---

115. *Incarnate Word*, 686–91.

116. Hans urs von Balthasar, *The Glory of the Lord: A Theological Aesthetics*, vol. 7, *Theology: The New Covenant*, trans. Brian McNeil (San Francisco: Ignatius Press, 1989), 144. Aquinas grants that Christ had a kind of hope (*STh* 3 q. 7 a. 4), and Maritain suggests an analogical sense in which faith might be attributed to him: *On the Grace and Humanity of Jesus*, 85n26.

117. John Greenleaf Whittier, "Dear Lord and Father of Mankind," in *The Hymnal 1940* (New York: Church Publishing, 1940), no. 435.

Conclusion

"Where did this man get these things?" (Mk 6:2; Mt 13:56); "No one knows the Father but the Son" (Mt 11:27; Lk 10:22). I do not wish to prove a thesis by citing a few lines from Scripture, but let me suggest a line of thought by recalling the testimony of the evangelists: Christ is no blind guide but one who sees, no prophet but himself the Word, the one who has gone into heaven and testifies to what he alone knows, who saw the glory revealed to Isaiah in his vision, who indeed was that glory dwelling in human form, who declares himself the way and says to everyone, without exception, 'Come, follow me.' Now, I grant that this testimony might be taken in many ways. But I would point out that the overwhelming tendency of the church was to take it one way: Christ knew the Father immediately. This tendency was not unaware of considerations to the contrary—that Jesus grew in wisdom, that he knew neither day nor hour—yet preserved its conviction. When the question was ripe, the necessary and sufficient conditions of this knowledge were worked out and affirmed. It was not divine knowledge, for divine knowledge is God. It was human knowledge. But it was not a knowledge he discovered or learned. It was not a knowledge by some analogy, some finite species. It was a knowledge immediate and proper.

Yet a contemporary sensibility rightly demands justice to the historicity of this man Jesus. It finds its apprehension of the traditional claims difficult to square with its suppositions about the entailments of historicity. The apparent conflict has been too easily resolved. Christ, too, is proclaimed a believer. He is called the definitive revelation but, implicitly, there is acknowledged some higher, finite analogue by which he himself understands. No one seems to be asking what that analogue could be.

Lonergan's reply is twofold. First, the mystery itself does not oblige us to choose. Indeed, the mystery does not permit us to choose. For the mystery of the Word made flesh involves not only the divine creativity of the Word as God but also the human creativity of the Word in his humanity. For us, to be is to become. For Christ, in his humanity, it was the becoming of the Word, not imperfectly but perfectly, not for himself but for others. Second, because this is a mystery held in trust, we are neither to expect perfect understanding nor to make the limits of our understanding the measure of our assent. Nevertheless, there is a basis for imperfect understanding. It lies in the analogical conception of ineffable and effable knowledge. Such a conception preserves the historicity of the Lord without negating his transcendence of history. He is the realized eschaton.

Scholastic distinctions between divine, beatific, infused, and acquired knowledge, between infinite and finite species, natural and supernatural knowledge, effable and ineffable knowledge, easily seem abstruse. But the issue here is not merely Christ's competence to be the definitive revelation of divine love. To detest sins perfectly, would he not have to take their full measure? To love me, to grieve for *my* sins, to give himself up for me, would he not have to know them? "They are," he says, "blind guides." "Follow me," he says, "take up your cross, every one of you." If we are each to risk all in this least trivial pursuit, may we not ask, does he know where he is going?

Conclusion and Epilogue

If you want to teach others how to live,

you must first take yourself in hand.[1]

ETTY HILLESUM

T HE GOTHIC CATHEDRAL MAY have been the perfect realization
in art of scholastic theology.[2] So sweeping a claim is not the object of
proof, of course. Still, the coincidence in a single civilization of two such
monuments of the spirit says much that is praiseworthy for its priorities,
values, and preoccupations. Our own civilization exhibits nothing like
this coherence, and one wonders if anything like it will ever be possible
again. If theology is not to abet cultural decomposition but promote
genuine healing and creating, it must find a new basis for coherence.

That basis, if it is to be permanent, will reside not in the structure
of a work but in the structure of the working. The great *summae* of the
thirteenth century are cathedrals of thought: transcendent in vision,
comprehensive in scope, permanent in intention, magnificent in their
structural articulation. Their achievement is prominent among the
reasons we are wont to think of the products before the practices of
scholasticism. The *lectio* and *quaestio* were communal practices before
they were literary forms. As literature, they are, as it were, byproducts
of common life in the medieval university. The same cannot be said of

1. Etty Hillesum, *Etty Hillesum: Essential Writings*, Modern Spiritual Masters (Maryknoll, N.Y.:
Orbis Books, 2009), 32.

2. Erwin Panofsky, *Gothic Architecture and Scholasticism: An Inquiry into Analogy, Arts, Philosophy and
Religion in the Middle Ages* (New York: Plume / Penguin, 1974).

the *summa* or the manual, however much they express a tradition and enact, in some way, a pedagogy.[3] Their pedagogical order is a function not of the order that produced a *summa* but of the order a *summa* aims to produce. As a product intended for study, rather than a byproduct of study, a *summa* may tend of its nature to supersede the public convivium of *lectio* and *disputatio*. Perhaps the pinnacles of scholastic achievement unwittingly encouraged the dissolution of scholastic practice. In a sense, what Lonergan is after is a rejuvenation of theological practice by attention to its personal and communal structure.

What is certain is that the scholastic dream of lasting entente between faith and reason slipped away. Scholastic thought went to seed in a riot of arcana, or stiffened into school traditions, or flew apart into the various philosophies of modernity, united in nothing so much as a deliberate turn from the Christian past. Its builders, ever less in touch with the mental habits of the age, played a shrinking role in an expanding world. As Christendom spoiled, theologians turned inward to reassure one another of their certitudes. Their cathedrals of thought became fortified keeps. The main forces of modern intellectual culture, and perhaps a good deal of religious culture, went right around them. Bailiffs occupied the chairs where architects once sat. Pressing questions were kept out and adventuresome thinkers kept back.

Lonergan was reared and educated and asked to teach in the "wooden old world"[4] of ahistorical orthodoxy. He felt its lack of probity keenly. Heidegger called it 'The System' and mistook it for Catholicism. Lonergan, who recognized the glory in the ruins, quietly soldiered on— not to save the keep but for love of the cathedral.[5] That there could be no simple reconstruction was plain to him from the outset. What could be instead, however, came to him only gradually.

Lonergan's brief was never with scholasticism but with its shabby shell. He was critical of a conversation that had gotten 'stuck' in certain ways and was investing tremendous energy in controlling the kinds of questions that would be allowed to come up and be permitted a serious

---

3. See Mongeau, *Embracing Wisdom*, esp. 91–117.

4. Santer, review of *The Way to Nicea*, 226.

5. On Heidegger's critique of 'the System' and Lonergan's efforts, see Lawrence, "Lonergan's Search for a Hermeneutics of Authenticity."

hearing. It is an attitude of alienated or perhaps disingenuous obscurantism that calls to mind Dostoyevsky's Grand Inquisitor. Hannah Arendt writes of the political significance of Socratic thinking in a way that seems relevant both to the present crisis and to Lonergan's contested place in it.

> Non-thinking, which seems so recommendable a state for political and moral affairs, has its perils. By shielding people from the dangers of self-examination, it teaches them to hold fast to whatever the prescribed rules of conduct may be at a given time in a given society. What people then get used to is less the content of the rules, a close examination of which would always lead them into perplexity, than the possession of rules under which to subsume particulars.[6]

It does not seem far-fetched to think that the anxiety crisis that gripped so many in the Catholic world before and after Vatican II was precipitated by the disarticulation of the prevailing rules that became inevitable with the demise of classicism.

Lonergan was not interested in political revolution but honesty in the face of historical questions. His form of Socratic thinking is not involved in the denial of dogma but strictly renounces a dogmatic reassertion of the old rules. It demands a penetration to their deeper roots. Lonergan's program is a wisdom of the concrete, a wisdom of self-attention and self-discovery, a wisdom of attention to data and openness to questions, and a wisdom of self-surrender in love. It means back to the questions and back to the questioners; it is a hard therapy, bound to be unsettling, but a way forward.

'Forward' has too often been the slogan for deracination, but deracination is just what progress cannot mean. Contemporary theology, like our culture itself, is a zone of profuse creativity. But that zone is too easily just a jumble of ideas without clear criteria for sifting them. Like most of the humanities today, theology's present tendency is centrifugal. This reflects the unresolved issue of postmodern hermeneutics: the relationship between the truth of existence to truth in the ordinary sense, the

---

6. Arendt, *Thinking*, 177; see 166–79.

truth of predication. The priority of the former may be so exaggerated as to renounce, in the name of perspective, the very possibility of predicative truth. In fairness the truth of existence is a perennial problem, and so is perspective. Still, understanding may be incorrect. It may be more or less correct. There may be no permanent solution to the problem of existential truth, but it hardly follows that no true judgments—qualified, perspectival, but true as far as they go—are possible. Indeed, familiarity in oneself with the elements of meaning and the possibility of their being assembled in various ways yields a methodical possibility of embracing multiple perspectives in a single—if perhaps dialectical—view.

One has to grow into this possibility. Correct understanding requires development and preparation. It is not enough to recognize authenticity as the problem before truth. One has to measure up, and measuring up means growth. In theology as in life, we have to become competent, and becoming competent is not merely mastery of material but also mastery of oneself as an observer, interpreter, judge, and agent. Becoming competent, measuring up, getting ready: this is the radical form of the problem 'before truth.'

It is just here that I find Lonergan so exceptionally helpful. We are not at the level of our time simply for living in it; we have to catch up with ourselves, and the catching up is not only assimilating contents but figuring out how to handle them. "Suppose," Kierkegaard complained, that

> someone wanting to learn to dance said: 'For hundreds of years now one generation after another has been learning dance steps, it's high time I took advantage of this and began straight off with a set of quadrilles.' One would surely laugh a little at him; but in the world of spirit such an attitude is considered utterly plausible. What then is education? I had thought it was the curriculum the individual ran through in order to catch up with himself; and anyone who does not want to go through this curriculum will be little helped by being born into the most enlightened age.[7]

---

7. Søren Kierkegaard, *Fear and Trembling*, trans. Alastair Hannay, Penguin Classics (New York: Penguin, 1985), 75.

Lonergan, I feel, faced this problem squarely. The business of catching up is not merely learning what our ancestors understood; it is also fitting it together in a way that is responsible to history. It is more than that, too, if Lonergan is right. It is entry, by self-appropriation, into a new stage in the control of meaning.

The climb this involves is not supersessionary; we cannot be on the level of the twenty-first century if we have failed to reach the thirteenth or the fourth. I do not mean reaching only the contents of past achievement, although the contents are at risk because the questions are being forgotten. I mean reaching the kinds of differentiation and development those contents demand. Scholasticism and gothic are magnificent constructions. They and all their like are the products of structuring activities, and undergirding the whole are the primitive structures of the spirit. It is to these that Lonergan directs our attention, for an understanding of them provide the first principles for the interpretation of every kind of cultural formation and every domain of inquiry. A *summa* of theology has become impossible because theology will not stand still. But what may be possible is a grip on the operators of theological development. That would make possible a reading of the tradition in its past transformations. It would make possible some collective responsibility for the tradition in its future.

Better than anyone I know, Lonergan has envisaged the contemporary problem of theological readiness and presented a practical path to it, starting with an adequate hermeneutics of interiority. A scientific and normative self-knowledge can reveal the truncations that yield a possessive individualism, an ideological secularism, an alienated postmodernism, and an impulse to liquidate traditions. Relativism originates in reaction to empiricism. The facts are not all 'out there' to be seen. Being is intelligible, and the intelligible is not imaginable. The facts have to be reached through inquiry, and inquiry is difficult. If one has no adequate mediation of judgment, inquiry is not only difficult but also in principle inconclusive. If one has no way of recognizing in the polymorphism of one's own consciousness the possibilities of philosophic error and its theological consequents, one also has no adequate way of understanding the order of history, which is not only (like natural process) nonsystematic but also dialectical. One is hard-pressed to find in the history of Christian theology anything more than an expression of the diverse forms of Christian experience. But Christian experience is the experience of infidelity as well as fidelity. By itself, it provides no sure basis for differentiating the message of the Gospel from whatever cultural milieu Christians happen to find themselves in. The exegesis of Christian experience, and that alone, is no basis for prophecy but only a recipe for captivity to the present.

Theology is a wisdom, or at least love of a wisdom higher than human wisdom. Its aim is not an exegesis of religious experience or a science of religious propositions. It is to know and make known a reality. That reality is God. It is God, however, not as known in himself but as known in the greatest of all works: the orderly communication of God's friendship to his enemies by the personal entrance of God's Word into human history and God's Love into human hearts. These are mysteries we hold only in trust, and the light sufficient for judging them is not ours. Our knowledge of them is participatory, for the communication of divine friendship is historical and in it we have our very modest role to play.

I find Lonergan a remarkable guide to discerning the wholeness in our tradition and in our manifold questions. This is not because he answers them all. It is mainly because he is a midwife. He is a midwife for the discovery in oneself of the elements of meaning, of the spontaneous and self-regulating activities of questioning, of their immanent criteria and their prospects of subversion. He brings to light the ontological structure of the hermeneutical circle. These discoveries are a basis for figuring out how the different voices and stages of the tradition might fit together. Those stages are also the stages by which the Gospel has been mediated into cultures. Theology is authentically theological in the measure it serves this mediation. By measuring up to the demands of theology's successive stages, we make our small but providential contribution to the greatest of all works.

The longer I study Lonergan, the more intriguing I find him and the more I admire the scope, the depth, and the dynamism of his mind. John Capreolus, *princeps thomistarum*, the first great commentator on Thomas Aquinas, remarked that he had sought to add nothing of his own but only to report the mind of the master.[8] Let me be bolder and humbler. Bolder, because I have perilously mixed advocacy with interpretation, and who knows whether to good or ill issue. Humbler, because I cannot claim to have understood Lonergan so well as to have reported his whole mind on the matters at hand. I have sought to add clarity by making explicit what Lonergan left implicit, by reformulating what he put obscurely, by relating his thought to some questions of today. But I am sure I have also added, without knowing where or how, constraints and oversights that narrow unduly his capacious vision. The end of a project like this brings home to me the difficulty of the climb still ahead.

Today, unfortunately, Lonergan barely registers. The reasons are many. Some, like his confinement to the world of Roman seminaries, are circumstantial. Some are self-inflicted, like his penchant for popularization and an oblique and sometimes fustian style. Culpably or no, his acolytes—I do not exclude myself—have added burdens of their own, not least by making 'Lonerganism' a school. The coup de grâce, finally, is a conventional nonsense that neither understands nor cares to understand Lonergan but wishes only to pin him down. Aquinas, Lonergan remarked, might have been far more successful had not "superficial opinions backed by passion . . . promptly buried [his work] under the avalanche of the Augustinian-Aristotelian conflict."[9] Our proclivity for superficial opinion has not gone away.

Lonergan was well aware of the fate most likely in store for his work in the short term. He remarked of Aquinas that

> besides being a theologian and a philosopher St Thomas was a man of his time meeting the challenge of his time. What he was concerned to do may be considered as a theological or philosophical synthesis but, if considered more concretely, it turns out to be a mighty contribution towards the medieval cultural synthesis.[10]

8. John Capreolus, *Johannis Capreoli Defensiones Theologiae Divie Thomae Aquinatis*, ed. Celsus Paban and Thomas Pègues, vol. 1, 7 vols., repr. (Frankfurt am Main: Minerva, 1967), 1.

9. Lonergan, "Belief: Today's Issue," 85.

10. Bernard J. F. Lonergan, "The Future of Thomism," in *A Second Collection*, CWL 13, 39–47, here 40.

Undoubtedly Lonergan understood his own labors as a contribution toward the cultural synthesis that must someday arise from the embers of our late modernity.

One may wonder, however, why he thought widespread adoption of his practices could ever be more than just a dream. He was well aware that methodological (and indeed, religious) options have metaphysical entailments. The deliberate selection of a method is itself a foundational decision, and the method foresees the necessity of scrutinizing other options as well as one's own. At least part of the answer, then, is that Lonergan took his stand on the fact that a correct metaphysics is latent in the structure of rationality just as an adequate realism is latent in adherence to the word of God. What Lonergan meant by method, while not a curative for every ill, would nevertheless promote the emergence and clarification of positions surmounting antitheses the likes of historicism and anachronism, rationalism and fideism, empiricism and idealism, that have rendered religious and secular thought ineffectual. The realities of nature, grace, and even sin are fifth columns pushing for methodical effectiveness, for wonder cannot stop asking questions, otherworldly love cannot relinquish its beloved, and a suffering race and planet cannot stop pleading for comfort. Starting with Lonergan's own surrender to the practical necessities of communication, the ascesis of self-appropriation has been hidden by facile summaries. We should not continue to let ourselves off so easily. To the extent that Lonergan's proposal depends on self-appropriation, one has to earn it through painstaking practice. No more than the *Spiritual Exercises* of St. Ignatius can it be learned simply by reading a book.

Our theme has been 'before truth.' Truth means conformity to being. That conformity has its conditions—intellectual, methodological, and existential—and 'before truth' is a conceit for naming them. The truth is not 'out there' to be seen. It has to be reached. Intellectually, our duty before truth is to prepare. It is to inquire soberly, diligently, with humble devotion. It is to gradually develop understanding. It is to love getting things right and despise merely 'being right.' The alternative to fulfilling these duties is not merely to be ignorant. It is to be culpable.

Methodologically, our duty 'before truth' is to give an honest account of ourselves and our tradition. The articles of faith are not our uninquiring possession, like manna collected with the morning dew. They are known through true judgments with a contingent history. Theologians are asked to confront that history and answer for their role in it. We have offices before the truth of doctrinal predication.

Reaching the truth, finally, is not only worthy of devotion but depends on it. There is needed, then, an existential and not only an intellectual readiness. It is a readiness to let go our own sufficiency and acknowledge another, the sufficiency of evidence. It is a readiness to yield before the truth we neither make nor control. Because we are not the primary truth or the primary good, our knowing and our loving must be forms of self-surrender. We should expect, as Augustine discovered, to be changed in more than our opinions. If we would be sufficient unto ourselves, we are diminished and fall away from the truly Sufficient.[11] In God, to be and to know are one, not by conformity but by ontological identity. God, therefore, is the primary truth, the Truth beyond access to any inquiry. In the light of glory his sufficiency will be self-evident to us, but still it will be known in the measure of our surrender.[12]

We must not, therefore, be wise in our own conceits. Our highest wisdom is another kind of readiness, not to apprehend, order, or judge but to be apprehended, ordered, and judged. Before Truth All-Sufficient, our best readiness is to kneel and confess:

> *O the depth of the riches and wisdom and knowledge of God! How*
> *unsearchable are his judgments and how inscrutable his ways!*
> *"For who has known the mind of the Lord,*
> *or who has been his counselor?"*
> *"Or who has given a gift to him*
> *that he might be repaid?"*
> *For from him and through him and to him are all things. To him be*
> *glory for ever. Amen.*[13]

---

11. "Plus autem appetendo minus est, qui, dum sibi sufficere deligit, ab illo, qui ei uere sufficit, deficit." Augustine, *De civitate Dei*, 14.3, ed. B. Dombart and A. Kalb, Corpus Christianorum, Series Latina 48–49 (Turnhout: Brepols, 1955), 48: 435, lines 62–63.

12. *STh* 1 q. 12 aa. 6 and 7.

13. Rom 11:33–36, RSV.

Works Cited

(For texts and decrees from the ecumenical councils, see Tanner et al., *Decrees of the Ecumenical Councils*.)

Aeschylus. *Oresteia, Agamemnon, The Libation Bearers, and The Eumenides.* Translated by Richmond Lattimore. The Complete Greek Tragedies. Edited by Richmond Lattimore and David Grene. Chicago: University of Chicago Press, 1953.

Alighieri, Dante. *Vita Nuova.* Translated by Dino S. Cervigni and Edward Vasta. Notre Dame, Ind.: University of Notre Dame Press, 1995.

———. *Paradiso.* Translated by Robert Hollander and Jean Hollander. First Anchor Books ed. New York: Anchor Books, 2008.

Allen, Jeffrey A. "Revisiting Lonergan's View of Natural Knowledge of God." Paper presented at the Lonergan Research Institute Graduate Seminar, Toronto, Ont., 2015.

———. "Ignatius's *Exercises*, Descartes's *Meditations*, and Lonergan's *Insight*." *Philosophy and Theology* 29, no. 1 (2017): 17–28.

Anatolios, Khaled. *Retrieving Nicea: The Development and Meaning of Trinitarian Doctrine.* Grand Rapids, Mich.: Baker Academic, 2011.

Aquinas, Thomas. "In Symbolum Apostolorum, scilicet 'Credo in Deum' expositio." In *Opuscula theologica* 2, 191–217. Edited by Raymund M. Spiazzi. 2nd ed. Turin: Marietti, 1953.

———. *Liber de Veritate Catholicae Fidei contra errores Infidelium, seu Summa contra Gentiles.* Edited by Ceslas Pera, Pierre Marc, and Pietro Caramello. Leonine ed. 3 vols. Turin: Marietti, 1961.

———. *Summa theologiae.* New York: Editiones Paulinae, 1962.

———. *De perfectione spiritualis vitae.* Opera Omnia 41, B. Leonine ed. Rome: Ad Sanctae Sabinae, 1969.

———. *Sententia libri Ethicorum.* Edited by R.-A. Gauthier. Opera Omnia 47. Leonine ed. Rome: Ad Sanctae Sabinae, 1969.

———. *Quaestiones disputatae De veritate.* Opera Omnia 12. Leonine ed. Rome: Editori di San Tommaso, 1970.

———. *Super Evangelium S. Ioannis Lectura.* Edited by Rafael Cai. 6th ed. Turin: Marietti, 1972.

———. *Sentencia libri De anima.* Opera Omnia 45. Leonine ed. Paris: Librairie philosophique J. Vrin, 1984.

———. *Opuscula IV.* Edited by H.-F. Dondaine. Opera Omnia 43. Leonine ed. Rome: Editori di San Tommaso, 1992.

———. *Super Boetium de Trinitate | Expositio Libri Boetii de Ebdomadibus.* Opera Omnia 50. Leonine ed. Paris: Editions du Cerf, 1992.

———. *Quaestiones de quolibet.* Vol. 2. 2 vols. Opera Omnia 25. Leonine ed. Paris: Editions du Cerf, 1996.

———. *Commentary on the Gospel of John.* Translated by Fabian R. Larcher. Thomas Aquinas in Translation. Washington, D.C.: The Catholic University of America Press, 2010.

Arendt, Hannah. *Between Past and Future: Exercises in Political Thought.* London: Faber, 1961.

———. *Thinking.* New York: Harcourt Brace Jovanovich, 1978.

Aristotle. *Basic Works of Aristotle.* Translated by Richard McKeon. New York: Modern Library, 2001.

Augustine. *De civitate Dei.* Edited by B. Dombart and A. Kalb. Corpus Christianorum, Series Latina 48–49. Turnhout: Brepols, 1955.

———. *De Trinitate.* Edited by W. J. Mountain and F. Glorie. Corpus Christianorum, Series Latina 50–50A. Tournhout: Brepols, 1968.

———. *Augustine: Confessions.* Edited by James J. O'Donnell. Oxford: Clarendon Press, 1992.

Ayres, Lewis. "'Remember That You Are Catholic' (Serm. 52.2): Augustine on the Unity of the Triune God." *Journal of Early Christian Studies* 8, no. 1 (2000): 39–82.

———. "Athanasius' Initial Defense of the Term *Homoousios*: Rereading the *De Decretis*." *Journal of Early Christian Studies* 12, no. 3 (2004): 337–59.

———. *Nicaea and Its Legacy: An Approach to Fourth-Century Trinitarian Theology.* New York: Oxford University Press, 2004.

von Balthasar, Hans Urs. *The Glory of the Lord: A Theological Aesthetics.* Vol. 7, *Theology: The New Covenant.* Translated by Brian McNeil. San Francisco: Ignatius Press, 1989.

———. *Theo-Drama: Theological Dramatic Theory*. Vol. 3, *The Dramatis Personae: The Person in Christ*. Translated by Graham Harrison. 5 vols. San Francisco: Ignatius Press, 1993.

Bambach, Charles. *Heidegger, Dilthey, and the Crisis of Historicism*. Ithaca, N.Y.: Cornell University Press, 1995.

Barnes, Michel René. "Augustine in Contemporary Trinitarian Theology." *Theological Studies* 56, no. 2 (1995): 237–50.

———. "De Régnon Reconsidered." *Augustinian Studies* 26, no. 2 (1995): 51–79.

Barter Moulaison, Jane. "Missteps on *The Way to Nicea*: A Critical Reading of Lonergan's Theory of the Development of Nicene Doctrine." *Studies in Religion/Sciences Religieuses* 38, no. 1 (2009): 51–69.

Bauckham, Richard. *Jesus and the God of Israel: God Crucified and Other Studies on the New Testament's Christology of Divine Identity*. Grand Rapids, Mich.: William B. Eerdmans, 2008.

Beatrice, Pier Franco. "The Word 'Homoousios' from Hellenism to Christianity." *Church History* 71, no. 2 (2002): 243–72.

Behr, John. *The Way to Nicaea*. The Formation of Christian Theology 1. Crestwood, N.Y.: St. Vladimir's Seminary Press, 2001.

Bellah, Robert N., ed. *Habits of the Heart: Individualism and Commitment in American Life*. Berkeley: University of California Press, 2008.

Bernanos, Georges. *The Diary of a Country Priest*. Translated by Pamela Morris. New York: Carroll & Graf Publishers, 2002.

Biemer, Gunter. *Newman on Tradition*. Translated and edited by Kevin Smyth. New York: Herder and Herder, 1967.

Blanchette, Oliva. *Philosophy of Being: A Reconstructive Essay in Metaphysics*. Washington, D.C.: The Catholic University of America Press, 2003.

Bonaventure. *Doctoris Seraphici S. Bonaventurae Opera Omnia*. Edited by the Fathers of the College of St. Bonaventure. Vol. 1. 11 vols. Ad Claras Aquas [Quaracchi]: Ex typographia Collegii S. Bonaventurae, 1882.

Boyle, Nicholas. *Who Are We Now? Christian Humanism and the Global Market from Hegel to Heaney*. Notre Dame, Ind.: University of Notre Dame Press, 1998.

Braman, Brian J. *Meaning and Authenticity: Bernard Lonergan and Charles Taylor on the Drama of Authentic Human Existence.* Toronto: University of Toronto Press, 2008.

Brotherton, Joshua R. "The Integrity of Nature in the Grace–Freedom Dynamic: Lonergan's Critique of Bañezian Thomism." *Theological Studies* 75, no. 3 (2014): 537–563.

Brower, Jeffrey E., and Susan Brower-Toland. "Aquinas on Mental Representation: Concepts and Intentionality." *The Philosophical Review* 117, no. 2 (2008): 193–243.

Brown, Patrick. "Classicism: A Prelude." Paper presented at the West Coast Methods Institute, Loyola Marymount University, Los Angeles, Calif., April 2013.

Brown, Raymond E. "'And the Lord Said?' Biblical Reflections on Scripture as the Word of God." *Theological Studies* 42, no. 1 (1981): 3–19.

Brown, Stephen F. "The Theological Role of the Fathers in Aquinas's *Super Evangelium S. Ioannis Lectura.*" In *Reading John with St. Thomas Aquinas: Theological Exegesis and Speculative Theology*, 9–22. Edited by Michael Dauphinais and Matthew Levering. Washington, D.C.: The Catholic University of America Press, 2005.

Buckley, Michael J. *At the Origins of Modern Atheism.* New Haven: Yale University Press, 1987.

Burns, J. Patout. *The Development of Augustine's Doctrine of Operative Grace.* Paris: Études augustiniennes, 1980.

———. "From Persuasion to Predestination: Augustine on Freedom in Rational Creatures." In *In Dominico Eloquio = In Lordly Eloquence: Essays on Patristic Exegesis in Honor of Robert L. Wilken*, 294–316. Grand Rapids, Mich.: William B. Eerdmans, 2002.

Burt, Julian. "Lonergan Doctrine: Is It Orthodox?" *Homiletic and Pastoral Review*, January 1986.

Byrne, Patrick H. "God and the Statistical Universe." *Zygon* 16, no. 4 (1981): 345–63.

———. "Lonergan on the Foundations of the Theories of Relativity." In *Creativity and Method: Essays in Honor of Bernard Lonergan*, 477–94. Milwaukee, Wisc.: Marquette University Press, 1981.

———. *Analysis and Science in Aristotle.* SUNY Series in Ancient Greek Philosophy. Albany: State University of New York Press, 1997.

————. *The Ethics of Discernment: Lonergan's Foundations for Ethics.* Toronto: University of Toronto Press, 2016.

Capreolus, John. *Johannis Capreoli Defensiones Theologiae Divi Thomae Aquinatis.* Edited by Celsus Paban and Thomas Pègues. Vol. 1. 7 vols. Repr. Frankfurt am Main: Minerva, 1967.

Cessario, Romanus. "Incarnate Wisdom and the Immediacy of Christ's Salvific Knowledge." In *Problema theologici alla luce dell'Aquinate*, 334–40. Vol. 44:5. Studi Tomistici. Vatican City: Libreria editrice Vaticana, 1991.

Coakley, Sarah. "What Does Chalcedon Solve and What Does It Not? Some Reflections on the Status and Meaning of the Chalcedonian 'Definition.'" In *The Incarnation: An Interdisciplinary Symposium on the Incarnation of the Son of God*, 143–63. New York: Oxford University Press, 2002.

Cochrane, Charles Norris. *Christianity and Classical Culture: A Study of Thought and Action from Augustus to Augustine.* Revised and corrected. New York: Oxford University Press, 1944.

Coelho, Ivo. *Hermeneutics and Method: The "Universal Viewpoint" in Bernard Lonergan.* Toronto: University of Toronto Press, 2001.

Congar, Yves. *I Believe in the Holy Spirit.* Translated by David Smith. Revised ed. 3 vols. New York: Crossroad Publishing, 1983.

————. *Journal d'un Theologien, 1946–1956.* Edited by É. Fouilloux, D. Congar, A. Duval, and B. Montagnes. Paris: Editions du Cerf, 2001.

Conn, Walter. "Bernard Lonergan and Authenticity: The Search for a Valid Criterion of the Moral Life." *American Benedictine Review* 30, no. 3 (1979): 301–21.

Conrad, Joseph. "Amy Foster." In *"Typhoon" and Other Tales*, 201–40. Edited by Cedric Watts. Revised ed. New York: Oxford University Press, 2009.

Cory, Therese Scarpelli. *Aquinas on Human Self-Knowledge.* New York: Cambridge University Press, 2014.

Cronin, Brian. *Value Ethics: A Lonergan Perspective.* Guide to Philosophy 13. Nairobi: Consolata Institute of Philosophy, 2006.

Crowe, Frederick E. "Bernard Lonergan as Pastoral Theologian." In *Appropriating the Lonergan Idea*, 127–44. Edited by Michael

Vertin. Washington, D.C.: The Catholic University of America Press, 1989.

———. "Eschaton and Worldly Mission in the Mind and Heart of Christ." In *Appropriating the Lonergan Idea*, 193–234. Edited by Michael Vertin. Washington, D.C.: The Catholic University of America Press, 1989.

———. *Lonergan*. Outstanding Christian Thinkers. Collegeville, Minn.: Glazier, 1992.

———. "St Thomas and the Isomorphism of Knowing and Its Proper Object." In *Three Thomist Studies*, 207–35. Chestnut Hill, Mass.: Lonergan Institute at Boston College, 2000.

———. "Universal Norms and the Concrete *Operabile* in St Thomas." In *Three Thomist Studies*, 3–69. Chestnut Hill, Mass.: Lonergan Institute at Boston College, 2000.

———. "For Inserting a New Question (26A) in the Pars Prima." In *Developing the Lonergan Legacy: Historical, Theoretical, and Existential Themes*, 332–46. Edited by Michael Vertin. Toronto: University of Toronto Press, 2004.

———. "Lonergan's Search for Foundations: The Early Years, 1940–1959." In *Developing the Lonergan Legacy: Historical, Theoretical, and Existential Themes*, 164–93. Edited by Michael Vertin. Toronto: University of Toronto Press, 2004.

———. *Christ and History: The Christology of Bernard Lonergan from 1935 to 1982*. Ottawa: Novalis Press, 2005.

———. "For a Phenomenology of Rational Consciousness." In *Lonergan and the Level of Our Time*, 77–101. Edited by Michael Vertin. Toronto: University of Toronto Press, 2010.

———. "The Puzzle of the Subject as Subject in Lonergan." In *Lonergan and the Level of Our Time*, 155–79. Edited by Michael Vertin. Toronto: University of Toronto Press, 2010.

Curran, Charles E. *Catholic Moral Theology in the United States: A History*. Moral Traditions Series. Washington, D.C.: Georgetown University Press, 2008.

Davis, Charles. "Lonergan and the Teaching Church." In *Foundations of Theology: Papers from the International Lonergan Congress 1970*, 60–75. Notre Dame, Ind.: University of Notre Dame Press, 1971.

———. Review of *The Achievement of Bernard Lonergan*, by David Tracy. *Journal of Religion* 53, no. 3 (1973): 384–87.

Dawson, Christopher. *The Age of the Gods: A Study in the Origins of Culture in Prehistoric Europe and the Ancient East.* New York: Sheed & Ward, 1934.

————. *Christianity and European Culture: Selections from the Work of Christopher Dawson.* Edited by Gerald J. Russello. Washington, D.C.: The Catholic University of America Press, 1998.

De Haan, Daniel D. "Perception and the *Vis Cogitativa*: A Thomistic Analysis of Aspectual, Actional, and Affectional Percepts." *American Catholic Philosophical Quarterly* 88, no. 3 (2014): 397–437.

De Nys, Martin J. "Lonergan and Radical Orthodoxy." Paper presented at the West Coast Methods Institute, Loyola Marymount University, Los Angeles, Calif., April 2017.

DeHart, Paul J. *Aquinas and Radical Orthodoxy: A Critical Inquiry.* Routledge Studies in Religion 16. New York: Routledge, 2012.

Denzinger, Henricus, and Adolfus Schönmetzer, eds. *Enchiridion Symbolorum Definitionum et Declarationum de Rebus Fidei et Morum.* 36th ed. Frieburg: Herder, 1976.

Dewart, Leslie. *The Future of Belief: Theism in a World Come of Age.* New York: Herder and Herder, 1966.

Di Noia, J. Augustine. "Karl Rahner." In *The Modern Theologians: An Introduction to Christian Theology since 1918*, 118–33. 3rd ed. Great Theologians. Malden, Mass.: Blackwell, 2005.

Dodds, E. R. *The Greeks and the Irrational.* Berkeley, Cal.: University of California Press, 1951.

Doorley, Mark J. *The Place of the Heart in Lonergan's Ethics: The Role of Feelings in the Ethical Intentionality Analysis of Bernard Lonergan.* Lanham, Md.: University Press of America, 1996.

Doran, Robert M. *Theology and the Dialectics of History.* Toronto: University of Toronto Press, 1989.

————. "Reception and Elemental Meaning: An Expansion of the Notion of Psychic Conversion." *Toronto Journal of Theology* 20, no. 2 (2004): 133–57.

————. *What Is Systematic Theology?* Toronto: University of Toronto Press, 2005.

————. "Are There Two Consciousnesses in Christ? Transposing the Secondary Act of Existence." *Irish Theological Quarterly* 82, no. 2 (2017): 148–68.

Dorr, Donal. "'Conversion.'" In *Looking at Lonergan's Method*, 175–85. Edited by Patrick Corcoran. Dublin: Talbot Press, 1975.

Dulles, Avery. *The Assurance of Things Hoped For: A Theology of Christian Faith*. New York: Oxford University Press, 1994.

———. "Faith and Reason: From Vatican I to John Paul II." In *The Two Wings of Catholic Thought: Essays on* Fides et Ratio, 193–208. Edited by David Ruel Foster and Joseph W. Koterski. Washington, D.C.: The Catholic University of America Press, 2003.

Eliot, T. S. *Four Quartets*. New York: Harcourt Brace Jovanovich, 1971.

Emery, Gilles. "Essentialisme ou personalisme dans le traité de Dieu chez saint Thomas d'Aquin?" *Revue Thomiste* 98, no. 1 (1998): 5–38.

———. *Trinity in Aquinas*. Translated by Matthew Levering and Teresa Bede. Naples, Fla.: Sapientia Press of Ave Maria University, 2003.

———. *The Trinitarian Theology of Saint Thomas Aquinas*. Translated by Francesca Aran Murphy. New York: Oxford University Press, 2007.

Fagles, Robert, and W. B. Stanford. "The Serpent and the Eagle." In *Aeschylus: The Oresteia*, 13–97. Translated by Robert Fagles. New York: Penguin Classics, 1977.

Fatula, Mary Ann. "*Contemplata Aliis Tradere*: Spirituality and Thomas Aquinas, the Preacher." *Spirituality Today* 43, no. 1 (1991): 19–35.

Fay, Cornelius Ryan. "Fr. Lonergan and the Participation School." *The New Scholasticism* 34, no. 4 (1960): 461–87.

Fehmers, Frank, ed. *The Crucial Questions: On Problems Facing the Church Today*. New York: Newman Press, 1969.

Finnis, John. *Fundamentals of Ethics*. Oxford: Clarendon Press, 1983.

———. *"Historical Consciousness" and Theological Foundations*. Toronto: Pontifical Institute of Medieval Studies, 1992.

———. *Religion and Public Reasons*. Collected Essays, vol. 5. New York: Oxford University Press, 2011.

Flanagan, Joseph. *Quest for Self-Knowledge: An Essay in Lonergan's Philosophy*. Toronto: University of Toronto Press, 1997.

Ford, David F. "Method in Theology in the Lonergan Corpus." In *Looking at Lonergan's Method*, 11–26. Edited by Patrick Corcoran. Dublin: Talbot Press, 1975.

Fortin, Ernest L. "A Note on Dawson and St. Augustine." In *The Birth of Philosophic Christianity: Studies in Early Christian and Medieval*

Thought, 115–22. Edited by J. Brian Benestad. Collected Essays 1. Lanham, Md.: Rowman & Littlefield, 1996.

———. "The New Moral Theology." In *Ever Ancient, Ever New: Ruminations on the City, the Soul, and the Church*, 113–29. Edited by Michael P. Foley. Collected Essays 4. Lanham, Md.: Rowman & Littlefield, 2007.

Fredriksen, Paula. Review of *Lord Jesus Christ: Devotion to Jesus in Earliest Christianity*, by Larry W. Hurtado. *Journal of Early Christian Studies* 12, no. 4 (2004): 537–41.

Frye, Northrop. *Fearful Symmetry: A Study of William Blake*. Princeton Paperbacks. Princeton, N.J.: Princeton University Press, 1969.

Gadamer, Hans-Georg. *Truth and Method*. 2nd ed. New York: Continuum, 2000.

Gaine, Simon Francis. *Did the Saviour See the Father? Christ, Salvation and the Vision of God*. New York: Bloomsbury Publishing, 2015.

Galot, Jean. *Who Is Christ? A Theology of the Incarnation*. Rome: Gregorian University Press, 1980.

———. "Le Christ terrestre et la vision." *Gregorianum* 67, no. 3 (1986): 429–50.

Gelpi, Donald L. *Inculturating North American Theology: An Experiment in Foundational Method*. AAR Studies in Religion. Atlanta: Scholars Press, 1988.

de Ghellinck, Joseph. "Denis Pétau." In *The Catholic Encyclopedia*. New York: Robert Appleton, 1911. Accessed September 11, 2015. http://www.newadvent.org/cathen/11743a.htm.

Gilbert, André, and Louis Roy. "La Structure Éthique de La Conversion Religieuse d'après B. Lonergan." *Science et Esprit* 32, no. 3 (1980): 347–60.

Gilson, Étienne. *Réalisme thomiste et critique de la connaissance*. Paris: Librairie philosophique J. Vrin, 1939.

———. *The Mystical Theology of Saint Bernard*. Translated by A. H. C. Downes. New York: Sheed & Ward, 1940.

———. *Le philosophe et la théologie*. Paris: A. Fayard, 1960.

———. *The Philosopher and Theology*. Translated by Cécile Gilson. New York: Random House, 1962.

———. *Le réalisme méthodique*. Paris: Chez Pierre Téqui, 2007.

Gregson, Vernon, ed. *The Desires of the Human Heart: An Introduction to the Theology of Bernard Lonergan*. New York: Paulist Press, 1988.

Griffiths, Paul J. "Theological Disagreement: What It Is, and How to Do It." ABC, Aug. 26, 2014. http://www.abc.net.au/religion/articles/2014/08/26/4074627.htm.

———. *The Practice of Catholic Theology: A Modest Proposal.* Washington, D.C.: The Catholic University of America Press, 2016.

Grillmeier, Alois. *Christ in Christian Tradition.* Vol. 2–2, *From the Council of Chalcedon (451) to Gregory the Great (590–604).* Translated by John Cawte and Pauline Allen. 3 vols. Louisville, Ky: Westminster John Knox Press, 1995.

Grindheim, Sigurd. *God's Equal: What Can We Know About Jesus' Self-Understanding in the Synoptic Gospels?* London: T&T Clark International, 2011.

Guarino, Thomas G. *Foundations of Systematic Theology.* Theology for the Twenty-First Century. New York: T&T Clark International, 2005.

Gula, Richard M. *Reason Informed by Faith: Foundations of Catholic Morality.* New York: Paulist Press, 1989.

Gunton, Colin. *The Promise of Trinitarian Theology.* Edinburgh: T&T Clark International, 1991.

Hadot, Pierre. *Philosophy as a Way of Life: Spiritual Exercises from Socrates to Foucault.* Translated by Arnold I. Davidson. Malden, Mass.: Blackwell, 1995.

Haight, Roger. *Jesus, Symbol of God.* Maryknoll, N.Y.: Orbis Books, 1999.

de Halleux, André. "Personnalisme ou essentialisme Trinitaire chez les Pères cappadociens." In *Patrologie et Œcuménisme: Recueil d'Études,* 215–68. Louvain: Leuven University Press, 1990.

Harvey, Van A. *The Historian and the Believer; the Morality of Historical Knowledge and Christian Belief.* New York: Macmillan, 1966.

Hastings, Adrian. "Obituary: Charles Davis." *The Independent,* February 5, 1999. http://www.independent.co.uk/arts-entertainment/obituary-charles-davis-1068782.html.

Hefling Jr., Charles C. *Lonergan on Development: "The Way to Nicea" in Light of His More Recent Methodology.* Ann Arbor, Mich.: UMI, 1983.

———. "Turning Liberalism Inside Out." *Method: Journal of Lonergan Studies* 3, no. 2 (1985): 51–69.

———. "The Meaning of God Incarnate According to Friedrich Schlei-ermacher; or, Whether Lonergan Is Appropriately Regarded as 'A Schleiermacher for Our Time,' and Why Not." *Lonergan Workshop* 7 (1988): 105–77.

———. "A Perhaps Permanently Valid Achievement: Lonergan on Christ's Satisfaction." *Method: Journal of Lonergan Studies* 10, no. 1 (1992): 51–76.

———. *Why Doctrines?* 2nd ed. Chestnut Hill, Mass.: Lonergan Institute at Boston College, 2000.

———. "Revelation and/as Insight." In *The Importance of Insight: Essays in Honour of Michael Vertin*, 97–115. Edited by David S. Liptay and John J. Liptay. Toronto: University of Toronto Press, 2007.

———. "Another Perhaps Permanently Valid Achievement: Lonergan on Christ's (Self-) Knowledge." *Lonergan Workshop* 20 (2008): 127–64.

Helmer, Christine. *Theology and the End of Doctrine*. Philadelphia: Westminster John Knox, 2014.

Hengel, Martin. *The Son of God: The Origin of Christology and the History of Jewish-Hellenistic Religion*. 1st American ed. Philadelphia: Fortress Press, 1976.

Hennessy, Kristin. "An Answer to de Régnon's Accusers: Why We Should Not Speak of 'His' Paradigm." *Harvard Theological Review* 100, no. 2 (2007): 179–97.

Higton, Mike. "Reconstructing *The Nature of Doctrine*." *Modern Theology* 30, no. 1 (2014): 1–31.

Hillesum, Etty. *Etty Hillesum: Essential Writings*. Modern Spiritual Masters. Maryknoll, N.Y.: Orbis Books, 2009.

Hopkins, Gerard Manley. *Poems and Prose*. Edited by W. H. Gardner. New York: Penguin, 1985.

Hurtado, Larry W. *Lord Jesus Christ: Devotion to Jesus in Earliest Christianity*. Grand Rapids, Mich.: William B. Eerdmans, 2003.

———. *One God, One Lord: Early Christian Devotion and Ancient Jewish Monotheism*. 3rd ed. Cornerstones. London: Bloomsbury T&T Clark, 2015.

International Theological Commission. "The Consciousness of Christ Concerning Himself and His Mission (1985)." In *International*

Theological Commission: Texts and Documents, 305–16. Edited by Michael Sharkey. San Francisco: Ignatius Press, 1989.

James, Charles. "Falling into Subjectivism." *New Oxford Review*, September 2003.

Jaramillo, Alicia. "The Necessity of Raising the Question of God: Aquinas and Lonergan on the Quest after Complete Intelligibility." *The Thomist* 71, no. 2 (2007): 221–67.

John of the Cross. *Collected Works of St. John of the Cross*. Translated by Kieran Kavanaugh and Otilio Rodriguez. Garden City, N.Y.: Doubleday, 1964.

———. *Obras Completas de San Juan de La Cruz*. Edited by José Vicente Rodriguez and Federico Ruiz Salvador. Madrid: Biblioteca de Autores Cristianos, 1982.

———. *A Spiritual Canticle of the Soul and the Bridegroom Christ*. Translated by David Lewis and Benedict Zimmerman. Grand Rapids, Mich.: William B. Eerdmans, 2000.

John Paul II. *Fides et Ratio*. Encyclical Letter. September 14, 1998.

Jones, Carleton P. "Three Latin Papers of John Henry Newman: A Translation with Introduction and Commentary." PhD diss., Pontificia Universitas S. Thomae in Urbe, 1995.

Jordan, Mark D. *Ordering Wisdom: The Hierarchy of Philosophical Discourses in Aquinas*. Publications in Medieval Studies 24. Notre Dame, Ind.: University of Notre Dame Press, 1986.

Jossua, J. P. "Some Questions on the Place of Believing Experience in the Work of Bernard Lonergan." In *Looking at Lonergan's Method*, 164–74. Edited by Patrick Corcoran. Dublin: Talbot Press, 1975.

Kaplan, Grant. *Answering the Enlightenment*. New York: Crossroad Publishing, 2006.

Kasper, Walter. *The God of Jesus Christ*. Translated by Matthew J. O'Connell. New York: Crossroad Publishing, 1984.

———. *Theology and Church*. Translated by Margaret Kohl. London: SCM Press, 1989.

Kempe, Margery. *The Book of Margery Kempe*. Translated by Barry Windeatt. 1st ed. New York: Penguin Classics, 2000.

Ker, Ian. *The Achievement of John Henry Newman*. Notre Dame, Ind.: University of Notre Dame Press, 1990.

Kereszty, Roch. *Jesus Christ: Fundamentals of Christology.* 2nd ed. Staten Island, N.Y.: Alba House, 2002.

Kerr, Fergus. *Twentieth-Century Catholic Theologians: From Neoscholasticism to Nuptial Mysticism.* Malden, Mass.: Blackwell Publications, 2007.

Kierkegaard, Søren. *Fear and Trembling.* Translated by Alastair Hannay. Penguin Classics. New York: Penguin, 1985.

Knasas, John F. X. *The Preface to Thomistic Metaphysics: A Contribution to the Neo-Thomist Debate on the Start of Metaphysics.* New York: Peter Lang, 1990.

———. "Aquinas's Metaphysics and Descartes's Methodic Doubt." *The Thomist* 64, no. 3 (2000): 449–72.

———. *Being and Some Twentieth-Century Thomists.* New York: Fordham University Press, 2003.

———. "Why for Lonergan Knowing Cannot Consist in 'Taking a Look.'" *American Catholic Philosophical Quarterly* 78, no. 1 (2004): 131–50.

Knox, Ronald A. *Essays in Satire.* London: Sheed & Ward, 1928.

ten Kortenaar, Neil. "Chinua Achebe and the Question of Modern African Tragedy." *Philosophia Africana* 9, no. 2 (2006): 83–100.

LaCugna, Catherine Mowry. *God for Us: The Trinity and Christian Life.* San Francisco: Harper, 1991.

Lamb, Matthew L. *Eternity, Time, and the Life of Wisdom.* Naples, Fla.: Sapientia Press of Ave Maria University, 2007.

———. "Bernard Lonergan SJ: The Gregorian Years." In *Lonergan's Anthropology Revisited: The Next Fifty Years of Vatican II,* 57–80. Edited by Gerard Whelan. Rome: Gregorian and Biblical Press, 2015.

Lambert, Pierrot, and Philip McShane. *Bernard Lonergan: His Life and Leading Ideas.* Halifax: Axial Press, 2010.

Lash, Nicholas. "Method and Cultural Discontinuity." In *Looking at Lonergan's Method,* 127–43. Edited by Patrick Corcoran. Dublin: Talbot Press, 1975.

———. Review of *The Way to Nicea: The Dialectical Development of Trinitarian Theology,* by Bernard J. F. Lonergan. *New Blackfriars* 58, no. 682 (1977): 150–51.

Lawrence, Frederick G. "The Horizon of Political Theology." In *Trinification of the World: A Festschrift in Honour of Frederick E. Crowe in Celebration of His 60th Birthday*, 46–70. Edited by Thomas A. Dunne and Jean-Marc Laporte. Toronto: Regis College, 1978.

———. "Language as Horizon?" In *The Beginning and the Beyond: Papers from the Gadamer and Voegelin Conferences*, 13–34. Edited by Frederick G. Lawrence. Chico, Calif.: Scholars Press, 1984.

———. "Dangerous Memory and the Pedagogy of the Oppressed." In *Communicating a Dangerous Memory: Soundings in Political Theology*, 17–33. Edited by Frederick G. Lawrence. Atlanta: Scholars Press, 1987.

———. "Lonergan's Foundations for Constitutive Communication." *Lonergan Workshop* 10 (1994): 229–77.

———. "Lonergan's Postmodern Subject: Neither Neoscholastic Substance nor Cartesian Ego." In *In Deference to the Other: Lonergan and Contemporary Continental Thought*, 107–20. Albany: State University of New York Press, 2004.

———. "Finnis on Lonergan: A Reflection." *Villanova Law Review* 57, no. 5 (2012): 849–925.

———. "Lonergan's Search for a Hermeneutics of Authenticity: Re-Originating Augustine's Hermeneutics of Love." In *Lonergan's Anthropology Revisited: The Next Fifty Years of Vatican II*, 19–56. Edited by Gerard Whelan. Rome: Gregorian and Biblical Press, 2015.

———. *The Fragility of Consciousness: Faith, Reason, and the Human Good*. Edited by Randall S. Rosenberg and Kevin M. Vander Schel. Toronto: University of Toronto Press, 2017.

Levering, Matthew. *Scripture and Metaphysics: Aquinas and the Renewal of Trinitarian Theology*. Challenges in Contemporary Theology. Malden, Mass.: Blackwell, 2004.

Liddy, Richard M. *Transforming Light: Intellectual Conversion in the Early Lonergan*. Collegeville, Minn.: Liturgical Press, 1993.

Lindbeck, George A. *The Nature of Doctrine*. Philadelphia: Westminster, 1984.

———. *The Church in a Postliberal Age*. Grand Rapids, Mich.: William B. Eerdmans, 2002.

Loasby, B. J. "Hypothesis and Paradigm in the Theory of the Firm." *The Economic Journal* 81, no. 324 (1971): 863–85.

Loewe, William P. *Lex Crucis: Soteriology and the Stages of Meaning.* Minneapolis: Fortress, 2016.

Lonergan, Bernard J. F. *De Deo Trino 2. Pars Systematica.* Rome: Gregorian University Press, 1964.

———. *De Verbo incarnato.* Rome: Gregorian University Press, 1964.

———. "Bernard Lonergan Responds." In *Foundations of Theology: Papers from the International Lonergan Congress 1970*, 223–34. Edited by Philip J. McShane. Notre Dame, Ind.: University of Notre Dame Press, 1971.

———. "Bernard Lonergan responds." In *Language, Truth, and Meaning: Papers from the International Lonergan Congress 1970*, 306–12. Edited by Philip J. McShane. Notre Dame, Ind.: University of Notre Dame Press, 1972.

———. *Method in Theology.* New York: Herder and Herder, 1972.

———. *A Second Collection.* Edited by William F. Ryan and Bernard J. Tyrrell. Philadelphia: Westminster, 1974.

———. *The Way to Nicea: The Dialectical Development of Trinitarian Theology.* Translated by Conn O'Donovan. Philadelphia: Westminster, 1976.

———. *Caring about Meaning: Patterns in the Life of Bernard Lonergan.* Edited by Pierrot Lambert, Charlotte Tansey, and Cathleen Going. Thomas More Institute Papers 82. Montreal: Thomas More Institute, 1982.

———. *A Third Collection: Papers.* Edited by Frederick E. Crowe. New York: Paulist, 1985.

———. "Christ as Subject: A Reply." In *Collection*, 153–84. Edited by Frederick E. Crowe and Robert M. Doran. Collected Works 4. Toronto: University of Toronto Press, 1988.

———. "Cognitional Structure." In *Collection*, 205–21. Edited by Frederick E. Crowe and Robert M. Doran. Collected Works 4. Toronto: University of Toronto Press, 1988.

———. *Collection.* Edited by Frederick E. Crowe and Robert M. Doran. Collected Works 4. Toronto: University of Toronto Press, 1988.

———. "Dimensions of Meaning." In *Collection*, 232–45. Edited by Frederick E. Crowe and Robert M. Doran. Collected Works 4. Toronto: University of Toronto Press, 1988.

———. "Existenz and Aggiornamento." In *Collection*, 222–31. Edited by Frederick E. Crowe and Robert M. Doran. Collected Works 4. Toronto: University of Toronto Press, 1988.

———. "*Insight*: Preface to a Discussion." In *Collection*, 142–52. Edited by Frederick E. Crowe and Robert M. Doran. Collected Works 4. Toronto: University of Toronto Press, 1988.

———. "Isomorphism of Thomist and Scientific Thought." In *Collection*, 133–41. Edited by Frederick E. Crowe and Robert M. Doran. Collected Works 4. Toronto: University of Toronto Press, 1988.

———. "Metaphysics as Horizon." In *Collection*, 188–204. Edited by Frederick E. Crowe and Robert M. Doran. Collected Works 4. Toronto: University of Toronto Press, 1988.

———. "The Natural Desire to See God." In *Collection*, 81–91. Edited by Frederick E. Crowe and Robert M. Doran. Collected Works 4. Toronto: University of Toronto Press, 1988.

———. "On God and Secondary Causes." In *Collection*, 53–65. Edited by Frederick E. Crowe and Robert M. Doran. Collected Works 4. Toronto: University of Toronto Press, 1988.

———. "Theology and Understanding." In *Collection*, 114–32. Edited by Frederick E. Crowe and Robert M. Doran. Collected Works 4. Toronto: University of Toronto Press, 1988.

———. *Understanding and Being: The Halifax Lectures on Insight.* Edited by Frederick E. Crowe. Collected Works 5. Toronto: University of Toronto Press, 1990.

———. *Insight: A Study of Human Understanding.* Edited by Frederick E. Crowe and Robert M. Doran. Collected Works 3. Toronto: University of Toronto Press, 1992.

———. *Topics in Education: The Cincinnati Lectures of 1959 on the Philosophy of Education.* Edited by Robert M. Doran and Frederick E. Crowe. Collected Works 10. Toronto: University of Toronto Press, 1993.

———. "Consciousness and the Trinity." In *Philosophical and Theological Papers 1958–1964*, 122–41. Edited by Robert C. Croken, Frederick E. Crowe, and Robert M. Doran. Collected Works 6. University of Toronto Press, 1996.

———. "Exegesis and Dogma." In *Philosophical and Theological Papers 1958–1964*, 142–59. Edited by Robert C. Croken, Frederick E.

Crowe, and Robert M. Doran. Collected Works 6. University of Toronto Press, 1996.

———. "The Origins of Christian Realism (1961)." In *Philosophical and Theological Papers 1958–1964*, 80–93. Edited by Robert C. Croken, Frederick E. Crowe, and Robert M. Doran. Collected Works 6. Toronto: University of Toronto Press, 1996.

———. "The Redemption." In *Philosophical and Theological Papers 1958–1964*, 6–28. Edited by Robert C. Croken, Frederick E. Crowe, and Robert M. Doran. Collected Works 6. Toronto: University of Toronto Press, 1996.

———. "Theology as Christian Phenomenon." In *Philosophical and Theological Papers 1958–1964*, 244–72. Edited by Robert C. Croken, Frederick E. Crowe, and Robert M. Doran. Collected Works 6. University of Toronto Press, 1996.

———. "Time and Meaning." In *Philosophical and Theological Papers 1958–1964*, 94–121. Edited by Robert C. Croken, Frederick E. Crowe, and Robert M. Doran. Collected Works 6. University of Toronto Press, 1996.

———. *Verbum: Word and Idea in Aquinas*. Edited by Frederick E. Crowe and Robert M. Doran. Collected Works 2. Toronto: University of Toronto Press, 1997.

———. *For a New Political Economy*. Edited by Philip McShane. Collected Works 21. Toronto: University of Toronto Press, 1998.

———. *Macroeconomic Dynamics: An Essay in Circulation Analysis*. Edited by Frederick G. Lawrence, Patrick H. Byrne, and Charles C. Hefling Jr. Collected Works 15. Toronto: University of Toronto Press, 1999.

———. *Grace and Freedom: Operative Grace in the Thought of St Thomas Aquinas*. Edited by Frederick E. Crowe and Robert M. Doran. Collected Works 1. Toronto: University of Toronto Press, 2000.

———. *Phenomenology and Logic: The Boston College Lectures on Mathematical Logic and Existentialism*. Edited by Philip J. McShane. Collected Works 18. Toronto: University of Toronto Press, 2001.

———. *The Ontological and Psychological Constitution of Christ*. Edited by Frederick E. Crowe and Robert M. Doran. Translated by Michael G. Shields. Collected Works 7. Toronto: University of Toronto Press, 2002.

————. "A New Pastoral Theology." In *Philosophical and Theological Papers 1965–1980*, 221–39. Edited by Robert C. Croken and Robert M. Doran. Collected Works 17. Toronto: University of Toronto Press, 2004.

————. "Doctrinal Pluralism." In *Philosophical and Theological Papers 1965–1980*, 70–104. Edited by Robert C. Croken and Robert M. Doran. Collected Works 17. Toronto: University of Toronto Press, 2004.

————. "The General Character of the Natural Theology of Insight." In *Philosophical and Theological Papers 1965–1980*, 3–9. Edited by Robert C. Croken and Robert M. Doran. Collected Works 17. Toronto: University of Toronto Press, 2004.

————. "Horizons." In *Philosophical and Theological Papers 1965–1980*, 10–29. Edited by Robert C. Croken and Robert M. Doran. Collected Works 17. Toronto: University of Toronto Press, 2004.

————. "Horizons and Transpositions." In *Philosophical and Theological Papers 1965–1980*, 409–32. Edited by Robert C. Croken and Robert M. Doran. Collected Works 17. Toronto: University of Toronto Press, 2004.

————. "Merging Horizons: System, Common Sense, Scholarship." In *Philosophical and Theological Papers 1965–1980*, 49–69. Edited by Robert C. Croken and Robert M. Doran. Collected Works 17. Toronto: University of Toronto Press, 2004.

————. "Philosophy of God, and Theology." In *Philosophical and Theological Papers 1965–1980*, 159–218. Edited by Robert C. Croken and Robert M. Doran. Collected Works 17. Toronto: University of Toronto Press, 2004.

————. "Questionnaire on Philosophy: Response." In *Philosophical and Theological Papers 1965–1980*, 352–83. Edited by Robert C. Croken and Robert M. Doran. Collected Works 17. Toronto: University of Toronto Press, 2004.

————. "Reality, Myth, Symbol." In *Philosophical and Theological Papers 1965–1980*, 384–90. Edited by Robert C. Croken and Robert M. Doran. Collected Works 17. Toronto: University of Toronto Press, 2004.

———. "Sacralization and Secularization." In *Philosophical and Theological Papers 1965–1980*, 259–81. Edited by Robert C. Croken and Robert M. Doran. Collected Works 17. Toronto: University of Toronto Press, 2004.

———. "The Scope of Renewal." In *Philosophical and Theological Papers 1965–1980*, 282–98. Edited by Robert C. Croken and Robert M. Doran. Collected Works 17. Toronto: University of Toronto Press, 2004.

———. "Bernard Lonergan Responds (1)." In *Shorter Papers*, 263–74. Edited by Robert C. Croken, Robert M. Doran, and H. Daniel Monsour. Collected Works 20. Toronto: University of Toronto Press, 2007.

———. "Bernard Lonergan Responds (2)." In *Shorter Papers*, 275–81. Edited by Robert C. Croken, Robert M. Doran, and H. Daniel Monsour. Collected Works 20. Toronto: University of Toronto Press, 2007.

———. "The Mystical Body of Christ." In *Shorter Papers*, 106–11. Edited by Robert C. Croken, Robert M. Doran, and H. Daniel Monsour. Collected Works 20. Toronto: University of Toronto Press, 2007.

———. *Shorter Papers*. Edited by Robert C. Croken, Robert M. Doran, and H. Daniel Monsour. Collected Works 20. Toronto: University of Toronto Press, 2007.

———. *The Triune God: Systematics*. Edited by Robert M. Doran and H. Daniel Monsour. Translated by Michael G. Shields. Collected Works 12. Toronto: University of Toronto Press, 2007.

———. *The Triune God: Doctrines*. Edited by Robert M. Doran and H. Daniel Monsour. Translated by Michael G. Shields. Collected Works 11. Toronto: University of Toronto Press, 2009.

———. *Early Works on Theological Method 1*. Edited by Robert M. Doran and Robert C. Croken. Collected Works 22. Toronto: University of Toronto Press, 2010.

———. "De Ente Supernaturali/The Supernatural Order." In *Early Latin Theology*, 52–255. Edited by Robert M. Doran and H. Daniel Monsour. Translated by Michael G. Shields. Collected Works 19. Toronto: University of Toronto Press, 2011.

———. "De Ratione Convenientiae: Methodus Theologica Ad Finem Incarnationem Applicata/The Notion of Fittingness: The Application of Theological Method to the Question of the Purpose of the Incarnation." In *Early Latin Theology*, 482–533. Edited by Robert M. Doran and H. Daniel Monsour. Translated by Michael G. Shields. Collected Works 19. Toronto: University of Toronto Press, 2011.

———. "De Scientia Atque Voluntate Dei/God's Knowledge and Will." In *Early Latin Theology*, 262–411. Edited by Robert M. Doran and H. Daniel Monsour, Translated by Michael G. Shields. Collected Works 19. Toronto: University of Toronto Press, 2011.

———. *Early Works on Theological Method 2*. Edited by Robert M. Doran and H. Daniel Monsour. Translated by Michael G. Shields. Collected Works 23. Toronto: University of Toronto Press, 2013.

———. *Early Works on Theological Method 3*. Edited by Robert M. Doran and H. Daniel Monsour. Translated by Michael G. Shields. Collected Works 24. Toronto: University of Toronto Press, 2013.

———. *A Second Collection*. Edited by John D. Dadosky and Robert M. Doran. Collected Works 13. Toronto: University of Toronto Press, 2016.

———. "An Interview with Fr Bernard Lonergan, S.J." In *A Second Collection*, 176–94. Edited by John D. Dadosky and Robert M. Doran. Collected Works 13. Toronto: University of Toronto Press, 2016.

———. "Belief: Today's Issue." In *A Second Collection*, 75–85. Edited by John D. Dadosky and Robert M. Doran. Collected Works 13. Toronto: University of Toronto Press, 2016.

———. "*Insight* Revisited." In *A Second Collection*, 221–33. Edited by John D. Dadosky and Robert M. Doran. Collected Works 13. Toronto: University of Toronto Press, 2016.

———. "Natural Knowledge of God." In *A Second Collection*, 99–113. Edited by John D. Dadosky and Robert M. Doran. Collected Works 13. Toronto: University of Toronto Press, 2016.

———. "Revolution in Catholic Theology." In *A Second Collection*, 195–201. Edited by John D. Dadosky and Robert M. Doran. Collected Works 13. Toronto: University of Toronto Press, 2016.

————. "The Dehellenization of Dogma." In *A Second Collection*, 11–30. Edited by John D. Dadosky and Robert M. Doran. Collected Works 13. Toronto: University of Toronto Press, 2016.

————. "The Future of Thomism." In *A Second Collection*, 39–47. Edited by John D. Dadosky and Robert M. Doran. Collected Works 13. Toronto: University of Toronto Press, 2016.

————. *The Incarnate Word*. Edited by Robert Doran and Jeremy D. Wilkins. Translated by Charles C. Hefling Jr. Collected Works 9. Toronto: University of Toronto Press, 2016.

————. "The Origins of Christian Realism (1972)." In *A Second Collection*, 202–20. Edited by John D. Dadosky and Robert M. Doran. Collected Works 13. Toronto: University of Toronto Press, 2016.

————. "The Subject." In *A Second Collection*, 60–74. Edited by Robert M. Doran and John D. Dadosky. Collected Works 13. Toronto: University of Toronto Press, 2016.

————. "The Transition from a Classicist World View to Historical Mindedness." In *A Second Collection*, 3–10. Edited by John D. Dadosky and Robert M. Doran. Collected Works 13. Toronto: University of Toronto Press, 2016.

————. "A Post-Hegelian Philosophy of Religion." In *A Third Collection*, 194–213. Edited by John D. Dadosky and Robert M. Doran. Collected Works 16. Toronto: University of Toronto Press, 2017.

————. *A Third Collection*. Edited by John D. Dadosky and Robert M. Doran. Collected Works 16. Toronto: University of Toronto Press, 2017.

————. "Aquinas Today: Tradition and Innovation." In *A Third Collection*, 34–51. Edited by John D. Dadosky and Robert M. Doran. Collected Works 16. Toronto: University of Toronto Press, 2017.

————. "Christology Today: Methodological Reflections." In *A Third Collection*, 70–93. Edited by John D. Dadosky and Robert M. Doran. Collected Works 16. Toronto: University of Toronto Press, 2017.

————. "Lectures on Religious Studies and Theology (3) The Ongoing Genesis of Methods." In *A Third Collection*, 140–59. Edited by John D. Dadosky and Robert M. Doran. Collected Works 16. Toronto: University of Toronto Press, 2017.

————. *Method in Theology*. Edited by John D. Dadosky and Robert M. Doran. Collected Works 14. Toronto: University of Toronto Press, 2017.

———. "Method: Trend and Variations." In *A Third Collection*, 10–20. Edited by John D. Dadosky and Robert M. Doran. Collected Works 16. Toronto: University of Toronto Press, 2017.

———. "Natural Right and Historical Mindedness." In *A Third Collection*, 163–76. Edited by John D. Dadosky and Robert M. Doran. Collected Works 16. Toronto: University of Toronto Press, 2017.

———. "Theology and Praxis." In *A Third Collection*, 177–93. Edited by John D. Dadosky and Robert M. Doran. Collected Works 16. Toronto: University of Toronto Press, 2017.

———. "Unity and Plurality: The Coherence of Christian Truth." In *A Third Collection*, 228–38. Edited by John D. Dadosky and Robert M. Doran. Collected Works 16. Toronto: University of Toronto Press, 2017.

———. *The Redemption*. Edited by Robert M. Doran, H. Daniel Monsour, and Jeremy D. Wilkins. Translated by Michael G. Shields. Collected Works 9. Toronto: University of Toronto Press, 2018.

Lonergan, Bernard J. F., and Michael Shute. *Lonergan's Early Economic Research: Texts and Commentary*. Edited by Michael Shute. Lonergan Studies. Toronto: University of Toronto Press, 2010.

Long, Steven A. *Natura Pura: On the Recovery of Nature in the Doctrine of Grace*. 1st ed. Moral Philosophy and Moral Theology. New York: Fordham University Press, 2010.

Long, Steven A., Roger W. Nutt, and Thomas Joseph White, eds. *Thomism and Predestination: Principles and Disputations*. Naples, Fla.: Sapientia Press of Ave Maria University, 2016.

Mackey, J. P. "Divine Revelation and Lonergan's Transcendental Method in Theology." In *Looking at Lonergan's Method*, 144–63. Edited by Patrick Corcoran. Dublin: Talbot Press, 1975.

MacKinnon, Edward. "Understanding According to Bernard J. F. Lonergan, S.J. - Part III." *The Thomist* 28, no. 4 (1964): 475–522.

———. "The Transcendental Turn: Necessary but Not Sufficient." *Continuum* 6, no. 2 (1968): 225–31.

Mansi, J. D., E. Baluze, Louis Petit, Gabriel Cossart, Jean Baptiste Martin, and Philippe Labbe. *Sacrorum Conciliorum Nova et Amplissima Collectio*. 53 vols. Arnhem: Hubert Welter, 1927.

Mansini, Guy. "Understanding St. Thomas on Christ's Immediate Knowledge of God." *The Thomist* 59, no. 1 (1995): 91–124.

Maritain, Jacques. *Existence and the Existent*. Translated by Lewis Galantiere and Gerald Phelan. Image Books ed. New York: Image, 1956.

―――. *On the Grace and Humanity of Jesus*. Translated by J. Evans. New York: Herder and Herder, 1969.

Marsh, James. "Postmodernism: A Lonerganian Retrieval and Critique." *International Philosophical Quarterly* 35, no. 2 (1995): 159–73.

Marshall, Bruce. "Reckoning with Modernity." *First Things* 258 (2015): 23–30.

Massa, Mark Stephen. *The American Catholic Revolution: How the Sixties Changed the Church Forever*. New York: Oxford University Press, 2010.

Matava, Robert Joseph. *Divine Causality and Human Free Choice: Domingo Báñez, Physical Premotion, and the Controversy de Auxiliis Revisited*. Boston: Brill, 2016.

Mathewes, Charles T. "The Presumptuousness of Autobiography and the Paradoxes of Beginning in *Confessions* Book One." In *A Reader's Companion to Augustine's Confessions*, 7–24. Edited by Kim Paffenroth and Robert Peter Kennedy. 1st ed. Louisville, Ky: Westminster John Knox, 2003.

Mathews, William A. *Lonergan's Quest: A Study of Desire in the Authoring of* Insight. Lonergan Studies. Toronto: University of Toronto Press, 2006.

Matustik, Martin J. *Mediation of Deconstruction: Bernard Lonergan's Method in Philosophy: The Argument from Human Operational Development*. Lanham, Md: University Press of America, 1988.

McBrien, Richard P. *Catholicism*. New ed., completely revised and updated. New York: HarperSanFrancisco, 1994.

McCabe, Herbert. *Law, Love and Language*. New York: Sheed & Ward, 1968.

McCarthy, Michael H. *The Crisis of Philosophy*. Albany: State University of New York Press, 1990.

―――. *Authenticity as Self-Transcendence: The Enduring Insights of Bernard Lonergan*. Notre Dame, Ind.: University of Notre Dame Press, 2015.

McCormick, Richard. "*Humanae Vitae* 25 Years Later." *America Magazine*, July 17, 1993.

McPartland, Thomas J. *Lonergan and Historiography: The Epistemological Philosophy of History.* Columbia, Mo.: University of Missouri Press, 2010.

McShane, Philip. "The Hypothesis of Intelligible Emanations in God." *Theological Studies* 23, no. 4 (1962): 545–568.

———. "Lonerganism." Edited by Walter Brugger and Kenneth Baker. In *Philosophical Dictionary*, 230–33. Spokane, Wash.: Gonzaga University Press, 1972.

———. *Process: Introducing Themselves to Young (Christian) Minders.* Halifax: Mount Saint Vincent Press, 1990. Accessed December 27, 2017. http://www.philipmcshane.org/wp-content/themes/philip/online_publications/books/process.pdf.

Meier, John P. "The Present State of the 'Third Quest' for the Historical Jesus: Loss and Gain." *Biblica* 80, no. 4 (1999): 459–487.

Mettepenningen, Jürgen. "The 'Third Way' of the Modernist Crisis, Precursor of Nouvelle Théologie: Ambroise Gardeil, O.P., and Léonce de Grandmaison, S.J." *Theological Studies* 75, no. 4 (2014): 774–94.

Meyer, Ben F. *The Church in Three Tenses.* Garden City, N.Y.: Doubleday, 1971.

———. *The Early Christians: Their World Mission and Self-Discovery.* Good News Studies 16. Wilmington, Del.: Michael Glazier, 1986.

———. *Christus Faber: The Master Builder and the House of God.* Princeton Theological Monograph Series 29. Allison Park, Penna.: Pickwick Publications, 1992.

———. *The Aims of Jesus.* Princeton Theological Monograph Series 48. San Jose, Calif.: Pickwick Publications, 2002.

Milbank, John. *Truth in Aquinas.* Routledge Radical Orthodoxy. New York: Routledge, 2001.

Miller, Jerome A. *In the Throe of Wonder: Intimations of the Sacred in a Postmodern World.* Albany: State University of New York Press, 1992.

Miller, Mark T. *The Quest for God and the Good Life: Lonergan's Theological Anthropology.* Washington, D.C.: The Catholic University of America Press, 2013.

Moloney, Raymond. "The Mind of Christ in Transcendental Theology: Rahner, Lonergan and Crowe." *Heythrop Journal* 25, no. 3 (1984): 288–300.

————. *The Knowledge of Christ*. Problems in Theology. New York: Continuum, 1999.

Mongeau, Gilles. "The Human and Divine Knowing of the Incarnate Word." *Josephinum Journal of Theology* 12, no. 1 (2005): 30–42.

————. *Embracing Wisdom: The* Summa Theologiae *as Spiritual Pedagogy*. Toronto: Pontifical Institute of Medieval Studies, 2015.

Moonan, Lawrence. "*...certo cognosci posse*. What Precisely Did Vatican I Define?" *Annuarium Historiae Conciliorum* 42, no.1 (2010): 193–202.

Morelli, Mark D. *At the Threshold of the Halfway House: A Study of Bernard Lonergan's Encounter with John Alexander Stewart*. Chestnut Hill, Mass.: Lonergan Institute at Boston College, 2007.

————. "Lonergan's Reading of Hegel." *American Catholic Philosophical Quarterly* 88, no. 3 (2014): 513–534.

————. "Meeting Hegel Halfway: The Intimate Complexity of Lonergan's Relationship with Hegel." *Method: Journal of Lonergan Studies*, n.s., 6, no. 1 (2015): 63–98.

————. *Self-Possession: Being at Home in Conscious Performance*. Chestnut Hill, Mass.: Lonergan Institute at Boston College, 2015.

Muratore, Saturnino. "Bernard Lonergan and the Philosophy of Being." In *Going Beyond Essentialism: Bernard J. F. Lonergan an Atypical Neo-Scholastic*, 175–81. Edited by Cloe Taddei-Ferretti. Naples: Istituto Italiano per gli Studi Filosofici, 2012.

Nachbar, Bernard A. M. "Is It Thomism?" *Continuum* 6, no. 2 (1968): 232–35.

Narcisse, Gilbert. *Les raisons de Dieu: argument de convenance et esthétique théologique selon saint Thomas d'Aquin et Hans Urs von Balthasar*. Studia Friburgensia 83. Fribourg, Suisse: Éditions universitaires, 1997.

Neuner, Josef, and Jacques Dupuis, eds. *The Christian Faith: In the Doctrinal Documents of the Catholic Church*. 7th rev. ed. Staten Island, N.Y.: Alba House, 2001.

Newman, John Henry. *Apologia pro Vita Sua: Being a History of His Religious Opinions*. Edited by Martin J. Svaglic. Oxford: Clarendon Press, 1967.

————. *An Essay in Aid of a Grammar of Assent*. Edited by Ian T. Ker. Oxford: Clarendon Press, 1985.

O'Callaghan, John. "*Verbum Mentis*: Philosophical or Theological Doctrine in Aquinas?" *American Catholic Philosophical Association Proceedings* 74, no. 1 (2001): 103–19.

———. "More Words on the *Verbum*: A Response to James Doig." *American Catholic Philosophical Quarterly* 77, no. 2 (2003): 257–68.

———. *Thomist Realism and the Linguistic Turn: Toward a More Perfect Form of Existence*. Notre Dame, Ind.: University of Notre Dame Press, 2003.

O'Callaghan, Michael C. *Unity in Theology: Lonergan's Framework for Theology in Its New Context*. Lanham, Md: University Press of America, 1980.

O'Connell, Matthew J. "St. Thomas and the Verbum: An Interpretation." *The Modern Schoolman* 24, no. 4 (1947): 224–34.

Ogden, Schubert Miles. "The Challenge to Protestant Thought." *Continuum* 6, no. 2 (1968): 236–40.

———. "Lonergan and the Subjectivist Principle." In *Language, Truth, and Meaning: Papers from the International Lonergan Congress 1970*, 218–35. Notre Dame, Ind.: University of Notre Dame Press, 1972.

Ormerod, Neil. "'It Is Easy to See': The Footnotes of John Milbank." *Philosophy and Theology* 11, no. 2 (1999): 257–264.

———. *Method, Meaning, and Revelation: The Meaning and Function of Revelation in Bernard Lonergan's "Method in Theology."* Lanham, Md.: University Press of America, 2000.

———. *The Trinity: Retrieving the Western Tradition*. Milwaukee, Wisc.: Marquette University Press, 2005.

———. "Gilson and Lonergan and the Possibility of A Christian Philosophy." *The Heythrop Journal* 57, no. 3 (2016): 532–41.

Panofsky, Erwin. *Gothic Architecture and Scholasticism: An Inquiry into Analogy, Arts, Philosophy and Religion in the Middle Ages*. New York: Plume / Penguin, 1974.

Patfoort, Albert. Review of *Divinarum Personarum Conceptio Analogica*, by Bernard J. F. Lonergan. *Bulletin Thomiste* 10, no. 2 (1959): 531–34.

Peghaire, Julien. "A Forgotten Sense: The Cogitative, According to St. Thomas Aquinas." *The Modern Schoolman* 20, no. 1–2 (1943): 123–40, 210–29.

Pernoud, Régine. *Those Terrible Middle Ages: Debunking the Myths.* Translated by Anne Englund Nash. San Francisco: Ignatius Press, 2000.

Perrier, Emmanuel. *La fécondité en dieu: la puissance notionnelle dans la Trinité selon saint Thomas d'Aquin.* Bibliothèque de la Revue thomiste. Études de théologie 3. Paris: Parole et silence, 2009.

Piaget, Jean. *The Psychology of Intelligence.* Edited by Malcolm Piercy and D. E. Berlyne. Routledge Classics. New York: Routledge, 2001.

Pius X. *Pascendi Dominici Gregis.* Encyclical Letter. September 8, 1907.

Plants, Nicholas. "Decentering Inwardness." In *In Deference to the Other: Lonergan and Contemporary Continental Thought,* 11–32. Albany: State University of New York Press, 2004.

Poe, Edgar Allan. *Complete Works of Edgar Allan Poe.* Vol. 3. 3 vols. New York: G. B. Putnam's Sons, 1902.

Pottmeyer, Hermann D. *Der Glaube vor dem Anspruch der Wissenschaft. Die Konstitution* Dei Filius *des 1. Vatikanischen Konzils.* Freiburg: Herder, 1968.

Rahner, Karl. "Dogmatic Reflections on the Knowledge and Self-Consciousness of Christ." In *Theological Investigations,* vol. 5, 193–215. Translated by Karl-H. Kruger. Baltimore: Helicon, 1966.

———. "Bemerkungen zum dogmatischen Traktat »De Trinitate«." In *Schriften zur Theologie.* Bd. 4, *Neuere Schriften,* 103–33. Einsedeln: Benziger, 1967.

———. "Der dreifaltige Gott als transzendenter Urgrund der heilsgeschichte." In *Mysterium Salutis. Grundriß heilsgeschichtlicher Dogmatik,* 317–401. Edited by Johannes Feiner and Magnus Löhrer. Mysterium Salutis 2, Die Heilsgeschichte vor Christus. Einsedeln: Benziger, 1967.

———. *Foundations of Christian Faith: An Introduction to the Idea of Christianity.* Translated by William Dych. New York: Seabury Press, 1978.

———. "*Theos* in the New Testament." In *Theological Investigations,* vol. 1, 79–148. Translated by Cornelius Ernst. New York: Crossroad Publishing, 1982.

———. *The Trinity.* Translated by Joseph Donceel. New York: Crossroad Publishing, 1997.

———. *Grundkurs des Glaubens: Studien zum Begriff des Christentums.* Edited by N. Schwerftfeger and A. Raffelt. Karl Rahner Sämtliche Werke 26. Zürich: Benziger, 1999.

Ratzinger, Joseph. *The Nature and Mission of Theology: Essays to Orient Theology in Today's Debates.* Translated by Adrian Walker. San Francisco: Ignatius Press, 1995.

———. *Introduction to Christianity.* Translated by J. R. Foster. Revised ed. San Francisco: Ignatius Press, 2004.

———. *Truth and Tolerance: Christian Belief and World Religions.* Translated by Henry Taylor. San Francisco: Ignatius Press, 2004.

———. *Dogma and Preaching: Applying Christian Doctrine to Daily Life.* Edited by Michael J. Miller. Translated by Michael J. Miller and Matthew J. O'Connell. San Francisco: Ignatius Press, 2011.

Rausch, Thomas P. *I Believe in God: A Reflection on the Apostles' Creed.* Collegeville, Minn.: Liturgical Press, 2008.

Régnon, Théodore de. *Études de théologie positive sur la sainte Trinité.* 4 vols. Paris: Victor Retaux, 1892.

Rende, Michael L. "The Development and the Unity of Lonergan's Notion of Conversion." *Method: Journal of Lonergan Studies* 1, no. 2 (1983): 158–73.

Reno, R. R. "Theology After the Revolution." *First Things* 173 (2007): 15–21.

Richardson, Cyril C., ed. *Early Christian Fathers.* Philadelphia: Westminster Press, 1953.

Richardson, William. "Being for Lonergan: A Heideggerian View." in *Language, Truth, and Meaning: Papers from the International Lonergan Congress 1970,* 272–83. Notre Dame, Ind.: University of Notre Dame Press, 1972.

Riestra, J. A. "La scienza di Cristo nel Concilio Vaticano II: Ebrei 4, 15 nella costituzione *Dei Verbum*." *Annales theologici* 2, no. 1 (1988): 99–119.

Rilke, Rainer Maria. *Letters to a Young Poet.* Translated by Stephen Mitchell. New York: Vintage, 1986.

———. *Letters to a Young Poet and The Letter from the Young Worker.* Edited by Charlie Louth. Translated by Charlie Louth. New York: Penguin, 2011.

Rixon, Gordon A. "Derrida and Lonergan on Human Development." *American Catholic Philosophical Quarterly* 76, no. 2 (2002): 221–36.

———. "Derrida and Lonergan on the Human Subject: Transgressing a Metonymical Notion." *Toronto Journal of Theology* 18, no. 2 (2002): 213–29.

———. "Understanding in the Word." Paper presented at the West Coast Methods Institute, Loyola Marymount University, Los Angeles, Calif., April 2017.

Rorty, Richard. "The Fate of Philosophy." *The New Republic*, October 18, 1982.

Rosenberg, Harold. *The Tradition of the New.* New York: Horizon, 1959.

Rosenberg, Randall S. *The Givenness of Desire: Concrete Subjectivity and the Natural Desire to See God.* Toronto: University of Toronto Press, 2017.

Rowland, Tracey. *Culture and the Thomist Tradition: After Vatican II.* Routledge Radical Orthodoxy. New York: Routledge, 2003.

———. "Catholic Theology in the Twentieth Century." In *Key Theological Thinkers: From Modern to Postmodern*, 37–52. Edited by Svein Rise and Staale Johannes Kristiansen. Burlington, Vt.: Ashgate, 2013.

Sala, Giovanni B. *Lonergan and Kant: Five Essays on Human Knowledge.* Edited by Robert M. Doran. Translated by Joseph Spoerl. Toronto: University of Toronto Press, 1994.

Sanks, T. Howland. "David Tracy's Theological Project: An Overview and Some Implications." *Theological Studies* 54, no. 4 (1993): 698–727.

Santer, Mark. Review of *The Way to Nicea: The Dialectical Development of Trinitarian Theology*, by Bernard J. F. Lonergan. *The Journal of Theological Studies* 29, no. 1 (1978): 224–26.

Schall, James V. *The Regensburg Lecture.* South Bend, Ind.: St. Augustine's Press, 2007.

Schillebeeckx, Edward. *Jesus: An Experiment in Christology.* Translated by Hubert Hoskins. New York: Seabury Press, 1979.

Sépinski, Augustin. *La psychologie du Christ chez saint Bonaventure.* Paris: Librairie philosophique J. Vrin, 1948.

Shakespeare, William. "Hamlet, Prince of Denmark." In *The Complete Works of William Shakespeare*, 1071–1112. New York: Avenel Books, 1975.

Shea, William M. "A Vote of Thanks to Voltaire." In *A Catholic Modernity: Charles Taylor's Marianist Award Lecture*, 39–64. Edited by James L. Heft. New York: Oxford University Press, 1999.

Shiffman, Mark. "The Eclipse of the Good in the Modern Rights Tradition." *Communio: International Catholic Review* 40, no. 4 (2013): 775–98.

———. "Response to Sherif Girgis." In *Subjectivity: Ancient and Modern*, 89–94. Edited by R. J. Snell and Steven F. McGuire. Lanham, Md.: Lexington Books, 2016.

Shute, Michael. *Lonergan's Discovery of the Science of Economics.* Toronto: University of Toronto Press, 2010.

Smith, Christian, and Melinda Lundquist Denton. *Soul Searching: The Religious and Spiritual Lives of American Teenagers.* New York: Oxford University Press, 2005.

Spitzer, Robert J. *New Proofs for the Existence of God: Contributions of Contemporary Physics and Philosophy.* Grand Rapids, Mich.: William B. Eerdmans, 2010.

St. Amour, Paul. "Lonergan and Gilson on the Problem of Critical Realism." *The Thomist* 69, no. 4 (2005): 557–92.

———. "Bernard Lonergan on Affirmation of the Existence of God." *Analecta Hermeneutica* 2, no. 1 (2010): 1–9.

Stead, G. Christopher. "The Concept of Divine Substance." *Vigiliae Christianae* 29, no. 1 (1975): 1–14.

———. *Divine Substance.* Oxford: Clarendon Press, 1977.

Stebbins, J. Michael. *The Divine Initiative: Grace, World-Order, and Human Freedom in the Early Writings of Bernard Lonergan.* Toronto: University of Toronto Press, 1995.

Stolina, Ralf. "»Ökonomische« und »immanente« Trinität? Zur Problematik einer trinitätstheologischen Denkfigur." *Zeitschrift für Theologie und Kirche* 105, no. 2 (2008): 170–216.

Strauss, Leo. *Natural Right and History.* Charles R. Walgreen Foundation Lectures. Chicago: University of Chicago Press, 1953.

———. "The Three Waves of Modernity." In *An Introduction to Political Philosophy: Ten Essays*, 81–98. Edited by Hilail Gildin. Culture of Jewish Modernity. Detroit: Wayne State University Press, 1989.

Taft, Robert F. "Mass Without the Consecration?: The Historic Agreement on the Eucharist between the Catholic Church and the Assyrian Church of the East Promulgated on 26 October

2001." In *Theological Dimensions of the Christian Orient*. Kottayam, India: Oriental Institute of Religious Studies, 2005. http://www.liturgia.it/addaicongress/en/study/3Taft_en.pdf.

Talar, C. J. T. "'The Synthesis of All Heresies'—100 Years On." *Theological Studies* 68, no. 3 (2007): 491–514.

Tanner, Norman P., Guiseppe Alberigo, J. A. Dossetti, P.-P. Joannou, C. Leonardi, and P. Prodi, eds. *Decrees of the Ecumenical Councils*. 2 vols. Washington, D.C.: Georgetown University Press, 1990.

Tavard, George H. "Commentary on De Revelatione." *Journal of Ecumenical Studies* 3, no. 1 (1966): 1–35.

Taylor, Charles. "A Catholic Modernity." In *A Catholic Modernity: Charles Taylor's Marianist Award Lecture*, 13–37. Edited by James L. Heft. New York: Oxford University Press, 1999.

———. *A Secular Age*. Cambridge, Mass.: Belknap Press of Harvard University Press, 2007.

Teevan, Donna. *Lonergan, Hermeneutics & Theological Method*. Marquette Studies in Theology 45. Milwaukee, Wisc.: Marquette University Press, 2005.

Teresa of Avila. *Collected Works of Teresa of Avila*. Translated by Otilio Rodriguez and Kieran Kavanaugh. 3 vols. Washington, D.C.: Institute for Carmelite Studies, 1980.

———. *Obras Completas*. Edited by Efrén De la Madre de Dios and Otger Steggink. 8th manual ed. Madrid: Biblioteca de Autores Cristianos, 1986.

Thornhill, John. *Modernity: Christianity's Estranged Child Reconstructed*. Grand Rapids, Mich.: William B. Eerdmans, 2000.

Tilling, Chris. *Paul's Divine Christology*. Grand Rapids, Mich.: William B. Eerdmans, 2012.

Torrance, T. F. "The Function of Inner and Outer Word in Lonergan's Theological Method." In *Looking at Lonergan's Method*, 101–26. Edited by Patrick Corcoran. Dublin: Talbot Press, 1975.

Torrell, Jean-Pierre. *Saint Thomas Aquinas: The Person and His Work*. Translated by Robert Royal. Washington, D.C.: The Catholic University of America Press, 1996.

———. "Saint Thomas d'Aquin et la science du Christ: une relecture des Questions 9–12 de la *Tertia Pars* de la Somme de théologie."

In *Recherches thomasiennes: Études revues et augumentées*, 198–213. Paris: Librairie philosophique J. Vrin, 2000.

———. "Le savoir acquis du Christ selon les théologiens médiévaux: Thomas d'Aquin et ses prédécesseurs." *Revue Thomiste* 101, no. 3 (2001): 355–408.

Tracy, David. *The Achievement of Bernard Lonergan*. New York: Herder and Herder, 1970.

———. "Lonergan's Foundational Theology: An Interpretation and a Critique." In *Foundations of Theology: Papers from the International Lonergan Congress 1970*, 197–222. Notre Dame, Ind.: University of Notre Dame Press, 1971.

Tyrrell, Bernard. "The New Context of the Philosophy of God in Lonergan and Rahner." In *Language, Truth, and Meaning: Papers from the International Lonergan Congress 1970*, 284–305. Notre Dame, Ind.: University of Notre Dame Press, 1972.

———. *Bernard Lonergan's Philosophy of God*. American ed. Notre Dame, Ind.: University of Notre Dame Press, 1974.

Vacant, Alfred, Eugene Mangenot, and Emile Amann, eds. *Dictionnaire de théologie catholique: contenant l'exposé des doctrines de la théologie catholique, leurs preuves et leur histoire*. Paris: Letouzey et Ané, 1908. Accessed May 28, 2016. http://archive.org/details/dictionnairedet03vaca.

Volz, John. "Domingo Bañez." In *The Catholic Encyclopedia*. New York: Robert Appleton, 1907. Accessed November 7, 2016. http://www.newadvent.org/cathen/02247a.htm.

Wakeman, Frederic E. *The Fall of Imperial China*. The Transformation of Modern China Series. New York: Free Press, 1977.

Wallace, William A. *The Modeling of Nature: Philosophy of Science and Philosophy of Nature in Synthesis*. Washington, D.C.: The Catholic University of America Press, 1996.

Walmsley, Gerard. *Lonergan on Philosophic Pluralism: The Polymorphism of Consciousness as the Key to Philosophy*. Lonergan Studies. Toronto: University of Toronto Press, 2008.

Wawrykow, Joseph Peter. *God's Grace and Human Action: Merit in the Theology of Thomas Aquinas*. Notre Dame: University of Notre Dame Press, 1995.

Weinandy, Thomas G. *Jesus the Christ*. Huntington, Ind.: Our Sunday Visitor, 2003.

———. "Jesus' Filial Vision of the Father." *Pro Ecclesia* 13, no. 2 (2004): 189–201.

Wendebourg, Dorothea. "Chalcedon in Ecumenical Discourse." *Pro Ecclesia* 7, no. 3 (1998): 307–32.

White, Thomas Joseph. "The Precarity of Wisdom." In *Ressourcement Thomism: Sacred Doctrine, the Sacraments, and the Moral Life. Essays in Honor of Romanus Cessario, O.P.*, 92–123. Washington, D.C.: The Catholic University of America Press, 2010.

———. *The Incarnate Lord: A Thomistic Study in Christology*. Washington, D.C.: The Catholic University of America Press, 2015.

Whittier, John Greenleaf. "Dear Lord and Father of Mankind." In *The Hymnal 1940*, 435. New York: Church Publishing, 1940.

Wilkins, Jeremy D. "'The Image of This Highest Love': The Trinitarian Analogy in Gregory Palamas's *Capita 150*." *Saint Vladimir's Theological Quarterly* 47, no. 3–4 (2003): 385–414.

———. "A Dialectic of 'Thomist' Realisms: John Knasas and Bernard Lonergan." *American Catholic Philosophical Quarterly* 78, no. 1 (2004): 107–30.

———. "Grace in the Third Stage of Meaning: Apropos Lonergan's 'Four-Point Hypothesis.'" *Lonergan Workshop* 24 (2010): 443–67.

———. "Method, Order, and Analogy in Trinitarian Theology: Karl Rahner's Critique of the 'Psychological' Approach." *The Thomist* 74, no. 4 (2010): 563–92.

———. "Grace and Growth: Aquinas, Lonergan, and the Problematic of Habitual Grace." *Theological Studies* 72, no. 4 (2011): 723–749.

———. "Trinitarian Missions and the Order of Grace According to Thomas Aquinas." In *Philosophy and Theology in the Long Middle Ages: A Tribute to Stephen F. Brown*, 689–708. Edited by Kent Emery, Russell L. Friedman, Andreas Speer, and Maxime Mauriege. Studien und Texte zur Geistesgeschichte des Mittelalters, Bd. 105. Boston: Brill, 2011.

———. "Love and Knowledge of God in the Human Life of Christ." *Pro Ecclesia* 21, no. 1 (2012): 77–99.

———. "Why Two Divine Missions? Development in Augustine, Aquinas, and Lonergan." *Irish Theological Quarterly* 77, no. 1 (2012): 37–66.

———. "(Mis)Reading Lonergan's *Way to Nicea*: A 'More Generous Interpretation,' in Conversation with Jane Barter Moulaison." *Studies in Religion/Sciences Religieuses* 42, no. 4 (2013): 429–447.

———. "Metaphysics and/in Theology: Lonergan and Doran." *Method: Journal of Lonergan Studies*, n.s., 5, no. 1 (2014): 53–85.

———. "Traduce Not the Inner Word: On Reading and Rendering Lonergan's Latin." *Method: Journal of Lonergan Studies*, n.s., 5, no. 2 (2014): 87–107.

———. "'Our Conversation Is in Heaven': Conversion and/as Conversation in the Thought of Frederick Lawrence." In *Grace and Friendship: Theological Essays in Honor of Fred Lawrence, from His Grateful Students*, 319–53. Edited by M. Shawn Copeland and Jeremy D. Wilkins. Marquette Studies in Theology 86. Milwaukee, Wisc.: Marquette University Press, 2016.

———. "What 'Will' Won't Do: Faculty Psychology, Intentionality Analysis, and the Metaphysics of Interiority." *Heythrop Journal* 57, no. 3 (2016): 473–91.

Williams, C. J. F. Review of *Verbum: Word and Idea in Aquinas*, by Bernard J. F. Lonergan. *Religious Studies* 8, no. 1 (1972): 80–82.

Wojtyla, Karol. *Faith According to St. John of the Cross*. Translated by Jordan Aumann. San Francisco: Ignatius Press, 1981.

Zizioulas, John D. *Being as Communion: Studies in Personhood and the Church*. Crestwood, N.Y.: St. Vladimir's Seminary Press, 1985.

Catechism of the Catholic Church. 2nd ed. Washington, D.C.: United States Catholic Conference, 2000.

"Philosophy 201 Flashcards | Quizlet," n.d. Accessed March 23, 2017. https://quizlet.com/182547159/philosophy-201-flash-cards/.

Subject Index

Index of Names